The Sense of Appropriateness

#824

in meeting
egs – what we did
in this other situ
was...

Comparative evaluation of
all available actions re their fairness
re family resemblances
Some are more fair than others (weighting)
not because they are closer to ideal
but because they exemplify, illustrate & teach
recognition of family "fair."

Fairest under the circumstances
re efficiency requirements

Proportion of F:E set by discursive evaluation
down to reflective equilibrium (in a real discourse)

SUNY Series in Social and Political Thought
Kenneth Baynes, Editor

The Sense of Appropriateness
Application Discourses in Morality and Law

Klaus Günther

Translated by John Farrell

State University of New York Press

Originally published as *Der Sinn für Angemessenheit. Anwendungsdiskurse in Moral und Recht.*
© 1988 Suhrkamp

Published by
State University of New York Press, Albany

© 1993 State University of New York

For information, address State University of New York
Press, State University Plaza, Albany, N.Y. 12246

Production by Diane Ganeles
Marketing by Dana E. Yanulavich

Library of Congress Cataloging-in-Publication Data

Günther, Klaus, 1957–
    [Sinn für Angemessenheit. English]
    The sense of appropriateness : application discourses in morality
and law / Klaus Günther ; translated by John Farrell.
        p.   cm. — (SUNY series in social and political thought)
    Includes bibliographical references and index.
    ISBN 0-7914-1551-1 (acid-free). — ISBN 0-7914-1552-X (pbk. : acid
-free)
    1. Appropriateness (Ethics)   2. Norm (Philosophy)   3. Prudence.
4. Law—Philosophy.   I. Title.   II. Series.
BJ1418.5.G86   1993
170—dc20   92-31385
                                                                CIP

10 9 8 7 6 5 4 3 2 1

Contents

Translator's Introduction

I

Moral philosophy is now commonly divided into two parts: normative ethics and metaethics,[1] on the one hand, and applied ethics or practical morality, on the other.[2] This division is considered self-evident and is generally accepted by philosophers and laypersons alike, and is currently institutionalized in the literature on moral philosophy and in university courses.[3] This is not of course incorrect, but it is this very self-evident character which contributes to the circumstance that the parts are more the *disjecta membra* than the differentiated components of an integral philosophical theory of morality.[4] So far, moral philosophy has failed to provide a systematic analysis of the interrelationship of these two aspects, without neglecting either one or collapsing one into the other.

If we may synecdochically express these elements in the form of the following questions *When is a norm valid? When is a valid norm appropriate to a concrete situation?* then we can recognize Klaus Günther's contribution as an attempt to distinguish between, interrelate, and answer these questions without having to sacrifice the deontological, cognitivist, or formalist features of a universalist moral philosophy.[5] Indeed, it is probably possible to read non-normative, skeptic, materialist, and contextualist (relativist) attacks on universalism as misguided critiques;[6] that is to say, what they are essentially critiquing is not the universalist justification of norms, but the absence of a sufficiently differentiated argumentative logic of the application of norms.

II

But up to now, moral philosophies of a Kantian provenience have really proposed an answer only to the first question, have failed to distinguish clearly between both, or have virtually mis-construed the second by reducing it to the first—the argumen-tative logic of application is assumed to be identical to that of justification. Curiously enough, this is due in no small part to the very type of universal principle which Günther takes as the point of departure of his analysis. Put simply, the universalization principle "(U)," as developed in discourse ethics by Karl-Otto Apel and Jürgen Habermas, states that a norm is valid only if all those affected by its general observance can accept (in a practical discourse) the con-sequences and side effects this observance could foreseeably have on their interests.

However, such a norm would be "perfect."[7] That is to say, to rec-ognize a norm as valid according to this version of (U), we would have to have unlimited time and infinite knowledge in order to be able to foresee all the possible situations in which this norm could find appropriate application in the future, thereby regulating each individual instance of its own application. For this reason, Günther drafts a "weaker" version of (U) by introducing a *ceteris paribus* clause, whereby a norm's validity is established only for its ob-servance under circumstances which are assumed to remain un-changed, and that means that particular situations of application are not considered.[8] This does not however mean that the appli-cation of norms is left to a context-bound *phronesis;*[9] rather, it is now necessary to first distinguish systematically between the "other things being equal" character of justification (the universal-reciprocal sense of impartiality) and the "all things considered" character of application (impartiality's applicative sense), where the specific situation is the focus of attention and the norm's appro-priateness refers only to the particular features of this situation. Günther can then demarcate justification discourses, which are concerned with the validity of a norm as a rule, from application *discourses,* which he derives from the idealizing presuppositions of argumentation[10] and which deal with the appropriateness of a (valid) norm in a specific situation.

Taking the work of Durkheim, Wittgenstein, Mead, Piaget, and Kohlberg as the basis for his analysis, Günther reconstructs this systematically introduced distinction between the justifica-tion and the application of norms within the framework of the development of moral consciousness and arrives at a three-level model of types of application.[11] The first level is characterized by the fact that justification and application cannot be distinguished:

validity entails appropriateness because both are established in
the same context-bound, situation-dependent manner. At the second level, ego's and alter's specific context can now be viewed from
the social system's perspective, but only from that of a particular
social system. That is to say, though norm and situation have been
separated, the distinction between validity and appropriateness
has not yet been fully developed because the paradigms provided by
the specific social system or group are the final point of reference in
the application of norms, which involves here simply the identification of typical situation features. Radically new situation features
are treated as exceptions to the rule and they generate problems
only when they go beyond the normative horizons of the particular
social system. It is at the third level that these problems can be resolved. The validity of a norm is now determined within the "universe of discourse," that is, in a situation-independent manner, and
this necessarily leads to the clear separation of the universal justification and the free, context-sensitive application of a norm.

This reconstruction can be formulated in terms of the relation
between equality and equity. At the first level they are indistinguishable in the sense that equality is mechanical: no exceptions
are tolerated. At the next level they are separated: extenuating circumstances are acknowledged, but only within a given normative
order. At the third level, equality and equity again become indistinguishable, but this time in the sense that each individual case is
unique, each is an exception.

After having established the philosophical and the sociomoral
necessity of the distinction between justification and application
and after having recognized the conflict of norms which is systematically generated in every application situation where we are
concerned with its specific constellation of features, Günther is now
in a position to identify the constituent elements of a logic of argumentation employed in application discourses.[12] The appropriateness of a norm can first be determined only after we have described
the situation completely in order to establish the relevance of its
particular features. This can involve a semantic analysis of the
terms used in the norm, which are in turn ultimately dependent on
an even more extensive (exhaustive) description of the situation.
Because a complete description of the situation unavoidably leads
to a conflict of norms, we are then faced with the task of resolving
this conflict. Only a formal criterion of norm appropriateness is
possible for discovering which of the conflicting norms best fits the

situation, and this is identified by Günther as the coherence of the norm with all the other (valid) norms (and semantic variants) of a specific form of life which are applicable in the particular situation.[13] This criterion of coherence is exclusive to appropriateness argumentation and also serves to reinforce the distinction between justification and application.

Because good reasons are weak in terms of effectuating a decision to act in a certain way and because conflicts have to be resolved within a limited period of time and with incomplete knowledge, law is reduced by systems theory to its function as a stabilizer of generalized expectations, thereby assigning an insignificant rhetorical role to appropriateness argumentation in law.[14] However, it is only against the background of the postconventional separation of justification and application that the situational appropriateness of legal norms as "rules" (in contrast to legal norms as "principles") can be decided in advance by the legislature positing the norms; but the increasing indeterminacy of even legal rules demonstrates the growing need for appropriateness argumentation in the application of law. The task of adjudication would then go beyond applying norms as rules (subsumption) to include the conduct of application discourses.[15]

Traditional hermeneutical solutions to the problem of indeterminacy rely entirely on the legal applicator's preunderstanding constituted within a specific legal order (and form of life) and thereby focus on the situation-dependent discovery of a legal norm, thus necessarily neglecting its situational appropriateness. By contrast, Dworkin's model, which is based on a concept of integrity that makes it possible to fit all arguments of principle (which go beyond a positive legal order) into a coherent political interpretation, ultimately requires that all relevant situation features be impartially considered in order to determine the appropriateness of a legal norm. Günther, however, wishes to avoid limiting the coherence of the political theory to a particular community and underscores the universalism of the right to equal concern and respect and thereby the proceduralism of the justificatory process. But this does not mean that the principle of integrity excludes relations of solidarity; rather, when it is read as a principle guiding application discourses, it lends expression to those elements of appropriateness argumentation which Günther has identified: a complete description of a particular situation unavoidably generates conflicts of norms which can be resolved only by establishing the coherence of all the applicable norms taken from the specific form of life.

III

In a very concise statement, Habermas brings together some of the essential elements of Günther's argument: "In justification discourse, we disregard the contingent context embeddedness of a proposed norm only for the reason that, if this norm passes the universalization test, it will be sufficiently open to a context-sensitive application. It may not be so selective as to permit only standard interpretations and curtail those differentiations which follow from the most exhaustive situation description possible and which have to be articulated in application discourse."[16] But, as Habermas implies, "standard interpretations" in the form of paradigms are permissible, if only because of their disburdening effects (in settings temporally restricted and because of the cognitive limitations of interpreters). However, understood as standardized situation descriptions, paradigms can be prevented from forming "interpretive monopolies" only if they are, not only in principle but also de facto in every situation, open to testing in application discourses.[17] This would not seem to be the case even in "modern" casuistry,[18] whose paradigm-centered structure all but dispenses with universally valid principles and relies on given "type cases" and analogies in the application of norms. Such an approach only elliptically acknowledges "the occasional situation" in which social or technical changes in the form of life warrant the paradigm being, "in some sense, demolished."[19] But it is in pluralist, decentered forms of life that paradigms have lost their received legitimacy, in the sense that their formation must now become reflexive,[20] and it is here that the need for application discourses, which determine the situational appropriateness of a universally valid norm, becomes all the more evident and illuminates the historical background for the revival of applied ethics.

To illustrate the fruitfulness of Günther's model let us restrict ourselves to just one other example. Habermas employs the distinction between justification and application discourses to criticize and better locate Walzer's theory of distributive justice.[21] After distinguishing between "material" principles of distributive justice, such as "to each according to his needs," and principles concerned with the "the protection of freedom and integrity," such as principles of due process and equal respect for all, Habermas continues: "Now, in that they appear to be universalizable all these [latter] principles of justice can be justified, and it can be asserted that they are prima facie *valid*. But only their application in particular concrete instances will show *which* of the various competing principles is the most appropriate in a *given* context. And that is the task of discourses of application. . . . I find the idea of matching principles of justice generally to a priori delimited total spheres of action highly problematical. In my view the sort of considerations Walzer entertains could be accommodated in discourses of application; but then they'd have to show themselves to be valid for each single case in its own right."[22]

Elster also criticizes Walzer for similar reasons (however, more for goods-specific and country-specific principles of distribution than for sphere-specific ones)[23] but does so against a non-normative background, which is to say that he contends that principles of allocation can be ascertained by empirically analyzing the institutions responsible for distributing goods and burdens, and this is the task he sets himself in *Local Justice*. Though this is not the place for a differentiated critique of Elster, we may, with the help of Günther's model, point out the following: Notwithstanding the fact that his research testifies to the enormous complexity of equitable distribution (and thus, of application problems), the pitfalls of such an empirical approach include the possibility of tacit normative assumptions finding their way into the analysis. Thus, for instance, if, at the moral-philosophical level, justice is reduced solely to distributive justice[24] a type of welfarism may be favored which could lead to the disavowal of individual rights. Throughout his analysis and in what he calls the commonsense conception of justice,[25] Elster concentrates on the second-order actors concerned with the decision on allocation (experts in institutions), thus marginalizing the other three agents he identifies: the claimants or recipients (third-order actors), politicians (first-order actors), and public opinion.[26] In terms of the logic of an application *discourse,* this privileging of second-order decision makers would have to be read as a disregarding of relevant situation features, at least in the form of the partial exclusion of the interests of those directly affected by, and those indirectly involved in, the decision on allocation.

If it is indeed the case that our decentered forms of life necessarily refrain not only from prejudicing the validity of norms (which can now be established only by universal justificatory procedures) but also from predetermining their situational appropriateness (which is now to be ascertained through application discourse and no longer by acquiring dispositions considered correct within a specific concept of the good life), and if, by implication, our universal principles require not consequentialist, skeptic, substantivist, or contextualist qualifications, but a context-sensitive application, then the prospects for better tackling some of the major moral conflicts of our time may not be so slim.

———————————

I would like to thank the author for the invaluable assistance he gave me in every phase of the translation project, and Jim Neuger, who also commented on a draft of the translation. Thanks are also due to Ken Baynes, who not only initiated the project but also guided its realization.

Author's Preface

If a grandson murders his grandfather in order to get his hands on the estate bequeathed to him in the latter's will, should he nevertheless be permitted to inherit it according to the rules of law? On the basis of the decision of this famous case in American legal history (*Riggs v. Palmer*), Ronald Dworkin illustrates the effectiveness of a "sense of appropriateness."[1] The principle that no one may gain advantage from his own illegal conduct—following which Riggs was refused the right to inherit his grandfather's estate—justifies an exception which had not been foreseen in the rules governing the statute of wills. Although it cannot be deduced from positive law, this principle leads to a decision in which subjective rights are taken seriously.

In cases of this kind, is it merely a matter of finding the correct principle? The following arguments ought to confirm the suspicion that, in cases of moral and legal conflict, we have major difficulties in appropriately judging the situation to which various rules and principles can possibly be applied. The sense of appropriateness reveals itself not only in following the correct principles, but also in impartially applying them while considering all the particular circumstances. That, when doing so, we cannot do without practical reason is the thesis of this book.

In a slightly altered version, this study was accepted as my doctoral dissertation by the law department of Johann Wolfgang Goethe University in Frankfurt am Main in the summer of 1987. The Tuesday seminar at the Institute of Criminology, the discussion group at the Institute of Economic Law, and the research group "Jurisprudence" of the philosophy department gave me the opportunity to present work-in-progress for discussion. I would like to thank my friends in the *"Gelber Hahn"* study group for their helpful criticism, also John Farrell, Reiner Frey, and Norbert Zimmer. Without the stimulation, encouragement, and support I have been receiving from Jürgen Habermas, Klaus Lüderssen, and Rudolf Wiethöler for many years, this study would not have been possible. I thank the Leibniz Program of the *Deutsche Forschungsgemeinschaft* for financial support.

Author's Introduction

Determining the relation between action, norm, and situation is one of the major problems of the theory of society. The general question concerning the possibility of societal order can be translated into the more specific one as to how actors coordinate their action plans with one another in situations. The intended action and its goals are in a single context with cultural norms as well as with the specific facts of a situation, be they experiential states, expectable events, or other actors' attitudes requiring interpretation. The attempt to thematize this relation in terms of the application of norms is based on the assumption that in this way one can find out more precisely how a society relates to itself via the individual actions of its members in particular situations. Even according to an altogether naive preunderstanding, it ought to be clear that the self-understanding of a society continually changes in the process of applying moral, legal, and social norms in specific, nonidentical situations.

Formulated in this manner, a journey through theories of morality, law, and society would be necessary for solving this problem in order to discover in detail how the application of norms is implicitly or explicitly thematized. By restricting myself in the following to cognitivist theories of morality and law, and of these only a few, I choose an approach that facilitates a productive comprehension of the problem. Cognitivist theories assert that moral judgments and norms claim a validity that rests on reasons which are plausible for, and can therefore be generally agreed upon by, everyone affected. In this way they differ from all other theories that reduce the validity or meaning of moral judgments and norms to statements of a nonnormative kind. For a theory of society, this means that the coordination of actions can—at least, additionally—come about on the basis of an agreement among those involved on the reasons for action, and cannot therefore be exclusively described from an external perspective. Thus, the possibility of describing the coordination of

1

actions from the perspective of single individuals is ruled out, along
with the possibility of reducing the topic of action coordination to
the choice of compatible means for subjectively chosen ends. The attempt to regard societal order solely as the product of systemic processes appears equally misguided.

The choice of an internal perspective aimed at the reconstruction of intersubjective justifications for action, and at their presuppositions, is to be extended in the following by the assumption that
reasons for action contain not only a validity dimension, but also an
application dimension. If reasons are relevant to action coordination, then neither referring to the situation alone nor referring to
the norm alone is sufficient in itself. In the first case, action would
be explained as a merely adaptive reaction to a situation; reasons
for the application of a norm would then be a matter of mere rhetoric, in the pejorative sense of the term. In the second case, the argument that the action is based on a justified norm is not enough
because no norm can regulate all the cases of its own application.
This insight suggests the alternative of resorting to habitual practices instead of norms, or of redefining the relationship between
norm and situation in terms of the contrast between "normal case"
and "exceptional state." Viewed from an internal perspective, however, the application of norms appears as a cognitive process in
which reasons also play a part—reasons, however, that are different
from those which can be advanced for the validity of a norm.

These reasons are concerned with the act of choosing the relevant situation features in an action situation. If we overlook or do
not appropriately consider an essential aspect of the situation, it
can have considerable moral consequences; and these cannot be prevented by simply checking the truth of the facts *taken into consideration* or the correctness of the *proposed* norm. This can be made
intuitively clear with the help of an example belabored both by Kant
himself and in the literature on Kant. Whoever betrays an innocent
person to an ill-willed pursuer because he does not want to make
himself guilty of lying screens out all those aspects which have
nothing to do with his original intention to lie. This intention is the
only relevant fact he singles out. One cannot argue about this choice
in terms of the aspect that the correspondingly defined situation (I
want to lie) contains false assertions of fact.[1] The other assertions of
fact (the person pursued is innocent, the pursuers are ill willed)
could also be argued about in terms of whether they are true. However, this would not do anything for the question of whether we have
considered all the relevant facts (expressed in true assertions of

fact) or whether the selection made is even appropriate. The same also applies both to reaching an agreement on whether the proposed norm (You ought not to lie!) is worthy of recognition and to the consensus about its correctness. We could probably reach agreement quickly that this norm could be accepted by everyone. However, we have not gained any information about the problem whether the proposed norm was also appropriate in view of all the facts of the particular situation. That other actions would emerge by considering other norms—for example, that one should protect innocent people from an expected misfortune if this is possible without considerable danger to oneself—cannot be discovered within the framework of an argumentation about the correctness of the norm not to lie, nor can we find an answer to the question as to which of the two norms is preferable in this situation.

Checking whether the conditions to be presupposed for applying the norm in the situation are given,[2] though at first glance plausible, does not help either. A norm can only be said to be correctly observed when the facts semantically presupposed by the norm are actually present. However, we have then considered as relevant elements only those facts belonging to the semantic extension of this one norm. From here we do not arrive at an appropriate consideration of the remaining facts, nor at other possible norms whose semantic extension includes these features.

The danger we are exposed to when leaving the act of selecting the relevant features of a situation to chance thus consists in an incorrect appraisal of, and an inappropriate reaction to, action situations. Then it would always depend on merely accidental individual dispositions and particular circumstances whether we happen upon the right answer in a situation. That we are not dealing here with a marginal problem in moral theory is made clear by the simple reflection—following the above example—that we know in most action situations which assertions of fact are true and which action norms—of those which could possibly be considered—are valid, and yet often enough act "immorally" because we—for whatever reasons and motives—overlook or incorrectly appraise certain aspects of the situation; or we underestimate the importance of particular precepts or prohibitions (worthy of recognition) in relation to the norms we then actually observe in the particular situation. Reproaches or critiques of this kind do not assert that I incorrectly appraised the facts or misjudged the importance of the norms *intentionally*. This reproach applies to those who merely feign acting morally, in truth, however, follow their own interests and deceive others about this fact. They are in a position to appraise the facts correctly and to judge the importance of the relevant norm accurately, but nevertheless act differently. In contrast, the other reproaches refer more to a lack of care in considering the relevant facts, to an absence of sensitivity to the particular circumstances, and to an insufficient aptitude for choosing the appropriate course of action in view of the particular situation. Of course, here we have only named various dispositional predicates which can be subsumed under the concept of judgment [*Urteilskraft*]. The normative or, at least, evaluative predicates like correct/incorrect appraisal, correct/incorrect assessment of importance, as well as the normative or evaluative comparisons, make the assumption appear plausible that the designated acts are accessible to a rational appraisal, at least to a certain degree. It would be meaningless to use expressions of this kind if it were not possible to reach agreement on their meaning.

There has been no shortage of suggestions on how this meaning should be determined. Traditionally, these acts of selecting the relevant features of a situation have been understood as an exercise of judgment—with the consequence that rational criteria for the appraisal are not to be found. Two reactions to the problem confront each other here, whereby each ascribes a different importance to judgment.

(a) In the tradition that essentially goes back to Aristotle, the problem of correctly choosing the features of a situation has always been regarded as being identical with justifying correct maxims of action. Whoever can correctly appraise the situation proceeds to act in a morally correct manner too—and vice versa. Here it is assumed that there is one form of life and that we, being its members, have always known how we have to grasp a situation. For the actor it is a matter of acquiring the correct disposition within a form of life—a disposition which will enable him to choose what is appropriate in unforeseeable situations. How he acts in situations, what features are relevant to him, depends on what is good for him,[3] and that means what conception of the good life he, in concurrence with others, aspires to. The features of the situation are therefore relevant only to the prudent choice of the action appropriate to the conception of the good life. Judgment is thus understood as the cultivated exercise of prudence [*Klugheit*], that is, cultivated by correct dispositions (virtues). What is right depends on the situation.[4] Naturalistic ethics has accentuated this perspective in claiming that moral predicates like "good" or "just" merely have a descriptive meaning.[5]

The advantage offered by this attempt at determining the concept of judgment is burdened by a considerable disadvantage—at least so much can be said after the introductory remarks. If we tie the appraisal of an action's moral quality to the successful judgment of the particular situation, we have to forgo isolating the justification of a norm and subjecting it to an independent test of its correctness.[6] Admittedly, at first glance one cannot see why this should be a disadvantage. This interpretation presupposes two premises, whose justification is not provided until later: that the claim to universality is tied to the correctness of a moral norm and that moral norms are universalizable only on the condition that the particular circumstances of the individual case are not considered. It was, however, exactly this separation of justification and application which posed for us the problem of precisely determining judgment. One can therefore tentatively object to the Aristotelian version of a solution to this problem on the grounds that it does not take seriously enough the necessity of distinguishing between the justification and the application of moral norms, but rather allows both to coalesce in judgment. Initially, one can only advance a historical-genetic argument for this: since the collapse of Aristotelianism's teleological worldview, we no longer have forms of life at our disposal which we could regard as binding for any individuals whosoever. Connected to this is the fact that the concept of prudence has dislodged itself from the semantic field which it still encompassed in the context of Aristotelianism (under the term "*phronesis*"). With politics becoming an autonomous realm, this concept became a category of this action sphere without moral or, at first, legal implications.[7] Precisely because moral conflicts of action can no longer be resolved by integration into a common form of life and because we are increasingly encountering conflicts between members of different forms of life, the abstraction of a norm's moral quality from the particular form of life, within which or to which it could be applied, was unavoidable. Whoever interprets this process in a different manner or maintains that a justification of moral norms independent of a form of life is impossible has to either accept the relativity of different forms of life or abandon the choice of the correct action in situations to a decision.

    (b) From the moral devaluation and invalidation of forms of life, universalist moral philosophies in the Kantian tradition drew the conclusion of neglecting the problem of a more precise determination of judgment in favor of a search for the conditions for correctly justifying moral norms. Whether a norm or a mode of action is morally correct should not be dependent on the particular situation, but rather—different versions in this tradition run thus—only on whether the norm or maxim can be generalized to such an extent that I would also observe it if I were in a similar situation and/or in the position of someone affected by the mode of action chosen by me, or if everyone else actually or virtually agreed. The disadvantage of these universalist moral philosophies consists not only in their neglecting the problem of a more precise determination of judgment, but also in the fact that they easily succumb to the danger of declaring it irrelevant. If this misunderstanding is to be found often enough on the side of their opponents, it is nonetheless frequently suggested by the universalist mode of argumentation, especially when it is combined with essentialist assumptions about reason—as in the idealist tradition. A universalist ethics then appears as an abstract, obstinate rigorism blind to facts and of service to immoral intentions at any moment. This danger always arises when the moral principle of universalization is treated as a concrete maxim of action, which, of course, can always only be the object of the universalization procedure. Thus Kant does indeed demand that the moral principle of the categorical imperative be applied to my maxims of action in such a way that I regard them as if they were a law of nature.[8] At the same time, however, he seems to suggest that the maxim of action, which has been justified in that manner, itself be also applied to the individual case as a law of nature. Confusing *pure* practical with *practical* judgment (for which, of course, Kant cannot be easily criticized) results in the generaliz*able* norm being applied without examining the situation, however *general* the norm is. If Kant's examples were only intended as illustrations for applying the categorical imperative to maxims, they would not be controversial. The lying example can be comprehended entirely undramatically if it is understood simply as a test for the generalizability of the maxim never to lie—although it is surely difficult merely to imagine following this maxim if, in doing so, I needlessly condemn an innocent person to death. Yet, Kant argues as if there could be no *application* situation at all where this maxim should yield to other maxims. He thereby identifies the maxim never to lie with the functional mode of the moral principle.[9] This tendency to confuse both can only be understood against the background of essentialist assumptions about an intelligible world which, in matters of morality in any case, stands opposite an empirical world merely as its negation. Nevertheless, even if these assumptions are moderated and the universalizability principle is determined as a rule of argumentation that should guarantee a qualified and (at least) virtual agreement among all those affected, the application problem remains acute. It does indeed appear intuitively implausible how a moral principle, which is supposed to assure the openness of the decision about the moral validity of a norm, can be so rigoristically misunderstood that even the reckless application of valid norms in situations should be mandatory; and yet this danger cannot be eliminated from the outset. Nor can it, from another perspective, be merely disregarded as a residual problem, one which will disappear by itself with the progressive implementation of different versions of universalist moral philosophies. Rather, it seems to be intensified by the fact that the destruction of norm-giving authorities by universalist critique has led to an intensification of the experience of contingency in situations. A lot of evidence points to the fact that modernity has accelerated the speed of change of reliable action orientations to such an extent that we are neither in a position to perceive adequately the situations in which we find ourselves acting nor able to apply a generalizable action orientation appropriately, not to mention develop an enduring conception of the good life. In contrast to the Aristotelian tradition, which was of course familiar with an experience of contingency in "the practical" and tailored the concept of "*phronesis*" especially to this,[10] modernity's experience of contingency exceeds everything that could still be jointly mastered by the participants within the cosmos of a polis. The realization that we can never know all the relevant aspects of a situation because we would never have sufficient time to consider all the aspects—this insight confronts us with a structural indeterminacy of application situations; because of this indeterminacy there remains only the alternative of once again attempting a rationalization of the application problem from the perspective of morally acting persons, or of completely changing the perspective and of no longer tackling the problem within the conceptual framework of moral action.

(c) In view of this alternative, citing yet a third "response" to the problem of a more precise determination of judgment suggests itself. Systems theories radicalize the experience of contingency and thus invert the issue: It is no longer a matter of how norm-guided action is possible *despite* contingency and indeterminacy, but of the conditions of possibility of social structures *on the basis* of contingency and indeterminacy. By taking the standpoint of contingency,[11] as it were, the problem is shifted out of the dimension of norm application and into that of the observation of system

formation and reproduction. Precisely because of the difference between norm and situation, normatively and, here especially, morally coping with contingent and indeterminate situations now
appears, by the same token, as a strategy inappropriate to a present
under the pressure of change.[12] Instead, systems theories connect
up with the concept of purposive-rationally operating prudence,
which was already de-moralized at the beginning of modern times;
they definitively free this concept of all connotations of both the
good life and political power maintenance, as well as of a means-end
scheme correlated to intentional actions. Viewed from the observer's perspective, social systems are formed by selecting from indeterminate possibilities, and are stabilized by strengthening these
selections with structures.[13] In order to be able to reproduce these
selections in various situations, systems adapt themselves to contingency by "temporalizing their complexity."[14] Their elements
themselves consist only of events (acts of consciousness, actions, information) which must be correlated anew at every moment, and
differently, so that the system can be perpetuated in time and determinacy. If social systems are successful in forming structures
that can deal with events as if they were information quanta (by tying selections of events to codes, for example), they can combine self-
reproduction with immense openness to information from the social
environment. In this way the application problem disappears
through the back door, as it were. However, it still remains questionable whether we are compelled to take this hasty step and solve
the problem of applying norms in contingent situations simply by
generally assimilating social structures to contingency. To be sure,
the systems-theoretic radicalization of contingency seems to be immediately plausible: "Time is the reason for the compulsion to select
in complex systems, for if there were an infinite amount of time
available, everything could be coordinated with everything else."[15]
From this perspective, even the traditional concept of judgment
proves to be a faculty pointing beyond reason because taste is able
to judge faster and can individualize the situation to be appraised
without having to justify rationally the transition from the general
to the specific.[16] Nevertheless, one could first of all ask whether
action-theoretic rationality is of absolutely no use to application because, supposedly, it has to be combined with the dimension of
infinity (infinite time, infinite knowledge). It could be that contingency can be separated from the justification of norms and that it
does not become a problem until actually applying norms. Then, one
would not be forced from the outset to surrender the claim, gained

from the actor's perspective, to a rational justification of norms and could consider in a second step whether this claim also has consequences for the application of norms. This presupposes that distinguishing between justification and application is possible and that one does not allow the attempt at a *rational* reconstruction of the application problem to fail as a direct result of the structural indeterminacy of situations; or, because of this, being then seduced into switching to the observer's perspective. It could possibly make sense to work for a while with the *assumption* that infinite knowledge can be acquired in infinite time. As long as we can proceed along this path, we do not need to get involved in the observer's perspective. Not until the end of this journey is the change in perspective necessary, and then it can be justified and does not have to be merely presupposed.

Up to this point it has been shown that the cited suggestions for a more precise determination of the application problem by means of the concept of judgment either avoid the problem or solve it at the expense of an essential element. We ran into the following dilemma: Either we had to assert that one can distinguish between justification and application with the consequence that the application problem was left indeterminate, or we could say something about the application problem but, at the same time, had to abandon claims to a rational justification of norms. Aristotelian attempts at a solution proved to be insufficient because they embed the concern with moral norms as such in the conception of a good life, which is no longer able to withstand the pressure of contingency generated by application situations; whereas systems theories stand up to this pressure, they do so only to absorb it in such a way that actually connecting the problem to moral action becomes superfluous. In order to show that a rational solution to the application problem is possible, at least to a certain degree, we have to take two steps in what follows. First, a distinction between the justification and the application of moral norms must be shown to be possible and meaningful. To this end, we shall refer to discourse ethics since it contains the clearest formulation of a cognitivist ethics, where the validity of moral norms is dependent on the quality of the justification. In addition, discourse ethics has so far been most vehemently confronted with the objection of insufficiently considering the particular situation. In this context, we shall also have to discuss objections which dispute that it is at all meaningful to claim such a distinction. If the demarcation between justification and application should succeed (Parts One and Two), it has to be examined in a further step whether rational standards for the application of norms can be explicated (Part Three). As our preliminary reflections have shown, it is not enough to leave this explication indetermined—by abstractly referring to judgment. In the course of attempting to distinguish between justification and application, it will become evident that the entire project of a cognitivist ethics depends not only on it being able to propose a procedure for the appraisal of good reasons for universally binding norms, but also on it being able to say something about the application of such norms in concrete situations. Not until we have explicated such standards shall we, on the basis of the legal system, turn to the problem of whether the structural indeterminacy of application situations does not condemn the entire enterprise to failure (Part Four).

Part One

The Problem of Application
in Discourse Ethics

The following section is concerned with the justification of the thesis that, in moral action, questions of norm validity must be separated from questions of application. As a first, preliminary reflection—still independent of any subsumption under a specific conception of ethics—it may be sufficient to point out that two distinct activities are involved: on the one hand, justifying a norm by showing that there are reasons, of whatever kind, to accept it, and, on the other, relating a norm to a situation by inquiring whether and how it fits the situation, whether there are not other norms which ought to be preferred in this situation, or whether the proposed norm would not have to be changed in view of the situation. This distinction does not alter the fact that the changed norm or the norm preferred to the one originally considered is itself in turn in need of justification and can be justified. The question whether ascertaining that a norm "fits" a given situation does not also take care of the justification problem is left open for the time being. What is first important is to separate and isolate the various aspects. Should it become apparent that this leads to absurd consequences, then we might well pursue the matter in the direction of that question.

Much more salient is the question whether norms can at all be justified without considering application situations. In what follows, we shall begin with this objection in order to sort out those phenomena which belong in the application dimension. In doing so I shall rely on the moral principle of the universalizability of norms as the justification principle suggested by Habermas in connection with his reflections on the justification of a discourse ethics. Every valid norm has to fulfill the following conditions: "*All* affected can accept the consequences and the side effects its *general* observance can be anticipated to have for the satisfaction of *everyone's* interests (and these consequences are preferred to those of known alternative possibilities for regulation)."[1]

At first glance, this principle of universalization (U) itself seems to presuppose the consideration of application situations when justifying norms, so that the necessity of distinguishing between justification and application could be demonstrated only inadequately using this principle. However, before examining this more carefully, we have to recall the distinction, mentioned above[2] in the discussion on Kant, between *pure* practical and *practical* judgment in order not to make the same mistake as Kant (in places) and his opponents and confuse the application of the *moral principle* with the application of a *norm* justifiable by the moral principle. Even independent of whether or not one combines essentialist assumptions about general reason with the predicate "pure" (which Kant liked to use), it is analytically constitutive of the concept of a moral principle that applying such a principle to a norm be separated from applying norms to a situation. If we keep this distinction in mind, three "application problems" associated with (U) can be isolated from one another, ones which lead us to the above-mentioned objection that a principle of justification without reference to application situations is really an empty formula.

I shall first turn to the question whether (U) can be applied to a norm hypothesis without referring to the application situations of the norm hypothesis—to put it another way: can the validity of a norm be justified independently of the situations of its application? I shall discuss this problem not on the basis of the rather complex version of the moral principle (U), but on the basis of the somewhat simpler version of a semantic universalization principle, as has been proposed by Hare and others. Here, the relationship between justification and application is already relevant because the semantic principle of universalizability presupposes that the norm hypothesis can be applied in different, but sufficiently similar situations. After this first step in section 1, I shall deal with the moral principle (U), which apparently even demands a reference to application situations if considering "the consequences and the side effects its general observance can be anticipated to have" belongs to the conditions of a valid norm. The difficulties, arising from the interpretation developed in section 2, in understanding this relation to application will be dealt with in section 3; I shall attempt to resolve them by proposing two formulations of the moral principle (U), of which only the stronger one connects justification and application with each other. As will be seen, this stronger formulation fully explicates the meaning of the idea of impartiality, but it cannot be shaped into an operational principle. In contrast, the weaker formulation permits an understanding of the idea of impartiality in the sense of a principle of justification, which explains why it has to be supplemented by an independent principle of impartial application. Following this, I shall examine (in section 4) the possibility of describing the impartial application of norms as a discursive procedure. This attempt will lead us once again to the converse problem of whether justification discourses can be replaced by application discourses. This objection, raised by Wellmer against the thesis of the distinction between justification and application, will be discussed in section 5. If the distinction can be implemented in the manner proposed here, there still remains one "application problem" to be discussed in section 6. Karl-Otto Apel has concerned himself with the question of how it is possible to apply the moral principle itself to a form of life.

1

Justification and Application
on the Presupposition of a Semantic
Principle of Universalizability

There can be no disputing the fact that a norm cannot exist
without showing a reference to situations, however weak this may
be. Every moral norm is "case-impregnated." Here, one can think of
Hare's analyses of the descriptive, as distinct from the prescriptive
meaning component of a moral norm,[3] or of Wellmer's discussion of
the unavoidable "situational index" of every norm.[4] The hermeneutical insights into the situation dependency of norms[5] are not to
be forgotten either, insights which, in existentialism, were height-
ened to the assumption of a kind of "situation ethics."[6] In order not
to lose sight of the systematic problem, let us summarize these insights as follows: Simply because of its semantic content, every
norm already incorporates a reference to situations, or to be more
precise, it contains descriptions of situation features. (How this content is to be appropriately explicated—whether hermeneutically,
semantically, or pragmatically—is not of consequence at the moment.) This observation is relevant to the application of (U) because
the "purity" of the justification principle and, as a result, the thesis
of the possibility of a distinction between justification and application could thereby be invalidated. If every norm in need of justification is tied to specific application situations in virtue of its case-
impregnated semantic content, then these application situations
must also become the object of any appraisal using (U). Then, however, it is no longer plausible why questions of application cannot
also be—at least implicitly—the subject matter of justification.
Furthermore, the distinction between justification and application
appears artificial since it operates with a fictitious kind of separation of powers in morality, according to which the decision on
the validity of a norm would be assigned to a justifying norm-
giver, whereas the application would be in the hands of a separate,

independent authority. Since this fictitious separation of powers is not compatible with the reality of the legal world, transposing it to questions of morality seems to lead to even more absurd consequences.

The response to this objection depends on what role the semantic content of a moral norm plays in testing conducted by (U). This in turn can only be determined when it is clear what is to be understood by the idea of a "universalization" of norms in need of justification. What is simply the reverse side of that objection is the misunderstanding that a "generalization" in the sense of indeterminate generality is necessarily connected to the testing of the universalizability of norms, so that cognitivist ethics could only justify the validity of "general" norms or would transform concrete norms into abstract ones. Similar to the confusion of the moral principle with moral norms, this objection rates arguments belonging to the validity testing of a norm incorrectly as arguments belonging to the appraisal of its semantic appropriateness.

The range in meaning of the terms used in a norm is irrelevant to the universalizability of this norm. This applies even when the universalizability principle is understood in a weak sense as the meaning of the expression "ought" and not, as Habermas comprehends it, as a principle of general and qualified agreement of all those affected. As R. M. Hare has shown, there are two different levels on which one can proceed when analyzing the generality of a norm. At one level, we distinguish between general and specific norms and, at the other, between universal and singular norms. Only the first distinction relates to the problem of the determinacy of norms, which is under discussion here. The semantic content of a norm can be, to varying degrees, situation-specific or not, depending on the level of detail employed by the terms used in the norm in describing possible situation features. The difference between a general and a specific norm is therefore only one of degree. General norms can thus also be specified at will, depending on how well we are informed about the facts of an application situation. It is only between universal and singular norms that there is a mutually exclusive difference. This difference depends on the logical properties of the expressions used in formulating a norm. Whereas singular terms designate an individual constant, universal terms consist of individual variables which can be fulfilled by more than one constant. "Briefly, generality is the opposite of specificity, whereas universality is compatible with specificity, and means merely the property of being governed by a universal quantifier and not containing individual constants."[7] Thus, even a highly situation-specific norm can still be universal as long as the terms relating to the situation features are applicable to more than one referent. This is for instance the case when the norm does not contain any proper names.

The two distinguished pairs are important for Hare because his thesis of the universalizability of moral norms is connected to the logical property of universal terms. We can justify a moral norm by showing that we would also observe or recommend it in every other situation that is sufficiently similar to the given one, and we do this even if we find ourselves in the place of others.[8] This presupposes that we can apply the proposed norm, at least hypothetically, to different situations on the basis of its semantic properties. Obviously, this cannot be done with singular terms. In *this* respect, universalizable moral norms do not differ from descriptive propositions whose meaning rule compels us to apply a predicate we ascribe to a thing because of certain properties to every other thing whose properties are similar in all relevant aspects to those of the first one.[9] For Hare, the special character of moral judgments, in contrast to purely descriptive ones, lies in their "prescriptiveness." The compulsion to apply a universal proposition to all similar situations does not only arise from the fact that the semantic properties of universal terms obligate us to observe this rule, if we do not want to pay the price of an incorrect use of language; rather, it also arises from the fact that, by using the predicate "ought," we commit ourselves to a recommendation or to a moral principle which we follow not only in the given situation, but also in all other situations belonging to the semantic extension of this norm. The logically compelling force, which inheres in a moral norm on account of the universal terms contained in it, cannot unfold, as it were, until I have already decided to regard a proposed norm as being motivationally binding (recommendable) for my action and that of everyone else.[10] Every moral norm is "synthetic" in virtue of its prescriptive meaning components.[11] Hare's metaethical position does not prescribe what norms we should choose; rather, it only explicates the fact that we are subject to certain semantic rules—by attaching the expression "ought" to a proposed action—*when* we recommend this action. What rules, maxims, or principles I decide on depends on what kind of person I am. "I have been maintaining that the meaning of the word 'ought' and other moral words is such that a person who uses them commits himself thereby to a universal rule."[12]

Already on the basis of these logical distinctions, it is clear that, with the choice of a specific moral norm, nothing has yet been decided about whether it is justifiable. We shall not know that until we have subjected the chosen norm to a test procedure, which for Hare consists in checking whether we would accept the same norm in other situations too. Nor does the specificity of the semantic content belong in this test procedure because the logic of the expression "ought" simply obligates us to formulate the norm hypothesis in universal terms and to regard it prescriptively as being motivationally binding for me and for others with regard to me. This is a necessary condition in order to be able to enter a justification procedure in the first place—a procedure by means of which the proposed norm is hypothetically applied to different situations. Every norm we subject to the universalization test has that specific semantic content we gave it when originally choosing it.

Our original question was, however, whether the universalization procedure enjoins us to consider the application situation in greater detail and, to this extent, is not neutral in respect of application, but can intervene in the semantic content of a norm, thus modifying it. After all, following Hare, we continually spoke about "situations" in our elucidation of his semantic analysis of normative propositions. Thus we still have to specify more precisely what is meant when the universalization principle demands that a proposed norm be accepted even when we find ourselves in a situation different from the original one.

For this procedure, a special aspect of the hypothetical comparison of situations is essential. The procedure can lead to the result that I reject a norm because of its nonuniversalizability only if I myself come to the realization that I cannot will the validity of such a norm under changed conditions. However, this insight remains inaccessible as long as I perceive the changed situation merely from my own perspective. What therefore also forms a part of the comparison of situations is that I put myself in the place of the other person affected by the consequences of my action and reflect on whether I still want to accept the proposed norm as binding for me and others now that I have also considered the needs and interests of the other person.[13] This requirement to change perspectives should not be confused with other versions of universalist ethics in the tradition of G. H. Mead,[14] according to which the change in perspective also incorporates the agreement of the other person; we shall return to this later. For the present, it is sufficient to understand this requirement—following Hare—in a weaker sense and simply attribute it to the meaning of the word "ought." According to that, the perspective of the other person is one of the variable situation features which, by reason of the universalization principle, I have to consider when reflecting on whether I want to observe the proposed norm in other situations too.[15] Since the word "ought" is used not only prescriptively—designating a norm that is motivationally binding for my will—but also in the sense of a universal rule, I have to combine my will hypothetically with that of another person in order to decide—according to my will thereby expanded to include the perspective of the other person—whether I can still will the application of the proposed norm.[16] If, having undertaken this expansion of my perspective, I nevertheless make a one-sided decision in favor of my own interests and without considering those of the other person although, had I done so, I would have actually had to reject the proposed norm, then not only do I use the word "ought" incorrectly for semantic reasons, but I also contradict myself.[17] What has to be examined now, however, is whether this hypothetical expansion of my perspective, which is linked to the comparison of situations, is necessarily coupled with a change in the semantic content of my proposed norm. When, on finding myself in a concrete situation, I universalize my mode of action in accordance with the perspective of the other person, don't I have to consider aspects belonging to this concrete situation where I want to perform this action and apply the corresponding norm?

Hare himself seems to give an affirmative answer to this question. He not only calls for the consideration of all the facts of the particular case and for the use of imagination,[18] but also compares the justification procedure of universal prescriptivism to "a kind of exploration," where we "look for moral judgements and moral principles which, when we have considered their logical consequences and the facts of the case, we can still accept."[19] By relating the justification of a norm to the specific case, to the external and internal facts, to the particular circumstances and the people affected, as well as to the consequences and side effects, Hare does not seem to distinguish between the justification and the application of a norm. Rather, it seems as if justifying a norm in an application situation focuses on proving that this norm is the one applicable under the particular circumstances of the case. To this end, we have to, as in any exploratory research process, advance hypotheses, experiment with the marginal circumstances of the situation and with the needs of the other person, and check the elicited results in respect of whether we could accept them without self-contradiction. But then the change of a norm hypothesis in a situation would also form a part of the process of moral justification.

In order to decide whether this impression is correct, we have to look at the entire construction of Hare's moral theory once again. The requirement of considering all the particular features of a given case is situated within the context of the justification of a norm, the criteria of which issue exclusively from the logic of the word "ought." The facts we refer to in this process thus only serve the examination of the legitimate use of the word "ought" in conjunction with a universal normative proposition. In order to establish the *validity* (as we could also say) of a normative proposition, we have to consider what consequences could arise from its application to particular facts and whether we are willing to accept these consequences. The facts, to which we relate a proposed norm in the context of these deliberations, need therefore be only hypothetical.[20] Then, however, it does not even matter whether they belong to the particular application situation or not. This does *not* mean that the particular features of the application situation could not be relevant to the deliberation on whether the norm could still be accepted if these or similar features were considered in a different situation. Yet, the consideration of these facts within the framework of these deliberations is logically independent of the circumstance that they are facts belonging to the application situation. The selection of the relevant facts is exclusively determined by the goal of testing the universalizability of the norm. What does not belong in this sphere are deliberations of the following kind: whether the proposed norm is the right or appropriate one *in this situation* too, whether it would not have been better to have favored a different norm on considering all the features of the situation, or whether the originally proposed norm should be modified in this situation. The only focus of interest in this sphere is the proposed norm and its semantic content, inasmuch as it is determined by universal terms. The situational index or case-impregnated character of a proposed norm, which cannot be circumvented even by restricting the terms to universal ones, does not in itself transform a deliberation aimed at justification into one oriented toward application. If we have arrived at the result that the norm is justified because we can also accept it in similar situations and if we were in the place of the person affected, this judgment is valid only to the point to which the semantic content of this norm extends. The semantic content is given prior to justification. It seems questionable that Hare himself would agree with this interpretation of his justification principle. Since he often condenses the argumentation situation of a justification to the application situation and thereby attaches his metaethical analyses to act-utilitarian positions,[21] the difference between justification and application is only of marginal significance for his position. That does not however affect our distinction. True, in every norm proposal which we subject to the universalizability test in an application situation, there is implicitly the claim that, with this proposal, we have suggested the right norm for this situation. If we believe our proposed norm to be appropriate, we need not expressly enter a deliberation on application after having completed the justification. However, we do not confirm this implicit claim by deliberating on whether we would still accept this norm as being valid if we considered still other features of the application situation, or put ourselves in the place of the concrete other. Merely by chance does it then *seem* as if, by establishing that the norm specifically related to this application situation is universalizable, we had also passed positive judgment on its appropriateness. In these cases it is improbable that we would declare a norm to be universalizable and justified but not appropriate to the situation. Nevertheless, because the set of features drawn upon when ascertaining universalizability is accidentally congruent with the set on which we would base our judgment of situational appropriateness, it does not follow that this has to be so in every case. The difference between the logical roles that the reference to situation features in justification and application situations plays in each case requires that the application problem be isolated, even though it seems at first glance as if the difference actually played only a minor role. In any case, Hare's semantic interpretation of the meaning of "ought" does not lead to an abandoning of the distinction between justification and application. It does not tell us what we should do when, in a situation, we have to select the relevant features which have to be brought into relation with a norm that is appropriate to the situation. It is not until we have hypothetically formulated a norm that we can, with the help of the universalizability principle, test whether it is morally valid.

2

Justification and Application
on the Presupposition
of the Moral Principle (U)

What still remains to be examined is whether this result is also consistent with a stronger version of the universalization principle as proposed by Habermas in the form of (U). Hare's semantic interpretation of this principle strongly suggests a blurring of the difference between justification and application because, in this interpretation, testing the moral quality of a norm is tied to a comparison of different situations and situation features belonging to the semantic extension of this norm. That gives rise to the impression that resolving the justification issue would also resolve the problem of application. Because of a special difficulty that inevitably arises with this procedure, it was suggested that the universalization principle be given a dialogical formulation. The change in perspective, also identified by Hare as an important indicator of the generalizability of a norm, quickly comes up against cognitive limits. It is only with difficulty, especially in complex situations, that I can put myself in the place of others. Moreover, I never completely leave my own perspective in favor of that of the other person. The deliberation required by universal prescriptivism—that, were another person to perform an action in the same situation with regard to me, I should still will that this mode of action be carried out—still leaves the decision up to me. There remains an egocentric residuum which could jeopardize the meaning of the universalization principle as a moral principle guaranteeing an impartial judgment.[22] The full meaning of this principle is not exhausted until the proposed norm, viewed from the perspective of each individual, can be collectively accepted by everyone.[23] This requirement stipulates that *everyone* put himself in the standpoint of the other person, that this be done *reciprocally,* and that all concerned judge *collectively* whether the norm corresponds to their common interests. Hare's version of the universalizability principle is not thereby invalidated, but it loses its status as a moral principle and becomes a component in a rule of argumentation which plays a role in the application of (U) in discourses.[24]

This version is also compatible with the distinction between the general or specific character of a norm, on the one hand, and its universal or singular character, on the other. Highly specified norms or modes of action can also be the object of a procedure in accordance with (U); however, they have to be formulated in universal terms since the minimal condition of a comparison of situations conducted from an egocentric perspective, as well as the possibility of a hypothetical application of the proposed norm to the situation of all other people, would otherwise be excluded *by these terms themselves.* Our original question was, however, whether expanding the principle of universalizability to include a dialogical dimension could have consequences for the distinction between justification and application. At first glance, this does not seem to be the case since the only difference between it and Hare's version consists in the fact that it is no longer one person alone who applies the norm to comparable situations, but rather everyone collectively. However, before we may accept this result, we have to inquire whether, when applying (U) itself, application situations do not perhaps play a role. After all, the discourse ethics version of (U) precludes a monological application[25] and requires that practical argumentation be conducted in the form of a discourse. For this reason, we have to examine whether the argumentation logic of practical discourses does not perhaps compel us to consider application situations.

The logical reconstruction of practical argumentation links up with the distinction between communicative action and discourse, which is however viewed not from the perspective of action theory, but from that of the logic of argumentation. The reason for this change follows from the fact that we do not relate directly to the objective, social, or subjective worlds in communicative action; rather, we thematize these world relations themselves as an issue in need of justification. If agreement, which is sufficiently effective for action, is be reached on this, the illocutionary meaning of those speech acts with which we establish a relation to a particular world in order to coordinate our actions in each case must itself become the object of an argumentation, that is, we have to justify the validity claim of an assertion, a norm, or an expressive utterance.[26] In the case of normatively regulated action—the only form of action of interest to us here—the distinction, as determined by the logic of argumentation, between communicative action and discourse can be summarized, as proposed by McCarthy, in the following way: "At a first (prediscursive) level, this [a justification for an action] can be provided by indicating the relevant data, the features of the situation that make this the 'right' or 'appropriate' thing to do or say, that is, the reasons for doing or judging things in this way in this situation. The warrant that establishes the connection between the proffered reasons and the problematic action or evaluation is in this case not a general law but a general norm or principle of action, or a general norm or standard of evaluation."[27]

It is not until a second level is reached that the general norm or principle of action itself must in turn be justified by referring to other principles or to relevant evidence which can support the principle of action at issue: "The relevant evidence is first and foremost the consequences and side-effects that the application of a proposed norm can be expected to have in regard to the satisfaction or nonsatisfaction of generally accepted needs."[28]

Let us stay with the first level for the moment. The fact that we have to refer to data and situation features when justifying an action seems at first glance to be strong evidence for the assumption that application situations play an important role in justifications, that is, as a criterion for the rightness or appropriateness of the action requiring justification. However, this impression changes when we ask how the data acquire the function of a criterion. Merely referring to situation features does not per se justify an action; this is not the case until the action can be based on a norm to which those features and data are relevant. The property of being a reason for action is not written all over the face of the data. They have this property only insofar as the action follows from a norm *together with* the situation features. This can be made clear by employing Toulmin's argumentation scheme. According to this, we represent the action requiring justification by "C" (for conclusion), the relevant data and situation features by "D" (for data), and the norm of action by "W" (for warrant). For the justification of an action we have the following simple scheme:[29]

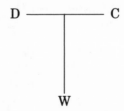

The level of communicative action thus refers to the relation between C, D, and W. W functions as a rule of inference[30] that permits
the transition from D to C. A practical argumentation can thus begin by citing data as reasons for an action (C) and, in the next step,
lead to the citing of a warrant that connects D and C. "If our chal-
lenger's question is, 'What have you got to go on?', producing the
data or information on which the claim is based may serve to answer him; but this is only one of the ways in which our conclusion
may be challenged. Even after we have produced our data, we may
find ourselves being asked further questions of another kind. We
may now be required not to add more factual information to that
which we have already provided, but rather to indicate the bearing
on our conclusion of the data already produced. Colloquially, the
question may now be, not 'What have you got to go on?', but 'How
do you get there?'. To present a particular set of data as the basis
for some specified conclusion commits us to a certain *step;* and
the question is now one about the nature and justification of
this step."[31]

The fully explicated justification for an action C thus consists
in a warrant W being applied to data and situation features D. By
advancing D as the reason for C, we have implicitly committed ourselves to a warrant which then recommends, calls for, or permits C
if D is present. Because Toulmin has the argumentation *begin* with
the citing of data and situation features, the fact that an implicit
decision has already been made on their relevance to the complete
justification remains, however, concealed. The application of a warrant to a particular set of data is then no longer a problem of
principle if, with the choice of this set, we have thereby already committed ourselves to an appropriate warrant. Toulmin seems to have
noticed this himself: "The data we cite if a claim is challenged depend on the warrants we are prepared to operate with in that field,
and the warrants to which we commit ourselves are implicit in the
particular steps from data to claims we are prepared to take and
to admit."[32]

On this presupposition, the transition from the data to the action C can also be analytically presented. Thus, Alexy has given this
kind of justification the following form:[33]

$$.(1) \quad (x) \quad (Fx \longrightarrow Gx) \quad (W)$$
$$.(2) \quad Fa \qquad\qquad\qquad (D)$$
$$(3) \quad Ga \qquad\qquad\qquad (C) \quad (1), \quad (2)$$

From this presentation it is completely clear that, with the justification of Ga by Fa, one avails of a universal rule (in Hare's sense) that already envisions a corresponding transition. Whether Fa is relevant to W depends on whether Fa belongs to the range of variables of Fx. If that is the case and Fa is present in the application situation, the norm W can be applied to D, and C can thereby be justified.[34] We have then already chosen the relevant situation features and we apply the norm only to the chosen domain. For this reason, the justification of action C does indeed refer to the application situation, but only to the extent that it is relevant to a (universal) norm from which C, together with D, issues. On the other hand, with the choice of W, we have already stipulated the domain of possibly relevant data. The justification of C thus comprises an application problem only in the narrow sense: C is considered to be justified not merely if there is a warrant W that permits the transition from D to C, but W must, in addition, be *applicable* to D and it must *be correctly applied* to D. This application problem is however to be separated from the question whether the transition from D to C is appropriate in view of various other data and situation features, and whether there are not perhaps still other warrants which can be applied to other situation features (or to the same ones in a different way) and thus lead, in this situation, to a different conclusion, one which should possibly be preferred to the original conclusion. When Toulmin states that, in argumentation, we have to *inter alia* "show that, taking these data as a starting point, the step to the original claim or conclusion is an appropriate and legitimate one,"[35] then both matters can be meant by this. Insofar as we have followed Toulmin, his proposed reconstruction of the logic of the uses of argument contributes nothing to the solution of the application problem in the wide sense, which is concerned not with the right application of a norm, but with the application of the right (appropriate) norm.[36]

This could change when we move to the second, discursive level. In discourse it is a matter of justifying the general action norm itself. Here, the universalization principle (U) plays the role of a rule of argumentation that should make it possible to pass from empirical evidence on the consequences for and side effects on each individual's needs, when a norm is generally applied, to the norm embodying a general interest.[37] This evidence or these descriptive references can be interpreted in Toulmin's scheme as "backing" for the norm in need of justification.[38] Applying (U) to a norm hypothesis (W) then serves to establish a bridge between the norm and the interests of all those affected, so that the validity of the norm can be tied to the agreement of all affected. It is possible that, in virtue of its meaning and functional mode, this bridging principle already includes the solution to all the problems associated with appropriately considering the particular features of an application situation. By applying (U), the interests relevant to backing a proposed norm are brought into a relation with the consequences and side effects of generally observing a norm. What consequences and side effects will arise, however, can only be ascertained when one anticipates possible application situations. Which of these consequences of applying a norm are relevant depends in turn on the interests of those affected. Thus (U) establishes a relation between the originally proposed norm and the interest embodied in it, on the one hand, and the interests of the rest of those affected, on the other. If (U) should serve as a test of whether the originally proposed norm embodies "an interest common to all affected,"[39] it evidently incorporates a "balancing of interests"[40] into practical argumentation, which can acquire its content only from possible application situations. Whether the consequences of applying a norm affect my interests and my own normative orientations (which are in need of justification), I will not know until I imagine in what situations an application of the proposed norm produces whatever kind of effects. On the other hand, already in our preliminary reflections, we became aware of the fact that not all of the possible application situations can be foreseen; for (U) itself speaks only of those consequences and side effects which "can be anticipated." Furthermore, the description of my interests—even if "the individual is the last court of appeal for judging what is in his best interest"[41]—is dependent on interpretations and traditions which can change. The interpretation of application situations in the light of affected interests is then also subject to such change.[42] Thus it seems as if only some, but not all of the possible application situations could be considered when applying (U). In order to clarify more exactly in what sense (U) is to be understood, we shall attempt in what follows to determine more precisely the meaning of such expressions as "general observance," "consequences and side effects" as well as "the interests of each individual." This will lead us to proposing a distinction between a stronger and a weaker version of (U). In the process, it will become evident that only the weaker version captures the meaning of (U) as a principle of justification and must therefore be supplemented by application discourses.

3

Two Versions of the
Universalization Principle

(U) requires the consideration of the consequences and side effects of a *general observance* or *application* of the norm in need of justification.[43] Only two things can be rationally meant by this: an observance by everyone who can be potentially considered an addressee (that is, if we exclude proper names, infinitely many), and an application in all situations. Both meaning components sound trivial when regarded within the context of (U). Precisely because the application of the universalization principle is aimed at ascertaining whether a proposed norm is in the common interest of everyone, it would be incorrect to limit the group of persons hypothetically entitled to observe the norm. Otherwise, an essential element of the universalization principle, contained in all the different versions, could not be fulfilled, one which consists in deliberating on whether the validity of a norm is still in my interest, not only when I observe it with regard to others (and thus possibly to my advantage), but also when others observe it with regard to me (and thus possibly to my disadvantage). Only if the consequences of a general norm observance for the life plans and conditions of each individual are expounded, can it be ascertained what is really in the common interest of all those affected.

The matter is more complicated with the second meaning component, application in all situations. Here too, there is at first a completely trivial sense: whoever speaks of a norm as of a rule combines with this the idea of a number of cases that are the same in a respect relevant to the rule and, because of this, are cases to which the norm can be applied. Whoever does the same in cases that are the same follows a rule: "The use of the word 'rule' and the use of the word 'same' are interwoven."[44] That there must be more than one application situation, at least potentially, already follows from the semantic condition, adopted from Hare, that a norm may not

29

contain any proper names, but rather only universal terms. What would then also belong to this would be the situation which differs from the original one only insofar as I find myself in the place of those affected by my intended action. Nevertheless, this kind of deliberation belongs to the application of (U) not only because I can thereby weigh the effects of observing a norm on my own self, but also because, in situations with different marginal conditions, there can be different consequences which in turn can be significant in different ways for the interests of each individual and thus ultimately for the common interest. Therefore, what is to be understood by the general application of a norm in all situations must now be clarified.

I shall try again to begin with the simplest possibility. The expression "general application of a norm" subsumes all the situations in which the norm is *applicable*. This means that those affected have to imagine situations in which all the features presupposed by the semantic content of the norm are given. Here I am disregarding the fact that not always, and usually seldom, can it be decided whether the particular features of a situation are included by the semantic extension of a norm; instead I am assuming that an application is possible in those situations imagined by those involved. The set of those situations to which the norm is applicable would then be formed from all the situation features to which the meaning of the universal terms used in the norm refers.

Now, a situation rarely consists of only those features belonging to the meaning of an applicable norm. In Kant's example of lying, there is not only the feature that I have the intention to lie, but also that an innocent person is affected by this. Nonetheless, the norm forbidding lying is applicable to this situation. If (U) is to be understood in this way, the number of situations which have to be included in the deliberations can scarcely be anticipated. For all that, let us not concern ourselves with this problem of knowledge yet; instead we shall attempt to clarify the meaning of the clause "all situations to which the norm in question is applicable" even more precisely. As the lying example demonstrates, every situation to which a norm is applicable contains the same features alongside, however, other features which can be different in every situation. Speaking of a rule as being applicable to different situations is only rendered meaningful in the first place by the possibility of various relations between the same and different features. (U) itself would also be superfluous, if it were always only the same situation to which a norm is applicable.

It is the diversity of possible application situations that first produces the material on which we measure the validity claim of a norm. We must now see to what extent this material is relevant to universalization. On the basis of the lying example it is clear that an application of the norm in different situations has, in each case, a different significance for the other situation features. If I isolate the element of my intention to lie and apply the norm forbidding lying to the situation, this has consequences for the fate of the innocent person. Now it seems to be exactly consequences of this kind, whose consideration (U) requires in the wording "consequences and side effects of a general observance of a norm." Here, however, the wording consciously leaves open what status the relation between the application of a norm and the succeeding events should have: whether it is a matter of empirically measurable causal effects or also normative ones. I attempt to take this into account by using the neutral expression "situation features," so that all those consequences and side effects are relevant to a consideration by (U) which arise from an application of the norm in all the various situations—that is, in every situation in which the norm is applicable to a constellation of features. This interpretation also makes sense; for applying (U) to a norm requiring justification is of major importance for deciding whether a norm is valid only if we can produce various examples on the basis of which we can illustrate what effects the application of a norm can have. However, we know this only if we also consider the remaining conditions of the situation. In doing so, we can also think of a wholly concrete situation here and now and reflect on what consequences and side effects observing a norm would give rise to for the concrete person facing me. Nevertheless, we have to keep in mind that, according to our interpretation (up to now), the term "consequences and side effects of a general observance of a norm" includes not only some arbitrary examples, but all the situations in which the norm is applicable.

Of course, not all the consequences of observing a norm in all situations are relevant to an evaluation of the validity claim; rather, only those which affect the interests of each individual. The fact that it depends on the interests of each individual captures the real sense of the principle of universalizability as a postmetaphysical moral principle. Instead of making the validity of a norm dependent on interest-independent criteria, fixed in a suprasubjective generality (however this may be further determined), only the interests of each individual affected by the norm should count. It is from the multiplicity of different, possibly conflicting interests affected by the consequences of a norm requiring justification that a common interest of all those affected must *first be formed*. Here, the polarizing formulation "interests of each individual" versus "collectively accepted by all those affected" guarantees that it is not the interests of the majority or of a certain group which are decisive; rather it guarantees that each individual has to assume the interest standpoint of every other one in order to be able to assess the intensity of every interest affected. It is not until clarity about the interests of everyone prevails reciprocally that one can speak of a common interest. As a result of this condition, (U) cannot be applied monologically; it can be applied only in practical discourses, where every participant has the same right to articulate his needs. The reciprocity of perspective-taking makes an impartial judgment possible, one that takes the real interests of all those affected into consideration, so that there is no need for an artificial restriction of knowledge about one's own or others' interests, as in Rawls' conception of the original position.⁴⁵

However, it still remains to be considered what it means for the application of (U) when the interests of each individual are connected with the consequences and side effects of applying a norm in the manner interpreted above. I assumed that only the consequences of observing a norm in every individual situation in which the norm is applicable can be meant. Accordingly, the interests of all those affected must also refer to this. Then it is a matter of the interests of each individual in every individual situation in which the norm is applicable. This interpretation also makes sense because only those consequences and side effects of applying a norm which are of positive or negative interest to us can be of importance. However, this interpretation also implies that each individual knows what interests he will have in every individual situation in which the norm is applicable. Thus, in the case of the lying example, I have to know that observing the norm forbidding lying will have effects on the fate of the innocent person, as well as what it would mean for my interests as an innocent person if another person, with regard to me and my pursuers, were to observe the norm forbidding lying.

If we accept this extensive interpretation of (U), we have then, however, done away with the application problem. If we pursue the lying example further, it will become clear that my interests as the innocent person are self-evidently directed toward the priority of the duty to save my life over the duty to observe the norm forbidding lying.⁴⁶ By articulating my interest—here: in averting the consequences and side effects of applying the norm forbidding lying to a situation—via a constellation of features which assigns me the role of innocent person, I claim the validity of another norm that in this situation is to be preferred to the one forbidding lying. Such an interest could probably be accepted freely by everyone as a common interest, so that the validity of the norm forbidding lying would have to be nullified or qualified by the restriction (to be formulated in universal terms) that, in the case of the innocent person, priority has to be given to saving his life. If we abstract from this example, it means that we have to consider, in every individual situation to which the norm requiring justification is applicable, all other situation features that are relevant to the interests of each individual and could therefore require the application of another norm or a modification of the original one. Balancing one norm against all other norms applicable in a situation would have already been anticipated by the application of (U) to that norm. We would have then decided not only that the norm is valid, that is, can be accepted by all those affected as embodying their common interest, but also that it is the appropriate norm in every individual situation in which it is applicable. Whether, in view of a particular situation, it is right (appropriate) to apply the norm would be a necessary component in the deliberation on whether the effects of generally observing a norm in every individual situation can be collectively accepted by everyone. In the scheme used by Toulmin, this can be expressed as follows: The evidence (B), with which the warrant (W) is justified, already contains all the relevant data and situation features (D) with which an action or singular normative proposition (C) can be supported. I therefore propose the following "strong version" of (U):

> A norm is valid and in every case appropriate if the consequences and side effects arising for the interests of each individual as a result of this norm's general observance in every particular situation can be accepted by everyone.

(U) would then include the semantic, as well as the universal-reciprocal and the applicative senses of impartiality.

On this assumption, a singular normative proposition could be justified even without referring to a warrant. The range of variables of Fx would be restricted to the single individual "a," and the evidence used to justify the norm's validity would support Ga as well. But Fx would then have to be either so general that this predicate could be applied to any situation whatever—whereby the norm would then be meaningless; or it would have to be so specific that it could be correctly applied only to one single situation in which all the situation features were obvious and the interests of all those affected were evident. Admittedly, when deriving the strong version of (U), we continually operated with an idealizing condition which now has to be investigated more closely; the condition that we can *anticipate* all the situations in which the norm is applicable. Only if our knowledge includes all the cases of a norm's application can we combine the judgment on the norm's validity with the judgment on appropriateness. However, it is obviously the case that we never have such a knowledge at our disposal. The function of the principle of universalization as a principle of impartiality that refers to the application of a norm in every individual situation thus collapses. However trivial, it does not follow from this that we cannot refer to any situation at all or can no longer engage in any reflection on consequences within the framework of justification discourses. In the lying *example,* it was, after all, already to be seen that even imagining hypothetical situations could produce plenty of material on the basis of which we can connect reflections on consequences with interests. Nevertheless, what is now problematic is the criterion according to which we distinguish a situation used as an example within justifications from a genuine application situation.

There cannot be such a criterion, since it would be incompatible with the meaning of the principle of universalization. The only trivial condition for the situations put forward as examples consists in the fact that the norm requiring justification must be applicable in the above-explained sense, that is, the minimal semantic presuppositions must be given in the situation. Otherwise, every restriction would result in certain application possibilities being suppressed and being deprived of a test of their relevance to each individual's interests. Seen from the objective side of the possible application situations of a norm, (U) is therefore an open principle. The limitation we are looking for is on the subjective side. It is dependent on the historical level of our experience and our knowledge. We can suppose only those application situations which we can imagine at the present point in time on the basis of our experience with ourselves as well as with the objective and social worlds. For this reason, in his wording of (U), Habermas himself already alluded to a weaker version: only those consequences and side effects which a general observance of the norm can be *anticipated* to have can be considered. In this way (U) is equipped with an index that ties its application to the level of knowledge at the current point in time.

This index also has an effect on the validity criterion put forward in (U): the common interest of all those affected. Only those interests expected to be affected by the consequences and side effects of applying a norm can be considered.

The circumstance that our interests can change in unimaginable ways also belongs to (U)'s time and knowledge indices. If we could foresee all the interests which will be affected by the repercussions of applying a norm in all application situations, we would not only have infinite knowledge about the objective and social worlds at our disposal, we would also be transparent to ourselves. This is why we can bring our interests to bear only in the manner and range in which we interpret them at the current point in time.[47] There is, however, no restriction with regard to the persons admitted: everyone whose interests are expected to be touched by applying a norm must be permitted to participate in the procedure of validity testing.[48] The cognitive problem that no one affected can anticipate all the possible application situations nor the development of his interests does not diminish his right to bring forward those disadvantages or advantages for his interests which he can foresee. Thus, despite the time and knowledge indices, it still makes sense to speak of the validity of a norm. Every norm justified according to (U) embodies, at that moment in time and corresponding to the current level of knowledge, a common interest—that is, it is valid for *everyone*. Although (U) speaks of a "general observance," the criterion for validity does not refer to all the situations foreseeable from an absolute standpoint; instead, it refers to the consequences and side effects foreseeable at that moment in time, insofar as they are relevant to the current interests of each individual and are collectively accepted by everyone. For this reason I propose the following "weaker version" of (U):

> A norm is valid if the consequences and side effects arising for the interests of each individual as a result of this norm's general observance under unchanging circumstances can be accepted by everyone.

Thus, we cannot rule out the possibility of being surprised, in the next moment, by a new situation in which we discover features different from the ones so far anticipated and which we interpret, in the light of changed interests, in a manner different from similar situations we had interpreted earlier. The fact that we live in a world where innocent people can be saved from an executioner's death only by a lie belongs to our sad experiences and is therefore foreseeable when we consider the consequences and side effects of generally applying the norm forbidding lying. It is already a different matter in situations where a doctor diagnoses that a patient has a terminal illness and asks himself whether he should truthfully inform the patient about the findings. This conflict has only really becomes acute since medical science improved its level of knowledge, and with the accurate prognosis of the course of an illness either destroys consolatory hopes or—in the case of withholding all or some details—violates the right to complete information. If the validity of a norm can be decided for all those affected but cannot be foreseen for all situations, it remains undecided how we should relate to the particular features in application situations, to the consequences and side effects, as well as to the interests— which we could not anticipate—of people concretely affected. The easiest answer would be to see again here simply a validity problem and to consider the new situation features and interests in a renewed application of (U) in order to decide afresh whether the norm is still valid when we incorporate the features of this situation into our knowledge, that is, into the set of what is foreseeable. That would, however, mean making the second step before the first. The correct sequence of these two steps will lead us to the distinction between justification and application.

In the weaker version of (U), we have abandoned the assumption of precisely knowing in advance, and with regard to every situation to which a norm is applicable, what situation features are relevant to the interests of all those affected. Forgoing this because of the time and knowledge indices means, however, that we are in danger of losing the applicative sense of impartiality. Whether it is right to apply a norm in a situation is no longer thematized by an application of (U) in its weaker version. One could leave this decision to judgment. Before making this precipitous step, it still remains to be carefully examined whether (U) does in fact leave us in a helpless position when it comes to the individual case.

(U) had to be equipped with an index simply because no one can anticipate all the application situations (i.e., every individual one) of a norm, but only those situations which can be hypothetically considered within the horizons of our enlightened experience of the world and ourselves. Be that as it may, we did interpret the expression "general observance" in such a way that it satisfies the meaning of the expression "rule," namely, to follow the same rule in every individual situation to which the rule can be applied. This aspect of the meaning of "general observance" does not get lost by introducing time and knowledge indices; it does, however, change into a mere assumption as a result. With the help of this assumption, we can anticipate various possible application situations and can scrutinize the consequences and side effects of an application in these situations. The subject matter of an application of the weak version of (U) is therefore our interests, insofar as they are affected by the proposed norm understood as a rule that is followed in every individual situation to which it is applicable. Thus, with (U), questions of the following kind cannot be thematized: whether it is right to apply the norm in a situation, how it should be applied, and so on; instead, all that is thematized are the consequences we anticipate it would have for our interests if it were applied in every individual situation. For this reason, validity concerns only the question of whether the norm *as a rule* is in our common interest.

However, if, with the weak version of (U), we can only partially redeem the claim that a norm is valid for everyone in all situations, then the meaning of the idea of impartiality is not fully exhausted. If according to the strong version of (U), the idea of impartiality comprises both validity and appropriateness, whereby, however, both cannot be thematized in a single act, we thus need yet another principle which obligates us to examine *in every individual situation* whether the requirement of the rule, namely, that it be followed in every situation to which it is applicable, is *legitimate* too. Since we screen out this question in the weak version of (U), we do not have to answer it for all application situations at once, but rather in the individual situation, and only for this situation. We can decide whether it is right to apply a norm in this situation only if we consider all the features of the situation and examine whether the norm is appropriate to the situation. The claim of a norm to be valid for everyone in all situations must be redeemed in two directions, as it were: in respect of the interests of all those affected, with the assumption of it being observed in all situations; and in respect of every individual situation, with the complementary assumption (but requiring justification) that the norm, appropriate in this particular situation, could also be accepted in different (all) situations by all those affected. What is relevant to justification is only the norm itself, independent of its application in a particular situation. It is a question of whether it is in the interest of all that everyone follow the rule. Whether a norm embodies the common interest of all does not depend on its application, but on the reasons we can advance as to why the norm ought to be observed like a rule by everyone. What

is relevant to application, in contrast, is the particular situation, independent of whether a general observance is also in the interest of
everyone. It is a question of *whether and how* the rule ought to be
followed in a particular situation in view of all the particular circumstances. In application, we have to take up the norm's claim
that it can be observed by everyone in every situation (i.e., like a
rule) from the side facing situations, as it were, and confront it with
all the features of the particular situation. The subject matter is
not the validity of the norm for each individual and his interests,
but its appropriateness in relation to all the features of an individual situation.

The judgment on the appropriateness of a norm does not refer
to all application situations, but always only to an individual one.
Thus, appropriateness means nothing other than limiting the
strong version of (U) to an individual situation. The absolute requirement that all situations be considered at one point in time is
proceduralized on the time axis, as it were, to the requirement that
all features be considered in an individual situation. Only in this
way can we hedge the risk which arises from doing without an absolute judgment on appropriateness in the weaker version. The decision about the validity of a norm does not imply a decision about
its appropriateness in a situation—nor vice versa. Yet both, in each
case, embody a certain aspect of the idea of impartiality: The requirement that the consequences and side effects which a general
observance of the norm can be anticipated to have for the interests
of each individual be acceptable to all operationalizes the universal-
reciprocal sense of impartiality; while, complementary to this, the
requirement that all the features be considered in an individual application situation operationalizes the applicative sense. By combining both aspects with each other, we approach the full meaning
of impartiality on diverse paths, as it were.

Speaking of "all the features in a situation" is admittedly very
vague. It remains unclear in what sense "all" is to be understood—
like Leibniz, for instance, as the absolute fullness of all perceptions,
or only in certain respects? This immediately links up with the
skeptical objection whether this requirement should not also be
equipped with an index since we will never know all the data in an
individual situation either. In Part Three I shall make a more precise proposal on how the requirement that all the features be considered can be operationalized. Since I am only concerned with
demarcating the problem of application at the moment, a few remarks ought to suffice here.

Features of a situation are not per se relevant. They first acquire this status in the light of interpretations, valuations, interests, life plans, or objectives. Depending on the degree to which these experiential patterns are differentiated, we perceive every situation differently, and every individual perceives a situation differently. Moreover, experiential patterns of this kind are changeable, so that we can perceive similar features in similar situations differently or discover new features. Now, the requirement of impartiality in the applicative sense means nothing other than that these different interpretations of a situation must be thematized because we should orient our actions according to a norm that we may consider not only to be valid, but, with justification, to be appropriate as well. It is the process where, in a situation, we debate these interpretations, compare competing and conflicting interests and normative expectations in order to form that norm which we can claim to be the appropriate one in view of the particular circumstances of the individual case. Not until we have completed this step can we step out of the parameters of the particular situation and examine whether the norm, which is appropriate in view of the particular circumstances, is valid too, that is, whether the consequences and side effects arising for the interests of each individual as a result of a general observance can be accepted by everyone. In no way can both steps be condensed into one. This presumption does indeed suggest itself because one could formulate (U) in such a way that, in a particular situation, we should collectively consider the effects of a general observance on the interests of each individual. However, with this version, the universal-reciprocal sense of (U) would become unclear because it confuses the tension between the particular situation and the interests of those concretely involved in it with the anticipated consequences arising for the interests of each individual as a result of generally applying a norm in different situations. The weaker version of (U) links up with a proposed norm, which has already been singled out, in order to put it into a situation-generalizing perspective and relate it to the interests of virtually everyone. That is why this version has to be supplemented by an application discourse which brings the situation-specific perspective to bear and relates it to the interests of concrete others. In application situations, it is not in itself a question of the generalizability of the interests affected, but first only a question of their discovery and relevance to the situation. Whether the interest embodied in the norm appropriate to the situation is also legitimate, that is, an interest commonly acceptable to everyone, is reserved for the application of (U) in the weaker version. If it is the case that only both kinds of practical argumentation together exhaust the full meaning of impartiality and that interest-related justifications are reciprocally dependent on situation-related applications, then it would have been proved that the application of norms in situations belongs to practical reason. Of course, we still have to reflect on the skeptical objection that we can never consider all the particular circumstances, even in a single situation. The microcosm of each individual situation is just as infinite as the macrocosm of all the situations to which the norm is applicable.[49] It would indeed be unrealistic to discard this objection. Yet, this does not rule out the possibility that the *claim* to a consideration of all the features of a situation is not only a possible, but also a practically effective component of the idea of impartiality. Only if we acknowledge this claim can we criticize the inappropriateness of applying a norm in a situation with the argument that a relevant feature has been overlooked or, in relation to other ones, inappropriately weighed.[50] The possibility of moral experiences in new situations also depends on the acknowledgement of this claim[51] since it compels us, when applying a norm in a situation, to pay regard not only to the presence of the application conditions presupposed by this norm, but also to other features—in terms of the claim, all of the features. The entire range of our available experiences should be employed to interpret the present situation appropriately (with all "retentions" and "protentions" in past and future). Being confronted with new experiences in application situations, we learn to recognize those norms in their relative inappropriateness which have thus far been regarded appropriate and to change them in view of newly discovered or differently interpreted features. Because, of course, we will never be able to discover all the features, there still remains a "gap" when we acknowledge a norm as being appropriate in a situation and as embodying a common interest. For all that, the dramatic character of this structural indeterminacy (the designation used above) diminishes to the same extent as we reduce its scope by combining rational justifications and sensitive applications and by incorporating the possibility of such a gap into our practical deliberations. It only assumes catastrophic dimensions, if we blindly insist on the validity of a norm and allow the problem of its appropriateness in a situation to be screened out by the pathos of existential decisions of ultimacy.

4

Application as Discourse

Up to now our discussion has dealt somewhat implicitly with application discourses, which have to supplement the universalization principle (U) in its weak version in order to exhaust the full meaning of the idea of impartiality. In what follows, it will be a matter of showing whether, and in what way, the application of norms in situations is possible as a discourse. This question must surely sound provocative for those who reduce the problem of application to judgment. To all appearances, everything militates initially against any possibility of relating discursive argumentation to the problem of application. Discourses specialize in justifying validity claims.[52] They serve the purpose of argumentatively redeeming the claim to truth connected with the illocutionary meaning of every assertion and the claim to rightness connected with the illocutionary meaning of every normative judgment. Whoever engages in argumentation by virtue of his demanding reasons for recognizing a validity claim has thereby accepted the presuppositions of argumentation, where discursive testing is possible. In practical discourses, (U) functions as a rule of argumentation that should make it possible to come to an impartial judgment on the validity claim of a norm (i.e., on the validity claim of a speech act referring to a norm). The validity claim of normative rightness refers to the general agreement which could be reached on the reasons that can be advanced for justifying the norm. The meaning of (norm) validity thus consists in the recognition of the norm by everyone, that is, as participants in a practical discourse. In this sense, instead of de facto validity, we always refer to "counterfactual" validity. Habermas distinguishes three levels in the presuppositions of argumentation, which direct a discourse to this counterfactuality.[53]

In analogy to the Aristotelian canon of logic, dialectic, and rhetoric, Habermas distinguishes between the logical level of products, the dialectical level of procedures, and the rhetorical level of processes of argumentation. In terms of the aspect of *product,* argumentation serves the purpose of producing cogent reasons with which a validity claim can be redeemed or rejected. Logical and semantic rules, the principle of noncontradiction, semantic consistency when using a predicate, and the identity of meaning among speaker and hearer when using a term are all part of this. As a *procedure,* argumentation is a process of reaching understanding in which the participants enter a competition that serves the cooperative search for truth under special interactive conditions. This is linked to the presupposition that they are relieved of the pressure of action and experience and that they reciprocally recognize each other as participants enjoying equal rights. This presupposition is made possible by rules such as reciprocal truthfulness, or recognizing a distribution of the burden of argumentation. Finally, as a *process,* argumentation serves the purpose of reaching a rationally motivated agreement among the participants. General conditions of symmetry must prevail, ones which exclude all force except that of the better argument. They can be reconstructed in rules that stipulate a general participation of all competent speakers, equal opportunities for speaking, and equal opportunities for availing of these rights. These three levels or aspects of argumentation are represented, each in its own way, within practical discourses by (U), so that (U) can be transformed into the principle of discourse ethics (D), according to which a norm is valid only if "all affected in their capacity as participants in a practical discourse" accept (or would accept) it.[54]

This brief sketch of the presuppositions of argumentation in practical discourses should only serve the purpose of again returning to the question of whether discourses are possible in application situations. An answer depends on how the meaning of the validity claim of a normative utterance is to be understood. The location of its analysis in speech act theory points to the interpersonal relationship which is established by the illocutionary force of a performative utterance.[55] The validity claim is directed toward the legitimacy of this relationship, that is, to its recognition by competent speakers or persons. For this reason, practical discourse is open to everyone. With this interpretation, however, one encounters another variant of the problem we already had with the expression "general observance" when analyzing (U). If norms claim to be valid for more than one situation—which Wittgenstein says is already given with the norm's property of being a rule—one must ask whether the validity claim refers not only to recognition by all potential participants in discourse, but also to all situations in which the norm is applicable. Worded differently: Doesn't recognizing a norm as a valid mean for every participant in discourse that he considers its observance appropriate in all situations in which it is applicable? The interpretation of (U) led to the result that this presumption would hold true if it could be assumed that we could foresee every individual application situation with all the features relevant to our present and future interests. For this reason, (U) was equipped with time and knowledge indices, which tie the decision about validity to the current level of our knowledge and our experience.

However, a closer look at the presuppositions of argumentation introduced by Habermas reveals a peculiar tension between the rule of argumentation (U) and the idealizing conditions of practical discourse. Argumentation is characterized as a procedure in the sense of an endless dialectical process, so that "proponents and opponents, having assumed a hypothetical attitude and being relieved of the pressures of action and experience, can test validity claims that have become problematic."[56] In this formulation, which should procedurally lend expression to the fact that practical questions admit of *truth*, there is no reference to time and knowledge indices. If we had an infinite amount of time and could have absolute knowledge at our disposal—that is, not having to act at the next moment, nor having to reckon with new, unforeseen experiences—we could anticipate each individual application situation too. As a rule of argumentation "that makes agreement in practical discourse possible whenever matters of concern to all are open to regulation in the equal interests of everyone,"[57] the weak version of (U), which is fitted with an index, is either in contradiction to this or is itself to be understood as an operationalization of this idealizing presupposition under conditions of time-dependent and limited knowledge. If the latter interpretation were true, the presuppositions of discursive argumentation would belong to the idea of impartiality in the *strong* sense. The *weak* version of (U) would then have to be understood as a rule of argumentation in justification discourses, which redeem the validity claim of a norm with respect to the common interest of all those affected under conditions of limited knowledge about possible application situations. Then, however, in a complementary step, the conception of an application discourse which proceduralizes the applicative sense of impartiality would also be possible, that is, an application discourse that has as its subject matter the appropriateness of a norm in a situation, taking into consideration all the particular features of the application

situation. The idealizing presuppositions of discursive argumentation would still be located above justification and application discourses, which, each in its own way, specialize in considering, under
specific limiting conditions, the interests of all those affected, on the
one hand, and all the particular features in a situation, on the
other. To that extent, practical reason would be possible in applications too.

   This would of course have consequences for the meaning of a
norm's validity claim. Understanding it in the sense of the strong
version of (U), it would also have to be comprehended as a claim
which includes the appropriateness of a norm in an individual situation and thus compels us to consider all the features in every application situation. It is only in this way that a "dialectical"
interweaving of general validity and concrete contexts can occur:
"The validity claimed for propositions and norms transcends spaces
and times, *'blots out' space and time;* but the claim is always raised
here and now, in specific contexts, and is either accepted or rejected
with factual consequences for action."[58] Application discourses connect a norm's validity claim with the particular context within
which it is applied in a situation. By tying its application to the appropriate consideration of all the particular features of each newly
emerging situation in space and time, these discourses "recontex-
tualize" the norm which was cut off from its context for the purposes
of testing its validity in the light of a common interest. In this way,
there arises a dynamism which in every situation introduces a surprising abundance of unforeseen aspects, subtleties, or alterations
to the semantic content of various, applicable norms and makes
modifications, restrictions, or emphasis shifts necessary in order to
satisfy approximately the claim of an appropriate consideration of
all features. Justification discourses have to halt this dynamism
and, with a hypothetical attitude and on the basis of the current
level of our knowledge, generalize a proposed appropriate norm beyond the concrete situation in order to test whether the consequences and side effects arising for the interests of each individual
as a result of a general observance can be collectively and freely accepted by everyone. It is not until this point that everyone, for himself and still carefully looking to all sides, plunges into the concrete
here and now.

5

Can Justification Discourses be Replaced by Application Discourses?

Against the possibility of distinguishing between the application and the justification of a moral norm in a manner like the one proposed here, Wellmer[59] has put forward objections which are essentially aimed not at expounding that justification discourses are in need of supplementation by application discourses, but, inversely, at treating norm justifications as a merely marginal problem of discourses in which we come to agreement on the right and appropriate mode of action in situations. In what follows I shall attempt to test the tenability of the above-proposed distinction in the process of discussing Wellmer's theses.

Wellmer sketches his objections against the background of a conception of ethics which is less concerned with the universal conditions of legitimate norms than with the conditions of an appropriate or correct understanding of oneself and the world. A universal morality that only deems those norms valid to which everyone can assent with reasons then appears as a possible interpretation of our conception of a good life—a conception which we cannot simply choose arbitrarily, but one with which we have always been living (at least since the Enlightenment) and which we cannot incessantly violate without falling into a false—ultimately, psychologically catastrophic—relationship to ourselves.[60] Ranking among these conditions of accord with ourselves are also those social conditions of reciprocal recognition between autonomous persons, which can only be abstractly reformulated in universalist morality; these are conditions which, after the loss of particular authorities, can only be violated at the cost of endangering our own identity.[61] For this reason, what is in the foreground in moral conflicts is not so much the issue of the individually accountable violation of general norms than that of producing an appropriate, common interpretation of the situation in which those affected act.

45

Whether a mode of action is generalizable in a universalist sense depends primarily on how we understand ourselves, others, and the situation in the context of the world in which we live.

By way of a critical analysis of the function and meaning of different versions of a universalist moral principle, Wellmer comes to this privileging of the "way of acting in a kind of situation" [*Handlungsweise-in-Situationen-einer-Art*][62] vis-à-vis valid norms and thereby to a prioritizing of situation interpretations over norm justifications. According to his interpretation, a moral principle, such as the categorical imperative, contains at the first level a generalization principle which simply follows from the semantics of the concept of a rule and can be characterized in the empirical sciences as an induction principle. As in Hare's interpretation of the logical universality of "ought," I am still obligated to accept those normative convictions I want to follow here and now, even when, in the same situation, I am in the position of the one affected. By choosing the expression "ought," I am obligated not to make any exceptions in my favor. It is not until the second level, according to Wellmer, that it becomes a question of the universalizability of a maxim of action and thus of the categorical meaning of the "ought," which refers to the common will of all rational beings in the Kantian version. Wellmer's intention is to understand the "can be willed" property of a maxim, implied in the categorical imperative by Kant, as that of a general maxim in a manner which does not compel him to dissociate the meta-principle of generalizability from the concrete content and referential context of a factual maxim of action.

According to his reading, the categorical imperative may not be "applied" as a supernorm to subnorms, nor may it be treated as a fixed procedure. Just as Hare ties the logical universality of "ought" to a prescriptive meaning, Wellmer interprets the moral principle as a kind of test which leads me to a contradiction with myself and my intentions when I hypothetically generalize my maxims. The categorical meaning of the moral "ought" reveals itself in maxims that I *cannot* will as general ones without falling into contradiction with myself. For this reason, nongeneralizable maxims have logical priority. It is only with these that the reference to our respective wills functions, that is, the reference which systematically produces self-contradictions. Norms, on the other hand, have a derivative status and are not already justified by reason of their generalizability, but by their internal negative reference to nongeneralizable maxims. They are thus necessarily addressed to exceptional situations in which we have to choose (in the situation itself) a different maxim of action that, in turn, can only be justified by its negative reference to a nongeneralizable maxim. These exceptions can scarcely be subsumed under normative regulations—in the sense of laws of permissibility—because every exceptional situation is different.

The negative interpretation of the moral principle does not tie the obligatory force of "ought" to insight into reasons for the validity of norms (irrespective of whether they are commands, prohibitions, or permissions), but to the concrete will in situations. Of course, this can still be dialogically expanded since one can no longer assume with the same certainty as Kant that what cannot be willed by me cannot be willed by all others either. However, the dialogical expansion is concerned not with the generalization principle as such, but with the appropriate understanding of the situation and oneself. "What we are dealing with here is, as it were, the 'communicative substructure' of Kantian ethics, i.e. that dimension of practical reason concerned with the *commonness* of relations to the world and the *appropriateness* of situation interpretations and self-understandings."[63]

By taking the following step, Wellmer radicalizes the distinction between norms and modes of action, which was developed during his discussion of the categorical imperative, to a contraposition at which Habermas's proposed version of the universalization principle (U) is carried *ad absurdum*. For Wellmer, there are two readings of (U) possible which arise from an interpretation of the expression "valid": (U) as a principle of the justice of norms, or as a principle of the rightness of action. In the *first* case, it is a question of a principle of legitimacy or justice that should tie the general agreement on the validity of a norm to an impartial resolution. According to Wellmer's interpretation, this version is however implausible because it is either tautological or merely an expression of the applicability of consensus theory to the problem of justice. In the *second* case, "valid" is interpreted in the sense of "right" or "ought to be." (U) then appears as a moral principle referring to "actions in a kind of situation." Analogous to his interpretation of Kant, Wellmer now understands (U) as a moral principle which only tells me in concrete situations what I *ought to* do. Understood in this way, however, the application of (U) leads to absurd results. Either one can only discover what norms, under ideal conditions of reaching understanding, are of equal interest to all those affected without knowing how I ought to act under real conditions,[64] or we try to apply it as a principle of evaluation for acting under nonideal conditions; but then we fall into unsolvable problems with the unforeseeability of

ιons under changed situation conditions. Then, the only way
..s to limit the applicability of (U) to *prima facie* norms and treat
..e question of the right action as a problem of application. However, this would have the meaninglessness of (U) as a consequence.

Wellmer has thus demarcated the parameters for his critique
and "fallibilist reconstruction"[65] of discourse ethics: questions on
the *justice of norms* concern procedures for argumentatively agree-
ing on the validity of legal norms and must therefore be separated
from the moral question concerning the conditions for distinguishing a *right mode of action* in situations. (U) is not suitable as a
solution for either problem because it operates with consensus-
theoretic presuppositions that suppress the element of facticity—
which is inherent in the decision on legal norms or in the
appropriate interpretation of my will in a situation—in favor of
idealizing conditions. For this reason, Wellmer follows up his critical interpretation of the universalization principle (U) with a detailed critique of the consensus theory of truth.[66] It is aimed
primarily at proving that it is either incorrect or meaningless to
link truth (and, following Habermas, always "rightness" too) in a
criteriological sense to ideal conditions of a forceless consensus. A
consensus under ideal conditions does not give us a criterion for the
truth/rightness of a consensus under factual conditions.[67] We would
either have to be able to call every de facto consensus true or have
to include the conditions under which we speak of the cogency of
reasons in the definition of ideal conditions. That would however be
meaningless because the evaluation of the cogency of reasons is
then no longer determined by formal and situation-independent criteria, but is dependent on our ability to judge in individual cases.
The formal criterion of ideal conditions would thus contain a material and situation-dependent element. Nor can the "demonstrating
or ascertaining function" (Habermas) of a consensus provide sufficient support for the truth of an assertion. Rather, this depends on
whether we recognize the reasons for a true assertion as "cogent,"[68]
that is, whether they concur with possible perceptions.[69] Consen-
suses merely link up with the prior satisfaction of purely semantic
conditions of truth. Whether a consensus is rational must be ascer-
tainable independently of its truth because what we consider true can
change, even if the conditions for the existence of a consensus are
fulfilled. It is only a kind of dialectical illusion within the participants' internal perspective that makes consensus rationality and
truth coincide for them.[70] Zimmermann has clearly articulated the
consequences of this separation of truth and consensus: "they lead

to the fact that the societal-communicative primacy of discursiveness does not imply the latter's fundamentality for the concept of language."[71] This in turn means that the necessity of discourses can no longer be justified by the fundamental norms of language-mediated intersubjectivity; instead, this necessity is justified for *politics* only by historico-political arguments,[72] for *ethics,* by our conception of the good life and its anchorage in our psychological identity as subjects capable of speech, and for *truth,* not at all. By disburdening validity claims of the ideal conditions of their discursive redeemability—conditions which must unavoidably be considered fulfilled—Wellmer has cleared the way for a dialogical ethics of the appropriate interpretation of situations.

If one still really wants to accept a universalist moral principle, it can only put forward the—negative—generalizability of modes of action as the criterion. In the end Wellmer drops this presupposition too by accepting universalist moral conceptions only as an ex post facto way of presenting our intersubjective conception of the good life. To make this step appear plausible, he interposes a fallibilist reconstruction of discourse ethics in which the universalist moral principle determines the moral argumentation on the generalizability of a mode of action in concrete situations: "My thesis is that, given this presupposition, moral argument is concerned almost exclusively with the interpretation of situations attendant upon actions and needs, as well as with the self-understanding of those who act and suffer—with the result that if we have reached agreement about the interpretation of situations and about self-understanding, moral controversies will as a rule dissolve. This means that the question whether *we* can (reasonably) will that *my* maxim should become a universal law is more or less synonymous with the question whether *my* interpretations of situations, *my* self-understanding, and *my* general interpretations are appropriate, accurate or truthful. The 'we' that so disquiets discourse ethics resides, so to speak, in the validity of my descriptions of situations, my understanding of reality, and my self-understanding. For the same reason, this is also the point at which to begin any critique or argumentative clarification."[73]

Wellmer explicates this thesis on the basis of the historical changeableness of collective patterns of interpretation and of moral argumentation in complex situations. Our moral views, on which we base the equal and unequal treatment of others, are dependent on prevailing collective patterns of interpretation which change under the pressure of the struggle for recognition and as a result of the influence of new experiences. An ethics which can react to such changes is fallibilist. In complex situations characterized by a barely resolvable conflict of different moral norms, the main thing is not so much the scarcely realizable generalizability of norms of permissibility which justify exceptions, but the norm-neutral choice of a mode of action whose generalizability or nongeneralizability is grounded on the "*appropriateness* and the relative *completeness* of descriptions of situations, including the various alternative ways of acting that are available in a given situation."[74] The functional efficiency and applicability of a moral principle of generalization (or rather, of the logical priority of nongeneralizability) to a mode of action depends on the range and intensity of the understanding of the situation. Thus, one could also speak of a direct applying of the moral point of view to the particular action situation: "In this way we could understand moral judgment as the ability to grasp those aspects of action situations upon which the non-generalizability (or the generalizability) of ways of acting depends. . . . But as far as this question is concerned, a consensus among a few individuals who are capable of judging and sufficiently close to the concrete situation is often more important for ascertaining [the] morality [of a mode of action] than a real agreement of everyone."[75]

From this perspective it is clear that Wellmer can and must contest the possibility of a distinction between justification and application.[76] His objection follows indirectly from a toning down of the highly idealizing presuppositions to which Habermas tied the reasons for the validity of a norm in his version of (U) and directly from the counterposing of norms and modes of action. The assertion that justification and application can be differentiated thus originates merely from the *appearance* that, in situations, we happen to be frequently concerned with given norms which, if they are at all relevant, can only have a *prima facie* character, which we have to limit in conflict situations by pointing out exceptions. For this reason, there is no need to wait for discourses to apply the moral principle to a given norm, which we would then, in turn, have to apply in situations; instead, since we liberated ourselves, during the Enlightenment, from this application thinking, which takes its orientation from the "dogmatism of the given," our real moral task consists in "applying" the moral principle itself in situations in order to find out which interpretation of the concrete situation is the more appropriate one. Wellmer suspects that an application problem in discourse ethics arises only as a result of a further confusion that follows from the already criticized "legalization" of morality:

Only in cases where we are concerned with authoritatively given norms, as in law, can we meaningfully distinguish between justification and application; whereas in morality, which does not have norm-giving authority, everyone is directly confronted with the situation and must act with moral sense, so that moral discourse and moral judgment belong together here—"practical reason expresses itself as moral judgment."[77] One could vary this objection as follows: the incorrect distinction between justification and application really concerns the distinction between law and morality.

There are two reasons why we should begin our response to Wellmer's arguments with a critique of this determination of the relationship between law and morality. First, there are also application problems in law which cannot simply be traced back to the fact that here we are concerned with general norms which are "justified" by the legislator and equipped with de facto, authoritative validity by an act of parliament, and have to be applied to individual cases by an institutionalized judiciary.[78] Applying legal norms, at least in complex societies (where there are just as many legally complex as "morally complex" situations, which can no longer be clearly specified as being one or the other) and under conditions of a postconventional refraction of the validity of law, is no longer conceivable without appropriately interpreting the application situation in the light of principles, which for their part are in need of justification. Secondly, it is at least unclear how, for Wellmer, a democratic procedure which secures a general agreement on legal norms could, for its part, be legitimated. According to his interpretation too, the development of ideas of legitimation and the development of procedures of legitimation for positing law are subject to a process of modernization.[79] Nevertheless, this compulsion to modernize cannot be justified following Wellmer's own conception of morality. Ultimately, this compulsion would have to spring from our form of life, which is tied to the existence and maintenance of relations of mutual recognition (and detached only at the cost of a loss of identity); these relations can be explicated ex post facto in universalist conceptions of morality.[80]

This does not however mean that the incontestable evidence for a separation of law and morality should be disputed. Wellmer puts forward the principle of statute, the primacy of the constitutive function over the regulative function of law, and the coercive character of law as such evidence.[81] However, it does not follow from this that it is only in law that norms have a primary status over modes of action and that therefore there is a distinction between justification and application only here; whereas in morality it is primarily a matter of modes of action in situations and only secondarily a matter of norm justification, on account of which justification discourses cannot be distinguished here from application discourses. The question is whether the institutional difference between law and morality can be extended to an analytical one and to a difference in the theory of justification. Since I shall go into the difference between law and morality in greater detail below, in what follows I would like to separate the application problem from this and discuss the distinction between norms and modes of action independently of an institutional classification. Wellmer's analytical arguments and those based on his theory of justification are already a challenge for the thesis that justification and application are distinguishable.

With the aid of the specific meaning of the categorical "ought," Wellmer explained that questions of moral correctness concern only modes of action in situations: only on the basis of the nongeneralizability of an action willed by me here and now can it be definitively discovered what I ought (not) to do. In contrast, norms have a derivative status because they are internally related to nongeneralizable modes of action in situations. Their proscriptive or prescriptive character is thus addressed to situation-specific exceptions which, however, can no longer be expressed in specific and generalizable rules of permissibility.

The difference between norms and modes of action, which are stylized into opposites, does not however appear that plausible if one considers that norms can be *reasons* for actions. By employing Toulmin's scheme, we attempted to illustrate this function of norms, which is based on a logic of argumentation. According to this scheme, the *first* step of practical argumentation consists, quite in Wellmer's sense, in referring to the data and situation features (D) (to which of course the particular understanding of oneself, the world, and the situation also belong), and these then justify an action (C). However, the data draw their justifying force not from themselves, but only from their connection to the prescribed action in the form of a warrant or norm (W) worded in nonsingular terms. Admittedly, the discussion of the scheme also showed that argumentation with the help of a warrant does not sufficiently justify evaluating the action as being "right." A judgment on the appropriateness of applying the norm in this situation must be added to this—a judgment, however, which can only be formed by considering all the particular features. It is at this point that the interpretations brought to bear by Wellmer play their decisive role. If he wants to limit moral argumentation to this, then the data and situation features can draw their justifying force, as reasons for or against an intended action, really only from themselves. This thought suggests itself when Wellmer speaks of "ways of acting in a kind of situation." What constitutes obeying a rule in an action can then be understood in Wittgenstein's sense as "*customs* (uses, institutions)"[82] or as an ethos-bound practice in Aristotle's sense. On this presupposition, situation features acquire their justifying force by our understanding situations always already in reference to a common practice or a form of life. In this understanding process, we gain insight into "the concrete demands that the situation makes."[83] Then, of course, what is important is not so much whether we justify an action by referring to a norm which, on fully considering all the features, is appropriate in this situation, but rather by referring to the appropriateness and completeness of our (interpretative) situation description itself.[84] Wellmer's proposal differs from neo-Aristotelian ethics only in that he retains an extremely weakened universalist element by his tying the judgment on the moral rightness of a mode of action to its nongeneralizability for a common practice. And yet, according to Wellmer, this judgment comes about automatically, if only we consider the situation correctly.

In contrast to this, discourse ethics makes the justifying force of situation features the explicit topic of moral argumentation, and this along *two* paths: First, *directly,* by ascribing to these features the status of a justifying reason only if they belong to the range of application of a norm which is appropriate in relation to all other data in this situation. For this reason, "appropriateness" is a predicate not of the situation description, but of the norm in a situation relative to all the features; secondly, *indirectly,* by being able once again to examine the appropriate norm, for its part, with respect to its justifiability in the light of the interests of all those affected. That was the second level in Toulmin's argumentation scheme, where it was a matter of backing the warrant with evidence. The moral rightness of an action must therefore be understood in a double sense: we call an action right because it is the result of the *right* (appropriate) application of the *right* (valid) norm. A "dogmatism of the given" is not being promoted in this way because the de facto validity of the norm is relativized, in application, by the features of the situation, and in justification, by the interests of all those affected. The dogmatism does not consist in there being norms that are applied, but in a certain authoritarian attitude toward the validity claim of norms and in an insufficient sensitivity vis-à-vis the particular features of an application situation. As opposed to Wellmer's proposal, discourse ethics does not implicitly leave norms within the horizons of the understanding of a situation; instead, it makes their validity claim the topic of the justification, over and above appropriate application in a situation.

By insisting, in opposition to Wellmer, on the moral relevance of norms for justifying the rightness of an action, it does not mean that we have already shown how we can avoid the disadvantages (expounded by him) of the "norm approach" and of the application of (U) as a criterion of right action. The advantage of his counterproposal was that the negative generalization of modes of action must unavoidably include the appropriateness of situation interpretations in its subject matter and that the validity of norms must always be considered with a situational index which points to nongeneralizable modes of action. For this reason, (U) could be understood either as a democratic principle of legitimation for the justice of norms, or as a moral principle which, however, leads to absurd consequences when applied to actions. The moral principle (U) does admittedly use the *argumentum ad absurdum* in the above-distinguished strong version, which contains a judgment on the consequences and side effects of generally observing a norm in all situations in which the norm is at all applicable. It is only for this reason that Wellmer can criticize this version for transfiguring the task of anticipating situation-specific differences, which would justify the necessity of exceptions or extensions, into a monstrosity.[85] This expectation combines appropriateness and validity together in *one* principle. Our interpretation of (U) showed, nevertheless, that this merging is not convincing. The attribute "can be anticipated" equips the justification of a norm's validity claim with a time and knowledge index and thereby *separates* the consideration of the unforeseeably particular features of each individual situation from the justification requirement. For this reason, (U) in the weak version should not be misunderstood as a principle which requires us "to act in the way that, as far as we are able to judge on the basis of our hypothetical assumption, we really would act if the conditions for acting and achieving agreement were ideal."[86] In this manner, we may apply (U) only on the presupposition that we have an infinite amount of time and absolute knowledge at our disposal. How we ought to act in real situations is not directly known as a result of applying (U); we will know this, only after having conducted an application discourse which compels us to consider all the particular features. The validity claim of every norm or mode of action is indeed simultaneously factual and infinite, but the infiniteness claim must be operationalized, on the one hand, in justification discourses which relate, independently of an individual application situation, the norm or mode of action to the interests of all those affected and, on the other hand, in application discourses which require, in a situation, that all the features of it be considered.

In this context, there is, however, a systematic ambivalence in Habermas's paralleling of truth and rightness claims, and it is to this that Wellmer links his *reductio ad absurdum*.[87] In the version

"It is right (or commanded) that *h*,"

the propositional component "that *h*" can only refer to a mode of action or norm *independent* of an application situation. This logical difference is however blurred when Habermas uses the following as an example for the content of "that *h*": "Under the given circumstances, it is right (or good in the moral sense) to lie."[88] On the one hand, what it is right to do under the *given* circumstances can be ascertained only after we have conducted an application discourse and arrived at the result that "*h*" is the appropriate mode of action in view of all the particular features of the situation; or, on the other hand, universally characterized situations are intended by the term "given circumstances" so that "*h*" is to be understood as a component of a proposed norm or action whose validity we have to examine in a justification discourse before applying it in a concrete situation. *Both* can be intended by "it is right . . ." To that extent, the explication of the meaning of the validity of the moral "ought" should, strictly speaking, refer only to the justification dimension. The systematic ambivalence may of course be due to the fact that in many moral conflict situations it *seems* as if the justification and application situations did not differ from each other. This impression is correct only when the range of situation features we consider relevant when forming a moral judgment in a situation is identical with the foreseeably unchanging set of those situation features which we hypothetically consider when weighing the consequences and side effects of a general observance of a norm and when, in addition, the interests of all those concretely affected in a situation are the same as the interests of all those potentially affected. Then, it is indeed the case that a common understanding of the situation is sufficient for establishing the moral rightness of a mode of action, and that (non-) generalizability can be measured according to whether we can will a corresponding common practice. To the extent that it allows a separation of justification and application, discourse ethics also facilitates moral reasoning even when we have to relativize the common understanding of our practice vis-à-vis other forms of life (and application situations).

With this response, however, we seem to have arrived merely at the third alternative of Wellmer's interpretation of the moral principle, according to which (U) relates only to *prima facie* norms and the real moral problem consists in situation-specific application. The consequence would be that (U) as a moral principle would become meaningless.[89] In connection with his other objections, this argument can be put more pointedly in the form of the question why discourse ethics still needs justification discourses at all. If what is morally decisive takes place in application discourses anyway, then there is a need for a justification discourse only if one adheres to the questionable idealizing concept formations of the consensus theory of truth and if one regards practical justification discourses as one of its special cases. Within the context of this study, I cannot engage in a discussion of the objections leveled directly at the consensus theory of truth. Such a discussion would presuppose a detailed critique of the premises of verificationist semantics.[90] In what follows, we shall only be concerned with presenting the philosophical plausibility of a universalist principle of justification as a moral principle.

As a principle of justification, (U) detaches norms and modes of action from their particular form of life and situation in order to place the validity claim at the disposal of the interests of all those affected.[91] It does not follow from this that norms and modes of action have no indexical situation reference, but only that the justifying force of situation features does not follow solely from situation interpretations, but emerges together with an appropriate norm that is to be applied to them and is itself in need of justification. The binding force of the moral "ought" may not be *solely* dependent on the fact that, in virtue of its situational indices, the norm or mode of action in question happens to belong to our common practice. That was the advance that Kant made beyond Aristotelian and moral sense ethics by establishing the categorical imperative as a universal moral principle. Only on this presupposition can we claim that our norms and modes of action are also criticizable on a universalist level, namely, independent of our contingent form of life. To that extent, it makes sense to locate a universalist validity claim in the illocutionary forces of *every* normatively substantive utterance. The fact that norms retain a *prima facie* character owing to their situation-independent justification does not in itself place them in an antithetical relation to actions. As I have attempted to show, norms can function as reasons for actions. But this also means that they belong to the form of life in whose context we interpret an application situation. When we choose an appropriate mode of action in a situation, this occurs in the light of norms which claim universal validity in the universal-reciprocal and applicative sense.

This can be proved using Wellmer's own example of the change in collective patterns of interpretation due to the influence of new experiences and the pressure of the struggle for recognition.[92] The fact that the new experiences[93] can subject an unequal treatment previously considered justified to revision presupposes not only a factual change in habitual views and established practices. Collective learning processes in morality require a principle which compels us to consider new experiences also in a normative manner and to change moral convictions formerly considered justified. This can be no other principle that that of impartiality, that is, both in the universal-reciprocal and in the applicative sense. It must be able to carry the burden of argumentation when confronted by someone who wishes to continue an existing practice of equal or unequal treatment despite newly discovered situation features. This burden of argumentation can only be grounded in a principle which ties the application of a norm to the consideration of all features of the situation (and it is from this application that it first of all emerges in what respects what is equal should be treated equally and what is different differently). Merely revising collective patterns of interpretation without referring to the norms which must be impartially justified and applied cannot set a moral learning process in motion. Our moral practice does not change until we have realized that we can no longer appropriately apply a norm in view of new features and that it contradicts the interest of all those affected not to accept as valid a norm whose range of application has been enlarged in that way. For this reason, the *prima facie* character of norms is not a disadvantage, but simply illustrates that moral norms admit of their being changed by new experiences in situations. Their indeterminacy is the consequence of a differentiation and recombination of justification and application discourses.[94] The principle of impartial application not only requires a reception of changes that have already occurred, but contributes to the production of changes because of the built-in compulsion to self-corrective application while considering all the situation features. For this, however, the universalist claim must first be given, so that groups who have so far been treated unequally can "lay claim" to it.[95]

As has been shown, a number of plausible arguments can be advanced for the assumption that Wellmer's contrasting of norms and modes of action is "askew." Together, both belong to the cultural, societal, and biographical context in which we experience every situation of action. The "norm perspective" merely isolates the aspect of universalizability in respect of the interests of everyone, whereas the "action perspective" is concerned with the appropriate application of valid norms in situations. Wellmer's distinction tears the context apart and reserves questions of justice for norms and questions of morality for modes of action. Thus, he does not seem to be really concerned with analogous differentiations between norm and mode of action, law and morality, or justification and application, but with the rehabilitation of an ethics of the good life as opposed to one of impartiality and justice.

6

The Application of the Moral Principle

From the moment the first Athenian sophists distanced themselves so much from their immediate lifeworld and daily common practice that they discovered the distinction between *"nomos"* and *"physis"* and thereby the changeableness of rules valid among humans beings, we have been accustomed to distinguishing between moral actions and norms, on the one hand, and conditions for good, just, expedient, or rational and right moral actions and norms, on the other. Since this revolutionary discovery, the philosophical dispute in morality has revolved around the appropriate explication of these second-order predicates which we can ascribe to or withhold from given, proposed, or changed moral orientations.

Just like other moral philosophies that can be placed in a rationalist tradition, discourse ethics insists on this strict separation between the level of moral judgments and those predicates of a higher level. One of the essential reasons for this is that it subjects the use of such predicates to especially strict conditions. It makes their employment dependent on an additional moral deliberation that may not, however, coincide with that of the first level, if the construction is to be meaningful. The features at which this moral deliberation is directed and which should apply to every valid moral judgment can be arranged according to three standpoints.[96]

(a) Moral judgments must be justifiable. We can understand what this means by contrasting it with skepticism's contraposition. The latter does not by any means contest the two levels of moral phenomena; it does however draw the inverse conclusion from this, namely, that it is meaningless to talk *morally* about the second level of moral values because all it does is simply disclose the multiplicity of various inclinations, interests, or existential decisions. In contrast to that, "cognitivist" moral philosophies attempt to show that one can advance reasons for the rightness of a moral judgment at this second level, reasons that are more than private opinions about emotive states or empirical observations.

(b) Every moral norm must be able to be accepted—with reasons—by all those affected. There is also an elucidating contraposition to this feature: like skepticism, relativism does not contest that there is a kind of second level to moral deliberations, but it simultaneously claims that deliberations of this kind can only justify the validity of a moral judgment for a specific culture or epoch. In contrast to that, "universalist" moral philosophies insist that moral validity is always addressed to everyone and is not limited to specific forms of life or groups of people.

(c) Finally, a moral judgment may not be valid because it has a specific content. The contraposition here, various forms of a "material" ethics, denies the possibility of this feature because, at the second level of moral deliberation, one encounters *yet again* only moral determinations of content. The two levels differ only to the extent that the contents at the second level are equipped with special additional features which render the question concerning a possible third level superfluous: an especially distinguished (ontologically speaking) form of life, a value a priori, a special natural property of man, or a special character feature of a few people. "Formal" ethics, on the other hand, disputes that, at this second level, it is at all a question of the good or bad form of life, of authentic or inauthentic values, of the true nature of man or corresponding way of life, or a question of the virtues necessary for a happy life. Such questions— which always presuppose a common moral content and are simply concerned with discovering exactly what it is—are actually still situated at the first level. At the second level, by contrast, it is a matter of identifying which of these value contents we can deem binding for each individual and demand that he observe them as orientations for action, independently of what form of life he happens to be a member of, independently of what character features he possesses, and of what kind of conceptions of happiness he has.

The moral principle (U) groups these features together for every moral judgment claiming validity. It belongs to a series of other moral principles, such as Kant's categorical imperative, which attempt to express, each in its own way, what it is we refer to when we judge moral norms from the standpoint of the second level. Speaking of "moral principles," however, involves a danger that repeatedly leads to misunderstandings and was clearly in evidence when explicating the three conditions of validity of moral norms. The status of principles is too similar to that of norms to be always able to avoid treating a moral principle as if it were a first-level norm in need of justification. Then, however, the question of a *third* level at

which the validity of principles is to be justified is unavoidable—
ad infinitum. If one wants to avoid this regress, the status of the
one moral principle of the second level, which should be valid for
every moral norm, must be explicated more precisely. For this reason, Habermas proposed understanding (U) as a rule of argumentation which is used in practical discourses, so that the moral
principle is transformed into a *procedure* of discourse ethics which
makes it possible to form an impartial judgment on the validity of a
moral norm.[97]

Distinguishing between these two levels and precisely defining
the status of the moral principle is necessary for our purposes because only in this way can we distinguish the problem of applying
moral norms from that of applying the moral principle itself. So
far we have ignored this difference, always with reference to the
Kantian one between pure practical and practical judgment. The
discussion of Wellmer's position showed, however, that we have to
specify this distinction more carefully in order to defend our thesis
of the separation of questions of justification from those of application. If, according to Wellmer's interpretation, a moral principle of
the second level, such as the categorical imperative, is characterized by the fact that it lends expression to certain features of an
intersubjectively shared form of life, then we cannot in fact differentiate between the application of the moral principle and the application of a moral norm—with the consequence that Wellmer's
thesis would prove correct: one cannot meaningfully distinguish between issues of justification and those of application. The judgment
on the validity of a norm or a mode of action, which we make on the
basis of the "moral principle of a form of life," would then always
include a judgment on the appropriateness of the norm or mode of
action because the moral principle itself is appropriate to the form
of life *within* which it is applied. Consequently, the morally right
would not be a question of justification by applying a moral principle to a moral norm dependent on a form of life, but a question of the
appropriate interpretation of the particular form of life in a situation. For this reason, Wellmer translates the categorical imperative
correctly from his viewpoint when he recasts it as the question of
whether the mode of action requiring generalization can become
"general practice." However, this question is posed within a form of
life, that is, at the same level at which we devise the mode of action.
Whether such a mode of action is generalizable is then determined
only within the horizons of our common practice. Consequently, the
limits of these horizons, our form of life, would also be the limits of

generalizability. If, however, we can never adopt a standpoint outside our particular form of life, speaking of the compatibility of a mode of action with a general practice is actually meaningless since it demands of us precisely that we establish this distance to ourselves. Wellmer's criterion should really be condensed to the question as to whether we can *perpetuate* our practice to date with the mode of action in question.[98]

In this reduction of the principle of generalizability to the horizons of practice given with a form of life, there is of course the confusion of the moral principle with its subject matter, individual moral judgments—a confusion to which Kant strongly objected again and again. Opposing his own "wordy and deedless times" which much favored the value of practice over theoretical reflection, Kant warns that "[a]ll is lost if empirical, and consequently accidental, conditions of the execution of the law are made the conditions of the law itself. Then a practice which is calculated in relation to the probable result of previous experience is accorded the right of determining the theory itself."[99] He likewise objected to all moral philosophies which want to include the "practical material determining grounds" of education, civil constitution, happiness, moral sense, perfection, or the divine will in the principle of morality on the grounds that "it is certainly undeniable that every volition must have an object and therefore a material; but the material cannot be supposed, for this reason, to be the determining ground and condition of the maxim."[100] Wellmer, however, converts contingent conditions of a form of life into components of the moral principle; this principle would then have to be able to make these conditions for each form of life the subject matter of evaluation. Then there is no longer a distinction between the question of how we "apply" a norm or execute a mode of action within our established practice, and the question of whether we can perpetuate our practice with this norm or mode of action. The application and the justification of norms have indeed become interchangeable.

Playing off Kant's position against Wellmer's does admittedly involve the danger of moving to another extreme and of eventually falling into a dilemma. Wellmer himself warns often enough against distortions of our moral intuitions which can come about as a result of also adopting the rigoristic consequences when these intuitions are reconstructed from the Kantian perspective. The strict separation between a moral principle and moral norms of the first level then leads directly to a "two-world ethics" which has to operate with questionable assumptions in order to maintain this separation.

Even without sharing the Kantian premises on an unbridgeable gap between empirical and intelligible subjectivity, it would surely be difficult for every person impartially concerned with reconstructing his moral intuitions to accept the assumption that the moral principle has nothing to do with the form of life in which we grow up, act, and reach an understanding with one another. If we accept Wellmer's assimilation of the moral principle to a "moral principle of a form of life," we have to indicate precisely what the difference and unity of moral principle and form of life consist in. We are thereby again exposed to the problem of the distinction between the application of the moral principle to moral norms and the application of moral norms to situations.

We can find access to the conditions of impartially forming a judgment only from the standpoint of *our* particular form of life. This has two implications:

(a) We can always only concern ourselves with a *reconstruction* of those intuitions which we *have always followed* when discussing controversial moral issues. As the result of an internal reconstruction, a moral principle of the second level cannot be a moral norm of the first, for which we could, again for its part, demand a moral justification. For this reason, cognitivist moral philosophies are theories of morality and are not morals.

(b) As theories of morality, reconstructions of continually practiced moral intuitions are necessarily *fallible*. Competing theories could locate our intuitions better. Cognitivist moral philosophies are concerned, however, with the fallible reconstruction of a specific kind of moral intuitions: those we may assume to be shared by *everyone*. "Except for questions aimed at the universal, philosophy here does not have an advantage over the sciences, and it certainly does not have the infallibility of a privileged access to truth. Although the spontaneous formation of the sequence of numbers cannot be easily 'contested', 'every theory of natural numbers is indeed fallible.' (Henrich, 2d Thesis). What is valid for the foundations of algebra is all the more valid for ethics."[101]

Discourse ethics reconstructs universal moral intuitions from the general presuppositions of argumentation which we must inevitably lay claim to and assume are fulfilled any time we become involved in a moral controversy. To the extent that this reconstruction is directed at a practice we have always engaged in, it remains tied to the form of life to which this practice belongs. To the extent, however, that it is directed at universal aspects, it—fallibly—transcends the particular form of life where it had its point of departure and aims at the conditions of this practice which do not vary from one form of life to another. It is only in this way that a second level is reached from where different versions of this practice can be judged. The step transcending the particular form of life does not however lead into a transcendental world, but merely into a "quasi"-transcendental one which does not even share the substantialist presuppositions of transcendental subjectivity continually laid claim to by Kant, despite his fear of paralogisms. The presuppositions of argumentation, which we must unavoidably assume are fulfilled when we participate in an argumentation, are universal, but only in an idealized sense. We merely lay *claim* to them when we argue. Because, in our daily practice, we cannot avoid—in an entirely noncontroversial sense—addressing validity claims to every potential participant in argumentation or assuming that they are fulfilled, we *simultaneously* perpetuate our established practice *and* transcend it, going beyond our specifically given form of life.[102]

There is however a normative thorn in the flesh of the difference between the particular form of life originally familiar to us, and the ideal, universal communication community to which we have "always already" addressed ourselves. This normative thorn does not question our particular form of life *in toto,* but it does unrelentingly query each individual act within the established practice: whether the act satisfies the ideal conditions which it claims are fulfilled in its facticity. This normative difference is not, however, to be understood in such a way that a beautiful ideal is abstractly contrasted with a terrible reality. It does not demand of us that we subject ourselves to the resentment of a moral ideal. The ideal conditions intend really nothing more than that each individual could agree to the claimed validity with reasons. The moral principle (U) attempts to formulate nothing but this condition for the case of norm-guided action and moral judgments. As a rule of argumentation, it cannot be abstractly applied by individuals or an elite to a disorganized moral reality; it is only applicable in practical discourses. For this reason, discourse ethics can reformulate the moral principle in such a way that only that norm which finds the agreement of all those affected as participants in a practical discourse may claim to be valid.

All the same, our forms of life cannot be exhausted by a practical discourse; the thorn of the "ought" remains. The reconstructive aspect of discourse ethics does indeed demonstrate the internal interwovenness of the moral principle with *every* form of life, but the normative aspect pits one against the other. This always becomes a problem when we consider the relation of the moral principle to the nongeneralizable components of a form of life, which are brought to bear by the skeptic, relativist, and material objections to a cognitivist, universal, and formalist ethics. The moral principle excludes inclinations, passions, particular interests, culturally determined ways of life, ethical [*sittlich*] value standards, and maxims of the good life from moral discourse. It places them under a justification proviso which comes into effect when they claim to be binding on others. Then, only those modes of action of a cooperative practice which embody a generalizable interest for each individual may claim validity.

Yet, in a form of life, how can the willingness be presupposed that such a task of selection will actually be performed by all those involved—the task, that is, of distinguishing between generalizable and nongeneralizable aspects? Even if, in moral controversies, we have always implicitly operated with idealizing presuppositions, as the moral principle (U) explicates them, it does not follow that we use (U) as a criterion *for us* (all), too, in order to decide on the validity of our moral judgments and proposed norms. In most cases, the generalizability of a norm solely within the horizons set by our lifeworldly practice is sufficient. But even if this criterion were used by us in at least a few cases, the problem of how to resolve the relation between what is generalizable and what is definitively nongeneralizable would remain unsolved. While the moral principle separates questions of the morally right from questions of the good life, it does not give any orientation at all for their mediation in concrete situations. Though not all questions of the good life are questions of the morally right, moral decisions *always* affect our particular conceptions of happiness. It would only occur to an orthodox Kantian philosopher to claim here that we have to thoughtlessly suppress our desire for happiness in the case of conflict with moral prescriptions (if one disregards here the poor consolation offered by the postulate of immortality). Finally, there still remains the problem of whether we may demand an application of the moral principle not only for our own form of life, but also for *other* forms of life. Though at least the fallibly *reconstructive* aspect of discourse ethics may seem plausible to members of Western traditions because this aspect itself operates with models of argumentation coming from this tradition (which makes it necessarily fallible in conjunction with the claim to universality), this does not necessarily apply to members of other traditions. All three problems concern the application of discourse ethics in a form of life.[103]

Apel has proposed discussing *this* application problem as "the problem, which is itself in principle still a moral one, of whether the application of a postconventional discourse ethics is a *reasonable expectation* [*Zumutbarkeit*], or more precisely: the problem of the *relativity of the reasonableness of the expectation* with reference to what Hegel called the 'substantive ethical life' of the commonwealth."[104] The principle (U) can be applied as an action-guiding principle in real discourses only if, within the particular form of life, application conditions are fulfilled which make it reasonable to expect of its members that (U) be applied. These conditions can only be historically reconstructed and identified from the tradition of the forms of life concerned. For this reason, Apel postulates a "critical mediation between transcendental ethics and historical hermeneutics" which constructively and reconstructively connects the "*counterfactual* anticipation of a 'reasonable reality' "[105] with "historically related application,"[106] and introduces this into discourse ethics as the moral principle of reasonable expectation. This part of ethics—designated by Apel as "Part B," as distinct from the formulation of discourse ethics itself ("Part A")—is supposed to satisfy the requirements of an ethics of responsibility in a radical sense since it claims to consider not only the consequences of applying a moral norm (first level), but also "the consequences and side effects of historically situation-related applications of the principle (U^a),"[107] that is, of the principle (U) as a principle of action in real discourses. In this way, the historically related application of the moral principle itself becomes in turn a case to which the moral principle is to be applied, namely as a principle of responsibility for the consequences of applying the moral principle (U). The obligation in an ethics of responsibility to reconstruct the conditions of reasonable expectation for applying discourse ethics in forms of life can, however, no longer mean the restoration of the concrete general in the sense of conceptionalized, reasonable reality. Rather, according to Apel, one can only reflect negatively on the obstacles hindering an application of the moral principle to the moral institutions of a form of life. The experience of these obstacles presents itself as an experience of difference whenever we ourselves reconstruct our own intuitions, which we have always presupposed in moral argumentation: as a difference between the ideal conditions and the *conflicting* lifeworldly practice. Acknowledging this difference as an obstacle to applying the moral principle implies, according to Apel, the obligation to remove it. Thus, following from the presuppositions of serious argumentation, which are unavoidably assumed to be fulfilled, there is, in addition to the moral principle (U), a "moral-strategic supplementary principle (S) for the justification of an ethics of responsibility"[108] which combines purposive-rational with communicative action in such a way that practical discourses can become real.

With the principle of reasonable expectation Apel himself has postulated a criterion of application which belongs to the category of appropriateness. In situations of moral conflict, an action may be reasonably expected of others not only if it is morally prescribed, but if the person obligated to act can also comply with it in view of the particular situation in which he finds himself. For this reason, the judgment on whether an action may be reasonably expected of others presupposes the consideration of the particular circumstances of the action situation in respect of their significance for the individual disposition of the person obligated to act. Reasonable expectation is subjective appropriateness. We usually accept the explanation of a person who, on not performing an action we would really expect of him, cites its unreasonableness in a situation which is special for him.[109] Apel does not however relate the criterion of reasonable expectation to individual situations in which a moral norm is applicable, but to forms of life and their historical reconstruction. Analogous to the colloquial use, for Apel, "reasonable expectation" is aimed at the "subjective" conditions of a particular form of life, at the cultural self-understanding mediated by tradition and at the concrete solidarity of its members—but in reference to the applicability of the moral principle itself. Apel explicitly distinguishes this problem from the question of the appropriate application of morally justified norms in individual situations. The moral principle itself cannot be applied to forms of life in the same way as moral norms are applied to situations. Either the postconventional moral principle would become a conventional norm (confusing the first with the second level), or we would fail to recognize the fact that, at the postconventional level, it is already a matter of "justifying the norms to be applied as historically situation-related ones, while considering the anticipated consequences of their general application."[110] Thus, if the applicability of the moral principle were institutionalized in a form of life, the problem of applying moral (in the sense of the moral principle, justified) norms would resolve itself in that the consequences and side effects of a general observance of the norm would have already been considered in (U). What would remain to be done would then only be a problem of judgment or prudent application. However, we already saw in the preceding

sections that the problem of the situation-appropriate application
of a morally justified norm cannot in itself be solved by simply applying (U) as a rule of argumentation in a practical discourse. That
is to say, a general institutionalization of practical discourses would
not yet take care of it. Apel thus presupposes that we already have
a norm "to be applied," that is, that a decision about situational appropriateness has already been made. I cannot contest here the fact
that in addition to the problem of applying moral norms, there is
still a further problem of applying the moral principle to forms of
life and that "reasonable expectation" proves to be a productive criterion in order to judge the appropriateness of the moral principle
to forms of life. Without wishing to question the distinction between
both application problems, I would nevertheless like to defend the
thesis that some of the problems of applying the moral principle can
be better understood as problems of applying morally justified
norms. A verification of this thesis would have the advantage that
discourse ethics could reduce the degree to which it sets its heart on
a dubious "moral-strategic" implementation of its moral principle,
which in any case could not be construed in the prisoner dilemmas
alluded to by Apel.

The criterion of appropriately applying a norm in complete consideration of all the situation features does not "supplement" the
moral principle, but relates its meaning—the idea of impartiality—
to the particular application situation. A violation of situation-
specific particularities is precluded in that the application of norms
itself falls under the supervision of the idea of impartiality. This
danger is much more prevalent if the application of morally justified norms is left to prudent application. The prudence of the application manifests itself of course precisely in the fact that, for the
sake of the goal of realizing a morally justified norm, those particularities of a situation which cannot be harmonized with the semantic content of a norm are treated strategically. In contrast to
that, the idea of the impartial application of norms compels us to
become involved with the particular circumstances of a situation
and to appraise them in the light of competing normative viewpoints. The relation of a norm to all other aspects of a situation has
to be determined anew in every application situation because
changes in the constellations of features cannot be foreseen. Then,
of course, deciding on a specific norm which is to be applied is again
selective, and this selectivity is further intensified by the fact that
the norm to be applied must not only be appropriate to the situation, but also embody a general interest in order to be justified. The

selection may however be considered *appropriate* if it has been preceded by the consideration of all the features of the application situation. Here too, judgment retains a residual competency because it is impossible to consider all the features of a situation. I shall investigate the implications of this "residue" later. The fact that we can never completely close the gap between norm and situation does not however mean that we may not presuppose in the idea of impartiality that it can in principle be surmounted in order, in the first place, to be able to give *meaning* to the argument that a relevant feature *D* has not been considered in this situation *S*. The idea of impartiality first makes it possible that different and, at first, competing normative situation interpretations can be brought to bear without being previously excluded by the application of a specific valid norm. According to this aspect, the prudent application of conventional norms is *always* partial because it considers and accepts as valid only those viewpoints in a situation which belong to the semantic content of a single norm. The norm is not yet relativized as one normative viewpoint *among others,* a viewpoint that has to be brought into a relation with all the other features. For this reason, application discourses are pluralist and always relate, in an entirely noncontroversial sense, to *prima facie* norms only. This relativization is, however, only possible at the postconventional level because it is only at this level that validity and situational appropriateness can be separated from each other. That is why one confuses different levels if, in situations, postconventionally *justified* norms are applied as conventional norms without considering the particular circumstances.

It is only in this way that we can at all succeed in exhausting the universalist content of moral norms in different situations over a long period of time. The justification of a norm endures only to the degree to which possible contexts of application are known to all participants in virtue of their historical experience. Only an impartial application puts us in a position to relate a universalistically justified norm to extended and changed contexts too and thereby exhaust all the semantic variants. Variations in context compel us to interpret situations anew, and we can thus bring forward new interests. Before we can decide whether a consideration of this interest also expresses a general interest, we first have to ascertain what interests are affected in a situation. Linked to this are specific cultural semantics, societal institutions, and biographical particularities—in short, all the essential elements of a form of life within which a "situation" exists and is interpreted as such. However,

these elements are just as constitutive of a universalist norm's semantic content, which is not unequivocally fixed, as their universal
justification is constitutive of its validity. New interpretations of
the situation then force changes, modifications, and revisions of this
content—with the consequence that a norm modified in such a
manner has be checked again as to whether, in view of the currently
known contexts, it can be accepted by everyone with reasons. But
the sheer fact that we have to consider new interpretations of the
situation at all follows only from the idea of impartial application.

So far I have only spoken generally about the "features of a situation." The requirement to consider all the features of a situation
does not itself distinguish between generalizable and particular
features. *This* distinction is of course only a topic for justification
discourses. When we enter an application discourse, we do not yet
"know," as it were, which of the relevant normative aspects of a situation belong to a general interest. In application situations we are
first confronted with the needs and interests of a concrete other as
well as with various interpretations of the situation, from which we
must first of all form an appropriate action norm in order to be able
to check whether the norm then "to be applied" is also generalizable
beyond the concrete application situation itself. Thus, in application discourses it is not in itself a matter of precisely expounding a
difference between generalizable and particular interests, but of
producing an interpretation which is coherent in the light of all the
features of a situation. The norm to be applied must be able to co-
here with all the other applicable norms (from whose applicability,
however, the relevance of a particular feature first follows) in this
situation *S* before we can decide on its validity *independently* of *S*
(that is, whether its general application in all the other situations
so far known to us is also in the justified interest of everyone). The
appropriateness of a norm or the degree to which all the particular
circumstances are considered is expressed in the degree of coherence of the norm to be applied with all the relevant situation features. In contradistinction to the consensual validity of a norm, its
coherent application can only be judged in the situation itself.

I shall investigate in greater detail possible ways of making
norms coherent for application in the section on appropriateness
argumentation below. The horizons within which we can bring various viewpoints to bear on a situation are determined by the particular form of life, its cultural semantics, societal institutions, and
modes of socialization. These elements form, as it were, the building
blocks of which situations are composed and with whose help we

construct new norm hypotheses. The plan according to which these components are, in each case, put together depends on the particular action situation. Which of the different possible norm hypotheses we finally choose is determined by the dimensions of the different weight of competing viewpoints, by dimensions of primacy, and of the greater or lesser degree of violation of others' particular interests. Deliberations on reasonable expectation—of the kind sketched above—relating to the concrete other and his individual situation also play a role here. All these dimensions are relational determinations which place the appropriate norm in relation to as many of the other normative viewpoints as possible.

As has been repeatedly stated, producing a norm which is situationally coherent for application is not sufficient to exhaust the idea of impartiality completely. There remains the universal-reciprocal sense of the principle of impartiality, which points beyond the particular situation and according to which the validity of a norm is determined. If we add this sense of the principle of impartiality to a norm's appropriate application in situations, which is dependent on the perpetual discovery of new situation features, we open a new perspective on applying the moral principle (U) in a manner appropriate to the form of life, a perspective which is possibly less conspicuous but all the more differentiated than Apel's proposal of a moral-strategic implementation. If the idea of impartiality is not simply restricted to the argumentative justification of the validity claim of a norm "to be applied," but already has an effect on application in situations and on the discovery of changed constellations of features, we have to engage in deliberations on reasonable expectation already at the first level of applying norms in situations, deliberations like those Apel demands for supplementing—in the sense of an ethics of responsibility—the moral principle (second level). In that every new situation, which reveals itself in changed interpretations, alters the conditions of coherence for the application of a norm, it exposes itself in this indirect manner to appraisal by the moral principle. In this way, a situation-specific moral rationalization of the lifeworld occurs. The application of the moral principle is itself once again materially and temporally proceduralized. Such a highly complex and, in its entirety, scarcely comprehensible process of moralization does admittedly depend on two strong presuppositions. First, this process requires the sensitive, imaginative, and innovative discovery of "new," previously unconsidered situation features which, by the agency of the principle of complete consideration of all the features of a situation, can be fed into the process of consensual justification and coherent application. This presupposes a highly integrative capability on the part of cultural semantics, a relative indeterminacy of existing normative orientations, and a high tolerance for competing interpretations on the part of individual conceptions of the good life. Secondly, an impartial application also presupposes that the idea of impartiality is at least implicitly recognized and partially effective as a rule of argumentation in a form of life. If this presupposition is not fulfilled, we are faced with the problem expounded by Apel, namely, that of applying the moral principle in a form of life. In order for a successive moralization (incorporating more and more contexts) and rationalization of a form of life to come about by way of impartial application, forms of life must at least "facilitate"[111] the idea of the impartial justification and application of norms. Of course, this application problem is probably less dramatic than Apel presents it. Insofar as the idealized general conditions of argumentation, from which the moral principle can be derived, are fallible, reconstructive insights, these insights must be accessible to a form of life if there are, at least in principle, other forms of interaction different from those of force in it. "Applying" the moral principle to a form of life then proves to be an unceasing effort to falsify those reconstructive hypotheses which are formed from the perspective of a particular form of life, a perspective that can never be completely transcended. On the other hand, the *explicit recognition* of the moral principle as the embodiment of the impartial justification and application of moral norms cannot be achieved by "strategic-moral" measures, but only by autonomously gained insight. There may well be various meaningful possibilities for combining purposive-rational with consensual action, and it may well be permissible, within limits, to promote instrumentally the objective of achieving general relations of reaching understanding, but the last leap toward autonomous recognition of the principle of discursively reaching an understanding must be made solely by the individuals themselves.[112] The moral principle only functions on this condition. It is only against those who undertake to annul the public validity of this principle in a form of life that there is the right to revolution.

Part Two

The Problem of the Application
of Norms in the Development
of Moral Consciousness

In the following chapter I would like to consider the problem of the application of universalist norms from a different viewpoint. So far I have concerned myself with a systematic distinction between justification and application and have attempted to introduce it by means of an extensive interpretation of the principle of impartiality. The debate with Wellmer's objections to the possibility of drawing such a distinction at all demonstrated the alternative which permits one to do without the distinction. It consisted in going back to concrete interactions in particular communities and differentiated forms of life in order to leave the choice of the norm, which is simultaneously appropriate and valid within the horizons of a form of life, to prudent deliberation within the interactive situation itself. We rejected this alternative because, as Wellmer explicitly admits, it is necessarily tied to abandoning universalist claims. Forgoing these claims is necessary if one limits, with Wellmer, the property of admitting of truth to assertoric or empirical propositions and contests this in respect of normative or practical propositions. In action situations we are then confronted not with validity claims in need of justification, but with various interpretative possibilities from which we, in collective processes of clarification, have to choose the appropriate one in order to be able to perpetuate the common practice. Questions of validity, just like questions of appropriateness, can then only be answered in the situation itself—and only *via negationis*—since both kinds arise within the horizons of one form of life or one common practice.

In what follows I would like to take this alternative indirectly as the departure point in order to show that the distinction between justification and application becomes unavoidable with the overcoming of an ethics of the good life dependent on forms of life. In doing so, it ought to become clear that the advantages that a situational ethics provides for the problem of the appropriateness of moral actions and norms in situations do not have to be forfeited at the level of a universalist ethics by the separation of justification and application; rather, they can only be appreciated in the first place at this level because the idea of impartiality requires the consideration of all the situation features and not just those which are relevant within the limited horizons of the interpretation of a norm valid in a particular situation. To this end, it has to be shown how the relationship between moral norms and situations is determined in concrete situations, how a situation-independent status for rules and norms can at all emerge from the generalization of communicatively interwoven perspectives, and how changes in the validity status of a norm from context-bound to universalist types are internally connected with changes in the manner of applying a norm.

It is scarcely still possible to take in at a glance the number of different theories on the social genesis of norms. The following selection is thus restricted to those theories which are especially relevant to our topic because they operate with a distinction between at least two moral levels where situation-related and universalist orientations are contrasted. Between the theories of Durkheim, Mead, Piaget, and Kohlberg, with which I shall be primarily concerned in what follows, there are also internal connections owing to one author's reception of another. Piaget extended Durkheim's distinction between mechanical and organic solidarity into the distinction between heteronomous and autonomous morality; Kohlberg linked up with this and, via a reception of Mead's model of reciprocal perspective-taking, differentiated Piaget's initial steps toward a connecting of moral stages with social relations of unilateral or bilateral respect. The theory of perspective-taking offers a useful background for the following reflections because it explains the emergence of norms from symbolic structures which, for their part, have emerged from a situation-transcending, generalized interweaving of perspectives. We can thereby trace how the problem of the situational appropriateness of moral norms changes from the level of simple interaction with concrete others, through the level of the "generalized other," up to procedures of universalist validity. These two steps can be provisionally characterized in the following way:

(a) As soon as ego and alter no longer adopt the particular standpoint of the other merely reciprocally but are able to observe their reciprocal relation from a common, third perspective, then the abstraction of a norm from various possible action situations is complete and a relation of application is given. The norm can still have a somewhat situational character and be interwoven with concrete relations of reciprocity. But it can be surmised that how the application problem is framed could depend on the degree of temporal, spatial, and social generalization of the norm embodying a common perspective.

(b) In the social generalization of norms, there is a jump to universalization. Then norms themselves can again be made the subject matter of a judgment. The third position, embodied in societal norms with varying degrees of generalization, is extended beyond all particular contexts to a criterion which ties the moral validity of a norm to the agreement of all those affected. At this level, so the thesis runs, justification and application are separated. The fact that this is an unavoidable process will be explained in what follows on the basis of the internal relations between validity, appropriateness, and the structure of perspectives.

In the course of this attempted explanation, the distinction between context-bound and impartial application will crystallize as an adequate characterization of these two levels (a) and (b). All the following sections of this part are concerned with its systematic justification and its reconstruction in terms of a developmental logic. In a highly condensed form, Durkheim anticipated essential aspects of this distinction in the pair of concepts, mechanical and organic solidarity, and linked them to a hypothesis in the logic of development. I shall begin with a presentation of this hypothesis in order to gather together those issues whose precise explication is the topic of the succeeding sections.

1

The "Free Application" of Indeterminate Norms as a Result of Societal Rationalization Processes (Durkheim)

Durkheim classes the indeterminacy (*l'indétermination*) of the collective consciousness and of the abstract rules in which it manifests itself among the secondary factors of the process which leads to the dissolution of the segmental type of society and to the emergence of the division of labor in the organizational form of organic solidarity.[1] It is an indication of the diminishing force of the collective consciousness and is one of the conditions which increases individuality's latitude for variability, and thus makes a division of labor possible. Along with the naturalistically explained primary factors of increasing social density and growing volume of population, indeterminacy really ought to be ranked among the internal factors, from which the modernization and rationalization of a society can be read.[2] Because even highly differentiated societies organized on the division of labor cannot entirely do without a collective consciousness,[3] indeterminacy characterizes the state of the collective consciousness under conditions of high complexity. For Durkheim, the fundamental problem of the social and moral integration of a modern society consists in the fact that a morality which has become abstract is no longer able to coordinate the centrifugal movements of individual deviations,[4] whereby a return to determinate forms would however impede the process of the division of labor. Using the opposition of determinacy and indeterminacy, Durkheim depicts this problem again from an internal perspective: " . . . for the division of labour to be able to arise, and to increase, it is not enough for individuals to have within them the seeds of special aptitudes, nor for them to be stimulated to veer towards these aptitudes, but individual variations must also be possible. Such variations cannot occur when they are opposed to some strong, well-defined state of the collective consciousness. For the stronger such a state, the more resistant it is to anything that may weaken it. The better defined it is, the less room it leaves for changes. Thus we can foresee that the division of labour will be more difficult and slower, the more vigour and precision the collective consciousness possesses."[5]

Those states of the collective consciousness are determinate in which common feelings of at least medium intensity and with high resistance are articulated clearly and precisely against deviations. Society (i.e., its segments) is integrated via the similarity of the sentiments to which the individual is "mechanically" assimilated.[6] Correspondingly, social rules express the self-description of society according to the aspect of similarity and dissimilarity; they are known to everyone and are recognized by everyone.[7] For this reason, the common consciousness or the "collective type" is embodied most precisely in the norms of criminal law.[8] The criminal is the one who attacks the psychic type of a society, a type which has been integrated via likenesses. An action is defined as criminal "when it offends the strong, well-defined states of the collective consciousness," so that the crime corresponds to the determinacy of the collective consciousness as a kind of determinate negation which posits an individual difference.[9] For this reason, the criminal is ostracized and is subjected to a repressive sanction in which the unity of the collective consciousness is restored. The transcendent authority falling to penal norms corresponds to the determinacy, accuracy, clarity, precision, and unequivocalness with which the states of the collective consciousness are described in these norms. The norms enforced by sanctions are fused with religious beliefs of faith, which give them a validity claim that is experienced as sacred, supernatural, eternal, and as "separated" from the remaining expressions of the life of individuals in the community.[10] Charismatic leaders or organized authorities administrate the transcendent authority, and they themselves have a share in it; they have the power to identify and suppress opposition to the collective consciousness. "The similarity of consciousnesses gives rise to legal rules which, under the threat of repressive measures, impose upon everybody uniform beliefs and practices."[11]

An essential consequence of the determinacy of states of consciousness is the concretist manner of connecting norm and situation. All the rules of law, morality, and religion necessary for the collective integration of the segment are tied to local particularities and traditions, which treat each new situation in the same, unchangeable manner. Not only are human beings kept "concrete and definite,"[12] each social practice in every individual case is also determined in advance. Durkheim describes this against the background of the "formalism" of segmentary societies: "The way in which men must take food or dress in every situation, the gestures they must perform, the formulas they must pronounce, are precisely laid down."[13] The specific determination and ritualization of modes of action in situations permits only low mobility but not changes or the formation of individual differences.

According to Durkheim's naturalistic interpretation, this is changed only by the increased interdependence of society's members and by population growth (density and volume of society). The compulsion to specialize that sets in with this and the intensifying struggle for survival produce differences[14] which can no longer be embodied centrally, nor integrated in a collective consciousness on the basis of similar states of sentiment. On the basis of the homogeneity of the collective consciousness, "a system of different and special functions united by definite relationships"[15] is differentiated. The division of labor effects (and is dependent on) a solidarity which does not unite the similar with the similar, but brings the dissimilar into a reciprocally supplementing, facilitating relation with the dissimilar: organic solidarity.[16] It is those moral and legal rules which are changing and are changeable that enjoy primacy, that is to say, those which are not dependent on the collective consciousness to the same high degree as the rigid rules of religiously enforced criminal law; they lose their transcendent authority. The relations between groups and individuals must be flexible and be able to vary according to function. The sanction prerogative devolves to restitutive forms, with which the vital cooperation of the various specialized units can be continued. Correspondingly, a society's integration prerogative changes from the repressive norms of criminal law to contracts. The network of obligations does indeed become more closely meshed than in mechanically integrated areas and the link to the state stronger, but at the same time duties and rights are restricted to partial aspects of the individual, that is, to different roles; they no longer apply to the individual as a whole.[17]

These changes are causally brought about by processes whose character resembles that of a law of nature; however, they do not come about without the influence of internal factors; nor do they transpire in their entirety at a single point in time. Rather, the transition from mechanical to organic solidarity consists in a shift of primacy. One of the essential accompanying phenomenon, a secondary factor of this process, is the emergence of an *awareness for application* in the collective consciousness. It is connected with the formation of individuality in the course of a function-specific division of labor. On the one hand, the collective consciousness must become increasingly abstract and indeterminate in order to take the variety of differences into account; on the other hand, however, it loses its transcendent authority, with which it made its presence felt in each particular case. "Conversely, the more general and indeterminate the rules of conduct and thought, the more individual reflection must intervene in applying the rules to particular cases."[18] Employing the example of religion, Durkheim traces how the collective consciousness becomes weaker and less clear, and the concept of God more general and more indeterminate in order to give more latitude to the individual's initiative and provide "freer rein for human forces."[19] The objective and social worlds which were still concretely represented in the collective consciousness are dissolved into universal and rational structures,[20] which the now freed individual "applies" cognitively or volitionally in particular situations: "Only abstract rules are fixed, and these can be *freely applied* in very different ways. Even then they have neither the same ascendancy nor the same strength of resistance."[21] The internal process of rationalization, to which the collective consciousness is exposed in the course of the division of labor, transforms religious interpretations of the world into abstract rules of rational thought; places legal and moral norms on the foundation of a few, indeterminate principles; and releases the individual from his kinship segment by forcing him to develop an individuality in the process of confronting his objective and social worlds. However, what is so revealing about this secondary factor for Durkheim is the correspondence between the indeterminacy of universalist norms and their free application by free individuals. The freedom of the individual consists not only in his emancipation from the collective consciousness; it is first of all constituted in the free utilization of the latitude now available in application; this latitude is provided by the indeterminate rules of the universally rationalized collective consciousness. Thus, the collective consciousness corresponds to the differences produced by and with the division of labor in three ways: in greater indeterminacy of universalist principles and rules, in a weakening of its authority, and in a free applicability of its rules by independent individuals.[22]

    Of course, Durkheim registers not only the progress that the division of labor constitutes for the social life of human beings, but also the greater proneness to crises which goes hand in hand with the indeterminacy of the collective consciousness and which can lead to anomie and disintegration. It was of course the very opposition between abstract moral rules and social reality's own specified logic that prompted Durkheim to conduct his study. However, Durkheim does not continue his search for mediating procedures which could take charge of the application and implementation of the abstract rules of the collective consciousness after the disintegration of the unquestionably valid, traditional consensus by the relativism and skepticism of differentiated urbane cultures;[23] that is, he does not continue this search within the internal perspective he adopted when identifying the application problem. This remains a mere secondary factor. Individuals, free in the application of indeterminate rules, find their concrete morality in professional organizations which regulate the categorical imperative of the society based on the division of labor[24] via corporative occupational ethics [*Standesethiken*].[25] The rules according to which these "intermediary associations"[26] are formed do have less authority and are not as general; nevertheless they are capable of "laying down in advance the functioning of each organ."[27] These rules make the division of labor of social functions possible by transforming the abstract indeterminacy of the collective consciousness into differentiated determinations. Society cannot let social functions remain "in an indeterminate state; moreover, they determine one another. It is like this that rules arise which increase in number the more labour is divided—rules whose absence makes organic solidarity either impossible or imperfect."[28] The indeterminacy of the rules of the collective consciousness is only indirectly left to the "free application" by individuals; rather, it is picked up by the formation of institutions, ones which, though no longer consuming the individual completely, fit him, by offering specific orientations, into the process of social functions which is that of the division of labor.

I shall deal with this alternative to the analysis of the application problem in greater detail under the heading "double contingency"; this was the alternative I already referred to in my preliminary reflections. For the purposes of our discussion here, it is sufficient to confine ourselves to Durkheim's description of indeterminacy as a secondary factor of the division of labor. "Free application" breaks the automatism of rule-following which, among other things, is characteristic of the state of mechanical solidarity. Indeterminacy and the weakening authority of norm validity correlate with one another. Application no longer takes its orientation from the imperative character of the norm, but from the rational deliberation with which an individuated person applies an abstract rule to an unforeseeable case. For structural reasons, it is in this way possible to apply abstract rules to highly differentiated cases which are comparable only in a few respects. Because they are no longer situation-dependent, indeterminate rules can admit of variations, are for their part changeable, and make changes possible, or at least they do not obstruct these changes. If we isolate these connotations and separate the application problem from external factors such as the increasing density and growing volume of society, and if we do not immediately have it correlate with horizontal processes of social differentiation and integration by means of intermediary associations, we have enough clues to keep us on the track of an internal reconstruction of the application problem in moral development. The fact that, in view of indeterminacy, there is "nothing fixed" anymore will not concern us until later. Now we can more clearly formulate our hypothesis that a universalist morality is confronted with a specific application problem which arises precisely as a result of the *changeover* from concretist to universalist structures. Attempts, such as Wellmer's, to revoke the distinction between justification and application had to, as a consequence, go hand in hand with the relinquishment of universalist claims—as Wellmer himself explicitly ascertains. The place of the mediation or contextualization of universalist principles with different situations is taken by the plurality of different forms of life in which the mediation has always already been conducted and is only in need of discovery through interpretive efforts. In contrast to that, we can now, following Durkheim, advance the hypothesis that the original fusion of justification and application in a certain state of the collective consciousness is differentiated as a result of the rationalization process, that is, differentiated into indeterminate norms, on the one hand, and an individualist awareness for application, on the other.

With Durkheim's distinction between mechanical and organic solidarity, as well as with the types of justification and application of social norms correlating to this distinction, all of those elements are given whose more precise determination will be the concern of the following sections. Corresponding to the line of our investigation, these elements can be roughly classified: A context-bound and an impartial "free" application of norms correspond to a conventional and a universalist moral consciousness, respectively. Both formations of moral consciousness are in a reconstructable evolutionary context. As evidence, one can put forward internal and external factors, which Durkheim regards as being still interwoven with one another. In the internal perspective, the reconstruction aims at the concept of "free application," which presupposes the separation of questions of justification from those of application and must therefore be explained as a consequence of the dissolution of context-bound norm application at the conventional level of moral consciousness. We shall require the external perspective later in order to show how a society deals with the unavoidable cognitive and motivational deficiencies of "free application."

All the attempts at reconstructing the development of moral consciousness from an internal perspective take their orientation from a model which was first extensively implemented by G. H. Mead.[29] Thus, in order to explain more precisely at what point in the development of moral consciousness the application problem appears in the sense understood here, it is obvious that we should turn to his interactionist model. Mead explicitly takes the internal perspective in order to reconstruct, from within this standpoint and *ex post facto,* the emergence of intersubjective meaning and validity.

For this reason I shall begin in the following excursus with Mead's theory of the emergence of meanings in social situations (section 1) since it can be shown with the help of this how the relation to a concrete other in a situation compels one to abstract from individual situation features, an abstraction to which the anticipation of behavioral expectations can be linked. This move to abstraction does not in itself refer to individual norms, but refers generally to identical meanings only. If there are situation-independent meanings, their appropriate application in the individual situation becomes a problem. Therefore, in the second section of the excursus, I shall refer to Wittgenstein's analyses of rule-following in order to clarify the internal connection between semantic generality and social intersubjectivity. Wittgenstein understands the intersubjectivity of rule-following from the outset in such a manner that it implies an appropriate application of the rule. Rule-following is characterized by him as common practice or "custom." The application of a rule thus always remains tied to a limited field of situations which are easy to grasp, and this field is common to the participants in such a language game.

Neither Mead's theory of the emergence of meaning nor Wittgenstein's analyses of rule-following can be related directly to moral norms. However, the fact that both authors analyze meaning conventions not in purely semantic terms, but as a result of social processes (Mead: perspective-taking; Wittgenstein: teacher-pupil relationship as the exemplary situation of a training—immanent to the language game—for rule-following), their arguments on situation-appropriate rule-following are also relevant to our topic. This becomes especially clear when we recall that Mead can seamlessly connect the draft of a universalist ethics to the explanation of the semantically identical use of symbols. I shall discuss this possibility, which is given with the model of perspective-taking, in a section on Mead's ethics following this excursus. If identical meanings emerge in virtue of the fact that alter and ego become mutually aware of their responses to the other's modes of behavior, then the reference points are already marked for an ethics that characterizes as morally right only those norm hypotheses which spring from a consideration of the perspectives of all those affected. Mead's draft is important for us because the concept of the social situation, which was introduced to explain the emergence of meaning, is extended to ethics, as it were. The social situation is also a moral one: Mead ties his ethical model of constructive hypothesis formation to the consideration of *all the "values" in a situation.*[30]

However, Mead connects the ethics of constructive hypothesis formation in situations directly to the idea of universal perspective-taking. As a result, he too fails to distinguish between a reciprocal and an applicative sense in impartiality. This distinction, however, becomes necessary when the normative standpoint of the generalized other is enlarged to the universe of discourse. With the help of the model of perspective-taking, we can now explicate more precisely what is meant by the distinction between a context-bound and an impartial application. The necessity of this distinction is still, however, in need of justification. This will be the topic of the third section. There I shall attempt to reconstruct the various types of application discourses which can be linked to the stage model of moral development as devised by Piaget and Kohlberg.

Durkheim traced the all-pervading force of the collective consciousness back to, among other things, the "transcendent authority" with which religious rules, and the institutions they regulate, are equipped. Because of this authoritarian, genetic residuum, objections to the supposed repressive character of universalist moral philosophies have been brought forward; I shall turn to these in section 4. The attribute "supposed" can be justified if, first, these objections can be traced back to an erroneous confusion of the justification and application dimensions and if, secondly, it can be shown that a universalist application does not by any means have to include an authoritarian and rigid application of norms. In attempting to do this, we shall again return to Wellmer's argument that an "application problem," in the sense intended here, arises only at the conventional level of the justification of norms.

Excursus:
The Emergence and Following of Rules in Social Processes

1. The Emergence of Situation-independent Meanings in Social Situations (Mead)

What Mead describes again and again in various ways in the first two sections of his book, and what he analyzes in ever-increasing detail in its presuppositions and consequences, is the process of transition from mere reaction to gestures to "self-perceivable" meaningful action.[31] Mead links this process to a multiplicity of motifs: the process of hominization and ontogenetic socialization, the formation of language symbols, and the emergence of consciousness and self-consciousness as well as societal institutions. Since I do not intend to provide an original interpretation of Mead, I shall proceed selectively in what follows and shall not be able to do justice to the wealth of his motifs.

The crucial feature of this transition consists in the fact that, in social intercourse between different beings, the first individual implicitly anticipates in his gestures the reaction or "response" the second individual (affected by the gesture as "stimulus") will explicitly give.[32] In the almost inscrutable complexity of this seemingly trivial process, the following elements are most important for Mead: a social process emerges between ego and alter; by anticipating the reaction of the second individual, the first individual develops a consciousness; in that the first individual ties his own mode of behavior to the anticipated reaction of the other, a preliminary form of self-consciousness emerges; to the extent that the anticipated gestures can be subsumed under identical types, preliminary forms of "meaning" emerge. In the process of internalizing the foreseeable reactions of others, the instinct-bound mechanism of stimulus and response is broken. The unconscious, one-sided adjustment via

simple gestures becomes a consciously controlled "mutual adjustment" intersubjectively refracted by meanings. As soon as the first
individual distances himself from his own stimulus and can not only
anticipate the response of the second individual, but also react to
his own stimulus as the other does, the original gesture has a
"meaning"—it becomes a "significant symbol." Here, of course, two
steps are to be separated from one another: one-sidedly taking the
attitude of the other, which puts the first individual in a position to
prognosticate the other's reaction to his own gesture and to causally
influence it accordingly; and, on the other hand, mutually taking
the attitude of the other, whereby the first and the second individuals rely on the *same* meaning, that is, both know and can normatively expect of each other that they use the *same* symbols. At
this level, the identity of the meaning of the symbol itself becomes
a topic for alter and ego—both rely on the "rules for the use of
symbols."[33] Mead, however, remains at the level of the simple use
of symbols, which he characterizes as already being "language."

What is decisive for our discussion is the decontextualization of,
or abstraction from, the particular circumstances of behavior, a decontextualization which goes hand in hand with the "semanticiza-
tion" of simple gestures. At the level of the identical use of symbols,
individual behavior is, as such, rule-governed. The less behavior is
determined by situational stimuli, the more clearly and the greater
the variety of ways which the relation between symbol, meaning,
and the concrete interactive situation moves to the center of attention. The place of an unconscious, instinct-bound mechanism which
"mediates" between stimulus and response is taken by the "application" of rules in situations. From the outset, Mead investigates
this process of abstraction in three directions at the same time:
with reference to the self, the other, and the action situation, without, in the process, precisely distinguishing between semantic, normative, and expressive aspects of the use of symbols. The significant
symbol, which for him completely represents language, has, like the
footprint of animal, a different meaning for the hunted than for the
hunter. I shall not consider this interweaving of meaning-theoretic
and action-theoretic questions here and shall attempt only to trace,
following Mead and in an ideal-typical manner, the process of abstraction which leads to a situation-invariant rule consciousness.

The mere taking of the attitude of the second individual by the
first still remains situation-specific and bound to the concrete dispositions of those involved. Of course, already by simple anticipation, ego ascribes to alter's anticipated response the status of being

premature in respect of the later-occurring action, as well as the status of being fictional in respect of the concrete modalities and the "whether" of the expected action. A step beyond the context of the situation is taken when ego not only prognosticates alter's response merely according to the given circumstances, but relates to alter's interpretation of ego's gesture. In this constellation, ego assumes that alter has the same relation to the intended gesture as he himself does. He can now comprehend alter's reaction as a response based on an antecedent act of interpretation and can expect that alter will behave toward him in the selfsame manner as ego toward alter. Both individuals interpret the gesture in the same way; it has the same *meaning* for them. Of course, situation features are still relevant to the production of a common meaning. Now, however, they are selected from the point of view that they belong to the same class of semantic features. If the meaning of a gesture is not to be laid down *hic et nunc* between person A and B— which in any case would not be possible without an understanding of universal "meaning"—the gesture must be able to have an identical meaning in different situations. A "third world" of meanings has thereby emerged between ego and alter, a world to which they can refer in situations: "What language seems to carry is a set of symbols answering to certain content which is measurably identical in the experience of the different individuals. If there is to be communication as such the symbol has to mean the same thing to all individuals involved."[34]

Mead interprets the function of symbolic meanings in line with the pragmatic tradition: they enable us to keep action-relevant situation features present in order to break the spell of the stimulus-response mechanism and step onto the level of conscious deliberation. "What such symbols do is to pick out particular characteristics of the situation so that the response to them can be present in the experience of the individual."[35] In this way, it becomes possible to experiment with situations, that is, with particular constellations of features, without the burden of having to act. Situation dependency opens the chance of better adjusting to situations with variable features. "Language does not simply symbolize a situation or object which is already there in advance; it makes possible the existence or the appearance of that situation or object, for it is a part of the mechanism whereby that situation or object is created."[36] Conversely, we are thus presented with the problem of correctly applying situation features in the concrete situation— situation features, that is, which have been abstracted from the abundance of individual features, generalized, and condensed to symbols with meaning.

Decisive for Mead is that the logical universality of linguistic signs is at the same time a social universality. "Meaning" is constituted not via the abstraction from individual features, but first via the use of symbols with identical meanings in communication. Those experiences with situations that "cause" us, in the pragmatic sense, to select specific features and to lay down their meaning are of a social kind.[37] Thus, Mead interprets the relationship between universality and particularity first behavioristically, in the traditional sense: "We can have, in this way, something that is universal as over against various particulars. I think we can recognize in any habit that which answers to different stimuli; the response is universal and the stimulus is particular. As long as this element serves as a stimulus, calls out this response, one can say the particular comes under this universal"[38]—in order then to pass over to "the social dimension of universality."[39]

> "Meaning as such, i.e., the object of thought, arises in experience through the individual stimulating himself to take the attitude of the other in his reaction toward the object. Meaning is that which can be indicated to others while it is by the same process indicated to the indicating individual. In so far as the individual indicates it to himself in the role of the other, he is occupying his perspective, and as he is indicating it to the other from his own perspective, and as that which is so indicated is identical, it must be that which can be in different perspectives. It must therefore be a universal, at least in the identity which belongs to the different perspectives which are organized in the single perspective, and in so far as the principle of organization is one which admits of other perspectives than those actually present, the universality may be logically indefinitely extended."[40]

Thus, the difference between various situations or various situation features is relevant only to the extent that it is brought to bear as a difference in the various perspectives of those participating in the communication process, that is, a difference in relation to the claimed identity of meaning. If what is meant has the same meaning for all the participants viewed from their respectively different perspectives, then it is a "universal." This state has been reached in differentiated human language.

The situation aspect and the intersubjective validity are thus simply *two different, equiprimordial sides* of a significant symbol.

When we apply a symbol in different situations in the same way, that is, with the same meaning, the interpretation of the situation as being "the same" always refers to all the potential interpreters of the symbol too. The symbol is situation-independent and impersonal at the same time: "What is essential to communication is that the symbol should arouse in one's self what it arouses in the other individual. It must have that sort of universality to any person who finds himself in the same situation."[41]

2. Rule-following as a "Custom" (Wittgenstein)

The relationship between the meaning and the intersubjective validity of a symbol can be specified more precisely with the help of the analyses of the concept of rule undertaken by Wittgenstein. The nature of this relationship reveals itself in the incorrect application of a rule in a situation: "The application is still a criterion of understanding."[42] According to Wittgenstein, the conditions of rule-conforming conduct can only be reconstructed from the internal perspective. Alter and ego have to participate in the same language game in order to be able to judge reciprocally whether the respective other has applied the rule correctly.[43]

The externally observable uniformity of conduct in different situations is unimportant for its characterization as rule-following; after all, it could be a matter of the regular reccurrence of a natural process. To follow a rule does not mean always doing the same thing in various, sufficiently similar situations; rather, it means always following *the same rule*. To that extent, the words "rule" and "same" are interwoven with one another—though, as Wittgenstein emphasizes, precisely only in the sense of "belonging to" and not of "fitting" one another.[44] Having accepted the primacy of the internal perspective for the analysis of rule-following, one is immediately faced with the problem of how the internal processes accompanying rule-following can be described. If no objective conditions can be stated for when one follows the same rule in different situations, one can no longer distinguish rule-following from the (subjective) belief that one is following a rule. For then one gets into the precarious position of having to distinguish particular mental states as being internally connected with rule-following. A large number of Wittgenstein's arguments serve the purpose of displaying the nonsense we produce when we associate expressions like "mean" and "rule-following" with mental events.[45]

If, however, taking recourse to the belief that one is following a rule is used as a criterion, it leads directly to rule skepticism. Thus, for Wittgenstein, there remains only common intersubjective practice: alter and ego have to understand each other as persons applying the same rule in different situations; they have to participate in the same language game in order to be able to judge whether the respective other is following the same rule in different situations. They have to step out of their roles as observers of unfamiliar behavioral events and become participants in a common practice. Thus, at least two action situations and two persons who apply rules and can judge rule application are constitutive of rule-following: "To follow a rule means to follow the *same* rule in *every* single case. The identity of the rule in the multiplicity of its realizations does not rest on observable invariants but on the intersubjectivity of its validity."[46]

The other, just like me, has to be able to apply the same rule; " . . . it is only in a situation in which it makes sense to suppose that somebody else could in principle discover the rule which I am following that I can intelligibly be said to follow a rule at all."[47] For this, there is no need for the presupposition that *A* should always do the same thing, only that *A* and *B* can collectively come to the conviction in each individual situation that what *A* does in each case is in agreement with the same rule. Then, if *B* for his part is at all competent to follow a rule, he has to be able to act in different situations according to the same rule without having to fear that *A* will reject his act as not conforming to the rule. The intersubjectivity of the "sameness" of a rule reveals itself in the possibility of criticizing incorrect applications. "Since rules hold counterfactually, it is possible to criticize rule-governed behavior and to evaluate it as successful or incorrect."[48]

How can we distinguish correct from incorrect applications? According to what has been said so far, the answer can, yet again, only be: What constitutes a correct application follows from the common practice. Wittgenstein examines two possibilities, whose implications he rejects.[49] Neither by looking at the rule alone nor by looking at the particular action in a situation can we find a criterion. The first position leads to what Kemmerling refers to as "rule Platonism," and the second to a "rule skepticism." According to the Platonic model, the rule, in virtue of its mere meaning, "inspires" me in a mysterious way to apply it correctly.[50] "Rule" and "situation" are as independent of each other as two different worlds. The application situation is of absolutely no importance for the decision on correct application because all application situations are already anticipated in the rule. Thus, Wittgenstein illustrates Platonism by the example of continuing a mathematical series: " 'All the steps are really already taken' means: I no longer have any choice. The rule, once stamped with a particular meaning, traces the lines along which it is to be followed through the whole of space.—But if something of this sort really were the case, how would it help?"[51] The criterion for the correctness of application is in the rule itself. The model can thus be reduced to the brief formula: "The rule regulates its own following."[52]

A more precise explication of this model leads to difficulties, however. Either the model would have to presuppose the usual internal states—"pictures," "voices" that tell us how a rule is to be applied.[53] Or it must be possible to put forward rules of application for which, in turn, there have to be rules of application—*ad infinitum*.[54] In addition, this model would have to be able to explain the phenomenon that there are situations in which various applications are correct, for example, when a commenced series of numbers allows various possibilities of continuing it. The skeptic draws a radical conclusion from this: If there is no rule of application and if various applications can be correct, every action can be brought into accord with a rule. Then, however, it is also meaningless to distinguish between "correct" and "incorrect" application. Rule skepticism claims: "No mode of conduct is a rule violation—all conduct is a rule-following."[55]

Wittgenstein's dissolution of this antimony between rule Platonism and rule skepticism is based on a dedramatization of the relationship between rule and situation. The attempt to ascribe primacy in the decision about what has to be regarded as the right application of a rule to one of the two sides, or to both sides together, leaves an important element out of consideration and thus produces the same antimony again and again. In §198 of the *Philosophical Investigations,* Wittgenstein advances all the essential arguments in a highly concentrated manner:

But how can a rule shew me what I have to do at *this* point?

With this question rule Platonism comes to an end; it had harbored the hope that the rule itself would be able to say what one has to do in each individual situation. Opposing this, the skeptic summarizes his experiences as follows:

Whatever I do is, on some interpretation, in accord with the rule.

The antimony is thus characterized by these two statements. Wittgenstein then rejects skepticism:

> That is not what we ought to say, but rather: any interpretation still hangs in the air along with what it interprets, and cannot give it any support. Interpretations by themselves do not determine meaning.

With mere interpretations, we remain in the Platonic world, as long as we restrict ourselves to the isolated meaning of the rule. All we do is have one interpretation follow another. It is not at all a matter of the arbitrary accord of rule (or its interpretation) and action, which was criticized by the skeptic, but of the fact that I do not arrive at the action at all if I take the rule alone, and its interpretations, as the point of departure. But how do we get our feet onto the "rough ground"[56] along which we can proceed? The skeptic merely varies his critique of Platonism:

> Then can whatever I do be brought into accord with the rule?

By radicalizing it in this manner, Wittgenstein can formulate the skeptic's problem more precisely and, at the same time, propose a solution that identifies the missing link between rule and situation:

> Let me ask this: what has the expression of a rule—say a signpost—got to do with my actions? What sort of connexion is there here?—Well, perhaps this one: I have been trained [*abgerichtet*] to react to this sign in a particular way, and now I do so react to it.

We have thus reached—at least for a great deal of cases—the ground that connects the interpretation of a rule in a situation with the action. What has to be added to this is the common practice of those who participate in the form of life in which following the rule is a practiced activity. Before I go into this in greater detail, a possible objection remains to be refuted, an objection that Wittgenstein himself promptly brings forward. If I simply "react," it could be a matter of a behavioristic scheme —as with Mead's interpretation of simple gestures. Wittgenstein, however, rejects physicalist reductions of this kind:

> But that is only to give a causal connexion; to tell how it has come about that we now go by the sign-post; not what this going-by-the-

sign really consists in. On the contrary; I have further indicated that a person goes by a sign-post only in so far as there exists a regular use of sign-posts, a custom.[57]

The reference to custom is to be understood at the same time as an elucidation of the meaning of "training" [*Abrichten*]. In this way Wittgenstein points to the intersubjective dimension of rule-following, which of course, as an established practice, is not fully at our disposal.[58] It is through socialization that we learn the ways in which we follow rules. Following a rule is thus "a practice" or a "common behaviour' of mankind."[59] Therefore, I follow a rule "blindly"—but not in a deterministic sense, rather as a matter of course.[60] However, with this rejoinder Wittgenstein has escaped the skeptic only momentarily. If following a rule, just like other activities, is simply part of a social practice, then this practice is in turn contingent. We can just as easily envision different customs. "Commanding, questioning, recounting, chatting, are as much a part of our natural history as walking, eating, drinking, playing."[61] However, this skeptical objection is brought to a halt at the boundary of the range of a practice. Within the institution, there obtains an intersubjective a priori that everyone who wants to participate in the language game must acknowledge. "It is constitutive of a 'form of life' that we cannot treat 'arbitrary' rules 'arbitrarily.'"[62] Thus, there cannot be independent criteria for correct or incorrect application; rather, there can only be criteria which are used within a form of life or within a common human mode of action when *A* judges whether *B* has acted in accordance with a rule. Similarly, the identity of the rule in various situations cannot be determined independently of the particular application practice. "The criteria for what is identical in a specific context are precisely those which stipulate what correct rule-following is for this context—and that is of course determined by the concurring way to follow rules."[63]

To this extent, Wittgenstein thus sticks to a skeptical position. The use theory of meaning applies to a multitude of language games. What the meaning of an expression is can only be discovered by participating in the game and thus by acknowledging the particular rules constitutive of it. For this reason, the interwovenness of "rule" and "identical" can likewise be understood only *within* the language game.

Whereas Wittgenstein links the relation between meaning and validity, between semantic identity and intersubjectivity, to the different contexts of rule-following and does not therefore go beyond the particular form of life in which the rule-following practice is embedded, Habermas radicalizes this relation to a system of unavoidable presuppositions which we must assume to be fulfilled in *every* language game.[64] From a Wittgensteinian viewpoint, the level of a meta-language game has thus been reached.[65] The accord itself between the participants now becomes the theme of a separate language game. The possibility of criticizing an incorrect application demonstrates the dovetailing of meaning and validity within a language game; however, those involved can now make this dovetailing itself the subject matter of critique. An intersubjective critique of incorrect applications of a rule is only possible if the participants harbor the mutual expectation that their particular action in a situation can be regarded as an intersubjectively correct application of a rule. In the case of disagreement, and with reference to these bilateral expectations, critique "can be repeated until one of the participants fulfills the other's expectation of recognition, the two arrive at a consensus grounded on critical positions, and are certain that R [i.e., the thematized rule] is intersubjectively valid for them—which is to say, that it has the same meaning for them."[66]

But can a disagreement about the correct application of a rule be reduced to the identity of its meaning for those involved? Habermas's introduction of a meta-language game allows a problem to become visible, namely, that a disagreement about the correct application of a rule can have at least two reasons: the rule does not have an identical meaning for A and B (which is *shown* by the fact that B would do something different in situation S than A) *or* there is a disagreement between A and B about the appropriate application of the rule in a situation S. The identity of meaning refers only to the rule and to a finite, but indeterminable number of examples, not however to situational appropriateness. Though Habermas refers to the disagreement about correct rule-following, he then however reduces it to the question of the identity of meaning, and thereby neglects the aspect of situational appropriateness.[67] Of course, one must concede that, precisely for a theory of meaning that is linked to Wittgenstein, the meaning of a rule cannot be separated from its application in a situation, so that a disagreement about the correct application of a rule always includes a disagreement about the identity of its meaning. Nonetheless, the question of situational appropriateness would then have to be thematizable in terms of the aspect of meaning identity.

Wittgenstein escapes this problem because he can leave the internal dovetailing of meaning, validity, and application unthematized in the concepts of custom, practice, or institution. For him, consensus is not a criterion for distinguishing correct from incorrect applications, established practice is. What we agree about in a practice can indeed be changed, but it can never be fully at our disposal within a single language game. " 'So you are saying that human agreement decides what is true and what is false?'—It is what human beings *say* that is true and false; and they agree in the *language* they use. That is not agreement in opinions but in form of life."[68]

Habermas's meta-language game can now be understood in such a way that it is this agreement, presupposed as an internal a priori in every language game, which is to be explicated against Wittgenstein's intention in order to escape language-game relativism.[69] Wittgenstein remains, however, at the object level relative to a language game, the level at which each language game has its own "criteria" of intersubjectively correct rule-following. Each language game solves the application problem for itself. In following a rule "as a matter of course," two things have already been combined with one another: the transition from the rule to the action in a situation, and participation in an intersubjective practice. Individually and collectively habitualized practices, customs, or institutions cannot be formulated in explicit rules, just as they do not admit of being restricted to specific application situations. If rule-following is a practice, then agreement must refer not only to the rule but also to the practice—for Wittgenstein, both are ultimately indistinguishable. For this reason, the language game for justifying an action by pointing to rules has a trivial end: "If I have exhausted the justifications I have reached bedrock, and my spade is turned. Then I am inclined to say 'This is simply what I do'."[70]

Habermas splits open "custom" in order to isolate the aspect of rule identity. Wittgenstein, on the other hand, recalls that agreement has to relate not only to the identity of the rule for all those involved, but also to the intersubjective practice of following it in situations. Because Wittgenstein rejects rule Platonism, the various ways of following a rule cannot all be anticipated in the identity of the rule. Wittgenstein does however preclude *a limine* the possibility that agreement in rule-following *practice* could ever become the topic of a language game. One can indeed call to mind, with Wittgenstein, that agreement must also refer to the situational appropriateness of the application of a rule, however he conceals this aspect in the concept of "custom."

We undertook this excursus with the intention of identifying the point at which the relation between identical meaning and

particular situation becomes crucial in the interaction between alter and ego. The application problem already presents itself as such
when ego relates anticipatingly to alter's reaction. In this constellation, however, it remains at the level of the occurrence of prognos-
ticated events. It is not until ego refers to a symbolic meaning that
is identical for both ego and alter that situational independence is
complete and the application problem explicit.

We were able to conclude from Mead's investigations that the
emergence of semantically identical and situation-independent
symbols can be explained and understood only in terms of a social
process. Thus, the reason for situational invariance is to be sought
in the requirement of intersubjectivity; situational independence is
the "price" we have to pay for being able to relate to one another via
meanings, without having to thematize anew in every situation all
its features and all the participants' individual dispositions. At the
same time, however, Mead's pragmatic reconstruction makes it
clear that we always have to consider the interactive use of semantically identical symbols against the background of selectively abstracting relevant features in situations. Now, it is precisely this
selection which can become problematic and require justification
with regard to the situation-appropriate use of symbols, that is to
say, problematic in relation to all the other features of the situation
and to the different perspectives of those involved.

Wittgenstein's analyses, on the other hand, led us to the application problem, with the conclusion that the problem of situation-
appropriate application cannot be solved simply by reaching
understanding on the identity of meaning. Judgment on the situational appropriateness of an application can be grounded neither on
the identity of the rule nor on the situation, nor on both; rather, it
too can only be based on an interactive practice. Participants' agreement has to be able to relate not only to the identity of the rule in
each individual case, but also to the appropriateness of its application in an individual case. By condensing, from the outset, the aspects of situation-invariant semantical identity, intersubjective
validity, and situation-appropriate use in the concept of "practice"
or "custom," Wittgenstein draws attention to the fact that thematizing one particular aspect should not suppress the others. By confronting Wittgenstein with Habermas, it became clear that the
focus on the aspect of the intersubjective validity of an identical
rule has to be widened to include the aspect of intersubjective,
situation-appropriate application in order to flesh out the full
meaning of Wittgenstein's concept of a form of life.

At this point, if not before, a problem we have so far neglected becomes acute: Both Mead's exposition on the emergence of the significant symbol and Wittgenstein's analyses of rule-following refer more to meaning conventions than to norms of action. The problem of situation-appropriate application does of course arise for both types of rules. But the sense is different in each case. It is one thing whether I appropriately play the language game of "commanding," "asking," or "chatting," it is another whether it is appropriate to command B to do a in situation S. Both cases are identical in respect of the semantic content of the norms. For this reason, certain arguments from the sphere of rule Platonism or rule skepticism will return again and again.

In what follows we shall restrict ourselves to the application of action norms. Here, language plays a part only to the extent that it is a medium for coordinating action and not just a medium for reaching understanding.[71] We shall take up the results of the preceding sections and concretize the thesis that the situation-appropriate application of action norms is an essential element of action coordination and can only occur in an intersubjective practice. The conditions of the intersubjectivity of appropriate norm application, and their change—which is reconstructable in terms of a logic of development—are the topics of the following sections.

2

Mead's Draft of a Universalist Ethics as a Method for the Constructive Formation of Appropriate Hypotheses

Mead moves from the level of the semantically identical use of symbols to the level of normatively regulated action when he examines the complementary emergence of self and society. The anticipatory adoption of others' responses not only coalesces to individual symbols imbued with meaning, it also relates to the different social roles connected with the interactive use of linguistic expressions. Ego thus adopts certain behavioral expectations of alter, expectations which are equipped with a normative claim. In this way, the other is experienced in a social role that comprises various aspects: not only that of speaker or hearer as the addressee of a communicative action, but also generally as a participant in an interaction stamped by normative experiences. Mead does not pursue the differentiation of these various aspects any further because he is solely concerned with the linguistically mediated, equiprimordial genesis of self and society. Habermas has distinguished three different domains to which participants in interaction relate at the same time as realizing the social roles of speaker and hearer: propositions and the perception of things, norms and role behavior, as well as identity and need.[72] For all of the three domains, the process of abstraction specific to each can be retraced, a process which Mead first described in general terms as the difference between universal and particular: the linguistic mastery of an objective world to which we relate with propositions and in which we can intervene teleologically; the social world of a "generalized other" which evolves from the spatial, temporal, and social generalization of behavioral expectations and to which we relate in a performative attitude; and the subjective world where we learn to differentiate between ego and superego and to which we can relate in expressive utterances.

Mead distinguishes two levels at which the process of abstracting intersubjectively binding norms occurs. The individual first relates to the attitudes and expectations of the *concrete* other whom he encounters in a situation. In doing so, he learns to reflect his own perspective on the specific situation in the particular perspective of the other. By confronting his perspective with that of the other, he distinguishes himself from the other and sees his own standpoint from that of the other. The multitude of social roles which the individual can take toward himself and others puts him in a position to generalize the role expectations not only beyond the contingent spatial and temporal circumstances of the particular situation, but also beyond the concrete context of the relationship to another. The individual takes his orientation from the *generalized* other, whom both ego and alter encounter as a third person. At the start of his study on the genesis of "self," Mead summarized the features of both levels as follows: "The individual experiences himself as such, not directly, but only indirectly, from the particular standpoints of other individual members of the same social group, or from the generalized standpoint of the social group as a whole to which he belongs. For he enters his own experience as a self or individual, not directly or immediately, not by becoming a subject to himself, but only in so far as he first becomes an object to himself just as other individuals are objects to him or in his experience; and he becomes an object to himself only by taking the attitudes of other individuals toward himself within a social environment or context of experience and behavior in which both he and they are involved."[73] According to this description, the process of the genesis of social norms consists of three interdependent elements: taking the attitude of the other, that is, as the concrete and generalized stages; the construction of a self; and the social context of common experiences and modes of behavior.

With the help of the distinction between "play" and "game," Mead specified these two levels more precisely. At the first level (play), taking the attitude of the other remains bound to concrete relationship and behavior patterns which have not yet been socially generalized and which the child experiences in everyday interactions.[74] The child playfully takes those roles toward himself which he perceives others to have from his perspective. He plays the roles of parent and child, teacher and pupil, and similar ones, with himself. The behavior patterns can indeed refer to different situations and are not bound to a specific point in time; they are however invariable in respect of the concrete role of specific persons. Rather, it is these persons themselves who concretely embody the behavior patterns—for example, in relations of caring—so that a disappointment of expectations always affects the particular interests of one of the persons involved.

It is not until the second level (game) that the behavior patterns also become socially generalized, that is, suprapersonal. The child can then distance himself from the expectations of the other and put these in relation to the expectational structures which relate to both his own expectations and those of the concrete other. In group and competitive games, the child must be in a position "to take the attitude of everyone else involved in that game"[75] in order to be able to participate. These multiple expectations of other participants can be only organized in a socially generalized form. They assume the character of rules of a game that are neutral vis-à-vis the changing concrete interests of all the participants and relate to those involved only in terms of the aspect of conformity or deviation. They simultaneously embody the common will of all the participants in a game, but the roles of the persons participating are nevertheless interchangeable. For this reason, breaking a rule not only violates the interests of the concrete other, it also disappoints the expectations—as embodied in the rule—of all those involved.

At this level, the perspective of a neutral third position has been reached, one from where ego can evaluate both his own and alter's perspective. To the extent that this third position disengages itself from the context of the game and embodies the common interest of the group in which the child grows up, this perspective coalesces to that of a generalized other.[76] It begins to determine not only individual phases of playing, but also the child's biography, as well as his social behavior. Complementary to this, the growing child begins to form a consistent self-consciousness. The moment an individual orients his actions according to generalized norms, he becomes interchangeable, when viewed from the perspective of the norm. He no longer takes his orientation only from the expectations of the concrete other in a particular situation, but also from a norm that is *valid* independent of the concrete interactive relationship. In this norm, he encounters the organized and generalized attitude of the group just like a concrete other, and in the course of socialization, he internalizes the condensed perspectives of all others, which he sets in relation to himself. On the basis of this internal relation between self and generalized other, Mead develops his model of the equiprimordial genesis of self and society.

A series of deliberations on the obligatory character of the moral ought, sanctions, and authority, as well as on the development of moral consciousness can—even independent of Mead—link up with the process of the formation of the third position.[77] In this context I am only concerned with the decontextualization associated with spatial, temporal, and social generalization. The specific character of decontextualization can be developed in two directions. In the generalized other, the action orientation is entirely independent of the particular application situation. Not only the specific spatial and temporal circumstances, but also the particular relationships to concrete others obtaining in each case, as well as one's own particular dispositions, are relevant only insofar as they belong to the particular features of the general norm of a group. Thus, they are not relevant as the particular features of the situation, but only as elements of an abstract class of features that can be found in different situations with different participants. On this scale, the third position signifies a standpoint of impartiality. Ego has to take vis-à-vis himself a perspective where it does not matter whether he finds himself in his own place or in that of alter. Viewed from this standpoint, alter takes the same perspective vis-à-vis ego as ego does vis-à-vis alter. On the presupposition of this third position, the perspectives in which the participants perceive the situation are decentered.[78] The third position acquires the status of an objectivating observer authority which makes it possible to relate neutrally, that is, with the attitude of the third person, to the perspectives that are interwoven in the concrete situation of interaction.[79]

On the other hand, however, the third position of the generalized other remains bound to the specific interactive relations of a particular group. The active norms do vary with specific individual cases, but not with the specific set of experiences in situations which has become part of the history of the cooperative relations of a particular group. To this extent, the norms remain bound to a restrictedly generalized context. After having introduced the concept of the generalized other, Mead does hasten to add that the specific context of groups can, for its part, be extended to "the one which is most inclusive and extensive . . . the one defined by the logical universe of discourse (or system of universally significant symbols),"[80] and he himself presents proposals for a universalist ethics. However, he does not provide an explanation for this process of extension because he is primarily concerned with the content side of this process, the side on which self and society are simultaneously formed: "What goes to make up the organized self is the organization of the attitudes which are common to the group. A person is a personality because he belongs to a community, because he takes over the institutions of that community into his own conduct. He takes its language as a medium by which he gets his personality, and then through a process of taking the different roles that all the others furnish he comes to get the attitude of the members of the community. Such, in a certain sense, is the structure of a man's personality."[81]

At this point, Mead does not yet fully exhaust the normative potential that is not only logically given with the "universe of discourse" of language, but also present in a social respect. He avails of this normative potential only to the extent that the community's expectations, as embodied in the third position, are constitutive of the genesis of the self. This has the implication, which is of interest to us, that he interprets the application of action norms in the context of the relation of self and society.

Mead describes the process of internalizing societal expectations as the development of the "me," which is encountered by the "I" as the specifically individual response and disposition. Societal norms are not altogether repressively internalized, nor do they occasion a conditioning of the individual by instituting conditioned reflexes; rather, the self's authority filters the adoption, application, and realization of generalized behavioral expectations within a reflexive process at the end of which, and not until then, stands the situational, spontaneous, and unpredictable reaction of the "I." "The 'I' is the response of the organism to the attitudes of the others; the 'me' is the organized set of attitudes of others which one himself assumes."[82] In a manner which appears peculiar at first glance, Mead links this distinction of different phases of the self to the application of norms in situations.

In terms of the *external relation,* the "me" is the "response" to the attitudes of others which the self takes anticipatingly. In terms of the *internal relation,* by contrast, the "me" represents the *social situation* to which the self as "I" responds with spontaneous conduct. In doing so, the "I" can be in accord or disaccord with the internalized expectations of others: "The self under these circumstances is the action of the 'I' in harmony with the taking of the role of others in the 'me'. The self is both the 'I' and 'me'; the 'me' setting the situation to which the 'I' responds. Both the 'I' and the 'me' are involved in the self, and here each supports the other."[83]

Thus, the relationship of the "me" to the "I" may not be thought of in analogy to an application relationship of norm to situation. Rather, Mead used the basic pragmatic-naturalistic model of the reaction of an organism to a situation that is defined by this organism as a problem requiring a solution. "The 'me' I have said, presents the situation within which conduct takes place, and the 'I' is the actual response to that situation. This twofold separation into situation and response is characteristic of any intelligent act even if it does not involve this social mechanism. There is a definite situation which presents a problem, and then the organism responds to that situation by an organization of the different reactions that are involved."[84] Unlike the case of a reaction to physical objects, the individual responds to the social situation as it presents itself in the form of the "me." The definition of the situation is the outcome of perspective-taking. In it, the various aspects of a situation have been adopted in the same way as the other participants appraise them for themselves, and these aspects open up different action possibilities for the self. The relationship of the "me" to the situation is thus determined by the social perspectives of those participating in a situation. The "I" is the act in which the various social perspectives on the particular situation are fused.[85]

In the process of spatial, temporal, and social generalization, the various social perspectives on individual situations are organized and standardized. The "me" then represents generalized and organized responses to social situations. By bringing his conduct into line with these responses in current situations, the individual becomes a member of society whose conduct is exposed to social control: " . . . the society in which we belong represents an organized set of responses to certain situations in which the individual is involved . . . ," and by taking over these responses via the perspective change with concrete others, the individual discovers "his cues as to what he is to do under a specific situation."[86]

Mead does not of course draft the model of a totalitarian society which subsumes every response of the individual under a rigid social discipline that would be cast over the socialized part of the self. Rather, the "I's" ways of reacting are at the same time the latitude for freedom and variation within which the socialized structures and the normative structures of society can as a whole be changed. If the self, mediated by the "me," participates in the community and forms a community [*vergemeinschaftet sich*] with others by appealing in a situation to the standards shared by the other members, it at the same time remains, mediated by the "I," autonomous and independent of the conventions of its community; it acquires the ability to distance itself from situations in which it finds itself, to subject them to critique, and to change them.[87] It is only both aspects together that constitute a complete individuality. Because no individual is like another in the specific manner in which the "I" reacts to the "me," every act of an individual in a situation changes the community as a whole. On the other hand, the "I" obtains its possibilities for expression only by availing itself of the relational patterns of the "me." "The novelty comes in the action of the 'I', but the structure, the form of the self is one which is conventional."[88] The ways the "I" will act are therefore in principle unpredictable, indeterminate, and contingent. The "I" is the situational application of the organized societal expectations of the individual self. One could designate it with a traditional term as "judgment." "In a society there must be a set of common organized habits of response found in all, but the way in which individuals act under specific circumstances gives rise to all of the individual differences which characterize the different persons."[89]

It is on these specifications of the relationship of the "I" and the "me" that Mead can base his theory of society. The precarious balance between organized intersubjectivity in a community and free intersubjectivity can be stabilized in institutions. The contingency of different individual modes of conduct is absorbed by certain, frequently occurring situations being typologized, so that responses can be normatively and cognitively expected. "There are, then, whole series of such common responses in the community in which we live, and such responses are what we term 'institutions'. The institution represents a common response on the part of all members of the community to a particular situation."[90]

Against the background of the relationship of the "I" and the "me," Mead does however distinguish different degrees of vigor with which the individual's freedom to change is subjected to social control by institutions. The continuum ranges from stereotyped responses, which rigidly restrict the possible latitude for conduct, to open institutions, which presuppose individuals who are capable of judging and acting: " . . . they do not necessarily represent or uphold narrow definitions of certain fixed and specific patterns of acting which in any given circumstances should characterize the behavior of all intelligent and socially responsible individuals . . . "[91] The introduction of institutions does not alter the fact that in every situation the individual takes over the various perspectives of the other members of the community and "applies" them in his biographically unmistakable manner by situationally reacting to the internalized behavioral expectations of others. Institutions can be traced back to the social process of taking the attitude of the other and play a no more demanding role than that of a means by which the individual realizes himself in social situations. They organize the responses of the other members of the community, so that the mode of conduct of the individual in a situation points in the direction of the generalized and not of the concrete other. By linking institutions back to the simple process of taking the attitude of the other, Mead relates them at the same time to that medium which alone makes a reciprocal taking of the attitude of the other possible; and, *per definitionem*, this medium points beyond both the individual institutions themselves and the particular community supporting them; that is to say, it points to the universe of discourse, which, in virtue of the semantically identical use of symbols, is open to all subjects capable of speech.

With the help of the distinction between the "I" and the "me," Mead redefined the problem of the application of norms in situations as the response of the self to a social situation. This shifting of viewpoint is instructive for us because it analyzes the problem of application from the standpoint of the situation. According to the basic model, by taking the attitude of the other, the self relates to the different viewpoints which are *socially* brought to bear in a concrete situation. This basic model is first of all dependent on whether the different viewpoints are spatially, temporally, and socially generalized, organized, or institutionalized to a greater or lesser degree. The concrete other is not simply suspended; rather, even under the conditions of an established generalized other, he represents a possible aspect in the particular situation, an aspect which could become socially relevant, that is, one which ego could be obligated to consider via perspective-taking.

However, this "obligation" only exists on a special condition which Mead explicitly formulated only in his proposal for a universalist ethics: it is only if we have to consider *all* the aspects of a situation that we are obligated to engage in situation-specific perspective-taking. Mead's pragmatism led him to develop universalist ethics from the standpoint of the situation. He compared the method of ethics with the logic of empirical research, which compels the scientist to consider all the facts associated with the concrete problem requiring a solution. Similarly in morality, it is a question of putting forward a "social hypothesis" which can claim to consider all the interests involved in the concrete social situation, that is, those that are an element within the conflictive occurrence which poses the moral problem. "We have to look at it from the point of view of a social situation."[92] Initially, every viewpoint in which an interest in the conflict situation is expressed is equally relevant to hypothesis formation. Because everyone affected interprets his interests in the same manner, namely, in terms of the internal self-relationship of the "I" and the "me," the relevant points of view embody individually different perspectives on the standards of the community. Mead terms them "values," which rank among the components of the conflict situation.[93] The social hypothesis which we construct while considering all the interests affected in a situation thus *reconstructs* at the same time the standards of the community—and does so anew and with a different result in every conflict situation which has to be resolved morally.[94] Mead describes the process of hypothesis formation in a situation as follows: "The only rule that an ethics can present is that an individual should rationally deal with all the values that are found in a specific problem. That does not mean that one has to spread before him all the social values when he approaches a problem. The problem itself defines the values. It is a specific problem and there are certain interests that are definitely involved; the individual should take into account all of those interests and then make out a plan of action which will rationally deal with those interests. That is the only method that ethics can bring to the individual. It is of the greatest importance that one should define what those interests are in the particular situation. The great need is that one should be able to regard them impartially."[95]

In this short passage, Mead describes a method for the construction of a situation-appropriate moral hypothesis. We have to consider all the aspects of the concrete situation which are put forward as interests of those immediately affected. The problematic situation determines what interests are to be considered; however, it must be all of these. The hypothesis (plan of action) has to relate "rationally" to all the interests involved. Mead does not elaborate this feature in the present passage, but just a few lines earlier, in the comparison with empirical hypotheses, he explains it by adding the term "consistent." Accordingly, the hypothesis may not be in contradiction to an unconsidered interest which would falsify it, just like a contradicting fact ignored in the empirical research process.[96] For this reason, the process of hypothesis formation is not subject to any material restrictions which exclude certain viewpoints from the outset. The only restriction is the field of the "problem." The standards of the community are simply values which have to compete with other ones that are likewise involved in the problematic situation.

Of course, Mead can characterize the process of hypothesis formation in this manner only because everyone involved already belongs to a universe of discourse, which puts him in a position to take a stand on a moral problem. Although Mead refers to Kant in his reflections on universalist ethics, he does not develop an explicit theory of the universal validity of moral norms. Rather, he aims primarily at a *practical reason of constructive hypothesis formation,* and not so much at a validity-testing reason, which he tacitly presupposes with the universe of discourse.[97] It is thus also this point—to have neglected the problem of forming norms in a situation—that he criticizes in Kant's idea of pure practical reason. In the form of the moral principle, legitimacy- and validity-testing reason can relate only to given norms, that is, to already constructed hypotheses, which it checks independently of the particular situation only in respect of their universal validity: "Any constructive act is, however, something that lies outside of the scope of Kant's principle. From Kant's standpoint you assume that the standard is there; and then if you slip around it yourself while expecting other people to live up to it, Kant's principle will find you out. But where you have no standard, it does not help you to decide. Where you have to get a restatement, a readjustment, you get a new situation in which to act; the simple generalizing of the principle of your act does not help. It is at that point that Kant's principle breaks down."[98]

The categorical imperative can only guarantee the impartiality of validity, which consists in the fact that I myself may not make an exception, in my favor, to a norm recognized as being valid. In contrast to that, Mead's method of impartial hypothesis formation presents first the task of discovering the interests of those affected in order first of all to formulate a situation-appropriate norm. But Mead even rejects the step to an explicit formulation of the norm: "You cannot lay down in advance fixed rules as to just what should be done. You can find out what are the values involved in the actual problem and act rationally with reference to them."[99] This rejection is however based on the same motif which awoke his mistrust in the categorical imperative. "Standards" or "fixed rules" cannot solve the problem of impartially forming appropriate hypotheses. They become mere "values" in which the interests, self-understanding, and societal meanings of those involved in the conflict situation are expressed, and thus become the material which is to be considered when constructing hypotheses. They can be degraded to this status only because the principle—put forward by Mead—of *impartially* defining the situation equips its claim to validity with a proviso. For this reason, and independent of Mead, the idea of a practical reason which is able to form hypotheses can be related to the problem of applying norms—to that extent, the processes of discovering and applying norm hypotheses are reversible.[100] My proposal—to understand the principle of impartiality in the applicative sense in such a way that it calls for the complete and appropriate consideration of all the features of the application situation—gives every valid norm the status of a hypothesis which is to be weighed in its relation to all the other features of the situation. Mead's idea that every hypothesis formed in a situation is at the same time a reconstruction of the community as a whole can also be understood in this sense.

We can now describe the dimensions of the application problem more precisely. Norms are applied in situations which are socially defined by the participants' interests as embodied in values, standards, and rules. While considering all of a situation's aspects relevant in this way, an impartial norm hypothesis is to be formed. Of course, impartiality requires not only that a hypothesis be formed in a situation-appropriate manner and that it refer to all the differences of a situation, but also—and Mead omits this aspect—that the norm hypothesis be universally valid for all potential participants in a (universal) practical discourse. With each application of a norm, the individuals involved in a situation continue the cultural tradition, their own biographies, as well as the solidarity with other concrete members of their community. With the requirement to observe situational appropriateness, which follows from the idea of impartiality, they simultaneously change these three aspects. What must be judged anew in every situation is the way in which cultural semantics describes the situation completely and appropriately, and whether the norm hypothesis formed within this semantics can be universalized; in every situation, concrete others must be recognized simultaneously in their difference and in their identity as participants in a discourse; and, at the same time, needs and interests—in each case particular, biographically unique, and generalizable—as well as their property as a need or interest shared or repudiated by others must be considered.

At the end of this section, there are still two problems to be noted, ones which will concern us more closely later. De facto we can neither consider all the aspects of a situation nor, by way of perspective-taking, make our own and others' interests completely transparent. For this reason, the process of hypothesis formation is tied not only to the principle of impartiality but also to a struggle for recognition, which Hegel after all described as a life-and-death struggle. These elements of double contingency will lead us back again to institutions later in our study.

For the moment, however, we shall remain independent of this and, in the next step, shall push the devaluation of institutions even further. In the above-cited passages on universalist ethics, Mead operated with two unsubstantiated premises: that the standards of the community become mere values in the process of moral hypothesis formation and that hypothesis formation itself must follow the principle of impartiality. The missing third premise is the devaluation of all conventions in the light of the universe of discourse. With this, however, we move to the level of the universal *validity* of moral norms. In posing the question concerning the justifiability of the universal validity claim, we move beyond the first level of Toulmin's scheme of argumentation, the scheme within which we have been operating throughout this second section. It was only at this level of universal validity that the devaluation of conventionally valid norms could occur, something which Mead already presupposed in his concept of impartial hypothesis formation. If the validity of conventional norms could not in turn be reflected and criticized in a universe of discourse, a situation-appropriate application of these norms would not be possible at all. Thus, it must be the differentiation between conventional and universal validity which leads to the emergence of the problem of application. In the following section, I would like to examine this hypothesis on the basis of theories of the development of moral consciousness.

3

The Differentiation Between Justification and Application at the Postconventional Level of Moral Consciousness (Piaget and Kohlberg)

If the validity of a norm is no longer unquestionably given, but dependent on the universe of discourse, what are the consequences for the application of this norm? Up to now we have assumed that the norms relevant to a situation are given in the community or have been crystallized in it through generalized perspective-taking. For this reason, we could concentrate on the problem of how given norms are appropriately applied in a collectively interpreted situation. However, at the end of the preceding section, it became apparent that a situation-appropriate, impartial moral hypothesis formation is only possible if *all* the possible normative aspects of a situation can be considered. This presupposes that there is no "validity" which prescribes the application of a certain norm without considering the particular circumstances of the situation. The relations of interaction must therefore be so "decentered" that the consideration of all the situation features is not restricted by the compulsion to observe a certain, authoritatively given norm. Furthermore, we voiced the assumption that a decoupling of the validity of a norm from specific situations of application does not occur until the validity claim becomes completely context-independent and no longer relates to a historically arbitrary community, but to all subjects capable of speech. It is not until then that a "free application" of norms, in the sense explicated by Durkheim, becomes possible, an application which can specialize in the appropriate consideration of all the features of the situation, without being burdened by decisions about validity. *The latter* are an independent concern of the justification of norms in the universal-reciprocal sense of (U). Cognitivist theories of morality have demarcated this level of norm justification, which is based on general and rationally motivated agreement, from earlier levels where a given authority, however this may be specified in detail, plays the role of the criterion of validity. Piaget distinguishes between autonomous and heteronomous morality,[101] Kohlberg between the three main levels of preconventional, conventional, and postconventional morality, as well as between a series of intermediate and transitional stages.[102] These theories are of interest to us not because they propose analogous formulations for the moral principle (U) at the highest level of moral development in each model, but because they reconstruct this level as the outcome of a development in which alternative moral principles have failed when faced with increasingly complex moral conflicts. By considering these theories more closely in what follows, I hope to get more precise particulars on the relation between justification and application in the transition from one level to another. If our systematic claim is correct, namely, that it is only a differentiation of the principle of impartiality into a principle of justification and one of application which fully exhausts the meaning of impartiality, then this differentiation may not be neutral vis-à-vis moral development, but can only come about at the highest level.

3.1 The Development of the Relation Between Equity and Equality in Piaget

In the example of the rules of a game, Piaget expressly begins his research on the development of the moral judgment of the child with the distinction between the "practice of rules" and the "consciousness of rules,"[103] but his observations on the actual application of rules serve him only as basic data for the further reconstruction of the internal attitude of playing children to the rules of the game used by them. Analogous to the levels of consciousness introduced by him, Piaget distinguishes between a motor stage at which simple individual regularities are repeated, an egocentric stage at which the child "plays in an individualistic manner with material that is social"[104] and attempts to imitate in his imagination the way older children play, a third stage at which the orientation toward cooperation with others begins but where the child is not yet capable of "legislating on all possible cases that may arise,"[105] and, finally, a fourth stage at which the child masters formal operations and can thus abstract from individual situations, so that he takes pleasure "in anticipating all possible cases and in codifying them."[106] What is characteristic of applicative conduct at this stage is that "the child must be able to reason formally, i.e., he must have a conscious realization of the rules of reasoning which will enable him to apply them to any case whatsoever, including purely hypothetical cases (mere assumptions)."[107]

These four stages of the *practice* of rules correlate not point for point, but only with three stages of a *consciousness* of rules. After the simply motor, assimilative stage, the child begins in the egocentric stage to regard the rules as holy and incontestable (though he frequently violates them in applying them in practice); he still believes at the stage of commencing cooperation in "the absolute and intrinsic truth of rules,"[108] from which he frees himself only at the third stage in favor of the ideal of complete cooperation; rules become arbitrarily changeable if these changes are in the mutual and general interest of those involved. Only the second and third stages are informative for the investigation of rule consciousness, and these are characterized by the contrast between "coercive rules" and "rational rules." Piaget's distinction between heteronomy and autonomy takes its orientation from this contrast. Coercive rules are a feature of asymmetrical social relations; they demand unilateral respect, with which the child is familiar from his relationship to his parents. The motivational basis and observance practice can by all means exhibit contradictory features: outward conformity, imitation, but also actual rule violations, which the child cannot at all perceive as such because he separates the supernatural and incontestable validity of rules from his own experiences of action. Piaget terms this kind of independent existence of rules "moral realism," and it is characteristic of the entire second stage. The child has an authoritarian relationship to rules, which he cannot relate to the particular features of the application situation: "We shall therefore call moral realism the tendency which the child has to regard duty and the value attaching to it as self-subsistent and independent of the mind, as imposing itself regardless of the circumstances in which the individual may find himself."[109] The reification of rules is exhibited by a heteronomy of duty, verbalism, and an objective conception of responsibility.

It is only with increasing cooperation among the partners of the game that this relationship to rules and to the application situation begins to dissolve. The stage of "mutual respect"[110] presupposes symmetrical relations of interaction in which the child learns both to distinguish himself from others and to relate to them. The ideal of cooperation itself becomes the criterion of validity for rules.

The motive for submitting oneself to valid rules is disengaged from the constraint to conform and makes rule-following dependent on whether cooperation can be continued and promoted in this way. Applying rules is experienced as a presupposition for cooperation. This includes the possibility of changing the rules if cooperation is maintained as a result.

Piaget's distinction between coercive and rational rules advances Durkheim's theory of mechanical and organic solidarity, frees it however from its "sociological reductionism," which was tied to naturalistic attempts at explanation.[111] Cooperation, reciprocity, and equal respect are not only the outcome of, but also the *reason* for, recognizing and following rules. The autonomy of the child also shows itself by his being able to apply rules independently, that is, by distancing himself from the validity of the rule and taking his orientation exclusively from the principle of reciprocity when applying it. The primacy of this principle over the obedient observance of a rule leads Piaget to a specification of Durkheim's concept of "free application." Using the example of reactions to rule violations and the principle of judgment prevailing therein, Piaget demonstrates clearly that it is only under conditions of cooperation that a non-retributive "sanction" can come about, one which focuses on the problems of the individual case and which is not in the service of punishment for the its own sake, but fosters the restoration of reciprocity. Whereas the mechanics of the retributive principle make one less sensitive "to the human side of the problem," the child interested in continuing cooperation tries "to understand the situation from within."[112]

The child's sense of justice is disengaged from obedience to authority and takes its orientation from the principle of equality. The restoration and continuation of reciprocity is now however compatible with a mechanical concept of equality. Equality in cooperative relationships requires the recognition of individual differences: " . . . justice itself is extended along a purely autonomous line of development into the higher form of reciprocity which we call 'equity', a relation based not on pure equality but on the real situation in which each individual may find himself."[113] Equality and reciprocity thus enforce "equity" as the highest level of moral judgments. True cooperation only comes about when all the particular features of all those involved in a situation are considered. Piaget thus distinguishes three levels in the development of the idea of justice: that of the priority of authority over equality, that of egalitarianism, and that of equity. Equity is "nothing but a development of equalitarianism in the direction of relativity. Instead of looking for equality in identity, the child no longer thinks of the equal rights of individuals except in relation to the particular situation of each. In the domain of retributive justice this comes to the same thing as not applying the same punishment to all, but taking into account the attenuating circumstances of some. In the domain of distributive justice it means no longer thinking of a law as identical for all but taking account of the personal circumstances of each (favouring the younger ones, etc.). Far from leading to privileges, such an attitude tends to make equality more effectual than it was before."[114]

Here we encounter a principle similar to Mead's constructive, impartial hypothesis formation. For Piaget, "equity" is the term for both a situation-appropriate and a reciprocal orientation in resolving conflicts of action. Like Mead, Piaget does not introduce this principle explicitly as a principle of justification or application, but designates it similarly as a "method of morality": the principle of cooperation is a "method for the elaboration of rules,"[115] that is, a meta-rule which we follow when dealing with concrete rules in order in this way to continue cooperation.

Focusing on a method of rule formation allows Piaget to link conceptually both concrete solidarity with the particular circumstances of a situation and abstract solidarity among equals. It is only on the basis of mutual respect that we are in a position to recognize others' particular perspectives as being different, but in principle equally justified—independent of every given rule. The point of reference for equal treatment is not a specific rule, according to which equals should be treated equally, but the idea of cooperation itself, in which the similar can be determined only relative to the dissimilar. The criteria for those features which we want to treat equally in different situations according to some rule must first be discovered in the cooperative process. This same process prohibits any rule fetishism in application situations and places the application of the rule under the restriction that no other situation features are discovered which, when considered cooperatively, could invalidate the original rule and thus lead to the formation of a new—situation-appropriate—rule. By "equity" Piaget characterizes different aspects of the principle of mutual respect: a universal aspect which obligates the participants to recognize each other as equals independently of individual differences and particular situations, and a particular aspect which obligates them to consider all the individual differences and particular circumstances of a situation. *Both* aspects can develop only at the level of autonomous morality. They determine the autonomous encounter with rules and norms, and this in three dimensions: when forming a rule which must take individual differences into consideration; when justifying a rule which must find the agreement of all those involved; and when applying the rule which, complementary to its being formed, must also take account of the relation to all the particular features of the application situation.

Thus, as Piaget's stressing of equity as the highest level of the idea of justice has shown, the dependency of a moral norm's validity on a principle of universal mutual respect seems not only not to rule out the situation-appropriate application of moral norms, but to make it possible in the first place. Only a decentered conception of reality allows the child to properly perceive individual differences in reality's characteristics. In contrast to that, the egocentric perspective at the level of moral realism only offers the alternative of an entirely ruleless obedience to the powerful or a rule fetishism that postulates blind obedience without consideration for individual particularities. The rule is experienced as an entity separated from the concrete experience of reality, an entity which either does not at all affect one's own action or is obsessively enforced. Since complex relations of cooperation presuppose the ability to perceive the perspectives of others and to perceive oneself from others' perspectives, a rule fetishism is not compatible with this level.

Yet, by invoking Piaget we have been successful in confirming only one part of the original thesis. A context-sensitive application of norms is possible at the level of autonomous morality, whereas the levels of heteronomous morality reify the relation of rule to situation. However, our concern was to show that, in addition to this, a *differentiation* between the application and the justification of norms comes about at the level of autonomous morality. We have only received pointers for this assumption from Piaget. That it wasn't anything more than this might be due to the fact that Piaget limited himself to the observation of children's games. The formation, justification, and application of the rules of a game occur in the same context, among the same participants, and within the clear horizons of possible conflict situations. As a result, however, a characteristic tension that could exist between the principle of universal cooperation and concrete cooperation in an individual case does not come to the fore clearly enough. That children cooperate with one another in an individual case does not in itself mean that they take their orientation from principles of *universal* reciprocity and equality. True, Piaget's interview material supports the latter assumption, but cooperation in an individual case could also be explained by the special conditions of the game, or by the friendship among the children, who had been playing with one another over a long period of time. The ability to perceive individual differences would then correlate, though not with a moral realism, certainly with particular relationships among participants in interaction and with concrete orientations in communities. The exclusivity of equity for the level of universal autonomous morality would then be questionable. Not until we are successful in distinguishing autonomous morality from these forms of a concrete, situation-related (but not necessarily egocentric) morality can we unequivocally say that the sense of equity belongs at the level of autonomous morality and possibly also find an answer to the question as to why the application of norms must then be differentiated from their justification. Curiously enough, Piaget observed *en passant* these forms of cooperation in girls' games. Carol Gilligan pointed out that Piaget attested an inclination to greater "tolerance" and "polymorphism" on the part of girls and set this off against boys' inclination to discuss conflicts of action in game situations heatedly and intransigently.[116] Even independent of their distribution across sex roles, these observations vouch for the relevance of a nonuniversal, but equity-oriented model of cooperation—and they lay the boys' inclination to hairsplitting "legal" discussion open to the suspicion of being more an indicator of a persisting authoritarian, rule-fetishistic attitude. Possibly Kohlberg's more complex model will inform us about the structure and function of such a second level and its significance for the problem of application.

3.2 A Provisional Developmental Scenario

By drawing on Durkheim's sociological insights, Piaget may have been spared from explaining the logic of the development of moral consciousness solely by way of changes in mental factors. *Social* experiences that a child has with objects and himself within interaction are reintegrated by formal operations at a higher level. That the child takes his orientation from intersubjectively valid truth and justice, which are independent of concrete situations or relationships to specific persons, is only comprehensible as a possible result of overcoming the egocentric perspective. For this reason, the contrast between egocentrism and cooperation is for Piaget the parameter according to which he sketches the development from a heteronomous to an autonomous morality. Through his reception of Mead, Kohlberg underscored the decisive significance of social perspective-taking for the change and development of moral structures.

The idea of development, which is characteristic of all of these theories, refers to the increasing self-reflection of structures of justice and cooperation. The authors are concerned with isolating the conditions of successful cooperation from factual and contingent experiences of cooperation, with disengaging them from particular contexts, and with reconstructing them reflexively. In this process, formal conditions of cooperation can be separated in an increasingly clearer manner from the problem-bound content, *about* which a cooperation can be achieved, and one which is sought by those involved. Of course, "success" is measured by the realization of cooperation itself and not by the successful outcome of a collective solution to the problem. Symmetrical relations with reversible positions, that is, the factors of equality and reciprocity isolated by Piaget as elements of justice, rank among the formal conditions. To the extent that those involved succeed in visualizing these conditions of successful cooperation, they can evaluate the particular content with respect to whether it satisfies these conditions or not. From this perspective of an intersubjectivity becoming more and more transparent to itself, there emerges the point of reference from which the logic of the development of moral consciousness takes it orientation: from cosmic worldviews, where the validity of moral or social norms depends on the transcendent authority of the "collective consciousness," through society itself, which is constituted by contract, to principles, in which the conditions of cooperation are embodied, and finally to procedures, where content cannot permanently escape the test of whether it is worthy of intersubjective recognition.

If the type of a norm's validity is interwoven with a certain type of social cooperation, this connection must also be of significance for the application of norms in situations. On the presupposition of the hypothesis that the development of social cooperation is characterized by increasingly reflexive formalization and universalization, the following two levels can be provisionally construed as ideal types ensuing from the insights we have gained so far:

Level 1: Norms are valid in concrete relationships. The set of all concrete relationships forms a particular community or primary group. The other encounters me in situations in which behavioral expectations are related to roles and the situation and are operationalized. By always being related to concrete others, perspectives are also tied to the particular situations in which those affected encounter one another. The *concrete* other encounters me only in a *concrete* situation. Thus, the change in perspective is always simultaneously directed at the particular situation in which alter and ego find themselves. One has to first construct a common perspective from which the particular actions can be considered. What is expected of one another can indeed be normatively symbolized, but it is determined primarily by the situation in which one directly finds oneself. For this reason, the justification of a norm takes place face to face with the concrete other in the particular situation of cooperation, and thereby always refers to the particular situation as well, or to a finite set of generalized situation features which tend to reappear regularly within the context of cooperation. In cases of conflict, it is a matter not of justifying or appropriately applying a norm, but of continuing cooperation in this situation and in the finite set of future situations. Even if we abstract from the concrete other in concrete situations and recognize him only in his membership in a particular community, the validity of norms remains interwoven with particular situations. For this reason, validity and appropriateness cannot be distinguished from one another; both categories are mutually substitutable. The fact that a norm at this level is appropriate has of course nothing to do with the applicative sense of the principle of impartiality. It merits the predicate "appropriate" not because it considers *all* the particular features of the situation in a coherent manner. Rather, the perspective the participants mutually take in a situation is limited by their membership in a concrete community. Incompatible situation features either jeopardize the entire system of cooperation or are ignored. As long as the relationships between the members of a community are still determined by the situations in which these relationships come about, validity and appropriateness cannot be separated. My perception of the other is as limited as my consideration of the situation's features is selective.

Level 2: Norms are valid because they can be justified by principles or in procedures in which the ideal conditions of cooperation are embodied. At this level, the conditions of cooperation are separated from concrete communities. These conditions are valid for virtually all participants; they constitute conditions of possible cooperation as such. The validity of a norm is no longer embedded in relationships to concrete others, nor located in particular communities; rather, it is addressed to everyone equally. It is only at this level that each individual can be recognized as autonomous because the idea of cooperation itself is the common ground on which those involved carry out the change in each of their own perspectives. Perspective-taking becomes universal-reciprocal. A valid norm has to be able to be recognized collectively by everyone when viewed from the particular perspective of each individual. In this way, the validity of a norm is radically separated from the particular situation and from the concrete relationships in a community. Everyone has to be able to judge independently of the particular situation whether a norm ought to be observed by everyone in every situation. Thus, the recourse to agreement with the ideal conditions of cooperation can only refer to the justifications of a norm's validity. This concentration on questions of justification follows that logic of an increasing self-transparency of the conditions of cooperation. Justifications by principles and procedures explicate these idealized conditions of cooperation by specializing in the moment of *universality*. Universality can only be produced by the cognitive element of *reasons* which "admit of truth" and which virtually *each* individual for his part could accept, just as in the empirical research process, where the truth validity of a hypothesis may not be limited to a specific group of people. To that extent, cognitivity, universality, and formalism are three interwoven elements of the impartial justification of norms.

With this specialization, however, the other aspect with which norm validity at the first level was still connected is left unconsidered: the situational appropriateness of the norm. When validity is universalized, the norm is removed at the second level from its context of concrete situations, relationships, and communities. Justifications have to concentrate on questions of validity and be addressed to the forum of a universal communication community. The rules according to which validity is determined are the rules of a procedure open to everyone and one in which only relations of reciprocal recognition are relevant. Because validity must be addressed to everyone, only those questions which concern everyone are thematizable in these procedures. The choice of an individual life plan and the choice of concrete relationships are not moralizable as long as the ideal conditions of possible cooperation are not affected by them. It is only if certain individual or collective values claim moral validity that they also have to be universalizable and capable of embodying an interest common to everyone. Thus, the relation of Level 2 to Level 1 is not abstract,

but concretely negativist: it selects those norms, values, or interests which are anchored in concrete relationships and observed
in particular communities, *if* they claim moral validity. If they
do so, Level 2 negates all non-generalizable aspects. Appropriateness is excluded as a criterion of validity. That moral norms are
only valid decontextually cannot of course mean that their application remains contextual in the sense of Level 1. Then, either
the application of a morally valid norm would be affected by the
same situation and perspective limitations which determined the
validity of a norm at Level 1, where validity was interwoven with
appropriateness. Or the application of the norm would take the individual particularities of the situation just as little into consideration as it *had to* during impartial justification. A contextually
limited application of *universally valid* norms presents itself as a
partial restriction or as moral terror—depending on whether one
judges application from the perspective of the norm or from that
of the situation. For this reason, the principle of impartiality must
become operative during application too; though not in the sense
of a rigid implementation of morally valid norms, but in the sense of
a complete contextualism of the particular application situation.
At Level 2, practical reason is specialized not only in the aspect of
the universality of the ideal conditions of cooperation, but also in
the aspect of situational appropriateness. As our analysis of the
moral principle (U) has shown, *both* specializations can no longer be
unified in *one* principle. They require analytical separation, so that
questions of validity can be clarified free of context and questions of
application clarified in terms of the specific situation. Of course,
both in turn refer to one another since it is only their combination
(not their confusion!) that exhausts the full meaning of the idea of
impartiality.

What happens to the concrete relationships, communities, and
life prospects of Level 1 in this ideal-typical construction? They lose
their moral validity to the conditions laid down by the second level's
principles or procedures. In this respect, the concrete normative
contexts are devalued [*entwertet*]. Their validity is now only hypothetical, that is, under the proviso that everyone, giving reasons,
can agree. But they remain relevant as aspects of the situation interpretation which are to be considered during application in the
particular situation. However, they are subject to the idea of impartiality insofar as *all* the possibly relevant views, and not just a contextually limited number, are to be taken into consideration. In this

respect, the de facto validity of concrete relationships, communities, and life prospects is suspended if this validity excludes competing aspects in a situation. The formation of a situation-appropriate norm comes about in abstraction from validity.

In reality, it may often seem as if justification and application discourses could not be separated analytically from one another. As has already been frequently remarked, this objection does not hold true; it arises as a result of the *appearance* that those arguments which are relevant in application discourses can also be relevant in justification discourses. But the criteria according to which their relevance is judged in each case are different in both discourses. Whereas in justification discourses it is exclusively a matter of the generalizability of articulated interests independent of a particular situation, in application discourses it is precisely a question of situation-specific interests, which are unimportant for the validity of a norm, at least at Level 2. As Hare has shown, the situation-specific content of a norm does not play a role in the issue of logical universalizability. Since it concerns everyone, justification discourse systematically screens out all features that are situation-specific and determined by particular interests. Of course, the norm itself, if it has a content at all, remains situation-specific and always determined by particular interests. However, one commits a category mistake if the content of the norm is made the criterion of validity. It was precisely the abstracting achievement of the post-conventional level to separate questions of validity from questions of content. For this reason, justification discourse is dependent on being provided with contents; it can neither produce them itself nor apply them in individual situations. With it, one can thus only check whether the given content embodies a generalizable interest. The fact that the proposed norm *also* affects particular interests may not influence the justification. Therefore, it is indeed conceivable for a norm to be situation-appropriate but not generalizable. In the first place, this can be the case if it is a matter not of a moral norm, but exclusively of questions of the good life or of the continuation of a cooperation. Secondly, this is always the case when in justification discourses it becomes apparent that, though the proposed situation-appropriate norm claims moral validity, it does not embody a generalizable interest. A norm is situation-appropriate to the same degree as it corresponds to the particularity of the specific situation in all its features. And the more features we discover, the more complex the requirements become which we set for the situational appropriateness of the norm. In this way, we enlarge that set of all application possibilities for which the norm is appropriate at a certain historical point in time. Whether a norm which is enhanced by an application possibility and is appropriate when viewed from the perspective of a particular situation is also valid, however, can only be decided in justification discourses, so that the combination of justification and application necessitates a historical process of mutual revisions. The principle of considering all the features in every individual situation and the principle of considering, independently of an individual situation, the interests of all those affected can be fused into one principle only at the utopian point where all those affected know the constellation of features of every individual situation to which the norm is applicable. The idea of impartiality is proceduralized by the combination of justification and application in three dimensions: in the *social* dimension by justification discourses, in which all those affected can participate; in the *substantive* dimension by application discourses, which make possible the consideration of all the situation features in every individual situation; and in the *temporal* dimension by the sequence of various unforeseeable application situations.

3.3 The Development of the Relation Between Equity and Equality in Kohlberg

The foregoing scenario of an ideal-typical development from situation-appropriate to universalist norms served the purpose of initially gathering together the characteristics which should make it possible to give a more precise description of the relation between justification and application. The relatively rough grid on which this was based—namely that of a heteronomous morality resulting from asymmetrical social relationships defined by unilateral respect and of an autonomous morality founded on symmetrical social relationships defined by mutual respect—was made more precise by Kohlberg by introducing a series of intermediate stages. Here, the covariance of three features is observed: moral judgment, its reasons, as well as social perspective.

In his critical appropriation of Piaget, Kohlberg distinguishes three main levels in the development of moral judgment:

I.   Preconventional Level

II. Conventional Level

III. Postconventional or Principled Level.[117]

By way of a provisional description, we shall present the brief characterizations (from an early study) with which Kohlberg described the basis of moral judgment for each of these three levels:
Level I: "Moral value resides in external, quasiphysical happenings, in bad acts, or in quasiphysical needs rather than in persons and standards."
Level II: "Moral value resides in performing good or right roles, in maintaining the conventional order and the expectancies of others."
Level III: "Moral value resides in conformity by the self to shared or sharable standards, rights, or duties."[118]

When these levels are portrayed in terms of the relationship between self and society's rules, we obtain the following general characterizations for each level: "From this point of view, Level I is a preconventional person, for whom rules and social expectations are something external to the self; Level II is a conventional person, in whom the self is identified with or has internalized the rules and expectations of others, especially those of authorities; and Level III is a postconventional person, who had differentiated his or her self from rules and expectations of others and defines his or her values in terms of self-chosen principles."[119]

Parallel to the levels of morality, Kohlberg distinguishes three levels of social perspective:

I. Concrete individual perspective

II. Member-of-society perspective

III. Prior-to-society perspective[120]

He characterizes them briefly as follows:[121] The concrete individual perspective "is that of the individual actor in the situation thinking about his interests and those of other individuals he may care about." Not until the second, the conventional level does the formation of a genuine *social* perspective actually come about, one which is "a shared viewpoint of the participants in a relationship or a group" and enables the actors to abstract from their own selves. The third, postconventional level reintegrates the individualistic perspective with the generalized perspective by making moral obligations dependent on their recognition by *every* individual; "it is the perspective of an *individual who has made the moral commitments or holds the standards on which a good or just society must be based*" (italics in the original).

Of course, this abstract classification does not in itself amount to very much. According to our hypothesis, an integration of the conventional level of moral judgments into the corresponding social perspectives would have to display a lower degree of situational flexibility than an integration of the postconventional level. Admittedly, the first impression militates against this, if one takes Kohlberg's early characterizations of moral levels as the basis. While Level II is characterized by orientations toward the concrete expectations of others or toward context-related role systems, conformity with abstract norms prevails at Level III. Kohlberg meanwhile specified his model of levels further. The following representation of the relations between moral judgment and sociomoral perspective is based on a total of six different stages, which are aligned in pairs with the three main levels. In what follows I shall however restrict myself to stages 3–6 (i.e., corresponding to Levels II and III) since the first two stages are not relevant to our topic.[122]

Level II (conventional)—Stage 3: Mutual interpersonal expectations, relationships, and interpersonal conformity. What is morally right is what people close to us expect or what one has to do in a specific role. One has to be "good" in this sense, and the corresponding intentions, motives, and attitudes have to be formed (trust, loyalty, respect, gratitude). Correspondingly, the reasons for doing right consist in being able to be a "good person" in one's own eyes and in those of others; observing a concrete interpretation of the Golden Rule, showing concern for others, having a desire to maintain rules and authority which support stereotypically good behavior. The sociomoral perspective relates to individuals in relationships with other individuals who can be aware of common expectations which have to take primacy over individual interests. However, there is not yet a differentiated third-person perspective.

Level II—Stage 4: Social system and conscience. What is morally right is that duties be fulfilled, except in extreme cases where they conflict with other duties. The reason for doing right is to maintain societal institutions ("if everyone did it"), or one's conscience vis-à-vis obligations acceded to. The sociomoral perspective differentiates between the standpoint of the community and interpersonal agreements. The latter must conform with the social system.

Level III (postconventional)—Stage 5: Social contract or utility and individual rights. What is morally right is to observe rules and norms which either can be justified by a social contract or comply with social utility. Independent of this, there are some absolute rights, such as life and liberty, which may not be violated by anyone. Correspondingly, the reasons for doing right are founded on the social contract which was freely entered into, or on insight into the social utility of abiding by the rules. The sociomoral perspective relates to the individual who enjoys certain rights, is an end in himself, and comes to agreement on specific norms with others by means of procedures.

Level III—Stage 6: Universal moral principles. What is morally the right thing to do is to follow self-chosen principles which claim to be universalist; equal human rights, and respect for human dignity. The reasons for doing right are belief in the validity of universalist principles and everyone's personal commitment to follow them. The sociomoral perspective is the "moral point of view," on which the validity of all normative orientations depends.

Even with this differentiated stage model, it can only be abstractly supposed that there is a connection between moral judgment, social perspective, and the consideration of all the relevant features of a situation. Kohlberg's sociomoral perspectives do not contribute much toward resolving the problem of application because he too fails to distinguish between questions of justification and those of application in the category of moral judgment. In Kohlberg's model, the sociomoral perspectives are relevant only to norm validity.

But, like Piaget, Kohlberg did undertake research on the development of specific concepts of justice.[123] A glance at the stage model permits one at first to suppose that higher stages imply more abstract justice orientations which operate with rigid concepts of equality and without considering individual differences. But Piaget had already observed how, in the autonomous morality of older children, the tendency to give priority to a "higher" justice over rigid normatizations becomes visible. Piaget's concept of "equity" signifies the ability to perceive individual differences and to strive for situation-specific resolutions to conflicts. Only in this way did it become at all possible to cast off the remaining traces of authoritarianism and to recognize the other in his individuality and particularity. Without explicitly referring to Piaget, Kohlberg based his research on the development of concepts of justice on the Aristotelian canon of distributive, corrective, and commutative justice, as well as on the principles of equity and equality. In the following table I shall parallel the results of the observations on "equality" and "equity" with moral stages and sociomoral perspectives.[124]

Kohlberg himself draws attention to the fact that the decisive step in the development of conceptions of equality and equity occurs at the transition from Stage 4 to Stage 5. At Stage 4, equality still refers to concrete norms, before which all those affected are regarded as equal without distinction of person, whereas concrete norms at the following stage are themselves in need of legitimation in the light of absolute rights, which protect each individual in his particularity. The concept of equality is detached from given normative reference points[125] and refers to individuals who are to be treated as equals, that is, who possess the same human rights and have same right to share in the welfare of society.

In the transition from Stage 4 to Stage 5, the specific function of these absolute rights also becomes clear. They protect the individual against those norms and procedures which infringe upon his absolute rights. Dworkin characterized absolute rights in this sense as "trumps" which can outweigh simple laws or political considerations of expediency.[126] In this way, they assume a function which was reserved for the "exceptional case" at Stage 4 and for the equity constitutive of this case. Equity at Stage 3 and 4 is also determined by the fact that there are norms that prescribe an observance which is equal and admits of no exception. At the conventional level there is only the rule-exception scheme. If one includes the sociomoral perspective and the concept of morality, a possible explanation for this presents itself: the conventional level is characterized by the priority of common normative action orientations over individual particularities, be it as at Stage 3 in the form of concrete relationships and role systems or as at Stage 4 in the form of a specific social system and its institutions. In both cases, norm and role expectation, on the one hand, and the specifically relevant cross section of the situation, on the other, determine one another mutually: as soon as the relevant situation features are given, a certain role expectation has to be fulfilled or a given norm applied; by the same token, a situation's zone of relevance is determined by the normative orientation. In neither case does the concept of morality permit a third position from which the application or observance of a given normative orientation could for its part be judged once again. Rather, such a position would itself be identical with the system of norms to be applied or with the concrete pattern of roles demanding fulfillment. The legitimate validity of a norm is dependent on that same context of a concrete community or a particular social system within which the norm is also applied. For this reason, diverging interpretations of the situation, competing structures of relevance, or different selections of features cannot refer in a concrete situation to a "higher" authority by means of which the original norm to be applied or the role-specific behavior pattern could in turn be relativized.

Stage	Concept of Morality	Equality	Equity	Sociomoral Perspective
3	Interpersonally Normative Morality	Among people who fulfill their roles well and have good intentions	Exceptions for deviations based on the recognition of extenuating circumstances and good intentions	Individuals in mutual relationships; concrete Golden Rule; concrete common expectations
4	Social system	Equality before the law (equality in the application of law)	Exceptions to the general application of norms in cases in which the norm is not open enough to be able to regulate each individual case appropriately	Societal point of view is differentiated from interpersonal agreement; social system defines roles
5	Human Rights and Social Welfare	Equal absolute rights and the absolute value of all individuals as equals	Reasserts the right to equal treatment when norms, laws, or procedures impede the exercise of absolute rights or disregard the value of human life	Prior to society. Values and principles have priority over agreements and contracts, problem with the integration of conflicting values
6	Universalization and Reversibility; prescriptive general moral principles	"Equality" and "equity" can as such be thematized, equity is detached from given criteria and related to all possible distinctions which must first be justified as being relevant to a common rule		Moral point of view from which societal agreements are derived; persons are ends in themselves

Corresponding to the sociomoral perspective, expectations appear at Stage 3 as particular states in the person. In complex, highly conflictive situations, or in unclear situations, a tragic conflict of roles can arise; this is the case when, for example, there are mutually exclusive loyalty obligations to various people which cannot be resolved without having recourse to a role-overlapping system of norms. Exceptions can then be justified via deliberations on reasonable expectation [*Zumutbarkeitserwägungen*]. Whoever violates a specific role expectation in the case of a conflict of duties is pardoned if he did it because of fulfilling another important role obligation, that is, he had a good intention. At the same level there are the "extenuating circumstances" cited by Kohlberg, which allow the reproach of violating one's duty to appear less serious if particular features of the person or his behavior are present, ones which impede a "good" fulfilling of the role expectation.[127] These types of exceptions are tailored to those situation features which are relevant to the system of relationships constituted by roles: persons and their characteristics, which they have to bring along with them as participants in interpersonal relationships. They represent, as it were, the remains of what dominated moral orientations at the preceding preconventional Stage 2 (not mentioned here). While the needs of the individual and the instrumental manner of their satisfaction determine the moral world of interacting persons there,[128] they are transformed at Stage 3 into those particular circumstances of a person which one can take into consideration, by way of exception. However, these exceptions may not become the rule, if the system of generalized behavioral expectations is not to collapse. It can only be maintained by disregarding situation-conditioned and arbitrary inclinations or needs.

Stage 4 presents the traditional understanding of equity as representing the exception to an applicable norm. Aristotle defines it as a "correction of legal justice": "When the law speaks universally, then, and a case arises on it which is not covered by the universal statement, then it is right, when the legislator fails us and has erred by over-simplicity, to correct the omission—to say what the legislator himself would have said had he been present . . . "[129] Of course Aristotle did already anticipate the following stage by characterizing equity not as a necessary evil but as a realization of that higher justice for which legal justice is unavoidably an inadequate expression[130] in view of the "fullness of life." The Stage 4 ideal type corresponds to this only in the manner in which it justifies the admissibility of exceptions from the social system as a whole. As an example Kohlberg cites the statement of a test person: an exception is justified "in order to demonstrate that the law can be fair or humane."[131] But it is the same system of laws which requires that all like cases be treated alike, that is, according to the criterion of equality which follows from the norm itself. Only because one cannot, in this way, make provisions for each individual case in which situation features incompatible with the norm appear, there is a need for the admissibility of exceptions. Here too, the particular case proves itself to be a potential regression to the preceding stage. Exceptions which ignore the general application of the norm can violate the principle of equality before the law by privileging individuals on account of their particular situation. In this way, the sociomoral perspective model typical of the preceding Stage 3 threatens to be activated, the model that ties the decision about rules and exceptions not to a generalized system of norms, but to the reciprocal relationship to others. The Stage 4 concept of equity considers this type as an exception. If, in an application situation, the norm to be applied may be disregarded in order to demonstrate that the system of laws is *fair* and *humane,* then it is exactly those concrete expectations of reciprocity defining the preceding stage's sociomoral perspective which are fulfilled.

At the following two postconventional stages, the rule-exception relation is reversed. With the moral concept of every individual's equal rights to life and liberty as well as to a share in the welfare of society, the de facto validity of norms in a particular society and, tied to this, the principle of equality in the application of law [*Rechtsanwendungsgleichheit*] can be transcended. Norms, laws, actions, and procedures must themselves be legitimated before the forum of these fundamental rights, and not just within the particular context of a specific community. This, however, applies not only to the justification of norms and procedures, but also to their application. If the application of a justified norm in a particular situation threatens to violate rights of this kind, then it must be revised for this case or invalidated. It is no longer only the identical application of a norm to all the addressees that guarantees equality (in the application of law), rather the norm itself and its application have to protect and promote the equal rights of everyone. This change in the meaning of the principle of equality is characteristic of many modern constitutions, which have included the right to equal treatment among their fundamental and human rights.[132] Thus, equity and equality prove to be different functions of the one principle of equal fundamental and human rights, which subject both the justification and the application of norms to certain provisos. The specific meaning of equity can in turn be explicated against the background of the sociomoral perspective characteristic of Stage 5. This perspective overcomes the rigid viewpoint of a generalized other. It seems almost as if it again adopted the person-centered perspective of Stage 3 in order to set the latter against the norm perspective of Stage 4. This impression is not however correct. It is only at the postconventional level that everyone can be recognized as an autonomous individual independently of his contingent concrete ties to other persons. This prior-to-society perspective universalizes the person-centered moral worldview of the first stage of the conventional level in favor of each single individual. "The individual point of view taken at the postconventional level, however, can be universal; it is that of *any rational moral individual.*"[133] As moral or rationally calculating individuals, we are all equipped with equal rights and, as bearers of such rights, we decide collectively and voluntarily to establish a societal system and corresponding institutions and norms. On this presupposition, the exception—whereby one could refrain from applying and implementing a socially valid norm on account of considerations of humaneness and fairness—becomes the rule in which the pre-state ("innate") and inalienable (cannot be manipulated in their substance by subsequent legislation) fundamental and human rights of every individual affected are to be taken into consideration by everyone.

At Stage 6, the preceding stage's sociomoral perspective does not change fundamentally; rather, it merely shifts its meaning from specific products, such as contracts or rights, to procedures (and their presuppositions) in which all those affected have to participate in order to reach an agreement.[134] This gives rise to a curious consequence for the relation between equality and equity: they become indistinguishable. "At Stage 5 law and moral norms are grounded on the operations of equality, equity, and so on. At Stage 6 these operations become self-conscious principles."[135] Those involved decide themselves which phenomena they want to treat equally and which unequally. In this way, equality and equity become entirely free of criteria, so that they can be related to any difference considered relevant by a participant in procedures. Thus, there is no primordial Archimedean reference point such as, for example, equal rights or equal rewards; instead, the equality operation becomes infinitely variable. Because ascertaining a relation of equality means factually, though not analytically, the positing of a difference, justifying a particular relation of equality necessarily requires justifying the difference posited thereby.[136] As an example Kohlberg cites the problem of distributive justice, whose solution at Stage 6 can only lie for him in the application of a principle of differentiation that is obviously borrowed from Rawls. According to this, the distribution of goods must not take its orientation from given, equal legal claims or from criteria of achievement; instead, it takes its orientation from the position of those presumed to be the least advantaged.[137]

The close consideration of Kohlberg's moral stages in terms of the aspects of equality and equity provided us with precise indicators for developments in the relation between social perspective, concept of morality, and the consideration of particular situations— as "exceptions." Conventional moral consciousness can cope with particular circumstances in a situation only as an exceptional situation because the sociomoral perspective restricts the selection of relevant features to what is relevant to the relationship to a concrete other or relevant to the fixed perspective of a generalized other. It is not until the transition to the postconventional level that the manner in which relevant features are considered is detached from the schematism of a norm to be applied. This is most evident at Stage 5, where absolute rights can block the application of a legitimate norm. This does not necessarily mean that the norm becomes invalid or illegitimate, but only that the individual's rights are affected in a particular case, rights which could be violated by applying the norm and by its resulting consequences. At this stage too, however, the selection of relevant features remains within a hierarchy of open and indeterminate principles or fundamental rights ("liberty," "life"), which are nevertheless firmly given as relevant aspects. In this way, a wealth of unforeseen, particular situation features can indeed be considered, but there is still no procedure for changing existing rights or principles, or creating new ones in concrete situations. The fixation Kohlberg ascribes to Stage 5 is the social contract hypothetically concluded at one time by all moral subjects. It determines the latitude for possible changes. Another problem characteristic of this stage in application situations is that of conflicting rights or principles in individual cases, that is to say, not *per se* but *per accidens*. Though conflicts of principles do not destroy the validity of one principle, the search for weighing criteria and appropriate coherence is a difficult problem to solve for this stage of moral consciousness.[138] A solution would presuppose the ability to go beyond rights and principles once more and, while considering all the relevant circumstances, to form an appropriate, possibly new or changed norm hypothesis. It is only Stage 6 which can make this move toward the extracontractual conditions of the contract in that it comprehends general principles now only as the embodiment of those normative conditions of procedure which all must accept if they want to come to a mutual agreement. All situation features can now become relevant, without having to consider whether they fit into a given set of rights and principles. For this reason, every norm to be applied has to be placed in relation to all the relevant situation features and be transformed into an appropriate norm that could be accepted by virtually all those affected.

Unfortunately, Kohlberg does not use the results of his study on the development of concepts of justice to differentiate at Stage 6 between the justification and the application of norms under conditions of procedural impartiality. This could be due to the fact that he takes the concepts of justice used as parameters from Aristotle's *Nicomachean Ethics*,[139] according to which equity, which thematizes the relation to the situation, is merely one concept of justice among others and, moreover, only becomes operative in a special corrective function when applying general norms.

However, because Kohlberg defines Stage 6 general principles in such a way that, on the one hand, they posit not only defensive rights against illegitimate interference but also positive duties, and, on the other, they are not solely applicable in specific areas, as are rights or simple rules, but "apply to all persons and situations,"[140] he cannot avoid at least an implicit distinction between justification and application. It is even more difficult to determine how positive duties are to be applied in each individual situation than it is for negative rights. Moreover, since these principles have to be so open and indeterminate that they can be placed in relation to every virtually relevant difference in a specific situation, it is no longer possible to construe an analytical connection between a norm that is valid for all persons and a norm that is appropriate in a particular situation. Kohlberg's dissolution of the contrast between equity and equality does force us to consider all the relevant features in every individual situation, but this principle can be combined, in *one* principle, with the principle of whether a norm is worthy of universal recognition only at a price: it assumes a form similar to the strong version of the moral principle (U), as presented in the systematic part of our discussion above.

4

Is There a Contextualist Alternative to "Stage 6"?— The discovery that "it depends"

The fact that introducing the difference between impartial justification and application of norms into the Stage 6 concept of morality is not merely of marginal significance can be illustrated on the basis of a problem that I already mentioned in my first rough sketch of two different types of application. Level 1 was to be defined by, among other things, the characteristic that the validity and the appropriateness of a norm refer to the same particular context. Following Kohlberg we can now describe this particular context more precisely with the help of the sociomoral perspectives of the two stages of conventional moral consciousness. It is then a matter of the system of concrete ties with corresponding mutual role expectations, on the one hand, or a concrete community in the sense of the generalized other, on the other. At both stages, the deliberations on justification and the evaluation of the individual case can be combined in one process. The concrete reciprocity prevailing at Stage 3 obtains the relevant situation features directly from the perspective of the concrete other and from the role expectations that structure this perspective ("What would you do in his/her place?"); at Stage 4 reciprocity is socially generalized and, in reflection on validity, includes as relevant those situation features which are essential within the horizons of the community ("What would happen if everyone did that?"). The contextual interwovenness of validity and appropriateness in concrete relationships and communities evokes the impression that the conventional stages are, at least in this respect, closer to the multiple particularities of individual situations than the universalist principles of the postconventional level. Kohlberg adopts this in his characterization of Stage 6 and places an "attitude of universal human care or *agape*" alongside universalist principles.[141] Furthermore, the conditions of procedure are dependent on a general "notion of trust and community."[142]

Supplementing Stage 6 with these aspects follows from the debate with objections advanced against an alleged rigorism and formalism, which are said to find expression in Kohlberg's preference for universalist orientations. Carol Gilligan tied these objections to the critique of a gender-specific bias because the Stage 3 concept of morality—concrete reciprocity, mutual trust, and care—has been displayed primarily by women.[143] Instead of supplementing Stage 6 with a principle of care as Kohlberg did in reaction to these objections, it can be shown in connection with our systematic reflections that universalist principles themselves already presuppose a specific form of solidarity and that concrete contextual conditions are taken into consideration when impartially applying these principles. Before going into this more closely (b and c), I would first (a) like to sketch, with reference to our topic, the objections leveled at Kohlberg.

(a) Kohlberg's contextualist critics refer to an altered interpretation of the so-called "relativist regression," which could be observed in longitudinal studies on adolescents in the transition to adulthood or in early adulthood. After having attained a principled moral attitude in the sense of the fifth stage of Kohlberg's model, some test persons began once again to take their orientation from relativist or contextualist standards after a certain period of time; they argued above all about the particular circumstances of the situation and the needs of those immediately affected, or they generally showed a considerable uncertainty in the moral appraisal of concrete conflicts of action. Because these phenomena are more characteristic of Stages 4 and 3, in part even of Stage 2, it was difficult to bring them into harmony with a model of development conceived as an irreversible sequence of stages; for this reason, they were described as isolated regressions. On the basis of new material and improved research criteria, Norma Haan, Carol Gilligan, and John M. Murphy opposed this interpretation with the attempt to identify a higher postconventional moral stage in later relativist and contextualist attitudes, a moral stage which leaves behind the abstract principled universalism of Stage 5 or of the hypothetically constructed Stage 6 in favor of a more sensitive perception of the individual case. According to them, a *different morality* reveals itself here, one which can be reconstructed on the basis of experiences with conflicts in concrete relationships and interactive situations ("real life problems"). Gilligan and Murphy characterized the contrast between the two conceptions of morality as follows: "The first, which we call PCF (postconventional formal), solves the problem of relativism by constructing a formal logical system that derives solutions to all moral problems from concepts like the social contract or natural rights. The second, which we call PCC (postconventional contextual), finds the problem in that solution which now appears as only one of several potential contexts in which moral judgments can be framed. PCC reasoning derives from an understanding of the contextual relativism of moral judgment and the ineluctable uncertainty of moral choice. On that basis, it articulates an ethic of responsibility that focuses on the actual consequences of choice. In the shift from PCF to PCC, the criterion for the adequacy of moral principles changes from objective truth to 'best fit', and can only be established within the context of the dilemma itself. According to PCC reasoning, the choice of principles for solving moral problems is an example of commitment in relativism, a commitment for which one bears personal responsibility and which allows the possibility of alternate formulations that could be equally or more adequate in a given case."[144]

The authors expressly distinguish this contextual relativism from the usual version of relativism, according to which there are a number of correct solutions to every moral problem, without it being possible to make a justified decision for one of them ("multiplicity"). In contrast to this, contextual relativism allows a differentiation between good and bad solutions, though not according to an objective standard, but according to the situation-dependent criterion of "best fit" or "adequacy." Nor can this version of relativism eliminate a final trace of genuine uncertainty in decisions, which is why the choice of the appropriate solution is ultimately the responsibility of each individual. Uncertainty in solving moral conflicts is the first experience which leads to the relativization of normativist "adolescent certainty."[145] It can be interpreted as an indication of a progressive development of moral consciousness if it is accompanied by a more complete consideration of different situation features than at the preceding stage. The precise perception of different aspects and a more comprehensive empathy with the particular needs of those concretely affected are expressed in the characteristically disconcerted response "it depends . . . ": "The discovery that 'it depends' renders his judgment more relativistic, but also more inclusive and more adaptive."[146] Responses of this kind are to be understood as constructive hypotheses which

ı according to different, even competing or conflict-
ıewpoints in order to find a norm hypothesis or
appropriate to the situation. Not only those fea-
ıuch are relevant to the application of universalist principles
are part of such a process, but also the concrete needs and expectations of others immediately affected and to whom the actor has a
relationship. Faced with the Heinz dilemma used by Kohlberg as interview material—a dilemma in which it is a question of whether
Heinz may steal a drug, which is sold by a druggist at a horrendous
price, in order to save his critically ill wife—the test persons classified as being at the PCC stage not only judge according to the priority of life over property, but also take the type of relationship
between Heinz and his wife into consideration.

Norma Haan ascribes contextualist attitudes, which in dilemmas are primarily concerned with the consideration of the concrete
needs and expectations of those involved, to an "interpersonal morality," which she distinguishes from a "formal morality."[147] The latter is characterized by "the formal system's aloofness from the
details of persons and situations and its focus on the moral agent's
capability of deductively drawing conclusions from principles given
prior to his experience," whereas the former is characterized by "the
interpersonal system's contextual orientation and its focus on persons' interactions and their mutually drawn conclusions."[148] Based
on a reinterpretation of Kohlberg's material in the light of her own
empirical investigations, Haan observes, like Gilligan and Murphy,
that test persons display a willingness, increasing with age, to
discuss moral conflicts in separation from principles and in terms
of aspects which are relevant in the particular situation to the concrete relationships between those affected. Empathy and trust
belong here more so than formal-operational capabilities. The
contradiction-free application of temporally, substantively, and socially generalized principles seems to neglect all the details not belonging to the applicative extension of these principles. It thus
expects of the moral subject less "commitment" than an interpersonal morality does, one that makes great demands in terms of following an interpersonal logic and a logic of the particular. To cope
with interpersonal conflicts, test persons thus value results, that is,
decisions actually made and actions actually taken, more than in-
tellectualized controversies, behind which they often suspect nothing more than strategies to fend off situational commitment or to
avoid action. Norma Haan identifies four characteristics of interpersonal reasoning:[149]

1. It requires dialogical reciprocity between participants, who strive for agreements on the basis of a mutual willingness to reach compromises or on the basis of common interests;

2. It is sensitivity to the context, which shows itself in the intention of those involved "to 'fit' a situation and thus reveal its possibilities for resolving action";

3. It is an inductive process, where new or unexpected solutions are more likely than in formal reasoning;

4. It demands commitment on the part of ego, who must coordinate different aspects of the situation and of the other's expectations, whereas reasoning with general principles encourages a detached and private conflict resolution.

Carol Gilligan radicalizes these aspects of an interpersonal morality to an ethics of care, interprets them in terms of specific sex roles, and contrasts them with the abstract justice thinking of men: "When one begins with the study of women and derives developmental constructs from their lives, the outline of a moral conception different from that described by Freud, Piaget, or Kohlberg begins to emerge and informs a different description of development. In this conception, the moral problem arises from conflicting responsibilities rather than from competing rights and requires for its resolution a mode of thinking that is contextual and narrative rather than formal and abstract. This conception of morality as concerned with the activity of care centers moral development around the understanding of responsibility and relationships, just as the conception of morality as fairness ties moral development to the understanding of rights and rules."[150]

More so than Norma Haan, Gilligan emphasizes the function of an interpersonal morality to form and stabilize identity. The experience of vital dependence on other persons and the importance of concrete ties for one's own existence allow interactions to appear not so much according to the viewpoint of rights and obligations but as a phase or as a part of a whole "network of relationships."[151] For this reason, moral conflicts are also always, and primarily, concerned with the continuance, change, or dissolution of relationship networks, as well as with the foreseeable consequences that a decision would have for the self of whoever is immediately affected. Thus, interpersonal morality does not by any means favor those solutions which spring from vague fantasies about the merging of self and other, or from a need for harmony which shuns conflict. Nor is the differentiation between self and other described as the result of a process of individualization in whose conflictive course moral subjects who are becoming autonomous demarcate themselves from one another. Rather, recognizing a difference between self and other ranks among the necessary conditions of the possibility of relationships, just as, conversely, these relationships first make the formation of a differentiated self possible. Thus, the specific experiences on which interpersonal morality is based deal again and again with the relation of nearness and distance in conflicts in life and relationships, just as Carol Gilligan investigated them exemplarily in women's abortion decisions.[152] She proposes distinguishing three levels, the first of which is characterized by a dominant caring for the self, a caring which regards everything morally good that promotes or does not interfere with one's own life plans. The second one begins with insight into the egocentrism of exclusively caring for the self and the harmful consequences for others connected with this, as well as insight into the dangers of an instrumentalization of the other for the purposes of continuing relationships. The reaction to this insight can first consist in a morality of self-sacrifice, whereby the woman refrains from satisfying her own needs in order to expend herself entirely in caring for others. It is only at the third level that the judgment of what is morally good is keyed to the balance between egoism and responsibility for others. This process draws its structuring dynamic from the increasingly comprehensive consideration of the context composed by the self, others, and their concrete relationship. Their factual interdependence is interpreted normatively: "This ethic, which reflects a cumulative knowledge of human relationships, evolves around a central insight, that self and other are interdependent."[153]

The fact that those involved take their orientation from contextual phenomena results in a characteristic change of theme, which is the point at issue in moral controversies. The resolution of a conflict within the framework of an interpersonal morality concentrates less on the *conditionally* relevant aspects of a proposed mode of action. The "whether" or "why" remains in the background; a universal right, which is valid independent of the concrete situation and which could justify a specific mode of action, appears less important for finding a common solution. Instead, primarily *modal* and *final* factors are considered. The "how" of a mode of action and the choice of a mode of action that, among various possibilities, is appropriate to the situation appears to be more important from the viewpoint of the common aim to continue, change, or dissolve a relationship without avoidable harm to one's own self or to others.[154]

(b) At least three phenomena can be isolated in the objections raised by Kohlberg's critics: the relation between moral universalism and concrete solidarity or reciprocity, the relation between questions of the good life and questions of justice, and, finally, the problem of the application of norms in concrete contexts. It is of course difficult to distinguish these phenomena from one another in the debate with Gilligan, Haan, and Murphy because their arguments connect a morality of interpersonal relationships and care to problems of appropriately resolving conflicts in life and to the moral capability of a context-sensitive appraisal of concrete situations. At first glance it seems clear that a morality of care is formed from experiences in concrete interactions and conflicts, experiences which existentially touch upon the life plans of those interconnectedly affected and require a high measure of empathy and sensitivity in order to be able to cope with them. For this reason, it can indeed be surmised that there is an internal connection between these three phenomena. Nonetheless, one can question whether this connection is so strong and exclusive that it justifies a *different* morality in comparison to the universalist one. Beyond an initially plausible and simple contrastive relation between formal and interpersonal morality, between cognitivist ethics and an ethics of care, it could be the case that some of the above-mentioned phenomena, each in a different way (analytically or complementarily), constitute a part of moral universalism when correctly understood. Since it is obvious that there is a connection between the topic of contextual sensitivity, discussed primarily in the studies on so-called relativist regression, and the problem of application under discussion here, I shall deal with this separately in (c) and shall first consider the other two issues. In the end, it will however become apparent that aspects of solidarity and questions of the good life are also a part of the problem of application.

The first problem concerns the contrast between moral universalism and an ethics of concrete relationships. It is connected with the second one—whether and how one can distinguish between questions of justice and questions of the good life—to the extent that only questions of justice can be resolved universalistically. For this reason, Kohlberg supplemented the principle of justice constitutive of the postconventional level with a "principle of benevolence," which essentially represents utilitarian principles of justice.

On the other hand, he does not consider it necessary to distinguish between a morality of justice and a morality of care.[155]

Kohlberg examines moral conflicts about concrete-reciprocal obligations in concrete relationships as a special case in a principled ethics of justice. "Thus, special relationship dilemmas may elicit care responses which supplement and deepen the sense of generalized obligations of justice."[156] Though questions of justice can only be resolved by principles, they cannot be completely separated from mutual respect and care. Conversely, conflicts in relationships, insofar as they concern questions of justice, cannot be resolved by care and empathy alone. To the extent that both sets overlap, care and justice belong together, that is to say, the particular obligations of a family member, for example, can accompany the duties which are justified according to principles of justice. Kohlberg thus assumes that there is a continuum between personal moral dilemmas, which require a high measure of empathy and care, and more or less pure problems of justice. This means, however, that we also have to solve our personal moral problems always within a framework drafted by universalist principles, that is to say, we cannot simply switch from one morality to another.[157] At Stage 6, principles of justice lose their rule-bound properties in favor of an orientation toward persons as ends in themselves, an orientation that can require a change in the principle in any situation. It is for this reason that the resolution of pure conflicts of justice is also dependent on a type of care that becomes manifest in mutual concern and respect for the other person as an end in himself. Sensitivity to the needs of the individual ranks among the presuppositions that a universalist morality must necessarily recognize if it binds the validity of norms to the agreement of each individual. But if this principle is the Stage 6 principle of justice, then justice and care are not mutually exclusive.[158]

According to Habermas, Kohlberg's attempt at linking justice and care, and the difference in degree of their relative importance— depending on whether the domain to be regulated concerns personal decisions or general questions of justice—is a somewhat inexact explication of the core idea of moral universalism.[159] Rather, even if it is understood in terms of discourse ethics, this idea already implies a principle of solidarity and mutual respect. This however gives rise to a strict separation of questions of justice and those of the good life. The latter can then no longer be answered with the help of principles because they are not at all concerned with questions of morality.

As we already made clear when interpreting the moral principle (U), the universal validity of a norm or a mode of action is dependent on the agreement *of every individual*. This subcriterion can only be meaningfully introduced into a moral principle if the participants in a moral discourse do not come forward as isolated individuals, but can recognize one another as members of a common lifeworld who are attached to each other in a relationship of solidarity. Otherwise, the application of a moral principle that designates as valid only those norms which embody a common interest would be meaningless. It could be replaced by more convenient techniques of mutual influencing which enable the individual to exploit his advantages strategically.

Relations of mutual recognition do however presuppose that the process we reconstructed in our interpretation of Mead and Durkheim has already been completed. According to Mead, the emergence of a self and of a personal identity is tied to taking the perspective of, first, the concrete other, then, the generalized other. Habermas interpreted this process as language-mediated socialization. Only if ego has a grammatical system of semantically identical linguistic symbols available is he in a position to distinguish between the communicative roles of speaker, hearer, and one who is present and, with the system of personal pronouns, to refer to various social objects linguistically. In the course of this process of a language-mediated socialization, religious authorities and illegitimate relations of domination are gradually placed under the legitimation pressure of validity claims which require justification, so that only those common agreements which have gone through the intersubjective process of achieving understanding may claim validity.

Discourse ethics takes up this process in a twofold manner: because the self can only exist in intersubjective relationships, it must be possible for these relationships as a whole to be simultaneously preserved and changed at certain points, to the extent that they threaten or repress the individual, or cause him to suffer unjustly, that is, insofar as they obstruct the formation of a self. Thus, the individual is to be protected in his individuality and liberty against illegitimate interference, as well as preserved and promoted in his dependence on intersubjectivity: "Since moralities are tailored to suit the fragility of human beings individuated through socialization, they must always solve *two* tasks at *once*. They must emphasize the inviolability of the individual by postulating equal respect for the dignity of each individual. But they must also protect the web of intersubjective relations of mutual recognition by which these individuals survive as members of a community. To these two complementary aspects correspond the principles of justice and solidarity respectively. The first postulates equal respect and equal rights for the individual, whereas the second postulates empathy and concern for the well-being of one's neighbor. Justice in the modern sense of the term refers to the subjective freedom of inalienable individuality. Solidarity refers to the well-being of associated members of a community who intersubjectively share the same lifeworld."[160]

Discourse ethics does justice to both principles by virtue of the fact that in the concept of discourse there is the right of each individual to safeguard his unmistakably particular interests, as well as the duty to recognize the interests of every other individual by putting himself in the place of the other in order to come to an impartial judgment about the common interest.

Discursive solidarity cannot however be tied to particular contexts or concrete reciprocities. In discourses, only the form of life as a whole can be continued; one cannot discover what is good for a concrete relationship or for the needs and life plans of an individual. This leads to a sharp distinction between questions of justice and those of the good life. The principle of solidarity constitutes a part of morality only insofar as it is related to the general conditions of a good life. It has to make self-realization and concretely reciprocal relationships as such possible by guaranteeing intersubjective relations of recognition, but it cannot lay down in a generally binding way what a happy life is, or what a successful form of life is. "The structural aspects of the 'good life', which from the perspective of communicative socialization in general are universally distinguishable from the concrete totalities of particular forms of life (and life histories), are included in its conception."[161] Unlike Gilligan, who puts forward a separate interpersonal morality, and unlike Kohlberg, who proposes a continuum between personal and universal moral problems, Habermas assimilates only those aspects from the world of concrete ethical relations which are also *constitutive* of a universalist morality of justice itself. Thus, Gilligan's and Haan's "real life problems," which they distinguish from Kohlberg's hypothetical dilemmas, are divided into two aspects. To the extent that conflicts in relationships and decisions about life plans also concern those questions which have to be answered by everyone identically—that is, are genuinely moral questions—they can also be judged according to Stage 6 moral principles. To the extent that it is a matter of the happiness of those involved, there can only be more or less appropriate, wise, and considerate decisions for which no generalizable principles can be found.

(c) In his discussion of Gilligan, Habermas has pointed out again and again that some of the shortcomings of a universalist morality criticized by her can be described as a problem in the application of principles.[162] However, he assigns the resolving of the problem to "prudent application" or judgment.[163] Since we are especially concerned here with the rationally reconstructable aspects of impartial application, we have to take up these pointers in the debate with Gilligan, Haan, and Murphy, and specify them.

In his reply to his critics, Kohlberg already hinted at the fact that universalist principles require a context-sensitive application if one does not want to confuse them with the rigid rules of Stage 4: "This growing relativism about factual interpretations is not in itself a questioning of the universality or validity of moral principles, like the principles of justice or human welfare, but it is a growing awareness of the difficulties encountered in getting clarity or consensus on their application to concrete situations."[164] If universalist principles themselves are nothing but embodiments of an ideal role-taking in Mead's sense, then a rigoristic application is not compatible with this criterion of validity. Rather, a reciprocal attitude-taking is needed in every concrete situation in order to find out what needs, interests, and expectations are at all relevant before evaluating them in the light of a principle. Principles correspond more to "*prima facie* rules" than to unshakable final decisions, which is why observing them requires constant "refinement and differentiation."[165] To the extent that Gilligan's construction of a morality of care is concerned with the contextual sensitivity of those involved in resolving a conflict, it does not stand in contradiction to the idea of moral universalism. As our interpretations of the development of the relation between equity and equality as components of the concept of justice have shown, Stage 6 differs from the preceding stages by virtue of the very fact that the norm perspective is surrendered in favor of a thematization of the differences in individual cases, differences on the basis of which those affected first of all agree on a common regulation or resolution of the conflict. A morality that employs the justified agreement of all those affected as the criterion of validity has to replace the simple application of given principles, which merely checks whether equal conditions of application are present, with a direct application of the "moral point of view" to each individual case. However, the moral point of view may not stop—as Wellmer claims—at the borders of a common lifewordly practice, but must be able to transplant the particularism of common lifeworlds that are different in each case into the universe of discourse. "Unlike a Stage 5 reliance upon notions of prior social agreements to resolve dilemmas, the principle of equal respect and the moral point of view of Stage 6 construct anew each case or dilemma in an effort to reach ideal consensus."[166]

However, our systematic interpretation of the moral point of view, explicated in the strong version of the moral principle (U), has shown that a direct application to individual cases is only possible if one distinguishes between a principle of impartial justification and a principle of impartial application. Although Kohlberg considers a context-sensitive application of universalist moral principles not only possible but even necessary in accordance with the meaning of moral universalism, he does not make this distinction. The reason for this is that he borrows the ideal of moral constructivism from Rawls which allows one to combine the components of application and justification in such a way that the moral point of view can become explicit both as a method of constructive hypothesis formation and as one of universalist justification. This constructivist idea forms the foundation of his reply to Gilligan's objections: "In the first place, they [Gilligan and Murphy] assume that our Stage 5 orientation of principled justice implies a rule-based rigor or fixity of application of a principle and a sense that such a principle is an immutable, absolute, defining choice. In fact, we use the term *principle* to mean a human construction which guides perceptions and responses to human claims in conflict situations (. . .)."[167] Principles are interpreted methodologically as procedural directives for finding a simultaneously appropriate and justified conflict resolution in concrete situations. "Unlike fixed and absolute moral rules, moral principles were characterized as methods or ways of seeing, and of constructing responses to, complex moral situations."[168] Stage 6 differs from all the preceding ones in that, at this stage, the procedure for the impartial formation of norms can itself be reflexively assimilated once again. Considering concrete circumstances and differences in individual situations from the perspective of each individual affected is a phase within this procedure, where norms simply play the role of normative criteria of relevance which we use to identify relevant situation features. The process of constructive hypothesis formation thus transpires as the reciprocal critique of normative viewpoints and of different individual features of the concrete situation.

However, as the solution to the problem of application, Kohlberg can integrate the method of constructive hypothesis formation into his explication of the moral point of view only if this method *simultaneously* guarantees a situation-appropriate and universalizable moral judgment. Nevertheless, a norm hypothesis, formed in consideration of specific context features, is not necessarily universalizable *for that reason*. This cannot be decided until it has been established that the norm hypothesis is also justified. A justification based on the agreement of virtually all the participants in a practical discourse must however abstract from the concrete situation and from the question of appropriateness. It would thus be more precise to describe Kohlberg's constructivist ideal as a combination of universalist justification and contextualist application. The fact that, here, the process of constructive hypothesis formation does not have to dispense with practical reason was already brought home with the help of our interpretation of Mead's universalist conception of ethics. The constructive method must take its orientation from the ideal of a consideration of *all* the features of a situation.

In the constructivist method, both components of practical reason are interwoven with one another in an indistinct manner. Contextualism and universalism cannot however be combined directly. The consideration of all the situation features, which precedes the construction of an appropriate hypothesis, is only possible in an attitude disburdened of the question of validity. It is aimed at an element that Gilligan, Murphy, and Haan constantly emphasize in their characterization of a contextualist morality: the compatibility, or "fit," of norm and situation. In Gilligan's morality of care, this element appears as a preeminent interest in the modal and final factors in choosing the appropriate mode of action (the "how"), in contrast to the conditional presuppositions. Gilligan and Murphy stress that it is precisely in this way that postconventional contextual relativism (PCC) differs from moral universalism: "In the shift from PCF to PCC, the criterion for the adequacy of moral principles changes from objective truth to 'best fit', and can only be established within the context of the dilemma itself."[169] The result is that a number of alternate appropriate norm hypotheses are in principle possible. Almost verbatim, Norma Haan puts forward among her four characteristics of an interpersonal morality the following attribute: contextual reasoning "is more likely to 'fit' a situation and thus reveal its possibilities for resolving action."[170] The criterion of "best fit" or "adequacy" can be understood as the requirement that all the situation features be considered appropriately. Meeting this requirement presupposes that the concrete situation itself becomes the focal point, the one at which appropriateness argumentation is directed in application discourses. In the process, however, the outright contextualism of application is in need of supplementation. Whether the appropriate norm hypothesis can be accepted by everyone can only be checked in justification discourses. Gilligan and Murphy are mistaken when they describe the transition from PCF to PCC as a shift "from objective truth to 'best fit.' " To the extent that what is intended by "objective truth" is not an irrevocable validity of norms, but the claim of a moral norm that it can be accepted by all those affected, it stands not in competition with the criterion of "best fit," but in a relation of supplementation. This can also be confirmed by the authors' own observation that some interview subjects could identify both universalist and situation-specific obligations when judging dilemma situations, without evidently perceiving the two as a contradiction.[171] Thus, "the discovery that it depends . . . " seems to signify not a completed transition to a relativist moral stage, but rather entry into an application discourse.

If one comprehends the contextualism of impartial application as a component of practical reason, the asserted connection to relativism dissolves. Gilligan and Murphy themselves have already distinguished contextual relativism from the stage of simple relativism, which they designate as "multiplicity." This position refrains entirely from using the predicates "right," "better," or "appropriate" to characterize a mode of action as being preferred to another; for this position there only remains the arbitrary decision. In contrast to that, contextual relativism is after all said to be able to permit decisions about which of the modes of action, responsibly chosen under conditions of uncertainty, is "equally or more adequate in a given case."[172] Thus, the criterion of "best fit" permits, it seems, only relatively appropriate moral judgments.[173] If an appropriate norm hypothesis is distinguished by the fact that it considers all the relevant features of a situation, then there can be only one which merits the predicate. Another question is whether the microcosm of a situation does not in fact appear to us as infinite, so that we will never be able to even identify all the features. I shall return to this problem below, one which primarily concerns situations of double contingency. The fact that we do not have such a capability at our disposal does not however preclude that we argue in application discourses on the basis of the assumption that there can be a single appropriate norm hypothesis which we could also discover, presupposing we had infinite time and infinite knowledge. It is only in this assumption that the idea of impartial application becomes apparent, the idea to which we appeal when we call for the consideration of a relevant feature hitherto overlooked. Our judgment on the mode of action more appropriate in relation to others is only possible on the basis of the assumption that it is the best one in consideration of all the particular circumstances. An alternative proposal would have to be able to show that a different mode of action can consider more features or other features better than the one originally proposed. In this way too, one can understand Norma Haan's point that an interpersonal morality operates inductively and thereby makes it possible to discover new resolution possibilities or develop alternative ones within concrete moral conflicts. It is only when the process of constructive hypothesis formation is forced to interpret the situation in a completely coherent manner that hitherto unconsidered features can at all be identified as new ones and included in the construction.

Norma Haan does of course assume that the inductive method of discovering new aspects cannot be applied by each individual alone and privately, from a distance to the conflict. Contextualism belongs to an interpersonal logic which requires a concrete change of perspective on the part of those immediately involved in the conflict, as well as empathy and commitment, a willingness to change one's own ego in view of others' concrete expectations. The procedure is dialogical, is not however limited to the exchange of arguments but includes emotions, wishes, and fears.[174] For Gilligan and Murphy, the resolution of a conflict is thus only possible within the horizons demarcated by the particular dilemma situation.

In this description of the contextualist method, that first level of types of application roughly sketched above can be recognized, the level at which neither norm and situation, nor justification and application can be separated from one another because the validity of the norm itself is tied to the context in which it is applied. When the question concerning the "how" of a mode of action supersedes the one concerning the "whether," the modality and situational appropriateness of the mode of action become the foundation for judging moral quality. The standards are taken from the particular interactive situation and from the context of relationships: the constitutive rules which are essential for the continued existence of a family, a love relationship, and for concrete institutions in general. These rules cannot be easily generalized; rather, they are formed in a different way in each case by virtue of the fact that there is a common practice in these institutions. Thus, for selecting an appropriate mode of action, rights and obligations are less important than actually clarifying the situation, that is, interpreting the conflict-laden problems, in order to find out what is "good" for oneself and for the relationship to the concrete other. In order to be able to constitute this teleological connection, however, those involved have to have already acquired knowledge of what a good life is for them, and they have to have collectively reached an understanding on what a successful form of life is for them.

At the postconventional level of moral judgment formation, the context-related standards of ethical life [*Sittlichkeit*] are not simply destroyed, which could be the impression given by the objections directed at Kohlberg. Only the unquestioned connection between validity and appropriateness is dissolved, the connection with which a contextualist morality blocks the transition to a perspective beyond the concrete relationship or institution. In this way, the rule structure of a form of life, or a mode of action that is good for a specific life plan, can in turn become the subject matter of a moral judgment if they claim general validity. What is said to be good for *everyone* can no longer be determined within the horizons of an individual form of life—and it could of course be the case that what an individual form of life prescribes as "good" cannot be accepted with reasons by anyone. Hegel drew attention to the fact that the immediate relationship between individuals can first take the form of a relation of master and slave and that a protracted struggle for recognition is required until an ethical relation has been developed. Thus, that a universalist morality isolates the validity of norms from their particular context in relationships and forms of life only means that the appropriateness of a norm does not suffice in order to declare it morally binding too.

On the other hand, it does not follow from this separation that universally valid norms could be applied without considering the particular circumstances of the situation. With the dissolution of the syndrome of validity and appropriateness and with the complementary separation of justification and application, application becomes "free" in Durkheim's sense, that is, independent of the de facto validity of given normative viewpoints. Application discourses can now consider *all* the normatively relevant aspects of a situation and are not confined to those which belong to the semantic content of individual, factually valid norms. On the one hand, disburdening the process of constructive hypothesis formation of questions of validity makes it open to all the various features which would have been left unconsidered in the application of a conventionally given norm. On the other hand, judgment on the correctness of the norm hypothesis remains dependent on an additional examination of the hypothesis' validity claim. The process of disburdening deliberations on appropriateness of conventional validity, which is given with the concrete context of relationships or with the ethical horizons of a community, is supported by a differentiated justification discourse specially tailored to determining an appropriate norm's universal worthiness to be recognized. A constructive hypothesis formation disburdened of questions of validity must therefore also consider questions of the good life insofar as they can be raised in a concrete situation. The appropriate application of legitimate norms may not harm forms of life without reason. These aspects belong to the situation just as much as those which are immediately relevant to a just resolution of conflict. However, on the other hand, this cannot mean that, in the dimension of application, questions of justice are again integrated into the horizons of a common form of life and thereby stripped of their universalist character. Then, absolutely nothing would have been gained by distinguishing between justification and application. Between the two extremes of a destruction of forms of life or a violation of conceptions of the good life, on the one hand, and a complete assimilation of morality and ethical life, on the other, there is a network of highly demanding presuppositions. First, the application of universalist principles is only possible on the condition that a form of life is, in general, facilitating to the moral principle. To this extent, the application of a moral principle in a form of life and the application of universalist principles to concrete situations are connected to one another. Secondly, conflicts between principles of justice and orientations of the good life at the postconventional level can only be resolved universalistically, that is, in favor of justice. A different order of priority would undo the distinction between morality and ethical life. Thirdly, the application of universalist principles to a concrete situation can be conceived at the postconventional level only as a process of constructive hypothesis formation. Only conventionally valid norms are to be applied independently of other viewpoints in every situation. In contrast to that, a postconventional construction of the application of norms presupposes that, in every situation, (a) various, conflicting principles are to be applied, which (b) are interwoven with certain conceptions of the good life and with a commonly shared form of life. Fourthly, aspects of justice and those of the good life cannot be substituted for one another. This does not however rule out that questions of the good life, to the extent that they are affected by the application of a principle in a situation, can be considered when interpreting the application situation.

5

Is Postconventional Moral Consciousness Rigoristic?

So far we have examined two different types of norm application as well as their specific relation to the justification of validity. In a first step, the model of perspective-taking served to illustrate the original genetic and validity dependency of a common perspective, or of a temporally, substantively, and socially semigeneralized norm, on its situational context of emergence in concrete interactive relationships. Wittgenstein's argument that following a rule is only possible as a common practice for which we are trained means, in terms of moral philosophy, that the interpretation of what is actually a mode of action practiced commonly in different situations seems to be more important than the justification and application of rules. This internal connection between rule, action, and situation within human practice does not present rule-following as a problem of applying norms in need of justification. According to this proposal, the right thing to do—right in the twofold sense of being simultaneously legitimate and appropriate—reveals itself in the particular situational process of interpretation. However, one cannot go behind this process if one interprets the practice of a language game in a quasi-transcendental or in a naturalistic sense. If one moves away from that internal connection within a habitualized and established practice in order to appraise it with the attitude of a neutral observer, one then shares a temporally, substantively, and socially generalized perspective from which one can question whether a practice is the result of an appropriate application of a legitimate norm. Even now, the generalized norm can still be the outcome of a common, situation-dependent interpretation, and as such is not only valid but also appropriate per se. Norm validity does not go beyond the concrete horizons of a particular context until the common perspective of a generalized other has been formed in such a way that the standpoint of each individual is taken

by everyone, and not simply the standpoint of a member of a form of
life by the other members. Then, however, a separation between the
situation-specific process of constructive hypothesis formation and
the universalist justification of a valid norm is required, as I attempted to show in connection with Mead's conception of a universalist ethics. The necessity of such a separation was made clear
with the help of the developmental theories of Piaget and Kohlberg,
and in the debate with those critics of Kohlberg who advance contextualist arguments. In doing so, a type of dialectical process—*sit
venia verbo*—emerged, a process in the course of which the context-
related assimilation of validity and appropriateness, characteristic
of the first concrete-reciprocal conventional stage, is disentangled
at the highest postconventional stage and thereby brought to self-
consciousness, as it were. In the idea of impartial application in
consideration of all the aspects of an individual situation, the early
contextualism, which is still tied to concrete-reciprocal perspective-
taking and to particular groups, is brought to bear, whereas the
idea of a commonness oriented by the needs and interests of those
immediately involved is expanded to a procedure of universal justification. For this reason, we could distinguish two types of application which relate, each in its own way, to the concrete context.
One type I designated above as Level 1, where justification and
application are confounded in the same context, whereas the other
type combines a context-sensitive application with a universalist
justification.

So far we have taken up contextualist arguments against the
idea of a moral universalism only to the extent that they defend sensitivity to situational and interpersonal details against the abstrac-
tive incision unavoidably connected with temporal, substantive, and
social generalization at the universalist level. However, these arguments still draw their persuasive power from another aspect which
we already saw alluded to in Wellmer's objections to the distinction
between justification and application. Wellmer justified his objections with the following argument (among others): a genuine application problem only arises with authoritatively given norms, which
must be related to arbitrary cases, whereas a postconventional morality is characterized by the fact that here it not a matter of norms
at all, but a question of appropriate modes of action in situations,
modes of action which we can discover by directly applying the
moral point of view to a situation. Gilligan, Murphy, and Haan justified the higher degree of accord with our moral intuitions which is
displayed by an interpersonal contextualist morality as compared to

a universalist one as follows: interpersonal morality does not need a system of formerly fixed and authoritatively given norms. For this reason, it remains to be asked whether the introduction of the distinction between the justification and the application of norms results in an authoritarian moral rigorism being defended, at least implicitly.

Hannah Arendt vigorously pointed out those dangers for the morality of action which are associated with the unexamined adoption of norms that require unconditional observance. They rob the actor of his own judgment, which, while listening to his conscience, he has to form in a concrete conflict situation; instead, they prize inconsiderateness toward oneself and others as a special moral polish. It is the perpetually repeated argument of those who do *nothing* but their duty. "By shielding people against the dangers of examination, it [nonthinking] teaches them to hold fast to whatever the prescribed rules of conduct may be at a given time in a given society. What people then get used to is not so much the content of the rules, a close examination of which would always lead them into perplexity, as the possession of rules under which to subsume particulars. In other words, they get used to never making up their minds."[175] With respect to this class of objections to normativist conceptions of ethics, at least three different topics can be distinguished from one another: (a) that the class of all strictly normative propositions, and thereby the moral ought in general, has authoritarian roots, so that normativity is to be equated with repression; (b) that the concept of the moral norm includes an obligation to obey which is usually connected with sanctions in the case of nonobservance and requires the subjection of inner nature to an internal or external authority; (c) that the introduction of the concept of a norm into ethics is necessarily connected to an abstraction from the concrete conditions of the context because norms as rules treat unlike cases alike, so that the duty to observe moral norms means inconsiderateness or "blindness" vis-à-vis the particular circumstances of a situation.

The first topic concerns the possibility of an ethical cognitivism, that is, the question whether the validity claim of moral judgments can at all be justified or is merely the expression of a relation of power between those involved; the second concerns the relation between moral judgment and action, that is, the question concerning the motivational agency which is to be presupposed for the actual observance of a moral prescription; and the third has to do with the relation between norms and application situations. Because the first two topics are in themselves of an extremely complex nature and have a long history in the controversies of moral theory, while the third one is of primary interest to us here, I would like to deal with these first two just briefly and only to the extent that they are relevant to our task.

(a) The *critique* of normativism in ethics is as old as normativism itself. One can interpolate this critique in the Christian critique of the Old Testament's trust in the law and find it embodied in the sentence from the Sermon on the Mount: "Judge not, that ye be not judged" (Mt 7:1)—as long as one does not understand it as simply a rule of reciprocity. Hegel took up this critique in his early theological writings and directed it at Kant's positivism of the moral law, where he could recognize nothing other than the establishment of an internal master-slave relation.[176] Paradoxically, Nietzsche's denunciation of the resentful character of the Christian moral tradition is based on the same motif and can be traced up to Adorno's paradoxically entangled meta-critique of Kant's critique of practical reason,[177] or to Foucault's archaeology of moral discourses as the product of societal struggles.[178] Naturalistic theories of ethics aim directly at a critique of the moral ought, according to which the meaning of a normative proposition can only be understood empirically or aesthetically after the end of metaphysics. In her discussion of the "norm model in ethics,"[179] Ursula Wolf relies on the thesis from Elizabeth Anscombe and Philippa Foot that the moral ought's claim to be binding is a relic of religion.[180] Ethics of this kind replaces a principle of norm justification with a naturalistic contextualism which judges the moral quality of an action teleologically according to whether the action contributes to the realization of a conception of the good life. The real moral problem does not merely arise in the question of whether social imperatives are worthy of recognition, but in the question as to "what principles for my action toward other persons correspond to my own conception of a correct life."[181] The meaning of the moral ought follows not from the reciprocal obligation to others, but from the obligation to myself. It is only in this way that an external imperative is transformed into a moral obligation imposed by me myself, that is, by my own conception of what kind of human being I want to be. If, according to this proposal, normative obligations and validity claims are again rescinded in an ethics [*Sittlichkeit*] of the good life, then everything depends on what is to be understood by a conception of the good life, if one does not wish to reintroduce a metaphysical anthropology. Wolf distinguishes a first level of subjectively valued goals, or goals considered valuable within a community, from a second level at which the question concerning the good life is posed "as the question concerning the interpretation of the existential situation of man and, resulting from this, as the search for an integral [ganzheitlich] mode of existence."[182] This can now only be characterized as "a kind of aesthetic undertaking."[183] Instead of this, Anscombe and Foot propose an empirical interpretation of what is good for us (all). Consistent with this, the predicate "good" is interpreted descriptively and draws its meaning from psychology. When we have a psychologically appropriate understanding [or account] of man at our disposal, then we also know what he needs, in a teleological sense, in order to be a human being in this understanding;[184] "and this 'man' with the complete set of virtues is the 'norm,' as 'man' with, e.g., a complete set of teeth is a norm. But in *this* sense 'norm' has ceased to be roughly equivalent to 'law.' "[185] For this reason, there is no logical gap between facts and values.[186]

Arguments against this position can be raised in at least two respects. The assertion that norms are orders backed by power relations can be contested with the point made by H. L. A. Hart that, if that were the case, norms could no longer be distinguished from a bank robber's "coercive order."[187] If, however, the concept of the binding character of moral norms presupposes voluntary recognition, which is only internally accessible, then the reasons for the recognition of a norm have to be intersubjectively thematizable too. For our topic, the second point is more important: that only a postmetaphysical morality does justice to the aesthetic or naturalistic interpretation of our basic existential situation and, for this reason, is a morality which can no longer prescribe binding norms, but, it is said, can only make recommendations for prudent action. Here, the contextualism we got to know with Wellmer as one dependent on the form of life, and with Kohlberg's critics as an interpersonal and situation-related one, is expanded to the whole situation of man, as it were. One can counter this, first, by pointing out that discourse ethics can also be traced back to a human *"factum"* in that it does not prescribe any concrete moral norms but reconstructs, in a fallible manner, the conditions of valid norms from the conditions of rational argumentation (conditions which do not have metaconditions). From the perspective of this presupposition, the situation of man can be interpreted as the outcome of a process of language-mediated socialization in which the individual communicatively gives of himself to the other and is thus dependent both on respect for his individuality and on a relation of solidarity to the members of a lifeworld.[188] Discourse ethics, however, uses these descriptions not in order to derive a conception of the good life, but in order to justify a procedural ethics that enables *every* individual to realize his life plan under conditions of mutual respect and communal solidarity. Secondly, one can rely on the same argument which we already put forward against interpersonal contextualism: the concrete conditions of the situation have to be considered when applying moral norms. Their range can be expanded by discovering new features because an impartial application is compelled to consider *all* the relevant aspects of a situation. Thus, both with the procedure of impartially justifying norms and with the principle of impartial application, discourse ethics can do justice to the human condition, without having to draw naturalistic consequences.

(b) The relation between moral judgment and action is known in the tradition as the contrast between duty and inclination. In Rousseau's definition of liberty as obedience to the self-given law, which Kant adopted for the explication of the concept of moral duty, there is the paradox of obedience and liberty. Due to the intention to cleanse the meaning of the moral ought of all sensualistic and social rank-related "impurities," the authoritarian residuum present while realizing and implementing moral norms seems to have been overlooked. Here too, discourse ethics can contribute to a defusing of the situation. For one thing, it is not forced to dichotomize moral and factually operative validity in the manner Kant did in his two-world doctrine. Validity claims, which are raised with the illocutionary component of every speech act, have a "Janus face: As claims, they transcend any local context; at the same time, they have to be raised here and now and be de facto recognized if they are going to bear the agreement of interaction participants that is needed for effective cooperation. The transcendent moment of *universal* validity bursts every provinciality asunder; the obligatory moment of accepted validity claims renders them carriers of a *context-bound* everyday practice."[189] This, however, only shows that there is no need for a leap in order to move from pure practical reason to motivated action; *how* the appropriate motivations can be made available still remains open. This is a question concerning personality structures and socialization, which a discourse ethics must presuppose for a concrete form of life.[190] In this context, finally, one can also ask about the external safeguards (sanctions) with which the implementation and realization of legitimate norms can be guaranteed. We shall return to this later.

(c) In our discussion of contextualist objections to Kohlberg's conception of the postconventional level, we already became aware of the fact that considering all the particular circumstances of a situation forms a part of the impartial application of a norm. The misunderstanding—namely, that because moral judgment takes its orientation from an abstract standpoint, this necessarily leads to a rigoristic application of justified norms—rests on an inadmissible connecting of the postconventional level of justification with a conventional concept of application. The properties which are thereby attributed to impartial application apply only to *this conventional* concept of application: orientation is taken from given rules because it is only in this way that the generalized other, the system's morality, can be maintained and the cooperative context sustained. Situation features lying outside the semantic range presupposed by an applicable norm can only be considered as exceptions since a single norm cannot determine all the cases of its own application in advance. Because the legitimacy of given norms can be checked only within an existing community, these norms remain tied to a particular context of defined interpersonal relationships, a context which renders them valid and within which they are at the same time appropriate. Within this context, the application situations, to which the collectively agreed norms are tailored, are essentially known. New, hitherto unconsidered constellations of features in an unforeseen situation are then indeed "exceptions," for which there is a principle of equity available, one that is to be used carefully and cautiously. However, the principle of equity can only be used *within* the boundaries of the particular social system. It serves the purpose of showing that the social system is humane even when exceptional cases arise. With an exception that goes beyond its boundaries, the social system can only react in that manner which is imputed to the postconventional level as a method of norm application: rigoristic, ostracizing, repressive. For it is then no longer a matter of normatively coping with a situation, but a matter of the self-assertion of the social system. In contradistinction to this, universalist principles or norms which are legitimate in the sense of the moral principle claim to be valid for *all* those potentially affected and to be appropriate for *all* application situations. Therefore, they can be disputed by anyone who puts forward a universalizable interest and can be checked in every individual application situation as to whether they consider all the features of the particular situation appropriately. Justification and application discourses are then no longer limited to the membership circle of a specific social system.

The rigid, inflexible type of norm application thus belongs more at Stage 4 of the development of moral consciousness. However, it is not conspicuous as such at this stage as long as norm validity and appropriateness are fused together within the particular context of a social system and within the corresponding horizons of situations which can be typified and are calculable. Norms valid in this sense can be applied without considering those circumstances of the situation which do not belong to the semantic extension of the specific norm. Deliberations on appropriateness are not thereby precluded, but have already been largely concluded with the fixing of validity. What remains are the hermeneutical and semantic deliberations when interpreting given norms. The provoking concept of "rigorism" appears only in the transition to the postconventional level if the application of given norms can no longer be harmonized with the impartial consideration of all, or at least other, relevant situation features. The context-bound application of a norm then reveals itself in its particularity.

How can one explain the mix-up which imputes a conventional concept of application to the postconventional level of norm justification? This confusion was suggested by the various conceptions of a universalist ethics themselves—that is, as long as the idea of the objective, universally binding validity of moral duties had to be interpreted in strict demarcation from the empirical world of social rank-related maxims of prudence and from the world of moral feelings. Because validity itself had to be completely context-free, should it correspond to a reason [*Vernunft*] obtaining prior to all possible experience, the appropriateness of a moral judgment was not in any event a topic of reason. One can even interpolate this misunderstanding in Kant's ethics, which is generally cited as the paradigm of a moral rigorism. Kant identified practical reason with the form of a law, which he had in turn developed in analogy to a causal-mechanical law of nature. At least in Kant's time, a law of nature was still defined as being valid without exception in every case to which it can be applied. For this reason, Kant's test procedure in which the moral law is applied to a maxim—the problem of pure practical reason—takes its orientation from the "type" constituted by a law of nature.[191] This implies not only the hypothetical idea whether I can will that all these maxims be followed (vis-à-vis me too) like a law, but also that they be applied in the same way in every conceivable situation. Kant did indeed stress that this comparison concerns only the form of the law and should not be regarded as the determining ground of the will. Freedom itself is the determining ground, and with the form of a maxim being analogous to a law of nature, I can only see whether the maxim is in agreement with freedom. However, if one understands him in such a way that the law-of-nature analogy is also valid for the application of a maxim which is in agreement with the moral law—because I am obligated to apply a maxim I can will as a law of nature in every application situation like a law of nature—then one arrives at the rigoristic consequences for which Kant is reproached by his critics. The moral maxim is then confused with the moral law itself: "A categorical imperative is simply a moral rule, and it involves a shift in the use of the term to suppose that a categorical imperative may under no circumstances be violated, that it is absolutely binding under any and all conditions. To suppose this is to confuse *a* categorical imperative, in the sense of a moral rule, with *the* categorical imperative, which is a moral principle."[192]

Kant was satisfied that the maxim was given in the material of the will and he was not concerned about its appropriateness. For him it was a problem of purposive-rational prudence, which is subsumed under empirical-theoretical truth claims, so that he could refer it to theoretical reason. On the basis of this deficiency, Hegel justifies the transition from morality to ethical life: "The proposition: 'Act as if the maxim of thine action could be laid down as a universal principle,' would be admirable if we already had determinate principles of conduct. That is to say, to demand of a principle that it shall be able to serve in addition as a determinant of universal legislation is to presuppose that it already possesses a content. Given the content, then of course the application of the principle would be a simple matter."[193] It is the same argument with which Mead distinguishes his draft of a universalist ethics from "Kant's principle": "But where you have no standard, it does not help you to decide. Where you have to get a restatement, a readjustment, you get a new situation in which to act; the simple generalizing of the principle of your act does not help. It is at that point that Kant's principle breaks down."[194] Yet, Mead's attempt to give effect to practical reason in the method of constructive hypothesis formation while considering all the normatively relevant features of a situation shows that Hegel's proposal to search for given principles in the ethical spheres of the family, civil society, and the state is not compelling.

In raising his objection, Hegel does however draw attention to a danger which arises when the choice of the appropriate maxim is left to subjective discretion. The consequences arising from the generalization of any maxims whatever can be extremely immoral if, in these maxims, the particular gives the impression of being the universally valid.[195] Then, precisely that assertion is correct which imputes a repressive particularism of application to the universalism of validity. As long as moral principles with universalist claims are applied particularly instead of impartially, this can only lead to the interminable detection of nongeneralizable interests and dependencies which merely hide behind a universalist claim. Yet, instead of viewing this as a problem of the neglected dimension of application, the idea of a universalist justification of moral judgments is itself abandoned. The objection can then be generalized to the suspicion that *all* moral judgments are *nothing but* the expression of historically and psychically changing intentions, motives, and interests. Both the rigoristic and the relativist interpretation and critique of a morality based on reason converge in the characterization of moral judgment as an instrument of domination.

It becomes apparent that these consequences are not compelling as soon as one distinguishes between justification and application. Justifications refer to the *validity* of a norm in the sense that it may not be dependent on an authority or on principles for which one cannot advance reasons that can be collectively accepted by all those affected from their particular, interest-determined perspectives. For this reason, cognitivist ethics, which uses a moral principle like the categorical imperative as a criterion of validity, aims at precluding the *privileging* of one's own or any other interest (or of a specific form of life) when it is a matter of the *validity* of a norm or the correctness of an action. If we adopt this perspective, which is exclusively concerned with universal validity, we cannot know how precisely and to what extent we must describe the situational conditions of the norm or the features and purposes of the action, or its context, until we have checked the norm, or the purpose of the action, in respect of its generalizability. The same holds true for a norm that in itself can be accepted by everyone when it is applied in a situation that is more complex than the set of relevant situation features presupposed by the norm itself. The moral principle does not itself determine the degree of specificity of a norm; even a mode of action in a situation can be universalized. This openness of the moral principle to a norm's content (which is generalized merely as a hypothetically fixed content and, *as such,* is checked in respect of its compatibility with everyone's interests) does indeed guarantee that no content remains excluded from the outset. But it does not provide us with a criterion for what is to be understood in each case as the appropriateness of the content of a norm. Appropriateness is a situation-dependent criterion which refers to the consideration of all the relevant situation features. For this reason, a norm that can be applied to a certain set of identical or similar situations by virtue of the features it contains can be acceptable to everyone affected, although situations are conceivable in which there are conflicting norms as a result of a changed constellation of features. G. M. Singer drew the following conclusion from this: "But if this is the case, then the rule derived from the application of the categorical imperative holds only for the circumstances to which it is applied, and, of course, for anyone in the same or similar circumstances, and does not thereby hold for all possible circumstances. Because it could not be willed to be a universal law that everyone should act in a certain way under certain circumstances, it does not follow that it could not be willed to be a universal law that everyone should act in that way under certain other circumstances. Indeed, on the basis of the categorical imperative, an act which would be wrong in certain circumstances may well be right in other circumstances."[196] In supplementing the idea of universalist justification by the principle of impartial application, the reproach of ethical rigorism leveled at universalist moral philosophies is no longer justified.

6

Summary:
Three Levels in the Development
of Types of Application

The introduction of the model of perspective-taking allowed us to reconstruct the societal dimension—as it were—of the relation between justification and application in its development more precisely than would have been possible with the concept of common practice as used by Wellmer in a different connection. At least three levels can now be distinguished at which validity and appropriateness assume a different relation to one another.[197]

At a *first* level, ego and alter can reciprocally take the perspective of the other and can view themselves from the other's perspective. At this level, only two things are possible: either situational and current behavioral expectations, and ones directed at the concrete other; or slightly generalized role patterns which remain dependent on concrete contexts of relations, where they can be activated. In the first case, the problem of application does not arise at all because the particular, collectively found regulation of the situation remains immediately context-related, situation-dependent, and individual. Justification and application cannot be distinguished from one another because alter and ego make a common decision about the situation here and now. The context in which this decision is "valid" is the same as the one in which it is also "applied"; it is thus appropriate from the outset. Speaking about validity and appropriateness is only metaphorical here. This level corresponds more to the model of unilateral causal influence than to that of bilateral reciprocity. In the second case, there already exists a socially, substantively, and temporally generalized, common perspective. However, it remains tied to concrete contexts of relations, where obligations to loyalty are developed among those involved. The validity of such obligations is dependent on the particular context of relations in each case, that is, on the system of

167

roles to which alter and ego can relate their common expectations. The same particular context of relations also determines the appropriateness of the common role expectations and of the specific reciprocal obligations to loyalty. The situations in which the system of roles is made present in a routine manner are essentially determined; one knows in advance what is at issue and which situation features are alone relevant. Unusual circumstances in an unforeseen situation or in the person of one involved (e.g., conflicts of loyalty) are considered as threats, or as exceptional cases where extenuating circumstances are regarded as admissible. Otherwise, the particular features of a situation remain irrelevant.

At a *second* level, the perspective commonly shared by alter and ego is already so highly generalized that both of them can step out of the particular context of relations and observe the latter from an explicit third, neutral position. Ego and alter relate to a common perspective from which they can reciprocally assume that the respective other will take this perspective vis-à-vis himself and the other. This kind of socially generalized perspective change is already implicitly present in simple role systems, but it is not until this level that the context of relations can also be put at a further distance. Behavioral patterns are disengaged from concrete interactions and become neutral toward the acting persons or those affected: it is the level of explicitly formulated systems of norms. This neutrality does not however extend to *everyone* being able to relate to a virtually common norm. Its context does not extend beyond a particular group or a specific societal system. Durkheim described this as the collective consciousness, which is defined by the mechanical assimilation of "the similar" and the exclusion of "the dissimilar." For this reason, validity and appropriateness are not yet discretely recognizable at this level, although situation and norm have already been completely separated from one another, that is to say, an explicitly formulated norm is applied to temporally and substantively different situations and socially different persons. But the difference between possible application situations remains easy to manage within the horizons of the particular group, so that one can limit oneself to selecting and normatively determining certain typical features and to treating every situation which displays such features equally. Norm application can thus be limited to checking whether the presupposed typical features are present. Of course, it is also clear that a norm cannot regulate all the cases of its own application. This circumstance is not however a problem at this level. New and changed constellations of features in unforeseen situations can be coped with as exceptions to the rule. It is only when they go beyond the scope of the legitimate normative possibilities of a group or of a particular societal system that difficulties arise.

The *third* level differs from the preceding one only in that it extends the validity of the generalized other to the "universe of discourse" (Mead). The validity claim of a norm or of a moral judgment is addressed no longer only to the common perspective of the members of a particular group, but to *everyone*. Going beyond the horizons of validity in this manner has far-reaching implications for the relation between validity and appropriateness. Being addressed to everyone, the validity claim of a norm can no longer be anchored in the same context which could guarantee the norm's appropriateness too. Rather, every individual must now be able to take the perspective of every other individual, without this universal-reciprocal change in perspective being substantively or socially restricted by a particular collective consciousness. For the validity of a moral norm to be able to satisfy this condition, there needs to be a special context-independent facility which enables all those affected to participate universally in establishing a perspective common to all. Potentially, this can come about in the form of principles that embody interests common to all, or in the form of procedures in which universality is guaranteed by virtue of the equal participation of all those affected. In both cases, the validity of a norm is determined by reasons which are legitimate not because they issue from a certain context, but because they can be accepted by everyone. In this way, justification and application are separated. Durkheim explained this process quite naturalistically in terms of the increasing volume and density of a society. With the cultural melting pot of urbane metropolises like Paris at the end of the nineteenth century before his eyes, he could determine the validity of universal norms only in such a way that it could do justice to a plurality of heterogeneous contexts connected to one another by the division of labor. If these norms were to be valid for everyone, they had to be necessarily indeterminate because the extreme complexity of different application situations and the fast change of individual constellations of features were no longer foreseeable, as was still the case within the closed horizons of a societal segment. With the universality of justification, application is also "free" and presupposes an autonomous individuality which applies universal principles in a situation-specific manner. This process can also be reconstructed in its logical genesis: With the devaluation of particular, context-related norm validity, the selection of relevant situation features is no longer given or determined prior to the application of a norm. Disentangling the perspectives also affects the perception of the individual situation. From now on, all the features which can be identified as being relevant according to a plurality of normative viewpoints requiring justification can be taken into consideration. Because validity per se no longer guarantees appropriateness too, the appropriateness of a norm in a situation must first be established in the process of considering all the relevant features. Because, conversely, an appropriate norm is not valid because it is appropriate, impartial justification and application are dependent on one another in order to constitute the meaning of a morally correct (valid and appropriate) judgment.

Following this rough sketch, a context-bound application can be distinguished from a free application. We find the criterion for this distinction in the variations in perspective structure. As long as the possibility of a universal-reciprocal perspective change is restricted in the temporal, substantive, or social dimensions by a particular context, validity and appropriateness remain conceptually undifferentiated, even though different institutions for these activities have been established, as for example in the legal system. Moreover, the institutional separation between legislating and applying the law is not connected in any analytical manner with the distinction between justification and application. Rather, it can be surmised that an institutional differentiation is possible only against the background of the assumption that a norm, valid according to parliamentary procedure, is also appropriate for a clear range of situations, so that it only has to be "applied" as soon as the semantically presupposed situation features are present.[198] As we shall see, in the legal system there are additional conditions which preclude a simple transference of the distinction between justification and application.

Thus, following this synoptic account, we can distinguish between context-bound application, which is assimilated to questions of validity, and free, impartial, but context-sensitive application. We found genetic reference points for our thesis that it is possible to differentiate systematically between the justification and the application of norms, and could also reconstruct the process which led to this differentiation and made it necessary. As the sketch of the three levels has shown, this process cannot be separated from a social perspective structure that defines specific kinds of contexts in which situation features acquire their relevance, and in which behavioral expectations vis-à-vis situations and persons are generalized to varying degrees, and where norms are justified or applied.

Excursus:
"Phronesis" as an Example of
Context-bound Application

1. The Aristotelian Theory

In a study on Kant's categorical imperative as a criterion of the ethical [*des Sittlichen*], Otfried Höffe drew attention to the fact that Kant's contribution to ethics does not exhaust itself in a deduction and an analysis of the moral law as a principle of generalization of any modes of action or rules whatsoever.[1] Rather, he distinguished a special kind of rules as being the subject matter of the categorical imperative: maxims, that is, rules with varying degrees of generality, according to which the actor himself determines his will in various situations. Whereas Kant is content to characterize maxims as subjective principles of the will[2] because, this being the case, it is then sufficient for judgment on morally correct action that there is a maxim of action at all, Höffe interprets them as principles in which it is expressed "what kind of human being one wants to be."[3] In this way, Höffe directs attention to the problem Hegel and Mead saw as the downfall of Kant's moral law. We must first have a set of maxims for our conduct in various types of situations before we can ask ourselves whether the concretely intended action is also morally justified according to the maxim on which it is based. According to Höffe, if this problem of a science of maxims, as it were, is taken seriously, ethics is divided into two parts: the justification or deduction of the moral law itself and its subjective anchorage in the autonomy of the will, on the one hand, and the moral legitimation of ethical [*sittlich*] maxims and their application in concrete situations, on the other. But the application of ethical maxims, Höffe adds, requires the assistance "of (ethical) judgment [*Urteilskraft*], expressed in Aristotelian terms, of *phronesis*, an 'ethical-hermeneutical task,' in which Kant showed precious little interest for various reasons."[4]

re Kant's seeing some need for judgment

171

By distinguishing between a moral principle as a justification principle for maxims and an "outline or layout knowledge" [*Umriß- oder Grundriß-Wissen*] of maxims for ethical action in various situations—a knowledge which must be concretized in the particular case—Höffe differentiates, in the sense we propose, between the justification and application of (subjective) norms (as maxims).[5] For Höffe, however, this differentiation has implications different from the ones drawn by us. If maxims are concerned with what kind of human being one wishes to be, what is of primary importance is the appropriate interpretation of the ethical context in which we grow up and have social intercourse with one another. Then, however, the application of this type of maxim also remains tied exclusively to the particular context. It is not subsequently subject to the principle of impartiality, which compels us to consider all the features of a situation independently of a particular context. Bubner pointed this out clearly. "No twisting of meaning can fail to see that the maxim only expresses what seems right to someone who is seeking orientation in a situation. He does not think about a law that is the same for all rational beings in heaven and on earth, valid under every condition, or one that purely and simply directs action. Against a certain background of historical determinants, with or without clear knowledge of the social conditions, and having cherished interests and acknowledged inclinations, he considers which of a number of alternative directions he should follow in order to realize his concrete action."[6] Characterizing the application of morally justified maxims as *phronesis* thus leads us to Aristotelian ethics, as an example of a context-bound application.

There is a good deal to be said for interpreting Aristotle's *Nicomachean Ethics* in terms of its opposition to the Socratic-Platonic thesis that the good is a universal and teachable knowledge which, in principle, makes appropriate action in every situation possible.[7] For Aristotle, on the other hand, it is a matter of appropriate action under unforeseeable and changeable conditions. For this reason, the good as the end of action cannot be determined in an abstract manner in advance, but must be demonstrated in each individual case and in a manner appropriate to the particular circumstances. It is only in this way that the actor can progressively realize and concretize his conception of a good life in various situations. *Phronesis* guides him in selecting and considering those situation features which are relevant to reaching this end.

Aristotle does not answer directly the question as to what a good life is. If it is not the realization of given ideas, then it can only be the manner in which a life is led as a whole. What leading a life consists in cannot be answered within the framework of ethics alone, but follows from ontology. This is described by the famous all-inclusive statement at the beginning of the *Nicomachean Ethics:* "Every art and every inquiry, and similarly every action and choice, is thought to aim at some good; and for this reason the good has rightly been declared to be that at which all things aim."[8] What is aimed at is determined by the being or essence of this. The reality of all modes of being, which are composed of material and form, consists in this aiming. Modes of being are changeable and can move or be moved. According to whether they have the end—the perfection of their form—in themselves or whether it is given to them from without, the types of movement and thus of reality differ. What distinguishes man from all other living beings is the "active life of that element that has a rational principle [*logon echon*]."[9] Because there can be varying optimum degrees in satisfying this, the best one can be distinguished as the one in which the essence can be optimally realized. Here, teleological ontology is combined with an ethics of perfectibility. To live in such a way that best corresponds to that element which has a rational principle, that is, to the essence, is the greatest good aimed at by man. Such a life is good or happy,[10] and what is specifically good for the acting man is guided by this end. Thus, the good life is not assessed according to whether private ends, which everyone follows individually, are achieved. Aristotle does not exclude these ends from ethics, but subordinates them to the end of the good life. Individual ends can indeed be heterogeneous, as long as their selection contributes to the realization of the good life, that is, if I set myself ends which are good as a means for my conception of life.

Because life as that element which has a rational principle is not an abstract principle to which every action in every situation is to be subordinated, but a more or less optimal self-objectivation of the essence, there are, depending on the particular circumstances, different modes in which the activities of the soul can unfold. The particular circumstances which characterize man are the rational and irrational parts of the soul, whereby the irrational parts are divided into a vegetative part common to all living beings and into a capability peculiar to man: a special "desiring element" (*orexis*) that enables him to wish anything or strive for any ends. This capability can subordinate itself or be opposed to the rational part of the soul.[11] Whether a life is successful is revealed in the degree to which we allow, in accordance with their determination, the rational and irrational parts of the soul to become operative in all situations of action. Aristotle designates the optimal degree "excellence" or virtue and, complementary to his classification of the soul, he distinguishes between intellectual (dianoetical) and moral (ethical) virtues.[12] The former can be taught, while the latter require successive acquisition and training over a long period of time. We have to make them a habit—Aristotle points to the etymological origin of "ethos" in custom, mores, and tradition.[13] The fact that we are able to realize our "desiring element" and our passions guided by the rational part of the soul is made possible by experiences in individual situations. We acquire virtues only by dealing with different situations of action where we choose the middle course between our extreme passions. "Whoever learns virtue and ethical life [*Sittlichkeit*] in the Aristotelian sense learns two things: the absolute determinations of what is, in itself and non-relatively, beautiful and disgraceful, and applications that are to be differentiated according to situations and to the circumstantial determinations of when, where, how, to what extent, toward whom, etc. [something is to be done]."[14] Thus, *for analytical reasons*, what also constitutes virtuous action, within which the good life comes about, are the appropriate modalizations which follow from the particular conditions of the situation. For this reason, virtuous action is to be understood as the appropriate concretization of ends under contingent conditions. Aristotle describes the relevant features of the individual case, its circumstances [*Peristasen*], by putting forward the various, corresponding pronominal structures: " . . . at the right times, with reference to the right objects, towards the right people, with the right aim, and in the right way . . . "[15] They are temporal, local, personal, final, and modal determinations, which can be expressed in corresponding adverbial clauses that characterize the action in a situation-specific manner.[16] Aristotle summarizes the two main factors of action as the "circumstances of the action" and its "aim" (*en hos he praxis kai hou heneka*).[17] Situativeness (*en hos*) and finality (*hou heneka*) appear again and again as characteristic features. Ethics must refer to this basic structure. It gives prominence to that action which is found to be a realization of the good life by way of its implicit end under situation-specific conditions. This acting is itself an end (but not an end in itself). As practice (*praxis*), Aristotle distinguishes it from production (*poiesis*), which has an arbitrary end outside of itself.[18] Such an ethics must presuppose that everyone already possesses a basic ethical attitude. It can then outline what modes of action we ought to adopt generally: that is the function of the catalogue of virtues. Moreover, it can explicate more precisely the capability we have to avail ourselves of in order to appraise the end and the situational circumstances of an action in such a way that it is, in accordance with our intention, also a virtuous action that we carry out *hic et nunc;* that is the function of the only ethically relevant intellectual virtue, practical wisdom or *phronesis.*

Thus, *phronesis* has a position which is directed at exactly this structure of action. On the one hand, it refers to the end of the good life as the end of all ends, which it does not choose itself but which is determined by the ontological constitution of man and by the orientation (which has become a habit) toward the domain-specific concretizations of virtues. Because "determined" does not mean that the end is clearly seen in a situation-independent manner, *phronesis* concretizes the final end of the good life to an end of action appropriate to the situation. It does not carry out this concretization deductively, but from the perspective of the particular individual case, the other structural element of action. The end is codetermined by the choice of means appropriate in a situation. *Phronesis* leads one into the process of deciding or choosing (*prohairesis*), at the end of which stands the *action* which conveys the good life. *Phronesis* is not therefore an instrumental prudence that puts actors in a position to fix any ends whatever and realize them in efficient action. It becomes operative only on the condition that the actor already has an ethos, that is, that he has always been directed to ethical ends in his endeavors. It is only then that he perceives the relevant features in a situation and does not allow himself to be carried away by those irrational endeavors which are harmful to him and detract from his true ends. Thus Aristotle opens his study of *phronesis* with the following observation: "Now it is thought to be a mark of a man of practical wisdom to be able to deliberate well about what is good and expedient for himself, not in some particular respect, e.g. about what sorts of thing conduce to health or to strength, but about what sorts of thing conduce to the good life in general [*poia pros to eu zen holos*]."[19]

Correct deliberation and consideration relate to the changeable, the contingent, and to what in turn can be changed by action. We do not need to be concerned in a practically relevant manner about what cannot be otherwise. On the other hand, correct deliberation does not judge what is to be changed from the viewpoint of instrumental rationality. The latter is a question of practical skill, of *techne*, which we employ wherever it is a matter of changes in respect of a heteronomous end, that is, in the domain of production, of *poiesis.* Unlike the latter, *phronesis* is not a capability that can be employed for arbitrary ends or be methodically learned. Like ethical virtues, it must be habitualized to a basic orientation, become a component of the ethos.[20] Correct deliberation clarifies the end immanent in the good action, an end which can be brought to the action from the outside. Whoever can act with such correct deliberation acts from a basic orientation which allows him to prefer the appropriate over what is "pleasant and painful." The guiding deliberations do not employ definite knowledge, they employ opinions, because we can have knowledge of the changeable only in the form of opinions.

We encounter the changeable only in the particular case. It is solely the knowledge of the philosopher which relates to the eternal laws of cosmic being. In the particular case, *phronesis* concretizes the end of the good life and synthesizes it with the relevant features of the situation into what is the outcome of prudent deliberation: action. "Nor is practical wisdom concerned with universals only [*ton katholon*]—it must also recognize the particulars [*ta kat' hekasta*]; for it is practical, and practice is concerned with particulars."[21] It is only the correct appraisal of the circumstances [*Peristasen*] of a situation—an appraisal which appropriately modalizes the action—that leads to the correct opinion of what is good for us here and now. Aristotle himself draws parallels to prudence in economics and politics ("wisdom concerned with the city"), which cannot be reduced to a universal nomological knowledge but requires the correct appraisal of the concrete conditions of action. This basic orientation is acquired not by the application of knowledge but by experience (*empeiria*) in individual situations of action: " . . . practical wisdom is concerned with the ultimate particular, which is the object not of knowledge but of perception [*aisthesis*]"[22]—that is, it is concerned with the circumstances of the case which are relevant to me, and indeed, in terms of their individual features. That is why *phronesis* starts with a prudent deliberation on the various aspects of a situation. Various possibilities which could lead to a situation-appropriate, good action are tried out in the "searching" and "calculating"[23] phase. Aristotle characterizes correct (and not instrumental) deliberation as "excellence in deliberation [*euboulia*],"[24] which has four features: first, it is "that which tends to attain what is good [*he agathou*];"[25] second, it can be described in the manner of a practical syllogism, to which it contributes both the major and the minor premise (the end does not therefore justify the means); third, it takes place within an appropriate length of time and finds that which is right with regard to the individual circumstances; fourth, it comprises both the final end of the good life and the concrete particular end. Of course, *phronesis* does not consist solely in the cognitive element of correct deliberation. It is also normative and leads into the volitional act of deciding and carrying out this decision. It "issues commands, since its end is what ought to be done or not to be done."[26] The whole process of deliberation is aimed at the "particular," the action to be carried out here and now. Whoever grasps this directly can determine, from here, the universal end, and then refer this end back to the action once again.

We have thus gathered together the essential determinations of *phronesis*. Aristotle closes his presentation with the resolution of a dilemma, whereby he summarizes all the elements of *phronesis* once again. This dilemma consists in the fact that those who already have the correct action at their disposal, that is, are in possession of a virtuous character, are not really in need of *phronesis* anymore because they know anyway what is to be done, whereas, conversely, those who are still striving for a correct basic orientation, that is, are not yet in possession of it, cannot avail of *phronesis* at all.[27] If these assumptions were correct, *phronesis* could not come into play in either case.

Aristotle resolves the dilemma by again underscoring the character of ethics as being directed toward perfect movement. Ethics is to assist man in being able to fulfill the function specific to him, that of realizing himself. All the strangeness of classical ethics disappears when we understand this in an entirely noncontroversial way, namely, as a successful life, which of course presupposes that one has enough to eat and drink, and sufficient clothing, and which, over and above this, consists in fulfilling one's own nature. And "the function of man is achieved only in accordance with practical wisdom as well as with moral excellence; for excellence makes the aim right, and practical wisdom the things leading to it."[28] Because, from the outset, we do not find ourselves in a perfect state, we have to bring the material and the possibilities of our as yet unshaped nature into that form which befits us and corresponds to our talents, so that we can realize ourselves in every respect. Aristotle does not provide any material ends for this, but determines human nature according to the special faculty which enables it to consciously relate to itself: our capacity for language or reason. If we do what corresponds to our nature as beings endowed with language and reason, we will achieve happiness. Ethical virtues are domain-specific concretizations of this striving, ones which spring from the experiences we have had during the course of our lives in individual situations while in search of happiness. Ethical virtues are thus themselves a product of experience and are not statically given. Through them we become aware of the characteristics we have to develop in order to be able to lead a good life in various situations. Thus, they make sure that the end in a concrete situation is right. However, that we learn to strive for what is good for us in each particular case also presupposes that we know what is good for us under the given circumstances. We approach the perfection of ourselves only if we live virtuously by reason of a conscious and reflected decision, and not by chance. For this we need practical wisdom or *phronesis*, which indicates the right way to the end. But this capability is also a product of experience with ourselves in various situations. We can employ our capability to deliberate on means-ends relations against our nature and put it in the service of harmful endeavors. It does not become practical wisdom until it contributes to the perfection of our nature as beings endowed with language and reason, that is, not until it is directed to the ends determined by the virtues and specifies these ends in the particular case in such a way that the good life can be realized with appropriate means. Practical wisdom as well as ethical virtues are necessary so that we can bring our natural talents into a form which befits them; this is achieved by a process of habitualization that is guided by experience. Practical wisdom and ethical virtues are mutually dependent and thereby enable us to approach the perfect state. Thus Aristotle concludes "that it is not possible to be good in the strict sense without practical wisdom, nor practically wise without moral excellence."[29] The latter "implies"[30] practical wisdom, and both properties have to coalesce into a unity in the course of the process of habitualization, a process which transforms our unformed nature into a reflected, ethically refracted second nature. The dilemma is thus resolved by a genetic determination of the interplay between practical wisdom and ethical virtue.

If ethical virtues and practical wisdom can, only as a unity, make correct decisions possible in particular cases, then the question concerning the relation between justification and application becomes superfluous. General knowledge about what is good for us, which we acquire with ethical virtues, cannot be separated from the experiences we have had in concrete situations. It draws its validity from the fact that it has solidified into being the basic orientation and is given in this way. Ethics does nothing other than explicate what is implicit in this second nature, the ethos. In the concrete particular case, *phronesis,* which has also become part of the basic orientation, seeks out the appropriate means for a continuation of the good life, that is, of the context where what is good for us has always been fixed in its outlines. Thus, in every individual case, the same process is structurally repeated, the process which led to the development of the basic ethical orientation; it is simply a matter of a situation-specific realization. Conjoining ethical virtue and practical wisdom allows the valid to appear as the appropriate, and vice versa. "Tying ethics back to a particular, lived ethos"[31] and restricting practical reason to the task of determining what is appropriate in the particular case—both relate to one another in a complementary manner. It is the same context of basic orientations acquired through experience in which we both concretize our striving for the good life and specify our striving for the appropriate means in the particular case.

However, it has not yet been stated what kinds of contexts determine the orientation toward the end of the good life. At first glance, the ontological definition of human life as *logon echon* permits various possibilities. It could be a matter of basic individual orientations, which everyone acquires alone and applies in an unmistakable manner in every situation. This reading is conceivable, at least at those points where Aristotle speaks about the individual actor. On the other hand, Aristotle did not write an ethics for individual persons. This interpretation is merely evoked by the translation of *"logon echon"* as "reason." But the basic ontological determination of man is to be understood preferably as the capability to use language.[32] It is this capability which enables us to distance ourselves from immediate endeavors and to pursue the good life consciously. We are equipped with this capability as individuals; however, at the *locus classicus* in *Politics,* Aristotle adds to this the definition of man as a "political animal" (*zoon politikon*)[33]; " . . . the power of speech is intended to set forth [*semainein*] the expedient and inexpedient, and therefore likewise the just and the unjust. And it is a characteristic of man that he alone has any sense [*aisthesin echein*] of good and evil, of just and unjust, and the like, and the association [*koinonia*] of living beings who have this sense makes a family and a state [*oikian kai polin*]."[34] Through language, each individual relates to the association of living beings and thereby determines what a good life is for him and what is specifically good. Though the good life is an independent end which cannot be surpassed, it cannot be acquired or realized independently of other human beings; "for the complete good is thought to be self-sufficient.

Now by self-sufficient we do not mean that which is sufficient for a
man by himself, for one who lives a solitary life, but also for parents,
children, wife, and in general for his friends and fellow citizens,
since man is sociable by nature."[35] That is why the ends of the individual are identical with the ends of the polis, and the latter's
ends represent the greatest good which the individual can strive for.
Thus, the context in which the acquisition of ethical virtues takes
place, where the end of the good life unfolds, and where the particular concrete situation of action is determined according to its
relevant circumstances [*Peristasen*]—this context is the concrete
political community, the form of life of the polis. That is why, for
Aristotle, prudent politics and economics, tactful and judicious
dealings with one's fellow human beings, and prudently leading
one's life are simply different modifications of the one virtue—practical wisdom. Gadamer summarized succinctly the function of *phronesis* in the ethical context of a political form of life as that "which
does not propose any new ethics, but rather clarifies and concretizes
given normative contents."[37]

   If the Aristotelian conception of ethics as the appropriate realization of the good life in each particular case is enlarged by this
dimension, which is "political" in the wider, classical sense, then it
is acceptable to interpret it as a specifically "contextualist" ethics.
To act in a morally right way in a concrete situation then presupposes that the given communal forms of life and the established
practices are appropriately interpreted. *Phronesis* becomes this
ethics' key concept, a concept which describes the thematizing task
of concretizing normative contents, a task which takes its orientation from a situation's multifarious circumstances. It has to shoul-
der the two elements which are separate for a postconventional
ethics. The aspired end of the good life is in need of concretization in
a situation of action, the particular features of which have to be considered when choosing appropriate means. The selection of relevant
features depends on the end requiring concretization, while the
concretization of the end is in turn directed by the particular circumstances of the situation and the corresponding modalizations of
action. In this way, virtuous action guided by practical wisdom per-
petuates the ethos of a form of life in individual situations.

   However, Aristotelian ethics cannot be classified in a scheme of
moral development in such a simple manner, and the debate would
not be very productive if this classification were the only result.
How the contextualism of this ethics ought to be understood depends on the meaning ascribed to the situation-related orientation

toward the good life. A Hegelian and a Kantian interpretation can be distinguished from one another. While the first one (a) grasps ethics as a hermeneutical self-understanding about lived contexts in concrete situations, the second one (b) attempts to take into account the ethos-character of ethics by demonstrating that the orientation toward the good life is a result of the detached reflection of practical reason. They differ primarily in their position on the validity claim of given normative contents. Whoever interprets the latter politically, in the sense of a substantive ethical life [*substantielle Sittlichkeit*], will assign a different task to *phronesis* than the person who considers them, for their part, to be in need of legitimation (c).

(a) Aristotle characterized the ends of the polis as the highest ones because the conceptions of life of many individuals are condensed in them. For this reason, the good life can only be realized in a political community. Politics is thereby given a special, ethically motivated task. It has to establish the ends of the polis, and the corresponding means, in such a way that every member of this form of life is able to direct his action in accordance with the end of the good life. That is why the *Nicomachean Ethics* closes with the transition to politics.[38]

Joachim Ritter interpreted this transition as follows: "ethics" prepares the way for "politics" by tying it to the polis's lived practices and forms of life. Political action presupposes the highest sensitivity to the ethos of a form of life, and the science of this ethos can only show how it is composed and how it is concretized by prudent deliberation in situations, so that it can be perpetuated in the particular case. "As 'ethics,' practical philosophy is politics."[39] Ritter determines the ethical as "custom, mores, tradition, modes of right and proper conduct as virtue, but also the institutions supporting these, such as the household, the cult of the gods, associations of friendship, communities in wars, at festivals, and at funerals. Thus, without being directed to existing norms and values, 'what is right,' in which action is 'ethically' determined, is concretely conveyed through the 'lived' institutional lifeworld and in the traditional forms of speech and action established in this lifeworld. 'What is right' belongs to the 'ethos' and the 'nomos' of the polis, to the habits of the household."[40] When concrete actions, in the sense of praxis (not *poiesis*), relate to the good life, they simultaneously realize the ethos of the polis. The self-perfection of man through praxis is based neither on the principle of freedom, nor on "the individual who is for himself, but on him [as he is] in his life composed of institutions."[41]

In this context, Ritter refers to §151 of Hegel's *Philosophy of Right*, which allows him to characterize the relation between praxis and ethos in its terminology: "The concept of praxis accomplishes for Aristotle the task of conveying the free independence of individuals to a unity with the general."[42]

Corresponding to the movement of objective spirit, Ritter does not stop at the merely received ethos when determining ethics as politics; for the situation in which Aristotle develops his practical philosophy is characterized by a crisis in tradition as a result of the Sophist enlightenment. Yet Ritter, like Aristotle, determines the good as the highest end not independently of the ethos, but relative to it. Because we have to proceed from our own experiences, reflection on our natural strivings—a reflection conducted in praxis as purposive and situationally appropriate action—remains bound to the ethical institutions by which we were originally and naively formed. Practical philosophy conceptualizes this reflection and thereby provides the justification for what is ethically right. It does not distance itself from received institutions, but clarifies and interprets them for what they are, namely, the origin and end of human praxis as the perfection of life. It relates to a life that has become "the substance of ethical institutions" within a polis.[43]

Ritter characterizes the procedure for this ethics as the "hermeneutical method."[44] While he thereby wishes to describe the appropriate procedure for ethical and political theories which take their orientation from the criterion of the free self-realization of man as a rational being bound to institutions, Gadamer explicates the specifically moral sense of this procedure. For him, the hermeneutical method itself, which relates to a lived ethos, becomes practical philosophy.[45]

Hermeneutics is then no longer merely a method for ethics and politics; it itself enters into the subject matter of ethics. That is why Gadamer can identify *phronesis* with hermeneutics. The normative contents of a form of life, which are given in the ethos, are relevant not only to an ethical-political theory, but primarily to morally right action in situations. In the concrete particular case, what is important is to concretize the habitualized strivings for the good in order to realize it with the appropriate means while considering the relevant circumstances [*Peristasen*]. *Phronesis* is tailored precisely to this task. In it Gadamer finds the great analogy to the hermeneutical method, whereby the interpreter concretely ascertains his position within effective-historical consciousness when faced with the situational experience of a received text. He relies on Hegel only indirectly, but he explicitly employs the definition of hermeneutics as practical philosophy to oppose Kant and his "ethical formalism."[46] What is decisive is not "knowledge of the general," but the appropriate interpretation of the "demand present in the situation" where an ethical choice must be made.[47] We gain access to the demands of the situation only by proceeding from our own empirical, ethical-political conditionedness, and not from the self-determination of reason in an intelligible sphere. Gadamer dedramatizes the two-world doctrine by understanding Kant's idea of unconditional self-determination or freedom—which can only be formulated by demarcating it from the empirical world—as being itself a component of a hermeneutically describable ethical life. It belongs to the ethical being of man, which is determined by socialization and political laws. Self-determined reason comes into its own when the given normative contents of an ethical form of life are appropriately followed. It becomes *phronesis:* "His [Aristotle's] analysis of *'phronesis'* recognizes in ethical knowledge a mode of ethical being itself that, as such, cannot be detached from the entire concretization of what he calls ethos. Ethical knowledge recognizes what is to be done [*das Tunliche*], what a situation demands, and it recognizes this on the basis of a deliberation that relates the concrete situation to what is considered right and correct as such. This deliberation thus has the logical structure of an inference, one premise of which is universal knowledge about the right, and this is grasped in the concepts of ethical virtues."[48] This mediating achievement of *phronesis* dissolves the rigid contrastive relation between the intelligible and empirical world, the formal and material world, or between the "subjectivity of knowledge and the substantiality of being."[49] Though this achievement can be represented as a practical syllogism, it cannot be compared with the application of universal norms to particular cases. "Ethical knowledge does not perfect itself in general concepts of bravery, justice, etc., but in concrete application, which determines what is to be done here and now in the light of such knowledge."[50] Virtues, as determinations of the mean, are regarded merely as schematic-typical constructions which have to be re-constructed with the help of *phronesis* in each individual situation.

(b) In debate with Gadamer's attempt to develop an ethics following Aristotle's conception of *phronesis,* Tugendhat raised objections which were intended to show how a "modern moral philosopher who has been through Kant would have to try to appropriate Aristotle's thoughts on *phronesis.*"[51] Linking up with Gadamer's

critique of Kant, Tugendhat interprets the problem designated
"phronesis" as a genuine problem of application which poses itself
not in competition with, but as a supplement to, Kant's concentration on the problem of justifying actions and norms by a moral principle. To convince a Kantian philosopher of the significance of the
conception of *phronesis,* one would have to show "that the Aristotelian problem of application arises precisely if one proceeds from a
principle of impartiality, which is what the categorical imperative
is. One could try to show that what is impartial in each case cannot
simply be deduced from the principle, but requires a situation-
related, non-deductive faculty of judgment."[52] If one constructs an
ethics in this sense along two lines, the normative contents of a
form of life that are situationally thematized by *phronesis* can for
their part be examined in terms of their claims to justification,
claims which do not simply embody the substantive content of the
ethos, as with Ritter, but adhere to the modern, Kantian principle of impartiality. The fact that *phronesis*—as a faculty for the
situation-related appraisal of what is appropriate here and now—
presupposes for its part an "affective disposition" acquired through
socialization does not preclude that the standards of socialization
are themselves in need of justification.[53] In this way, Tugendhat reduces the value attributed to *phronesis* in all those theories of ethics which expect it to be able to carry two burdens simultaneously:
that of justifying the morally valid and that of appropriate application. In the context of this interpretation, the ethos loses the normative force attributed to it as the content of a form of life, a content
requiring situational interpretation: "Aristotle himself never characterized the given as being the standard. He did indeed raise a
claim to justification, but it was one that, in the final analysis, could
not work."[54] Just as the ethos for its part is in need of justification
in the light of the modern principle of impartiality, the determination of what is impartial in a situation must also be criticizable.

Tugendhat takes up the Aristotelian claim to the justification
of a teleological ontology once again. Of course, he does not refer to
it in order to find a replacement for the Kantian concept of justification by the moral principle, but rather to extend ethics by the dimension which Kant wanted to repel with this concept: the question
concerning the good life as the end to be aimed at by my will, an end
that also *includes* taking my orientation from a universalist moral
principle because this is in my own, clearly understood interest. It
is only by answering this question that each individual can acquire
those determinations of the will which Ritter and Gadamer want to

leave to the reflected, lived ethos. These determinations of the will then include the *motivation* to act morally in the first place— because it is good for my happiness. Of course, Tugendhat no longer poses this question within the framework of teleological ontology, but reinterprets it empirically: "We thus need a formal concept of mental health."[55] Here, the Kantian penetration of the Aristotelian conception also leads to the fact that, with this formal concept, no concrete desirable ends, like virtues, can be normatively determined anymore, only the empirical conditions which must be fulfilled if we want to choose and realize our own ends in a free and self-determined personal disposition.

Höffe attempted to combine Kantian and Aristotelian motifs in a similar way. For him, just as for Ritter, ethics as practical philosophy is a form of reflection of the ethos, which, however, is concerned not with the presentation of a substantive ethical life in the sense of Hegel's philosophy of right, but with a type of transcendental reconstruction of the greatest good as the rational standard for concrete ethical life: "the original synthesis of the a priori with the a posteriori of life's concrete reality."[56] As has already been seen in his explication of the Kantian concept of maxim, Höffe constructs his version of a conception of ethics oriented by Aristotle on two levels: as a principle of justification for legitimate ethical life, on the one hand, and as a procedure for the application and continuation of this ethical life in individual situations, on the other.

That is why ethics can refer to the ethos in an entirely noncontroversial manner which is still disburdened of validity claims: "In order to concern oneself with ethics in a promising way, one has to possess, in principle, not only the capability to know, one must also belong to a context of communication and interaction, more precisely, to that context, the polis, where it is a matter not of mere survival or material prosperity, but of the good and ethical life."[57] Belonging to an ethos is less a hermeneutical than a practical presupposition of ethics. One must already be practically at home in the ethical life, and have the corresponding experiences, in order to be able to allow oneself to be guided by philosophical reflection on morals. This has implications for the interpretation of *phronesis:* it is a form of prephilosophical knowledge which is expressly thematized and brought to consciousness only by ethics as practical philosophy. "While prephilosophical knowledge, prudence (*phronesis*), recognizes how meaningful action has to be concretely carried out in the personal, economic, and political spheres, its own essence as prudence and, come to that, the elements and principles of ethical action, are not transparent to it."[58] While prudence determines the appropriate means solely in the particular case, ethics thematizes the element that is simply given to prudence as an end. Virtues as concretizations of the highest end, which is not a means for any other end, are checked in respect of their rational justifiability for the rational human being, the *logon echon*. The ethos of concrete ethical life is separated from an ethical science of principles in a methodologically and intersubjectively controllable manner. Because ethics enables the individual to step out of the original strivings of his action consciously and with reflection and to strive for the end of the good life voluntarily and with knowledge of the concrete circumstances, it makes a critical distance possible "to himself, his factual action, and his factual ethos."[59] Ritter's concept of hermeneutical method is thereby supplemented by a second step in which the given ethical institutions are not only appropriately interpreted and clarified, but also checked in respect of their compatibility with the reflected ethical being of the actor as *logon echon*. For Höffe too, however, the introduction of justification claims as conditions of the possibility of a critique of ethical life remains tied to the immanence of ethical life: "The emancipatory force of Aristotelian ethics consists not in its objecting to this primary ethical life sedimented in the institutions of the polis, its objecting to an action within the framework of the ethos, but in negating the formal coercive character of the ethos. This ethics is liberating in the sense that, by virtue of reflection, existing laws, customs, and habits—as that which merely exists in reality—are dissolved, their connection to the happiness of those individually and socially affected is made transparent; and, as a result of this, a life in the ethos, hitherto somewhat naturally lived because unquestioned, is transformed into a life guided by one's own reason as well."[60] That is also why the formal freedom of the individual—who orients his action according to the end of the good life and who chooses the means appropriate in a particular case with the help of an ethically reflected (no longer naively prephilosophical) *phronesis*—is not abstracted by Höffe to a formal moral principle which, as a pure principle of justification, would be neutral vis-à-vis every concrete form of life. As to its contents, the science of principles remains a material science. For this reason, the subject matter of ethics is to be understood "as the genuine synthesis of an unconditional—ethical life—and a conditional—the circumstantial (sociocultural and individual) conditions; it is a culturally and situationally dependent ought."[61] Because the element of the unconditional remains immanent to concrete ethical life, Höffe does not draw the consequence of separating validity and appropriateness. The orientations that an ethics can give are always related to concrete contexts, a particular community, or a particular situation. That is why it cannot draw up an abstract catalogue of norms, but restricts itself to being a typological outline science [*Grundbiß-Wissenschaft*]. Supported by Aristotle's definitions of the concept of type, Höffe uses it to characterize that specific property of virtues which synthesizes validity and appropriateness. Virtues fall short of the criterion of cognitive completeness and merely trace the domain-specific outline of where the mean of right action is to be encountered in the individual situation.[62] "The Aristotelian concept of the 'mean for us' is thus to be interpreted as the universal form of concrete ethical forms, as the essence of ethical life as virtue, which, in the indeterminacy of the two things related, is open to the concretely different claim in changing situations, without having to fix the action dogmatically, on the one hand, or dissolve it relativistically and declare it arbitrary, on the other."[63] In this way, Höffe can link up with his interpretation of the Kantian concept of maxim. As it is the case there, the main topic of ethics as practical philosophy is neither the justification of a moral principle, nor the application of individual virtues or maxims with the help of *phronesis,* but the discovery, legitimation, and concretization of typologically describable outlines of good, ethical life in various spheres of an ethically and politically constituted community.

(c) All attempts to rehabilitate the contextualism of Aristotelian ethics against formalist positions in the Kantian tradition maintain a precarious relation to teleological ontology. One can read from their respective positions on the latter how contextualist theories of ethics deal with the problem which Aristotle could solve very easily: what a good life is and what is good for each individual follow from the ontological determinations of man.[64] Because the ontological *ens et bonum convertuntur* can no longer be easily accomplished after a long period of empiricist and rationalist critique, all reconstructions endeavor to maintain the validity claim of the human-ethical context as the *definiens* of the *zoon politikon logon echon,* without paying the price of an ontology operating with unchangeable determinations of being. It is only in this way that they can rescue the original dovetailing of validity and appropriateness, one which attributes a special significance to *phronesis.* Efforts are then directed toward an ethical-political theory of the reflexive appropriation and conservation of ethical traditions (Ritter); toward a hermeneutical theory of the appropriate clarification and situation-specific concretization of tradition, which has its validity in effective-historical consciousness (Gadamer); toward an empiricist reinterpretation of ontology, which does however assimilate the radical justification claim of a modern moral principle (Tugendhat); and toward a rationalist anthropology, which, on the basis of the fundamental structure of human praxis, simultaneously justifies the conservation, continuation, and immanent critique of ethical relations in the form of an outline science of appropriate principles (Höffe). Despite all the important modifications and those that lead to significant differences in the details, none of these attempts moves beyond the given validity of concrete ethical life. The only exception is Tugendhat's reconstruction, which, though filtered through Kant's moral philosophy, nevertheless makes the validity claim of normative judgments dependent on a universalist principle of justification which must adapt to a formal empirical theory of the good life.

Nonetheless, Tugendhat's proposal alone points to the only alternative available if one wants to take seriously the problem associated with the concept of *phronesis* without wishing to forgo universalist justification claims. In order to find out what is impartial in a concrete situation, we have to assume that there is a separate, application-related faculty that differs from the moral principle, which is specialized in moral justifications. Of course, this faculty is no longer related to a particular ethical context, within whose horizons it is trained and employed; rather, it is related to the idea of impartiality itself.[65]

With this presupposition, the practical reason of *phronesis* itself is adapted to a universalist claim and detached from the particular validity claim of ethical contexts. As a result, the circumstantial [*peristatisch*] determinations of a situation—the temporal, final, local, personal, quantitative, and similar modalizations of an action—become relevant features of the situation and have to be fully considered when forming an appropriate norm hypothesis. It is only then that the particular validity of an ethical context is dissolved, a context within which the task of *phronesis* merely consists in a concretizing interpretation of normative contents which are already valid and appropriate.

In terms of this aspect, *phronesis* can be reconstructed as a method for the appropriate formation of hypotheses. In a "bare outline . . . of a neo-Aristotelian theory of practical reason,"[66] David Wiggins attempts to grasp the concept of *phronesis* as a situation-specific procedure of discovery. Entirely in Aristotle's sense, however, he relates this procedure not to impartial moral judgments, but to the idea of the good life. Having practical wisdom then means "to be able to select from the infinite number of features of a situation those features that bear upon the notion or ideal of existence which is his [i.e., he who has practical wisdom] standing aim to make real. This conception of human life results in various evaluations of all kinds of things, in various sorts of cares and concerns, and in various projects."[67] In every situation, all those features are relevant which follow from the various viewpoints constituting my conception of a good life. In order to consider all "the relevant features of the situation,"[68] the capacity, presupposed by Aristotle, to perceive the particular is required: *aisthesis*, which is aimed directly at the particular, and this can be represented as the minor premise of the practical syllogism.[69] The various viewpoints cannot however be brought into a consistent system—no theory "can treat the concerns which an agent brings to any situation as forming a closed, complete, consistent system"; rather, only the varying weight of different aspects can be justified in a situation.[70] Nevertheless, Wiggins does introduce a criterion which is directed toward completeness when considering all the relevant features: "The man of highest practical wisdom is the man who brings to bear upon a situation the greatest number of genuinely pertinent concerns and genuinely relevant considerations commensurate with the importance of the deliberative context."[71] The more particular features we consider, the more convincing is the justification for the weight attributed to a certain viewpoint which we regard to be the appropriate one in this situation. According to Wiggins, this is shown by the fact that the practical syllogism is compelling in that a normative viewpoint belonging to our conception of a good life is related to the concrete situation. That is why, in addition to the criterion of completeness, Wiggins introduces a kind of criterion of adequacy: "the larger the set of considerations that issue in the singling out of the said feature, the more compelling the syllogism. But there are no formal criteria by which to compare the claims of competing syllogisms. Inasmuch as the syllogism arises in a determinate context, the major premise is evaluated not for its unconditional acceptability, nor for embracing more considerations than its rivals, but for its adequacy to the situation. It will be adequate for the situation if and only if circumstances that could restrict or qualify it and defeat its applicability at a given juncture do not in the practical context of this syllogism obtain."[72] The evaluation of the norm hypothesis, which can be represented as the major premise of the practical syllogism, is determined not by criteria of validity, but by its appropriateness in relation to a situation which is characterized by the problem of how I can realize a good life here and now. Whether the evaluation is appropriate or not depends on there not being any relevant situation feature which could render the proposed hypothesis inapplicable. It is the same criterion of "fit a situation" which we already observed in the discussion on contextual relativism.[73] As it is the case there, Wiggins' interpretation of Aristotle also endorses a plurality of various possible practical syllogisms which are "applicable" in a concrete situation.

Thus, for Wiggins, completeness and appropriateness do not go beyond the form of representing a practical syllogism whose major premise can be enlarged to the conception of the good life which the actor follows in each case. It is only when this conception is devalued to one viewpoint among other ones, which also have to be considered when forming an impartial judgment, that the meaning of "completeness" and "appropriateness" changes. Virtues are then no longer the presuppositions of a man's character which have to be fulfilled in order for a life in a particular community to be successful; rather, they are simply normative viewpoints that are fed into an appropriate norm hypothesis whose validity claim must be acceptable to all those affected.

2. Appropriate Understanding: Hermeneutics

In moral conflict situations, we have to interpret our self-understanding and our understanding of the world in order to discover what is right—we became acquainted with this in different variations in Wellmer and Aristotle as a thesis of moral philosophy. For Gadamer, however, the discussion about morally right action does not take priority; rather, it is taken by the ontological determination of finite modern man interpreting himself within the horizons of effective-historical consciousness. From *this*, Gadamer draws consequences for moral philosophy. Understanding [*das Verstehen*] must submit to the normative claim of tradition by clarifying and interpreting in a situation-appropriate manner. In this way, the received context not only becomes the standpoint for interpretation in situations, it also acquires a validity claim sui generis.

Gadamer thereby expects deliberations on appropriateness to be able to fulfill the task of justifying validity claims and thus restricts them to the horizons traced out by the event of tradition [*Überlieferungsgeschehen*]. Along with Heidegger, he does indeed take seriously the experience of radical historicism and of the resulting devaluation of everything which was originally normatively binding. However, in the transition from history to historicality, traditions again acquire their own normative force. Because we have to understand these in order to be able to understand ourselves in the particular situation, the claim of traditions becomes an element originally belonging to and constitutive of our ontological make-up. The validity of meaning is assimilated to normative validity: "We are able to open ourselves to the superior claim the text makes and, through understanding, correspond to the meaning with which it addresses us."[74] In this perspective, the "application" of texts to the situation of the interpreter—an application guided by understanding—and the application of ethical norms to the situation of action can no longer be distinguished from one another. That is why, for Gadamer, "the problem of method [acquires] a moral relevance."[75] The requirement that all the features of the situation be considered is explicated as a method for the gradual revision of one's own prejudices within their historical horizons; and this requirement is absorbed by the concrete demands emanating from the situation itself. Understanding application is historical understanding—with this original variation of the Heideggerian theme of the historicality of being [*Dasein*], Gadamer continues the existential-ontological tradition in a self-chosen direction: "The general structure of understanding acquires its concrete form in historical understanding, in that the commitments of custom and tradition and the corresponding potentialities of one's own future become effective in understanding itself."[76] The circle of understanding is thus of relevance to our topic: it becomes—in the original sense of the word—a "paradigm" for appropriateness argumentation.

In what follows, I shall be concerned with limiting this paradigmatic function by attempting to show that, with the proposal to differentiate impartial justification and application, the advantages of the hermeneutical procedure can be preserved without having to accept the ethical obligations attached to it. *What* appears to us to be the situation's concrete demand is thematized in application discourses, where it is required that all relevant features be taken into consideration, whereas its property as a *"demand"* needs to be universally justified in justification discourses.

Art and history are the exemplary experiences on the basis of which Gadamer reconstructs the basic hermeneutical experience, and he elevates them to the model of a theory of the human sciences, in which tradition "in its truth comes to speech. . . . [and in this truth] one must try to share."[77] That is why, in terms of method, the human sciences do not stand at a distance to an isolated object, but participate in the event through the process of understanding—the event which tradition has always been. For this reason, understanding and interpretation are to be comprehended as "the further elaboration of an event coming from far away."[78] The human sciences thus simply assimilate the basic ontological determination of our finite and temporal existence. It is only the event of tradition that we can clarify, the event in which we have always been and which we perpetuate in every situation.

However, it is not entirely plausible how Gadamer can be so certain about the assumption of a constantly forming and effective common tradition. Of course, this certainty does not mean that we have to submit ourselves to an unquestioningly accepted tradition. Yet, we have to criticize our prejudices, which are caught in the present, by clarifying their hidden historical references and not by argumentatively redeeming validity claims. But tradition can no longer offer argumentative support of this kind. The finiteness and limitedness which Gadamer establishes for our understanding of the event of tradition apply not only to one, but to an immeasurable number of traditions. A commonness in traditions can no longer be established even within the old European humanist tradition, to which Gadamer refers. The compatibility of a plurality of different traditions in a specific instance depends on the reversibility of standpoints and not on being inserted into an event of tradition. For this reason, traditions are now only suitable as interpretative viewpoints, which we have to consider fully and weigh against one another in situations before checking, in a separate discourse, the validity of what we recognize as being right.

Within the stock of tradition, which he assumes to be secure and whose validity is given at the outset, Gadamer can, in accordance with the model of Aristotelian *phronesis,* elevate the situation-appropriate clarification of normative contents to the status of a principle of method—for all his aversion to the assimilation of truth and method. The demand for an understanding which gradually expands the original horizons of preunderstanding and approaches the ideal of a fusion of the original horizon with the ever-present received one—this demand does not issue from the idea of an impartial consideration of all the particular circumstances. What is appropriate is always that which is valid within the received context. Validity is measured according to degrees of belonging [*Zugehörigkeit*] to a specific context which is a common form of life. For this reason, Gadamer can refer to the rhetorical-dialectical virtues of tact, good taste, communal sense, and prudence—virtues through which the old European tradition absorbed Aristotle's concept of *phronesis*. "By 'tact' we understand a particular sensitivity and sensitiveness to situations, and how to behave in them, for which we cannot find any knowledge from general principles."[79] The generality in which the "viewpoints of possible others"[80] are present is the generality of an intersubjectively shared event of tradition. The sense of what is right establishes community. In the mot juste we encounter what is normatively right. Following this rhetorical tradition, Gadamer describes common sense [*Gemeinsinn*] not in terms of its formal structure, that structure oriented to the idea of generalizability, but in terms of the binding character of its contents: " . . . *sensus communis* is not primarily a formal capacity, an intellectual faculty that has to be used but already embraces a paragon of judgments and judgmental criteria that determine its contents."[81] The binding character of these criteria determines the moral motif of judgment: "Judgment is not so much a faculty as a demand that has to be made of all. Everyone has enough 'sense of the common' [*gemeinen Sinn*], i.e. judgment, that he can be expected to show a 'sense of the community' [*Gemeinsinn*], genuine moral and civic solidarity, but that means judgment of right and wrong, and a concern for the 'common good.' . . . The *sensus communis* is an element of social and moral being."[82] Of course, Gadamer sees quite clearly that Kant separated precisely this moral motif from the concept of judgment and explicated it in the form of a moral principle that, for morally justified norms and modes of action, requires a validity independent of an existing community and of the situational appropriateness of its judgments. However, the strict objectivity of the moral law for all rational beings, an objectivity reified by Kant to the two-world doctrine, leads to the consequence criticized by Gadamer that the judgment on appropriateness loses its ethical claim and is "subjectivized" to a judgment of taste, and the person judging can only ask of others that they simply approve it.[83] What Gadamer does not see with his critique is the distinction between justification and application, which was necessitated by Kant's separation. It is justification which demands strict generality in the sense of validity for everyone and cannot therefore be responsible for determining what is appropriate in the particular case. Conversely, the determination of what is appropriate loses its inherent reference to validity as a result of this distinction. Solidarity with individual differences must therefore come from a different source than the fusion of validity and appropriateness in a concrete communal context. With the idea of impartially considering all the particular features, solidarity acquires a basis independent of justification. It is only in this way that it becomes open to *all* differences and not only to those which can be discovered within a common context.

Instead of this, Gadamer follows the theme of Kant's *Critique of Judgment,* its determination of the concept of genius, and Romanticism's reception of this concept up to Dilthey's concept of experience. According to Gadamer, in this movement, the subjectivization of de-moralized aesthetic judgment is brought to a close in the abstraction of "aesthetic differentiation" [*ästhetische Unterscheidung*],[84] which posits the work of art as being autonomous. Opposing this, Gadamer reconstructs the ontology of the work of art, whereby the reference to the interpreting observer is constitutive of this. The "being [*Sein*] of the work of art" cannot be separated from "the 'contingency' of the conditions of access" of all those involved in the process of production, reproduction, and reception.[85] Understanding the work of art is thus simply an exemplary case of understanding oneself from the standpoint of finiteness, as is overwhelmingly clear in the experience of tragedy. "It is never simply a strange world of magic, of intoxication, of dream to which the player, sculptor or viewer is swept away, but it is always his own world to which he comes to belong more fully by recognizing himself more profoundly in it. There remains a continuity of meaning which links the work of art with the world of real existence and from which even the alienated consciousness of a cultured society never quite detaches itself."[86]

Aesthetic experience from the standpoint of finiteness also means, however, that the process of understanding can never be concluded because we can never become totally transparent to ourselves. The historicality of being [*Dasein*] has "always already" obtained, that is, primarily and never to be outstripped. Therefore, hermeneutics does not offer any method guaranteeing objectivity. With this argument, Gadamer criticizes the other two foundations in the history of the theory of understanding which are used by him to rehabilitate this concept: Schleiermacher's romantic hermeneutics with its claim to making possible the congenial understanding of what is strange in the biographical development of the thou, and historicism with its claim to being able to understand the epochs of universal history as objectivations of life, that is to say, to understand them from their own perspectives, but nevertheless fully and comprehensively, at least in principle. Both predecessors of hermeneutical consciousness are casualties of the same misunderstanding, namely, that though they recognize their particular subject matter—the other and history—in its individuality, they do not reflect on the finiteness of their own understanding. It was not until historicism was applied to itself that the standpoint of finiteness was fully revealed. Thus, with his thesis that life interprets itself in history, Dilthey still follows the romantic model of congeniality, despite all criticism of it. Against this model, Gadamer directs the question: "But if life is the inexhaustible, creative reality that Dilthey conceives, then must not the constant development of the meaningful context of history exclude any knowledge attaining to objectivity?"[87] Gadamer carries out this transition with Husserl and Heidegger. Though the relativity and historicality of experience is uncovered by Husserl's concept of the lifeworld as the presupposition of scientific objectivity, it is nevertheless still tied to the structures of consciousness. It is Heidegger who dissolves this connection in the ontology of temporality: "What being is was to be determined from within the horizon of time."[88] Thus, Gadamer can take stock of his debates with aesthetic consciousness, romantic hermeneutics, and historicism. The historical relativity of understanding is unfolded in the sense of the *genitivus objectivus* and *subjectivus,* namely as a procedure that, in the relativity of traditions, experiences its own "belonging" [*Zugehörigkeit*] to these traditions. Preunderstanding is not only an extrascientific presupposition of motivation in Max Weber's sense, but is constitutive of experience itself:

> "that we study history only insofar as we are ourselves 'historical' means that the historicality of human being [*Dasein*] in its entire movement of awaiting and forgetting is the condition of our being able to represent the past. What appeared first to be simply a barrier that cut across the traditional concept of science and method, or a subjective condition of access to historical knowledge, now becomes the centre of a fundamental enquiry. Belonging is not a condition of the original meaning of historical interest because the choice of theme and enquiry is subject to extra-scientific, subjective motivations (. . .), but because belonging to traditions is as original and essential a part of the historical finiteness of being [*Dasein*] as is the latter's projectedness towards future possibilities of itself."[89]

Here Gadamer brings about the transition from existential analysis to the recognition of the normative claim of tradition. By means of this detour, insight into the de-normativizing force of modernity and the recognition of the standpoint of finiteness lead back to Aristotle. The circle of understanding serves only to unfold methodologically our original belonging to the cultural circumstances in which we grow up and which shape our self-understanding and our understanding of the world; and this, without us ever being able to rise to questioning the validity of tradition or burst through the horizons traced by the circle of understanding in every situation anew. The idea of rational, impartial justification itself proves to be spellbound in this circle, which it apparently can only break at the cost of self-delusion. "In fact history does not belong to us, but we belong to it. Long before we understand ourselves through the process of self-examination, we understand ourselves in a self-evident way in the family, society and state in which we live."[90] Because the circle of understanding is not a methodological, but an ontological one, we can orient ourselves in situations only by participating in the event of tradition, within which we have always oriented ourselves from the outset.

The ontologically justified assimilation of appropriateness and validity is based on a peculiar confusion of the reciprocal aspect of reaching understanding [*Verständigung*] about something and the applicative aspect of an application of something, and this confusion finds expression in the concept of a fusion of horizons. It is only in this way that Gadamer can identify understanding and application and elevate the Aristotelian concept of *phronesis* to the status of a paradigm of hermeneutics.

Again and again, Gadamer paraphrases the presupposition of understanding a text as the willingness "to allow it to tell us something."[91] Historical consciousness refers to "the historically other."[92] He describes this process according to the model of putting oneself in the situation and horizons of the other. In this fictitious dialogical situation, we are concerned with "finding the right question" with which we can revise our own prejudices in the light of the "thing" [*Sache*] pertaining to the other. Though there can never be a complete, mutual transparency, as is claimed in romantic hermeneutics, there is nonetheless an "anticipation of completion"[93] by means of which we attribute the unity of a meaning to the other; and there is also the ideal of the "fusion"[94] of one's own horizons with those of another at a higher level of communality; it is in this ideal that "effective-historical consciousness" is constituted.

Gadamer also describes this process as "application" in the sense of *phronesis.*[95]

Critics have repeatedly drawn attention to this tacit connection between understanding a text and communication. This illegitimate connection is important for us because it leads to the core of the assimilation of questions of justification and those of application. In our systematic interpretation of the moral principle (U), we related the principle of justification to the universal-reciprocal sense of impartiality and the principle of application to its applicative sense. Viewed from this perspective, Gadamer interprets questions of justification, which belong in the sphere of reciprocity, as questions of application. Now, it has been shown that the application of normative contents to a situation also has a dialogical structure because it has to consider all the features of a situation. But we encounter the other in situations of application in a sense that is different from the situation of justification, namely, as "viewpoints of possible others,"[96] as Gadamer himself says, following the topos tradition rehabilitated by Vico and alluding to Adam Smith. In that the other appears to us as a "viewpoint," we adopt an attitude toward him which differs structurally from the attitude we take when he appears to us in his role as an addressee of validity claims. In the performative attitude in which another demands of me that I recognize something as being valid, we have to presuppose a reversibility of standpoints in principle. In this respect, and only in this respect, we are identical. It is a different matter in application discourses: here I encounter the other in the substantive difference of his interpretation of needs, which I must be able to bring into agreement with my interpretation. Thus, in concrete situations, I have to put myself in the place of the other and compare his interpretation of needs under the concrete circumstances with my own in order perhaps to change mine or his, or weigh one against the other. I apply my interpretation of needs as a norm hypothesis to the particular situation and must expand my interpretation of the situation by (all) those viewpoints which ensue from the need interpretation of the concrete other. It is exactly this distinction which is included when Gadamer, in drawing the parallel between hermeneutical and interpersonal experience, ascertains that "[o]penness to the other . . . includes the acknowledgment that I must let something be brought to bear on me, even though there may be no one who brings something to bear on me."[97] In situations of application in which the other is only a "viewpoint," it is a matter not of the other *bringing* something to bear on me, but of my considering the different viewpoints or relevant features of the situation, that is, of my *letting* these be brought to bear on me (or my situational need interpretation). This is independent of the other's role which he takes toward me with a performative attitude in that he demands of me that I recognize a validity claim. I am obligated to consider all the features of the situation for another reason: because the idea of impartiality obligates me to take the different circumstances, indeed (virtually) all of them, into account. Gadamer describes this process precisely: "Reaching an understanding in conversation presupposes that both partners are ready for it and are trying to let what is alien and opposed to them be brought to bear on them. If this happens mutually, and each of the partners, while simultaneously holding on to his own arguments, weighs the counter-arguments, it is finally possible to achieve, in an imperceptible and non-arbitrary interchange of viewpoints (we call this an exchange of views), a common language and a common statement."[98] Here too, however, one must pay heed to the fact that language and statement, reaching understanding and understanding, are not congruent. The commonness of the statement depends on the appropriateness of the normative content to the particular situation, whereas the commonness of language consists in the ideal conditions of reaching understanding which are assumed to be reciprocally fulfilled. But Gadamer brings both together, so that "language" and "thing" [*Sache*] become interchangeable.[99] For this reason, he can locate the element of normatively binding commonness in understanding's appropriateness to the thing, an element which can only be the result of a justification discourse. "To understand what a person says is, as we saw, to agree about the thing, not to put oneself in the place of another and relive his experiences. We emphasised that the experience of meaning which takes place in understanding always includes application."[100] Gadamer radicalizes this assimilation still more by taking the Aristotelian concept of *phronesis* as the paradigm for explicating hermeneutical experience and by attributing exemplary significance to legal hermeneutics.[101]

The implications of this assimilation are shown in Gadamer's interpretation of *phronesis*. Two elements come to the fore: the actor's tie to given ethical knowledge, the ethos, and the model of *epieikeia* (equity) for the application of legal norms. In both cases, what is designated by *phronesis* is the faculty for appropriately articulating in a situation the already given normative ties to the community. Virtues, and what Aristotle designates as natural law and the "nature of the thing," are simply types or schemes which trace out, as yet indeterminately, in what direction and manner the good is to be encountered in concrete action. Actually discovering what is right is however assigned to *phronesis*. It depends on the concrete situation. Virtues as well as deliberations on justice, which are to be conducted in terms of the nature of the thing when the law is to be corrected, form a part of the concrete case, where it is only possible for us to determine what is right from the perspective of the basic, reflected orientation of our characters.

Phronesis is thus the embodiment of the method by which what is normatively valid and what is appropriate in a situation are brought into correspondence with one another. Here, the certainty of the event of tradition simply assumed by Gadamer proves to be especially problematic. The question is: What becomes of *phronesis* when the ethos, to which it is constitutively related, loses its unquestioned validity? "The problem for us today, the chief characteristic of our hermeneutical situation, is that we are in a state of great confusion and uncertainty (some might even say chaos) about what norms or 'universals' ought to govern our practical lives. Gadamer realizes—but I do not think he squarely faces the issues that it raises—that we are living in a time when the very conditions required for the exercise of *phronesis*—the shared acceptance and stability of universal principles and laws—are themselves threatened (or do not exist)."[102] If there is no longer unquestioned validity which claims to be already appropriate, then the validity of a norm for every individual without ties, as well as the appropriateness of a norm in a situation must first be established. The moral sense of *phronesis* is then divided into the universal-reciprocal and the applicative sense of impartiality. The task of *phronesis* thus changes. When Gadamer describes the task of the person who possesses practical wisdom as having to be able to "see in the concrete situation what is asked of [him]," or to see "the concrete demands that the situation makes,"[103] then this is to be understood, after the loss of the ethos, in a sense that is disburdened of questions of validity. In order to fulfill the task described thus, we have to consider all the features of the situation appropriately. This includes prudent weighing of different interpretations as a precondition for choosing an appropriate norm. These elements no longer follow from the tacit reference to a valid tradition, as in the Aristotelian concept of *phronesis*, but from the idea of impartiality itself, to which the "demands" as well as their belonging to a "situation" are subject. The moral relevance of the hermeneutical method is cut back to giving effect to the sense of impartiality in application. Prejudice, which Gadamer rehabilitated for this method against the Enlightenment, loses its validity claim and becomes an element of constructive hypothesis formation. "Actually 'prejudice' means a judgment that is given before all the elements that substantively determine a situation have been finally examined."[104] What all the elements that determine a situation are can be discovered only if the application of our prejudices is guided by the criteria of completeness and appropriateness, which guarantee impartiality. In terms of this aspect, recognizing tradition, prejudice, authority, and ethical life means nothing other than recognizing the differences of possible interpretations in a concrete situation. It is only here that ethical knowledge is relevant. It can no longer justify its validity from within itself, but only in justification discourses.

For this reason, the critique of the assimilation of justification and application should not however lead in the opposite direction, namely, to a curtailing of the problem of application for its part. Böhler drew attention above all to the hermeneutical difference between the interpretation of received texts and the interpretation of authoritatively given norms.

> "The interpretation of institutional texts, whose validity is presupposed in the community, is assigned the task of bridging the differences between the text and the particularly given situation in such a way that the institutional texts have a current bearing on the orientation of action, that is to say, that they are applied to the present situation of the interpreter. This task of thematizing a binding practical meaning, of appropriating and applying this meaning, is reflected in and methodologically accomplished by *dogmatic hermeneutics,* which was developed by Jewish and Christian theology as well as by jurisprudence, and whose social-philosophical predecessor may be considered to be the Aristotelian doctrine of *phronesis.*"[105]

This description is only true of a conventional system of norms in which the "social system's morality" (Kohlberg) forms the final background for legitimation, a background originally fused with appropriateness. This background can be supported institutionally by authorities, so that the system of norms appears as if its appropriate validity were also authoritatively given for *internal* reasons. At the postconventional level, however, the element of authoritative givenness loses its function for the application of norms and, as explicit institutionalization, withdraws to a different level behind the validity requiring justification and the impartial application. Under these conditions, the restrictive dialogical situation described by Böhler cannot be true for a "dogmatic" application either, insofar as a claim to validity is also raised for the institutionalization itself. "For the institutional interpreter and/or actor who takes his orientation from such an [institutional] text, there only remains the task of availing himself of the interpretative latitude felicitously by means of a prudent appraisal and by reflection on the means, and while doing justice to the situation—such that the interpretation can be accepted as being correct in the sense of the text orienting action and regarded as being suitable to the situation of action."[106] This presupposition is true only if it is a problem of the semantically consistent application of a previously chosen text (a norm) to a certain set of situation features. What Böhler has in view here is the problem of application in the narrow sense, which also encompasses the reciprocal constitution of norm and concrete case, inasmuch as the semantic extension of a norm hypothesis is affected. The problem of application we are concerned with at the postconventional level is however characterized by the fact that we have lost the certainty of given, valid, and appropriate norms. What we are looking for is "guidance in the presence of conflict and equivocation,"[107] or in Bernstein's words, we want to find out "what we are to do in a situation in which there is confusion or conflict about which norms or universals are appropriate, or how we are to evaluate a situation in which we question the validity of such norms."[108] This, no more than Wellmer's analogous argument already mentioned above, is not to deny that there is an institutional restriction to free application. However, this restriction has nothing to do with application itself and cannot, above all, redress the loss of certainty in valid normative orientations.

Part Three

Appropriateness Argumentation in Morality

The discussion so far has produced primarily two results. On the presuppositions of a universalist moral principle like the principle of universalization (U), the idea of impartiality is divided into a situation-independent justification discourse and an application discourse which takes all the features of a situation into consideration. For reasons following from the development of moral consciousness, this separation proved to be unavoidable because, in the transition from the conventional to the postconventional level, the dovetailing of the validity and the appropriateness of norms within a particular context of common perspectives can no longer be maintained. Validity which relates to the universal-reciprocal change of perspectives cannot give a guarantee anymore that the valid norm is appropriate in the particular case. In this way, application becomes "free" in the sense that it has to take all the contexts into consideration which are relevant in a situation. An applicative sense of the idea of impartiality thus assumes a position alongside the universal-reciprocal sense, and we characterize the appropriate consideration of all the particular features of a situation by this applicative sense.

Impartiality in the application of norms is thus judged according to a criterion different from the one used for impartial justification, even though both belong to practical reason. What remains to be considered is how these criteria are to be exactly described. The provisional characterizations given so far do not admit of precise conclusions: As relevant viewpoints of a situation, we designated all possible aspects of a lifeworld which do not have previously fixed validity. In order to be able to claim appropriateness, it must be possible to relate these viewpoints to the situation coherently. A norm hypothesis can be designated as being appropriate only if it is compatible with all the other normative aspects of the situation. As long as this predicate is not attributed to it, it is to be regarded as one viewpoint among other ones, whose interrelation has to be appraised with respect to the situation.

A typical problem on the basis of which the relation between one-sided and appropriate norm application is frequently discussed is the conflict of norms in a situation. This problem is instructive for our purposes because the principle of impartial application systematically requires that a conflict of norms be produced in concrete situations.[1] If all the aspects of a situation are to be considered, then this leads necessarily to a conflict of norms because all the aspects can first be relevant only in different respects. The resolution of the conflict depends on there being rules which establish a kind of *context of consideration* between conflicting norms. Such rules are usually discussed under the title of "weighing," but rules of weighing are not the only ones which make a relation between conflicting norms possible. However, the problem of constructing appropriate norm hypotheses is in itself not solved by reconstructing these rules as long as criteria are not specified according to which the relative weight of a norm placed in the weighing procedure can be judged. The theory of argumentation does not lead us any further on this point.

In what follows I shall attempt to approach the task of describing appropriateness argumentation in a number of steps. I first wish to discuss the various proposals for describing the problem of a conflict of norms. Here, it is primarily a matter of distinguishing between norms which have a *prima facie* character and definitive or absolute norms. Because this distinction is connected to the problem of determining different classes of norms or two different kinds of validity, I shall adopt a proposal from Searle to distinguish instead between an obligation under unchanging circumstances ("other things being equal") and the normative proposition that, considering all the circumstances ("all things considered"), one ought to do something. This proposal is important for us because it justifies the distinction on the basis of how we conduct a conversation about reasons for acting, and not on the basis of a specific concept of a norm or of an analysis of the meaning of ought. Following Searle, I shall therefore propose regarding norms which are valid under unchanging circumstances as the possible outcome of a justification discourse, whereas in application discourses it is a matter of norms that are appropriate, considering all the circumstances. I would like to consolidate this proposal by discussing Alexy's attempt to differentiate between principles and rules, and I also wish to demarcate it from two alternative models suggested by Hare and Tugendhat.

The distinction between the attributes "under unchanging circumstances" and "considering all the circumstances" provides us with a first indication of what lines of argumentation play a role in appropriateness argumentation. If one relates both attributes to each other, some very simple lines of argumentation become evident. The first one presupposes a claim to equality which was necessary in justification discourses in order to abstract from the differences in possible application situations and which can now be used as a starting point for critique. Appropriateness argumentation regularly begins by pointing out that the unchanging circumstances presupposed by the originally applicable norm are not present in this concrete situation *S1*. However, pointing to the inequality or differences of the other features assumed by the norm to be unchanging can become an argument only on the strength of the presupposition that an appropriate norm has to consider all the relevant circumstances of a situation. Of course, the relevance of a different feature can only be shown in the succeeding step in argumentation, where it is related to another norm which can also be applied to the situation. If the application of the remaining norms leads to moral judgments which exclude one another in this situation, the problem of a conflict of norms arises.

For this reason I shall take up Alexy's proposal of resolving a conflict of principles on the basis of a conflict axiom [*Kollisionsgesetz*] which makes possible the formation of a deliberative, case-specific principle of preference. Weighing procedures are an example of how a complete context of consideration can be established between all the normatively relevant features in a situation. In the process, however, there emerges the problem that weighing is dependent on criteria according to which the relative weight of norms interconnected in a complex relation can be judged.

1

The Problem of a Conflict of Norms: *Prima Facie* and Definitive Norms

The distinction between norms which prescribe, only on the basis of a general assumption, that something be done and norms which prescribe absolutely or definitively that something be done is a topic frequently discussed in moral philosophy. With its help, one attempts to solve a problem which typically appears when it is tacitly a matter of appropriateness argumentation: the conflict of valid norms. A conflict of norms exists when at least "two norms, each independently applied, lead to results incompatible with one another, viz., to two contradictory concrete . . . moral judgments."[2] The standard example is the case of *X*, who promised Smith to attend his party; meanwhile, however, *X* hears that his best friend, Jones, is seriously ill and needs his help. If *X* decides to meet his obligations as a friend and his obligation to help Jones, he breaks the promise given to Smith. Since the promise and the duty to keep promises have not simply become invalid or null and void as a result, it has been attempted to characterize the recessive norm as a *prima facie* obligation, which is to be distinguished from a definitive obligation. This example does of course seem somewhat fatuous since the solution is obvious. A definitive norm, such as the following one, can be formed: "In situations of the type *S1*, priority is to be given to the duty to help over the duty to keep promises." The triviality of the example should not however delude us about the fact that, with this solution, it has not been clarified how the validity character of originally applicable norms is to be determined in relation to the definitive norm, nor in what way we can find an appropriate definitive norm, especially in complex situations.

Baier distinguishes between two stages which we have to follow successively, if we wish to consider what mode of action is the best one in a situation:[3] surveying the relevant facts which furnish a reason for or against a mode of action, and the weighing of the reasons themselves. Going back to Toulmin's scheme, we can characterize the deliberations to be conducted at the first stage as follows: we choose the relevant data in a situation in the light of different possible rules of inference or warrants. By means of the reference to a warrant, data become reasons for an action. Baier does not restrict the kind of warrant to strictly normative rules; rather, every reason-giving conviction is acceptable to him. After having viewed the relevant facts, we are able to weigh the reasons for or against. For this we need "principles of the superiority of one type of reason over another" (e.g., moral reasons over reasons of self-interest), or "rules of superiority" within a given type of reason.[4] We adopt this type of rules from our "social environment"[5] and can examine them, for their part, with respect to their correctness. The appropriateness of the outcome of deliberation depends essentially "on the correctness and completeness of the first step,"[6] the surveying of the facts.

The difference between the two stages is expressed in the two corresponding types of reasons: *prima facie* reasons and reasons on balance. The first type simply justifies the presumption that an action ought (not) to be carried out: " . . . the fact that I have a reason for or against entering on the proposed line of action *does not entail* that I ought or ought not to enter on it—it merely 'presumptively implies' it"; it is a matter of "reasons *other things being equal.*"[7] Baier designates reasons on balance as those which propose that, *all things considered,* we ought or ought not to do something. In this way, the proponent expresses the conviction that "no other contrary reason could be offered capable of overriding the reason or reasons on which he bases his judgment."[8]

Baier extends this distinction between the two types of reasons to the meaning of their validity. A norm which is a *prima facie* reason has, accordingly, only the character of a *"prima facie* ought," whereas the predicate of balance characterizes an " 'ought' *on balance.*"[9]

This extension of the distinction has problematic consequences for the obligatory character of a valid norm. If a *prima facie* reason does not, in Baier's words, "entail" that I must act, or may not act, in such and such a way, then everything depends on how the conditions of entailment are to be understood. One could object to this interpretation on the grounds that a reason which does not obligate me to do something is not a reason, that is, does not possess any obligatory content whatsoever. In his critique of the distinction between *prima facie* obligations and absolute ones (or obligations on balance), Searle suggested three possibilities.[10]

According to the first interpretation, *prima facie* norms only seem to obligate us to do something, or simply show a certain direction, whereas absolute or "actual" norms obligate us here and now, in the concrete situation, to do something. The statement that "1. *X* has a *prima facie* obligation to do *A*" would not entail that "2. *X* has an obligation to do *A*" because in a real situation it can emerge that, on considering all the situation features, *X* does not have an obligation to do *A*.[11] This distinction has the disadvantage that the obligatory force of the ought can only refer to the judgment of obligation in a concrete situation, whereas *prima facie* obligations are not obligations. If, in a concrete situation, *X* finds himself in the conflict of either keeping his promise to Smith and attending his party or of fulfilling an obligation to help Jones, an interpretation of promising as a *prima facie* obligation would mean that *X* never made a promise. Then there would be no conflict situation at all.[12]

The second interpretation distinguishes two different kinds of obligations. There is a logical relation between the above-mentioned judgments of obligation, (1.) and (2.), only on the condition that the *prima facie* obligation (1.) overrides all other obligations in this situation and thus becomes an absolute obligation in the sense of the judgment of obligation (2.). Relative to other *prima facie* obligations in this situation, it would then be an absolute obligation. In this case, even the original relative *prima facie* obligation would possess a weak obligatory content. Norms applicable in a situation are then divided into two classes—an absolute (strong) norm and various (weak) *prima facie* norms. The class in which a norm belongs cannot be laid down at the outset. " . . . [W]hether or not an obligation was *prima facie* or absolute would depend on the particular conflict situation under consideration, and we would not be able to specify two separate classes of obligations independently of specifying different conflict situations."[13] Ascribing a status to norms depends on the situation in which a norm overrides all others. Then, however, all the norms would be *prima facie* norms except one, which overrides all the others.

In a third interpretation, Searle proposes giving up the distinction as a viewpoint for the classification of norms or obligations and, instead, suggests making it dependent on a maxim of conversation. Accordingly, the difference between the two judgments, "what one has an obligation to do and what one ought to do all things considered,"[14] can be understood in such a way that it refers to the amount of information which one conveys in a conversation about the reasons for action. The statement that there is a (*prima facie*) obligation to do *p* can then be regarded as an indirect way of saying that *p* ought to be done. There is not a relation of deduction, in the conventional logical sense, between a *prima facie* norm and an absolute norm; rather, it is a matter of two different ways of giving reasons for actions, ways which depend on the amount of information given and which are compatible with one another. Between the utterances "(a) Jones has an obligation to do *A*" and "(f) All things considered, Jones ought to do *A*," there is not therefore a deductive relation ([a] does not entail [f]), there is simply a conversational one. Thus, conversationally, utterance (a) is also compatible with the utterance "(g) All things considered, Jones ought not to do *A*."[15]

If Searle's critique is correct, the distinction between *prima facie* and absolute obligations (norms) should not be related to the property of obligation because otherwise one would be forced to draw absurd conclusions. The outcome would be two different concepts of validity: a *prima facie* validity, whereby it is unclear to what degree it obligates, and an absolute validity which may not be limited. Searle's own proposal of explaining the distinction in terms of an implicature of conversation is not exposed to this problem because it is simply concerned with the manner in which we speak about reasons for actions.

I would like to extend this proposal further. It has the advantage of separating the distinction from the concept of norm and the validity of normative judgments in order to anchor it, instead, in the presuppositions of action, which lay down how we handle norms in situations. We can thus inquire further how a conversation is structured in which the attributes "under unchanging circumstances" (other things being equal) and "considering all the circumstances" (all things considered) are used. When a proponent speaks of an "obligation under unchanging circumstances," he does not expect any information about the application situation, except the information that is implied by the sameness of the relevant features in different situations. The attribute applies only to all the known situations at the point in time when the judgment of obligation is expressed. If a norm is valid in situation *S1*, then it is valid in the situations *S2*, *S3*, ... *Sn*, if the particular circumstances remain unchanged.

As our systematic interpretation of the moral principle has shown, this assumption must be made when justifying the validity claim of norms. It serves the purpose of disregarding possible changes in the constellation of features in a situation and of thematizing the norm solely from the viewpoint of whether all those affected can will that it be generally observed under situational conditions Sx, known at time tx. It is only on this presupposition that it is at all meaningful to justify the universal validity of a norm without at the same time appending an unforeseeably large number of exceptions. This includes the possibility of justifying highly specified norms (in Hare's sense) because the attribute "under unchanging circumstances" in neutral vis-à-vis the degree of specification. We can thus say that the validity of a norm always only refers to universal agreement on its applicability under unchanging circumstances.[16] The implicit assumption we make with this *ceteris paribus* clause in justification discourses develops its true effect in application discourses. In justification discourses, it serves the purpose of artificially excluding the consideration of different application situations. In application discourses, however, this fiction can no longer be maintained. We will not know whether the circumstances of the application situation are the same as those assumed in the justification until we have considered all the features of the situation, and that is to say, until we have conducted an application discourse.

Now, various cases can however be the same in some respects and different in others. If the presupposition that all the features of a situation are to be considered is valid, then none of the features which are different relative to a viewpoint of comparison may be excluded from the appropriateness argumentation as being irrelevant. But the *ceteris paribus* clause only takes into account those features that are the same in different situations in relation to the justified norm, and it artificially suspends the possibility of relevant dissimilarities. We can contest this requirement in application discourses by pointing out features which are not the same as those presupposed by the proponent as unchanging features.[17] In this way, we expand the range of phenomena to which argumentation refers. The proponent does have the possibility of leaving the additional features unconsidered and of insisting on the application of the norm hypothesis proposed by him. But then the opponent could reproach him for a one-sided, partial application of the norm and, thus, for arbitrarily treating unlike cases alike. The other two possibilities consist in continuing the appropriateness argumentation: in that the proponent disputes that the additionally considered, dissimilar features are relevant; or in that he considers—by way of correcting his originally proposed norm or by weighing—the normative viewpoints according to which these features acquire relevance in order to find an appropriate norm.

Thus, it is in application discourses that we encounter the problem of a conflict of norms. Norms which are valid under unchanging circumstances can conflict with one another when all the circumstances of a situation are considered. In justification discourses we simply establish that there is no norm which, under unchanging circumstances, conflicts with the norm requiring justification.[18] The conflict of norms would then be a problem of their appropriateness and not of their validity.

With this argument, we could of course be still exposed to the objections which Searle brought to bear on the distinction between *prima facie* and absolute. If it is solely the *prima facie* clause which refers to the validity of a norm, then it is unclear what exactly we are definitively obligated to do. Because the clause "considering all the circumstances" only characterizes the appropriateness of the norm, it seems as if there were no obligation tied to this. Thus, we would have only reproduced, in an inverse manner, the paradoxical outcome of the distinction related to the ought because we would then have only an obligation to engage in, or abstain from, actions which are prescribed under unchanging circumstances. This objection is however only half correct. Because we have separated the distinction from the ought, we can relate the *validity* claim to a situation-*appropriate* norm too—and, indeed, we have to do this if we want to know whether what the appropriate thing to do in a situation corresponds to a valid norm. To question whether the obligation which is appropriate, considering all the circumstances, is also valid under unchanging circumstances is by no means ruled out. A norm which is appropriate in *S1* can be valid for *S1, S2, . . . Sn* if relevant changed circumstances do not appear. In order to ascertain whether we have an obligation to do what is appropriate, we therefore have to again operate with the hypothetical assumption that the circumstances on which we based our judgment on appropriateness remain unchanged in different situations. We thereby switch from an application to a justification discourse.

Alexy defended the distinction between the *prima facie* and the definitive character of norms as a difference in the structure of norms and in their prescriptive quality. This proposal draws its persuasive force primarily from Alexy's relating this distinction to the different structures of principles and rules.[19] According to this, principles contain only *prima facie* prescriptions or reasons, whereas rules definitively prescribe an action. The consequence of this classification of the structure of norms is that principles can be restricted by conflicting rules or principles; rules in cases of conflict, by contrast, are to be equipped with a clause for exceptions, or they require a decision on which of them is to be regarded as valid and which invalid. "Because a principle is pertinent in a case, it does not follow that what the principle demands in this case is valid in the final outcome. Principles represent reasons that can be discarded by opposing reasons. . . . By demanding that exactly what they prescribe be done, rules contain a determination [*Festsetzung*] within the range of legal and actual possibilities. This determination can be thwarted by legal and actual impossibilities, which can lead to its invalidation; if however it is not thwarted in such a manner, then what the rule states is definitively valid."[20] Alexy's proposal of relating the distinction between the *prima facie* and the definitive character of norms to principles and rules does not affect the validity of norms. Both principles and rules raise a validity claim of the same kind and are in need of justification. The distinction does however have an effect on the structure of norms and on the fate of validity in the case of a conflict of norms.

The difference in the structure of norms consists in the fact that principles, as *prima facie* prescriptions, have the character of optimizing prescriptions. They "prescribe that something be realized to the highest possible degree, relative to the legal and actual possibilities."[21] Alexy thereby ascribes a teleological structure to principles. They prescribe that a state of affairs be striven for or realized in accordance with the available means and while considering competing legitimate ends. Optimizing a state of affairs in concrete situations follows from this constellation. In contrast to that, rules are "norms that can be either observed or not observed. If a rule is valid, then it is prescribed to do exactly what it demands, nothing more and nothing less."[22] In this sense, rules are "determinations within the range of actual and legal possibilities." They possess a determinate or definitive structure which is based on the selection of legal and actual possibilities. They are thus comparable to a conditional structure in which the facts of a case as circumscribed by the legal norm [*Tatbestand*] (if-component) are connected to a determinate (legal) consequence (then-component).[23]

The effect of this distinction is shown in the case of conflicts of norms. If the application of two norms leads to contradictory judgments on what ought to be done, this has different consequences for rules and principles, respectively:[24] either only one of the two rules is valid, or one of the two rules must be equipped with a clause for exceptions. This follows from their structure as definitive prescriptions. In contrast to this, principles incorporate the possibility of conflicts by virtue of their open structure. For this reason, both principles retain their validity, though, under the concrete circumstances, which are determined by the particular actual and legal possibilities, one of them has to recede. "However, this means neither that the recessive principle is to be declared invalid, nor that a clause for exceptions is to be built into the recessive principle. Rather, one principle has priority over the other *under certain circumstances. Under different circumstances,* it can be that the question of priority has to be answered the other way round" (italics added).[25] From the different reactions in the case of conflicts of norms, Alexy draws the conclusion that only the dimension of weight is decisive for principles, depending on the particular circumstances of the case. Rules, on the other hand, conflict with one another in the dimension of validity, with the consequence that only one of them can be valid.[26]

Alexy's description of the reactions in cases of conflict does however make it highly probable that the distinction between rules and principles has less to do with the structure of norms than with the application of norms in concrete situations, where the impartial application of norms requires that all the situation features be taken into consideration. For this, one can perhaps better rely on Searle's proposal that the distinction located by Alexy in the structure of norms can be reconstructed more appropriately in the presuppositions of conversation, on the basis of which we take a position on the obligations in a situation. Then the difference would consist in whether we treat a norm as a rule, in that we apply it without considering the changed features of the situation, or whether we treat a norm as a principle, in that we apply it on considering all the (actual and legal) circumstances of a situation. The different kinds of treatment result from the fact that deliberations on appropriateness are precluded by virtue of institutional restrictions in the case of applying a rule and are permitted in the case of applying principles. Because precluding deliberations on appropriateness violates the principle of impartial application, one must be able to justify it: for example, in the sense of a conventional concept of justice, by regarding the anticipation of deliberations on appropriateness as the task of the political legislator. The latter would then have already decided, in the sense of the "social system's morality," about the appropriateness of a norm, so that transgressions would only be admissible in "exceptional cases." The structure of norms itself would not however be affected by this institutional distinction.[27]

The assumption that Alexy's proposed differentiation actually concerns the application of norms becomes even more plausible when we turn to his construction of a conflict axiom: " . . . the resolution of the conflict consists in determining [*festsetzen*], in view of the circumstances of the case, a *conditional relation of priority* between the principles. Determining the conditional relation of priority consists in stating, with reference to the case, the *conditions* on which one principle has priority over the other."[28] From this conditional relation of priority, a definitive rule can in turn be formed, a rule in which the condition of the concrete case, as the facts circumscribed by the legal norm (if-component), is linked to a legal consequence (then-component). Then "the case can be subsumed" under this norm with the character of a rule.[29] This conflict axiom corresponds to the structure of weighing values or legal goods, which is customary above all in rulings by the German Federal Constitutional Court.[30] What Alexy is however concerned with is to impose a rational model on the weighing procedure. The conditional proposition of preference can in turn be justified argumentatively. It must correspond to a "weighing axiom" [*Abwägungsgesetz*] that clarifies the case-specific relation of a principle (a relation which is laid out in the norm structure of the principle) to other legal possibilities (other principles). Merely ascertaining that the principle *P1* has priority over the principle *P2* in the situation *S* is not sufficient. Rather, one can justify why the principle *P2* has to recede in this case by showing that fulfilling it under the given circumstances is less important in relation to fulfilling principle *P1*: "The higher the degree of nonfulfillment or infringement of one principle, the greater the importance of fulfilling the other one."[31] This is not to say that it is already known when an infringement or when a higher degree of importance exists, but this can in turn be empirically and normatively justified within the framework of rational legal argumentation.[32]

In this way, Alexy tailors the problem of a conflict of norms to the concrete case.[33] With the help of the conflict axiom, and its extension in the form of the "weighing axiom," highly specified propositions of preference relating to the particular circumstances of the case can be formed, and their case-specific features as circumscribed by the legal norm—in combination with a determinate legal consequence—can be transformed into a definitive rule.

The appropriateness of a principle follows from the determination of its relation to all the other principles applicable in the situation, and to the actual conditions on which the realization of the principle depends. Alexy does not of course provide any criteria according to which we could judge the appropriateness of a proposition of preference. But the concept of norm structure already restricts the possible viewpoints in that principles as optimizing prescriptions are limited to optimally realizing a state of affairs relative to the actual and legal possibilities. The weighing axiom defines the kind of relation according to degrees of importance and infringement, so that it is possible to state exactly what specifically requires justification.

It remains unclear why this type of appropriateness argumentation should be prescribed by the structure of principles. That certain norms require appropriateness argumentation only becomes apparent in application situations themselves. The requirement that a norm be applied relative to the actual and normative (legal) possibilities in a situation can however be directed at *every* norm. It does not depend on the norm itself whether we apply it with or without consideration of the particular circumstances of a situation. Alexy has to combine two prescriptions in one: the prescription connected with the deontological sense of a norm ("you ought to do *p*") and the prescription which stipulates a specific manner of application ("considering/not considering the circumstances, you ought to do *p*"). But then the difficulty arises of finding criteria which permit a clear decision about what manner of application is prescribed in each case, when one cannot make a distinction like the one in a modern legal system between the norms of fundamental rights and simple legal regulations.[34] That is why it seems easier to me to separate the manner of a norm's application from its deontological content. If our hypothesis on the separation of justification and application at the postconventional level of moral development is correct, then the prescription that a norm be applied only on considering all the circumstances is valid for every norm in virtue of the principle of impartial application. This does not rule out that, for reasons requiring justification, certain norms are artificially kept at a conventional level, with the result that changes in rules, for reasons of appropriateness, are only possible in exceptional cases or require a decision about their validity.

That appropriateness argumentation does not have to be limited to the application of principles is clear from the example—which Alexy himself puts forward—of so-called teleological reduction in the application of legal rules.[35] In this case, legal norms are related to a certain end, such as the will of the legislator, protection, or a legal good, and, from the perspective of this means-ends relation, are restricted or broadened in their range of application.[36] Here too, the norm is related to other normative possibilities in a situation. Alexy does however add that the tacit introduction of exceptions into a rule presupposes that a principle expressly prescribing the definitive application of rules may be overridden: for example, the principle that rules which are authoritatively posited must be followed.[37] However, this principle, which, at least as a principle of legal certainty [*Rechtssicherheit*], is a constituent part of a legal system, can only be explained in terms of the particular institutional conditions of this system. Based on this principle, the admissibility of appropriateness argumentations when applying simple laws can be restricted because such deliberations are reserved for another institution, such as the political legislator. Then, the distinction between principles and rules is not a distinction within the concept of norm, but one within the presuppositions of action on which norms are applied. This does not however rule out that every norm, taken alone, can be applied in such a manner that all the actual and normative features of a situation are considered. In complex societies, this is probably an unavoidable development, precisely with such norms that seem to be definitive "determinations" [*Festsetzungen*] within the range of possibilities.

Against this background, one could ask whether and how those definitive rules which are the outcome of a weighing procedure on fundamental rights differ conceptually from the other definitive rules. Situation features, which, as universal features of the legal norm, constitute the concrete rule's if-component, were selected in preceding appropriateness argumentations. Is this connection constitutive of the rules of fundamental rights? Can it be required of a definitive rule that it be justifiable in appropriateness argumentation? It would not be very meaningful to determine something definitively within the range of what is actually and legally possible if one had to reckon with conflicts of norms in every situation. Then, however, it can at least be assumed that every definitive rule could have emerged from an appropriateness argumentation. We would then ascribe definitive status to a norm because we regard it appropriate in situations which we can have a clear view of. Only because we have already considered all the relevant circumstances is it possible for us to call for the application of the norm without considering the remaining (irrelevant) circumstances. But also when applying definitive norms to situations, we have to find and justify rules for word usage which make it possible to check the congruence between the features of the legal norm and the description of relevant situation features. This does not transcend the scope of what is determined within the range of legal and actual possibilities as long as the particular features can be numbered among those belonging to the semantic extension of a norm. In changed constellations where the assumption of appropriateness is no longer valid, there is then a need to engage once more in an appropriateness argumentation.

From this perspective, the problem of a conflict of definitive norms also acquires a different profile. Precisely because appropriateness argumentation is ruled out in their case, one of the two norms must be declared invalid. Because it has always been presupposed in the case of definitive norms that all the particular circumstances have been considered, a conflict of two norms, which prescribe something on considering all the circumstances in the same situation, cannot be resolved except by admitting only one norm.

If the requirement of appropriate application is detached from the concept of norm structure, it can be justified only on the basis of the idea of impartiality. In this way, it is also possible to abandon the other problematic premise in Alexy's proposal: the characterization of principles as optimizing prescriptions. With this, principles are related to a concept of teleological action. In application, it is then only a matter of attaining a legitimate end with the suitable and necessary means, and while considering the degree of encroachment upon other, equally important ends or goods.[38] Only because the intensity of violation and the degree of fulfillment of principles cannot be quantified, Alexy refrains from conceptualizing the model of optimization according to cost-benefit calculations.[39] In comparing degrees of optimization of various states of affairs, only comparative, and not metric, value judgments are possible.[40] It is only in this connection that it is also plausible why Alexy can draw parallels between principles and values: what is prescribed in each case is the best state of affairs which can be attained on considering all the other values. This paralleling is thus already contained in the concept of optimizing prescriptions. Because Alexy defines principles not on the basis of their justification and application, but according to their norm structure, he can ascribe a quasi-material content ("state," "end") to them, one which has its own normative status ("weight") and which prescribes a particular type of application ("optimization"). The type of application follows from the norm structure and not from procedures that are valid for all norms.

With this definition based on norm structure and requiring a weighing of values in situations, Alexy does indeed avoid the reproach of speaking in favor of a "tyranny of values." With it, however, he rules out the possibility of being able to criticize values themselves in the light of principles or in discursive procedures.[41] According to his model, everything that appears as "value" in a specific instance would have to be put through a weighing procedure without it being possible to question this value itself. This leads one to conclude that, in weighing, the criteria for judging the degree of importance of conflicting values follow from the existing order of priority in each case. What that means can be made clear by Alexy's proposal to give up the distinction between principles and policies, which was introduced by Dworkin. This does indeed correctly characterize the de facto state of adjudication in constitutional courts, but its characteristic confounding of principles and the administrative or economic systems' functional imperatives is also taken over at the same time.[42] For a procedural theory of justification and application, on the other hand, values as collective need interpretations would have to remain criticizable.[43] However, this can only be achieved if particular types of justification and application are not already predetermined by a particular norm structure.

2

Appropriateness Argumentation as an Experimental Procedure and as a Moral Learning Process

Before summarizing and expanding, in the following section (3), the first indicators for possible lines of argumentation in application discourses—indicators obtained in the discussion on the distinction between *prima facie* and definitive norms—I would like to discuss two positions which, like Wellmer, but without abandoning universalist claims, link appropriateness argumentation directly to a procedure for the impartial justification of norms. These positions are instructive for our topic because, on the one hand, they explicitly maintain the possibility and necessity of appropriateness argumentation, which has as its requirement the complete consideration of all the relevant features of a situation. On the other hand, they incorrectly conjoin this presupposition with the justification principle of impartiality. Hare proposes a two-level procedure for "moral thinking" which makes an experimental handling of different situation features possible. We can insert different features into different principles and in this way form highly specified principles which consider virtually all the features of the situation. The criterion according to which we then determine the moral quality of a specific principle consists, on the one hand, in the degree to which relevant features are considered and, on the other, in the semantic universalizability of the proposed principle. But because Hare requires yet another criterion according to which the relation between the principles representing different features can be determined, he falls back on the utilitarian method of comparing the different intensities of needs affected in a situation. In this way, however, he introduces a material criterion into appropriateness argumentation. Tugendhat also attempts to explicate the appropriateness of a norm as a component of the principle of impartiality. The requirement of appropriateness is the propelling element of moral learning processes: it is only because we can—with critical intention—relate to this requirement that moral learning on the basis of new experiences is possible. Appropriate norms must be able to integrate these experiences. But Tugendhat also conjoins the principle of adequacy with a principle which is directed toward the agreement of all those affected: it then has the function of a directive of judgment [*Urteilskraft*] with which we make a new impartial moral judgment in new situations, one that considers the additional features. In this way, Tugendhat replaces argumentation on the resolution of conflicts of norms and on the selection of a situation-appropriate norm with an act of judgment.

Drawing on his earlier proposal[44] to understand the justification of moral norms as "a kind of exploration," Hare outlined a two-level procedure with the help of which we can construct and justify appropriate and, at the same time, semantically universalizable norms. He distinguishes between the "intuitive and critical levels of thinking."[45] Both are to be strictly distinguished from the metaethical level, at which it is solely a matter of the analysis of the meaning of moral words. Only the first two are "concerned with moral questions of substance."[46]

Hare's description of the intuitive level can be compared to our characterization of the first lines of argumentation on appropriateness. When, under normal circumstances, we follow our intuitively anchored and habitually accepted principles, we pay no attention to specific differences in situations. Principles of this kind originate from time-tested experiences in dealing with the different circumstances of situations. Conflicts do not emerge until changed features become relevant, as is above all the case in conflicts of norms. Then, intuitive principles prove to be inappropriate. Since we have nothing but our intuitive principles available at this level, resolutions of cases of conflict do not present themselves, as is the case at Kohlberg's Stage 3. In order to resolve a conflict, we would have to distance ourselves from our intuitions and habits, so that we could modify them for the specific situation. "Since any new situation will be unlike any previous situation in *some* respects, the question immediately arises whether the differences are relevant to its appraisal, moral or other. If they are relevant, the principles which we have learnt in dealing with past situations may not be appropriate to the new one. So the further question arises of how we are to decide whether they are appropriate. The question obtrudes itself most in cases where there is a conflict between the principles we have learnt—i.e. where, as things contingently are, we cannot obey them both. But if it arises in those cases, it can arise in any case, and it is mere intellectual sloth to pretend otherwise."[47] Whoever remains at the intuitive level has to regard problems of this kind as being irresolvable and accept a solution by decision only. The validity claim of intuitive principles is not criticizable because they are anchored as dispositions in our identity.

On the other hand, we can however distance ourselves, if not from habits, at least from the circumstances under which we acquired these habits and ask whether they are "good" or whether they can be justified in another manner. Finally, we can also ask whether the principles applied in our moral reactions were the right ones in this situation, or whether others would have been more appropriate. With these questions, we are already at the level of "critical thinking."

This second level does not simply take the place of our original moral intuitions, but presupposes them. Nor does it establish a higher or more substantial principle under which the conflicting principles of the first level would simply be subsumed; then the problems with the first level would merely be repeated. The only rules we follow in critical thinking refer to the semantics of moral terms and the collection of relevant facts in a conflict situation. It is thus Hare's metaethical theory of universal prescriptivism which defines the level of critical thinking. "Critical thinking consists in making a choice under the constraints imposed by the logical properties of the moral concepts and by the non-moral facts, and by nothing else."[48]

With the help of critical thinking, we can thus distance ourselves from our intuitive principles of the first level by confronting them with all the relevant features of the situation ("facts") and with the semantic conditions on which the term "ought" may be used in connection with a recommendation ("logic"). In the process, we do not have to take the original principles in the degree of universality or of binding character with which they are intuitively given to us in a situation; rather, we can consider all the relevant features of a situation which are not covered by an intuitive principle. The moral quality of a critical principle depends on whether we have considered all the relevant facts and can semantically universalize the principle thus specified, that is to say, whether we can still regard it as binding if we are in the position of the one affected. From this perspective, conflicts of norms present themselves as the result of an inadequate appropriateness of our intuitive principles. *Prima facie* principles are so selective and situation-specific that they cannot consider other features which are relevant. *Prima facie* principles lead to conflicts "because one of the principles picks out certain features of the situation as relevant (e.g. that a promise has been made), and the other picks out certain others (e.g. that the failure to show my friend the colleges would bitterly disappoint him). The problem is to determine which of these principles should be applied to yield a prescription for this specific situation."[49]

Critical thinking makes it possible to find a highly specific norm that is appropriate to the situation and to universalize it (semantically) by comparing it with other similar situations in which it is applicable (as a rule, those in which I find myself in the position of the other, and he finds himself in mine). Critical principles "can be completely specific, leaving out no feature of an act that could be alleged to be relevant."[50] Thus, at this level we can consider *all* the features of a situation. Hare personified this ideal in a moral "archangel" who can instantly grasp all the relevant circumstances in every situation. "When presented with a novel situation, he will be able at once to scan all its properties, including the consequences of alternative actions, and frame a universal principle (perhaps a highly specific one) which he can accept for action in that situation, no matter what role he himself were to occupy in it."[51] As the antitype, Hare establishes the "prole" who is dependent on being given *prima facie* principles, which he applies in every new situation in an unspecific manner and without considering the particular circumstances. It is a contingent decision which of the two ideal types we choose for ourselves. Under the restrictions of the human condition, that is, especially under conditions of limited time and incomplete knowledge ("neither the time nor the capacity"),[52] we will not be able to correspond fully to either of the two personified ideal types. Even if we decide on the role of the prole, we rely on, at least in conflict situations, a minimal effort on the part of critical thinking in order finally to decide on one of the conflicting norms. The fact that we will never actually be able to play the role of the archangel does not however rule out our being able to consider relevant circumstances in every situation which are not covered by the *prima facie* principles.

For our purposes, it is decisive that, with the personified ideal of the archangel, Hare tacitly introduces a two-part principle, one part of which complies with our characterization of deliberations on appropriateness in that it locates these deliberations at the level of practical reason. One the one hand, this principle corresponds to our reconstruction of the presupposition of impartial, complete description, which we can employ in appropriateness argumentation. We rely on this presupposition when we anticipate that only those norms which consider all the features of the situation may be regarded as appropriate. At the same time, however, Hare connects this principle to a second one, that of semantic universalizability. This means that, ultimately, we cannot judge the relevance of a feature until we have universalized the principle containing this feature. The experimental procedure of critical thinking then consists in putting virtually all features into different hypothetical principles and in fictitiously checking whether we would still accept each of these principles if, under unchanging circumstances, we were in the position of the one affected. For this reason, Hare describes appropriateness argumentation as follows: "We have therefore to proceed initially by guesswork. If we think that a feature of a situation *might* be relevant, we experiment with principles mentioning the feature; to accept the principles will be to accept the relevance of the feature, and to reject them will be to reject *those* reasons why it might be relevant, though there may yet be *other* principles which make it relevant."[53] Hare can of course use the principle of semantic universalizability implicitly as a criterion of appropriateness only because it distinguishes, by virtue of its structure, an entirely specific class of situation features. If universalization consists in me putting myself in the position of the one affected and in considering whether, from my perspective, I could accept the proposed principle, then it is primarily the particular situational consequences of the intended action for the *needs and preferences* of the other which are relevant.[54] But since it is at least theoretically possible to weigh competing needs against one another according to degrees of their intensity, Hare obtains in this way a principle which is simultaneously appropriate and universalizable. The experimental procedure of inserting various essential features into hypothetical principles is supposed to correct the deficiency of intuitive principles of not being able to consider all the relevant features. In this dimension, Hare's procedure is tailored to finding appropriate principles. To this end, it can be meaningful to universalize a hypothetical principle because additional information about essential features of the situation can be acquired in this way. In order to grasp a situation completely, I have to be able to know how the other sees it in the light of his preferences. In this sense, the principle of universalizability is simply a function of the presupposition of complete description. It is a different matter with the principle of universalizability as a criterion of validity. Here it is a question of the problem of whether everyone could accept the principle already framed, if one put oneself in the position of the other. Hare regards this agreement on the validity of a norm as already given with the norm's appropriateness in respect of the preferences of all others affected. He thereby identifies validity and appropriateness on the basis of semantic universality. We can thus follow Hare's two-level model to the extent that it implies the presupposition of a complete consideration of all the circumstances of a situation which are relevant to the need interpretations affected. On the other hand, we may not construe the process of revising and modifying *prima facie* norms according to purely utilitarian criteria, if we do not wish to again sacrifice the distinction between justification and application or the related advantages of a universalist moral principle.

Tugendhat also undertakes an analogous assimilation when he interprets the principle of impartiality as a directive of judgment. In doing so, he wishes to solve the problem of how moral learning processes resulting from experience are possible. If we have to interpret the principles to which we refer in moral conflict situations from the perspective of the first person, then this results in our not being able to integrate experiences we have as observers in the role of the third person into moral principles. On the other hand, however, the experience of the relativization of our moral convictions— an experience which recurs incessantly in history—points to the fact that we can obviously put forward the argument that certain experiences have been overlooked against the validity claim of moral principles. If that is not to lead to abandoning moral claims, then it must be possible on the basis of these experiences to change our moral principles. The precondition for this is that we are able to integrate the "outside view," from which we observe the relativity of our moral judgments, into the "inside view," from which we make moral judgments.[55] This is always and unavoidably tied to a claim to universality, whereby we claim to be able to show every other person that our judgment is right (or, in Tugendhat's mode of expression, is "good").

As a solution to the above problem, Tugendhat proposes understanding the justification principle of impartiality as a principle of judgment. This connection does not find expression in all those conceptions of morality which, like the Kantian, regard the appropriateness of concrete norms as already given with the application of the moral principle to them. The individual norms would then be ascribed the same certainty as is ascribed to "the departure point to which they owe their certainty," namely, the moral principle of the categorical imperative itself.[56] However, such a structure in the relation between moral principle and norms precludes the possibility of moral learning processes because the concrete norm may always only be derived from the moral principle without being exposed to changes by new experiences.

Two possibilities for methodologically construing the integration of experiences are ruled out for Tugendhat: deductive and weighing models. The deductive model, in which a general norm—as the major premise—is connected to a specific judgment of experience—as the minor premise—to form a concrete moral judgment, is not suitable for this purpose because the experiential component "remains purely theoretical."[57] Practical consequences, in virtue of which the moral conviction expressed in the major premise could be changed, are not admissible for this scheme.[58] Though the weighing model makes it possible to consider various—that is, in principle, all—norms applicable in a situation, it is not able to provide a criterion by which the weighing procedure could orient itself. This model is therefore correct only insofar as "in the moral judgment to be formed, none of the relevant norms may be disregarded, all have to be considered. But this idea of weighing is misleading because weighing presupposes a common standard or a uniform reference point in relation to which it is decided to what extent each of the norms ought to apply."[59] Now, Alexy has shown, however, that the weighing model can be specified methodologically in the form of a conflict axiom and a corresponding weighing axiom. Nevertheless, the problem of standards could not be completely resolved in this way. Moreover, it presupposed a teleological reinterpretation of principles and reduced the justification problem to justifying decisions of preference.

That is why Tugendhat introduces the idea of impartiality as a standard of weighing: "[W]hat the judgment aims at is a new norm appropriate to the concrete case, a norm that distinguishes itself only by impartiality, and by balanced consideration only to the extent that the correct balance between the norms has to consist precisely in this impartiality itself."[60] However, Tugendhat does not go so far as to derive the idea of impartiality itself from the unavoidable presuppositions of moral argumentation, but simply characterizes it as a "directive for judgment."[61] Its application depends on the individual's autonomy in judging. Thus, like Wellmer, Tugendhat favors an interpretation of the moral principle as a mere operationalization of the moral point of view, from which we have to judge each individual situation directly.

Tugendhat does however give the principle of judgment a peculiar sense. Unlike Wellmer, he does not wish to restrict it to a judgment on the continuation of a common practice, but wants to retain a universalist claim in order thereby to explain the possibility of moral learning processes. If the moral principle as a principle of judgment has a universalist claim, by virtue of which only those norms that consider all the aspects of a situation are to be distinguished as moral, then it is possible to put forward the critical argument that a relevant feature was overlooked in a concrete situation. This results in it being possible to criticize the original judgment as being partial and in it being necessary to make a new judgment which considers this feature too, in order to satisfy the requirements of the principle of impartiality. This, however, compels Tugendhat to tacitly supplement the principle of impartiality in the universal-reciprocal sense by a principle of adequacy, which the idea of impartiality embodies in the applicative sense: "Because every moral judgment that is rational in the narrow sense aims at impartiality, but of course also at grasping the practical problem adequately, and that is to say, from every point of view, conceding that a moral problem was judged partially, or otherwise inadequately, i.e., one-sidedly, leads to withdrawing the judgment and demanding that the judgment aiming at impartiality be repeated, a repetition that incorporates the aspects formerly not considered."[62] The principle of impartiality thus seems to be combined with a principle of adequacy in the moral point of view; but Tugendhat still maintains at least a terminological distinction and does not imply a reciprocal substitutability.[63] But then something else must be meant by an impartial judgment which relates to all those affected—something that is different from what is meant by an adequate judgment. This reveals itself in Tugendhat's description of the structure of moral learning processes as following from the "self-destructivity" of the principle of impartiality. The principle of adequacy, in the sense of considering all the relevant features, is violated if adhering to an original judgment precludes the reception of knowledge modified by an expansion of the phenomenal domain of our descriptive knowledge of a thing (as Tugendhat calls it)—an expansion, that is, resulting from new experience. In contrast to that, the principle of impartiality as a principle of justification is violated if the interest of someone affected is left unconsidered or dismissed without reason.

3

Elements of a Logic
of Appropriateness Argumentation

The reflections so far undertaken on the problem of a conflict of norms, and the debate with the solutions proposed by Searle, Alexy, Hare, and Tugendhat, permit a circumspect systematization with the goal of distinguishing the individual steps in an appropriateness argumentation. If the rationality of application is measured by the successively extended consideration of situation features and by the conflict of various applicable norms systematically produced by this consideration, a logic of appropriateness argumentation has to show with what argumentative means we can assert an extended situation description in application discourses and resolve the resulting conflicts. In what follows I shall first characterize more precisely those situations of argumentation in which the proponent has an obligation to support the claimed relevance of a situation feature by at least tacitly presenting a complete description of the situation. This is always the case when the opponent has reasons to ask the question: "Why do you rely on these data and not on others?" Possible reasons of this kind would be the untruth of the situation description given by the proponent, or the missing congruence between norm and situation description, or, finally, the lack of consideration of those situation features which are relevant to the application of other norms. Following this, I shall propose the introduction of a second level of argumentation where it is a question of the coherence of norms applicable to a situation and semantic variants.

3.1 Complete Description of a Situation

What is common to all the above-mentioned authors is the introduction of a first level at which the relevant facts are viewed and a hypothetical description of the situation is made. All the authors also point to the fact that the section of the situation identified as relevant in the first line of argumentation is determined by the *prima facie* norms which we apply under unchanging circumstances. With Toulmin's scheme of argumentation, it can be shown that the relevance of the selected data is determined by the claim that the proponent wishes to justify and by the warrant he relies on for this. With the choice of specific data as reasons (D) for a claim requiring justification (C), a specific warrant (W) is implicitly considered which permits the transition from D to C.[64] For this, the proponent can refer to the rule of semantic consistency, according to which a norm that is valid under unchanging circumstances must be applied in every situation in which these same circumstances are present. Alexy designates this requirement a basic rule of general practical discourse.[65] It is Hare's principle of universalizability which compels us to apply a predicate—one that we apply to a certain object—to every other object which is like the first one in all respects. An opponent who challenges the appropriateness of applying a norm with the question "Why do you rely on these and not on other data?" must thus give reasons as to why these other data are to be considered.

To illustrate this, let us return again to the example of a conflict of norms. The singular normative proposition requiring justification runs:

(C) I ought to go to Smith's party now.

The relevant data are

(D) I told Smith yesterday that I would attend his party today.

As a warrant, one can put forward the following:

(W) One ought to keep promises.

The opponent can now dispute that D is relevant to the justification of the singular normative proposition C. Because the proponent could justify his first argumentative move by pointing out that the relevant data belong to the unchanging circumstances of W, the opponent has to accept a rule for allocating the burden of argument which follows from the principle of semantic consistency.[66] He has to justify why he does not wish to treat like cases alike, which the proponent proposed with his hypothesis for application. The justification can be convincing only if he puts forward other features of the situation which justify a relevant difference to the features presupposed as being the same. For this, he has three possibilities available:

(D1) You did not tell Smith yesterday that you would attend his party.

(D2) What you said to Smith when he invited you was not a firm pledge, but a casual arrangement to meet.

(D3) You did indeed make a firm pledge to Smith, but your friend Jones is in serious difficulties at the moment.

The first objection (D1) contests the truth of the data that the proponent claimed to be relevant in his description of the situation. With (D2), the opponent doubts that the relevant data belong to the semantic extension of those expressions used in W—that is, whether what the proponent said to Smith was a firm pledge, and thus a promise, or just a casual arrangement to meet, which does not fall under the term "promise." Finally, the third objection (D3) is aimed at the lack of consideration of other relevant data in the description of the situation.

(1) If necessary, the truth of statements with which a situation is described must be checked in a theoretical discourse.[67] If the truth cannot be established, then this implies that the conditions asserted by the proponent for the application of the norm are not present. The participants in the argumentation have to agree that the facts of the external, social, and inner worlds, referred to when advancing reasons D, actually exist. The truth of each individual statement is a necessary condition for a complete description of the situation.

(2) The second possibility concerns the manner of referring to a situation. The opponent can contest that a feature belonging to a true description of the situation ranks among the conditions of application of a norm. Here, it is not disputed that the data put forward by the proponent are actually present, nor is it doubted that the unchanging circumstances presupposed by the norm itself would permit a transition to the conclusion. Rather, it is a matter of whether the description of data contained in the norm is in agreement with the true description of the situation. This is primarily a problem when it cannot clearly be established whether an

agreement between both exists or not. The meaning of a norm is not laid down once and for all; the unchanging circumstances are not finitely countable. Without agreement between the features of D and the features presupposed by W, D could not however be put forward as a reason for C. Problems of this kind appear above all in legal discourses, which is why, in what follows, we shall be dealing mainly with analyses of argumentation which have been conducted in legal theory. The universal character of a logic of appropriateness argumentation is not however affected by this; Toulmin discusses similar problems, simply in less detail.[68]

What arguments the proponent can use to ward off the objection of a lack of agreement depends on what is understood by "referring" the terms used in the norm to descriptions of the facts. Alexy has proposed characterizing the reasons used to prove, in cases of doubt, that there is an agreement as "word usage rules."[69] We then justify that the usage rule of the term used in the norm permits application to the feature of the case's facts. In our example, the participants in argumentation contest whether the kind of pledge that Smith was given by the proponent is a promise or just a casual arrangement to meet. The proponent would now have to state what features belong to his use of the expression "promise" in order to show that also those features are included with which the participants in argumentation unanimously describe the kind of pledge given to Smith. The proponent can expect of the opponent, who contests that the feature of the circumstances "a" is a "T," that he justify how he used the predicate "T." Thus, we can claim to apply a rule only if we use the expressions contained in it in a semantically consistent manner and can justify this in cases of doubt. In this way, it is required that "rules for the usage of the expressions used in the preceding stages of the justification" be stated.[70] These rules follow from the principle of semantic universalization: "In the absence of such rules it would be possible to treat two individuals a and b, who are alike in all the relevant aspects, as T in the one case and not in the other."[71] In the process, one has to state as many "decompositional steps" as are necessary in order to be able to establish congruence between the expressions used.[72]

Word usage rules secure the internal transition from the description of the situation and the norm to the conclusion by either establishing [*feststellen*] or determining [*festsetzen*] (postulating) the semantic identity of the terms used in D and W.[73] As rules, they are for their part in need of justification. If they only explicate an established word usage, then referring to language usage is sufficient. It is a different matter if they determine a new word usage. Then they are in need of justification according to the scheme W-D-C, just like a norm whose validity under unchanging circumstances has yet to be ascertained: "The justification of premises used in the process of internal justification is the subject-matter of external justification."[74] In legal discourses, the canons of interpretation, justification by precedent, and the principles of legal doctrine serve this purpose; in morality, determining [or fixing] the meaning of terms can only be justified by other valid norms. Only those changes in meaning which follow from a changed self-understanding of those participating in a practical discourse have to be checked with regard to their validity in a justification discourse.[75]

As in those cases, it is also possible here to thematize not only the validity of the rule, but also its situational appropriateness. For word usage rules not only explicate or postulate the correct usage of the expressions used in a norm, they also select at the same time certain features of the particular situation. Their function consists precisely in justifying the congruence between the term used in the norm and the description of the situation by carefully decomposing meanings until an identity of meanings has been attained.

Koch and Rüßmann have attempted to express this double function—the justification of the internal transition and the selection of situation features—by speaking not of word usage rules, but—following Carnap—of "semantic interpretations."[76] By fixing meaning (intension), semantic interpretations also lay down the conditions for the correct application of a sign to objects (extension). "The usage rule names the properties that an object must have so that the sign connected with the usage rule is correctly applied to it."[77] By choosing this theory of meaning, the double function of word usage rules seems to follow from itself, as it were. The possibly relevant situation features then belong to the extension, which is fixed with the intension of a term used in a norm. "In the premise that describes the circumstances of a case [Sachverhalt], it is stated whether the event that is up for legal judgment belongs to the extension of the terms that represent the semantic interpretation of the facts circumscribed by the legal norm [Tatbestand]."[78]

However, it is questionable whether the appropriateness of the decision fixing the extension selectively can also be justified in this way. The authors do expressly point out that, by laying down the semantic interpretation, the relevant features of a case's circumstances are also fixed, but they do not thematize whether and how the features of the particular situation have been considered in the process. "The semantic interpretation expresses what properties of the matter to be decided are important. Why it should be these particular properties that are important is a question which is to be answered in the justification for the semantic interpretation."[79] *What is justified,* however, is only that a rule containing such features as are found in the description of a case's circumstances is generalizable and valid according to various forms of external justification. However, the justification cannot again thematize the selection, which is presupposed as having already been made; this is so because it is now only a matter of the situation-independent determination of a meaning.

But the task of justifying the situation appropriateness of the determination of a meaning in relation to other semantic variants does not differ from the task of justifying the situational appropriateness of a norm in relation to other applicable norms. Whether what the proponent said to Smith was a firm pledge or merely a casual arrangement to meet can be decided by the participants in argumentation only if they put forward additional features which describe the event in greater detail and if they relate the features subsequently introduced into the argumentation to the differentiated intension of the term "promise." Hare described this procedure for selecting various norms which are applicable in a situation as proceeding "by guesswork." In legal theory, Engisch coined for this the phrase: "casting one's glance back and forth between the major premise and the circumstances of life."[80] What is decisive here for the impartiality of norm application is that all the semantic variants be related to all the features of the description of the situation.[81]

Different semantic variants of a term used in a norm can thus negate or confirm the claim to relevance of a situation feature with respect to other situation features, or they can link this claim to the latter. But then reasons must again be put forward for the word usage rule which the participants in argumentation advance as a reason for the determination of a meaning. But this is preceded by the "exhaustion" of all the possible semantic variants in a situation. To exhaust meanings and to check the generalizability of *an exhausted* meaning are two different argumentative operations. The exhaustion of semantic possibilities is for its part guided by the basic question: "Why these data and not others?" that is to say, even when we dispute a claim to relevance with the argument that the feature of the situation description does not fall under the term used in a norm, or does so differently, we have to fall back on an extended description of the situation.

The fact that a complete description of the situation is also necessary here for an impartial application is shown in the case of alternative or competing semantic possibilities. If the individual "a" is compatible with both the intension $m1$ and the intension $m2$ of the term "T," then it could be that an extended description of the situation will produce additional features, the consideration of which will lead to a change in the meaning of "T" with regard to its intension—for example, that one should treat casual arrangements to meet as a promise if there are no serious obstacles to keeping to these arrangements. Not until we have "gone through" different semantic possibilities in a situation can we check whether one should still recognize a norm like "one ought to keep promises" as universally valid if the features of the expression "casual arrangement to meet" belong to the properties of an action to which the predicate "is a promise" is applied in a semantically correct manner. This is a step in argumentation which is different from the formulation of a description of a situation that contains the feature concerned and also different from the justification of the determination of a meaning to whose extension this feature belongs.

Alexy, Koch, and Rüßmann assigned these operations to the "context of discovery."[82] That is correct insofar as the *validity* of a word usage rule is independent of the processes which led to a determination of a meaning. The norm is valid independent of whether and how one exhausts its meaning in a situation. However, the element of the decision on selection connected with this, the element requiring justification, consists in our having an obligation in practical discourses to go through all the semantic variants which are *possible in a situation,* if we do not wish to violate the principle of impartial application. For this, we need a complete description of the situation—even though it is often the case that this can only be *discovered* by our determining the extension of possible semantic variants. Precisely because selecting this or that feature of a case's circumstances is always connected with the determination of a meaning, this decision on selection has to be able to be justified with respect to all the other features of the situation.

The fact that what is important is not only the validity, but also the appropriate application of a word usage rule, is hidden by the analogy between the semantically correct application of the terms used in a norm and the correct application of the norm. "If the semantic interpretations did not lay down which circumstances the legal norm (qua their interpretation) is to be applied to, or not applied to, then they could not fulfill their ascribed bridging function between legal norm and description of the circumstances of the case."[83] Thus, the applicability of norms depends on the expressions contained in the norm being applied in a semantically correct manner, that is, being applied according to their rules of meaning and usage. On this presupposition, the appropriateness of the application of a norm would be given if the terms contained in it could be applied to the objects which possess the corresponding property. But it seems to be questionable whether the situations of the correct usage of the expressions contained in a norm are identical with the situations of appropriate application of a norm.[84]

As an outcome of this, we can conclude that the meaning of a norm, or what is meant by "unchanging circumstances," is by no means fixed. Frequently, meaning must first be laid down by a word usage rule, which for its part has to be justified. We know what meanings are relevant only in the situation itself. The principle of impartial norm application thus states in this case that the norm is to be applied on exhausting all the semantic possibilities which can be obtained in a complete description of the situation.

The description of the situation has to be complete not only in the sense that the features are described in such a manner that they agree with the features of the norm. In addition to this, different possible variations and varying degrees of generality in describing the same situation feature are to be considered. Here too, a corresponding mistake can give rise to a partial application. Included in the first group are cases in which different descriptions are applicable to the same situation feature. The fact that the doctor did not tell the terminally ill patient the truth about his condition can be described as a lie or as a considerate treatment. Included in the second group are cases in which different degrees of abstraction result in mutually exclusive norms.[85]

(3) The third case of an inappropriate norm application also rests on an incomplete description of the situation, which leads to a partial decision on selection. It concerns what we have so far thematized under the heading of a conflict of norms. If the opponent can show that other norms are applicable to the same feature or to other features of the same situation, the proponent must justify why the situation features selected by him are relevant, in contrast to all the others. The opponent could object: "Why do you rely only on the fact that you gave Smith a promise to attend his party, and not on the fact that your best friend Jones is in serious difficulties?"

In this example, it is especially clear how the choice of data already determines the further course of argumentation, in that a conflict of rules present in this situation is being obscured—"one has already—in effect—prejudged the ethical issues involved."[86] If I justify the judgment "I ought to comply with Smith's invitation" by referring to the situation feature that I gave Smith a firm pledge and I justify the transition by saying that one ought to keep promises, then there is no basis anymore to assert the remaining features of the situation. Here it is clear that the choice of reasons is based on a decision to select certain features of a situation description. The selective character of this claim to relevance does not reveal itself until the relevance of certain features is contested by referring to other features.

Referring to a certain feature of a situation is thus also in this case an argumentative move sui generis, one requiring justification. With the claim to relevance, a feature of a situation (or a set of features) is attributed normative significance, that is, it enters the set of reasons which justify an action. How can this decision on selection be justified? At this level of argumentation, referring to an applicable norm merely restates the claimed relevance of a selected set of features. If the opponent wishes to contest it, he has to refer to other features of the situation. If the proponent wishes to stick to his claim, he has to put forward reasons for discarding the other features. Thus, by claiming relevance for a feature, one always claims in addition that one can justify why all the other features of the situation description are disregarded. With this move, appropriateness argumentation establishes a relation with practical reason because the justification of the claim to relevance rests on the presupposition of a complete description of the situation. Only by comparing the selected set of situation features with a complete description of the situation can we establish whether the justification is also convincing. Wolfgang Wieland described this step in argumentation as a common figure in moral controversies:

> "One does not need a special acumen in order to track down and highlight in a concrete individual case those features that are not covered by the necessarily schematized norm. In such cases, one does not even have to appeal to a special rule for exceptions. The validity of the norm can remain intact, if one points out that an exceptional situation exists, one not foreseen by the norm, and indeed, one that is not foreseeable. This is one of the most common defensive figures in moral discussions, where of course the validity

of a norm is only rarely questioned *in abstracto.* One usually pre-
fers to interpret the situation in such a way that it no longer seems
to be covered by the norm."[87]

What is described conventionally here as a strategy for the exceptional case, or for generating such a case rhetorically, is an admissible step in appropriateness argumentation, one prescribed by the
principle of impartial application.

Nevertheless, merely extending the description of the situation
does not itself ensure a successful conclusion to appropriateness argumentation. The other situation features taken into account by the
opponent are, for their part, not without a reference; they in turn
are relevant to other norms. We thus have to relate the complete
description of a situation to all the other applicable norms. If the
opponent objects that "your best friend Jones is seriously ill," then
the description of the situation extended by this datum refers to the
norm that one ought to fulfill one's obligations as a friend. The complete description of the situation is subjected to a "normative exhaustion" which puts forward all the norms that can possibly be
applied. We are thereby operating at the stage of a conflict of
norms, which makes it necessary to transfer to the level of critical
thinking.

Thus, we do not immediately reach the level at which it is a
matter of justifying the warrant itself—independently of the situation—by casuistic evidence; we are first at the level where we are
concerned with justifying the warrant or rule of inference in relation to other rules which refer to a different selection of data in the
situation, or refer to the same selection but in a different manner.
What can then be designated as appropriate is the relation of a
norm to virtually all the other norms whose common feature consists in being applicable in this situation *S:* "Moral judgment
aims at the appropriate application of *moral* rules to particular circumstances insofar as their application requires choosing among
morally different alternatives."[88] Using traditional terminology, one
could characterize the capability presupposed for this as a kind of
imagination [*Einbildungskraft*] which consists in weighing various
possible, normatively relevant viewpoints and in judging their relations, consequences, and side effects. What is crucial, however, is
that it should proceed from the requirement of a complete description of the situation.

Toulmin proposed designating conflicting norms as "rebuttals"
which modify the inferential transition from W to C.[89] These make

it possible "to emphasize different aspects of the situation."[90] Accordingly, one commits a "fallacy of accident" if one "fails to acknowledge that some particular aspect of the present situation makes the general rule inapplicable to it."[91] But this proposal is meaningful only if we can already class an exception among the unchanging circumstances and thus foresee it. In all the other cases in which a conflict with other norms first appears in the situation—a conflict that qualifies or modifies the transition from W and D to C—the argument belongs to appropriateness argumentation.

3.2 Norm Coherence

The following level of appropriateness argumentation concerns the resolution of those problems of conflict which were systematically produced by argumentatively fulfilling the presupposition of complete description. The fact that we now argue on the basis of norms should not however mislead us into switching to a justification discourse or expecting the resolution of the conflict from that norm which can be proven to be valid independent of the particular situation. It is a precipitous step to claim that, by pointing to another relevant feature of the situation, "the question concerning the relevance of the differences shifts to the one concerning the rationality of the reasons for a moral judgment."[92] Tugendhat also takes this precipitous step when he rejects the weighing procedure and applies the idea of impartiality as a principle of adequacy directly to a situation. Nor does Hare succeed in solving the problem of a conflict of norms when he reduces critical thinking to the procedure of semantically universalizing a norm previously extended in its meaning by additional features. Both proposals to solve the problem presuppose that we already have a modified norm at our disposal and that it is now only a matter of its claim to validity.[93]

The conflict of norms cannot be reconstructed as a conflict of validity claims because conflicting norms or competing semantic variants enter a relation with one another only in a concrete situation. A justification discourse would have to abstract from this very property of the problem of a conflict of norms, namely, from its situational dependency. Leaving aside the case of a logical inconsistency ("You ought not to lie under any circumstances" versus "You ought to lie under some circumstances"), conflicts of norms are not foreseeable since we know neither all the application situations nor all the possible constellations of features in situations. What other norms or semantic variants are possibly applicable can only be known in the particular situation itself. This result agrees with the idea of the procedural justification of norms, as is characteristic of the postconventional level of moral reasoning.

According to what criterion can conflicting norms in a situation be weighed without implicitly stepping out of an appropriateness argumentation and into a justification discourse? Baier characterized norms on balance as those which we select on the basis of "rules of superiority." As such, these rules thus establish the relation between all the norm hypotheses relevant in the concrete situation. The criterion according to which we conduct this weighing cannot of course be drawn from the situation itself. Baier traces it back to the ethical context of a form of life and, as an example, mentions the fact that it is customary under present societal conditions to give priority to moral viewpoints over those of self-interest. With the help of such a rule of superiority, we can thus select, in a particular case, the appropriate norm from the set of all norm hypotheses pertaining to the situation.[94] This rule of superiority can in turn be justified. Alexy formulated this model of weighing in a methodologically clearer manner. As optimizing prescriptions, principles already have an inherently open, connective structure which makes it possible to relate them to the actual conditions of a situation (description of the facts) and to all the other rules and principles applicable in this situation. The priority of one principle follows from a case-related proposition of preference which can be justified according to the weighing axiom in such a way that the degree of violation of one principle depends on the importance of the other one. In this way, we can be sure that all the normatively relevant viewpoints have been related to one another before determining a norm appropriate. In addition to this, still other methods of relating can be put forward: Alexy himself mentions the principle of proportionality [*Verhältnismäßigkeit*], which ties the application of a norm to the selection of suitable and necessary means with respect to the actual possibilities present in a situation; as well as, generally, all comparisons and quantitatively determined conditions that allow a decision in favor of a norm, on considering all the other normative viewpoints. But the criterion problem is not entirely excluded in this way[95] because the degree of importance must itself be justified.

The criterion according to which we orient ourselves when weighing conflicting norms may not, for its part, have a predetermined material content which gives priority to certain normative viewpoints over others. Alexy's conception of principles as optimizing prescriptions already drew our attention to the danger that can arise when, for instance, a value model is projected onto a theory of norm structure. The decision on an appropriate norm is then reduced to deciding on the relatively better state of affairs, which is also the optimum in the particular situation. The problem thereby alluded to consists in the danger of already introducing material criteria when determining the structure of argumentation, criteria which should themselves be the subject matter of an appropriateness argumentation. A procedural concept of appropriateness, or a procedural application of norms, would have to refrain from using such implicit material criteria. If appropriateness is to consist in considering all the features of a situation, then the *method* of considering may not, for its part, be determined by material criteria.

The conditions of appropriateness should not prejudice the validity of a norm. Kant already cautioned us against that: "For the canon of practical reason is involved in this realm. Here the value of [a given] practice depends upon its appropriateness to the theory upon which it is based. All is lost if empirical, and consequently accidental, conditions of the execution of the law are made the conditions of the law itself. Then a practice which is calculated in relation to the probable result of previous experience is accorded the right of determining the theory itself."[96] Now, we have seen that the requirement to consider the accidental is entirely compatible with the idea of impartiality if—and Kant was probably also thinking of this—one keeps this requirement separated from all the conditions of validity.

Because the appropriate application of rules cannot be completely reconstructed rationally, Aristotle presupposed certain character features, whose formation depends on the biographical experiences of the individual and on the establishment of a political community. Whoever is "good" (brave, circumspect, just) knows with the help of practical wisdom what the appropriate thing to do is in a situation. Kant also assumed that this capability concerns a disposition that, once acquired, can be exercised well or badly, improved by examples, but cannot be applied methodologically.[97] The attempt to formulate rules of application leads to a paradox, which motivated Wittgenstein to characterize rule-following as a "custom" or "practice" for which we are trained. If a rule does not contain the rule for its own application, then rules of application in turn require separate rules for their application. "If it [general logic] sought to give general instructions how we are to subsume under these rules, that is, to distinguish whether something does or does not come under them, that could only be by means of another rule. This in turn, for the very reason that it is a rule, again demands guidance from judgment. And thus it appears that, though understanding is capable of being instructed, and of being equipped with rules, judgment is a peculiar talent which can be practised only, and cannot be taught."[98]

Kant could however exclude the categories from this paradox. He tied their application to a schematism in which the imagination has already synthesized them and the intuitively given. Adopting this solution for our attempt at determining the concept of appropriateness more precisely is out of the question because of the different, epistemological context and the problems associated with transcendental philosophy. With his solution, Kant nevertheless happened upon something which is also relevant to us: that element of agreement, of "fit," which we associate with an appropriate norm in a situation. We strive for this element in appropriateness argumentation when, on the basis of the presupposition of complete description, we put forward changed, relevant features against the unchanging circumstances presupposed by the original norm hypothesis, and when we try to weigh conflicting norm hypotheses against one another in order to find an appropriate norm.

The attempt undertaken so far to describe the logic of appropriateness argumentation permits only a formal criterion. What proved to be the argumentative move requiring justification was the claim to relevance with which a certain set of situation features is selected and distinguished as being normatively significant. This line of argumentation rests on the presupposition of being able to justify the decision on relevance in the light of a complete description of the situation. As viewpoints from which we extend and complete a description of a situation, other norms or different semantic variants of a norm are taken into consideration, ones which in turn distinguish other situation features as being normatively significant. If this description of the logic of appropriateness argumentation is correct, then a norm can be applied in consideration of all the circumstances if it is compatible with the application of all the other norms in a situation and with all the semantic variants possible in a situation. Thus, the formal criterion for appropriateness can only be the coherence of the norm with all the other norms and semantic variants applicable in the situation.

Even now one can still ask what coherence is guided by. In order to see to what extent the criterion of coherence can be formally specified, it is advisable to ask about the type of norms to which a *prima facie* norm is related in a situation. As conflicting norms, only those which are also valid can be suitable. In all other cases, the primacy of the *prima facie* norm would be indisputable. If we include this property, we can thus formulate a first criterion of coherence:

(1) A norm Nx is appropriate in the situation Sx if it is compatible with all the other semantic variants $NSVn$ and all the norms Nn applicable in Sx, and if the validity of each individual semantic variant and each individual norm could be justified in a justification discourse.

This criterion has the disadvantage that we never know which norms in a situation could ever be justified in a justification discourse. For this, we would have to possess an infinite normative imagination which would make it possible for us to anticipate every virtually universalizable norm applicable to a particular situation. This would be another version of the strong formulation of the principle (U). It would be based on the utopia of a complete correspondence between situation and norm. When we make a decision on relevance, however, we avail ourselves of norms already proved to be valid. For this reason, we can always refer only to those valid norms which belong to a—our—particular form of life. Thus, we can formulate a second criterion of coherence:

(2) A norm Nx is appropriately applicable in Sx if it is compatible with all the other norms NFL applicable in Sx which belong to a form of life FLx and can be justified in a justification discourse. (The same applies to all the semantic variants.)

With this form-of-life index of valid norms, it is not a matter of a restriction qualifying the validity claim or of a concealed tying of the rationality of application to the existing ethical life. The valid norms belonging to a form of life are not unchangeable, nor are they to be brought into a system of transitive relations (social system's morality) prior to every application, whereby it would then be merely a matter of interpreting them appropriately in an application situation. With the universalization of the validity claim at the postconventional level of moral reasoning, there can no longer be a prior determination of the application situation. Decentered forms of life do not have "ethical systems" at their disposal. Rather, in each individual situation, we have to apply all the valid norms in order to satisfy the requirement of a complete description of the situation. By being disengaged from a particular situation, valid norms become possible viewpoints within a form of life, and their application depends on the consideration of all the other normative viewpoints applicable in the particular situation. Modernity's rationalized and decentered forms of life are characterized by a plurality of virtually universalizable, but abstract, normative "stereotypes" which, by virtue of the various constellations of features in concrete situations, combine to form a matrix of conflicts of norms. In morally justifying an action or a corresponding singular normative proposition, we are now just concerned with the different kinds of reasons we employ—depending on the alternate rules of argumentation—in order to check appropriateness in respect of the particular situation, on the one hand, and the universal reciprocity of a norm's validity, on the other. Such a lifeworld requires a high degree of constructive fantasy and normative imagination in order to relate all the features of a situation to the normative claims in which a universal-reciprocal interest is expressed, and this, in order to do justice both to the "simultaneity" of the absolute difference of every individual situation and to the universal validity of moral norms.

In appropriateness argumentation, the moral validity of norms is simply presupposed and recognized as "given"; in justification discourses, it is suspended and can thus be contested and relativized at any time. This validity no longer determines the manner of a norm's application, that is, its relation to other valid norms in a situation. That is why the coherence of valid norms belonging to a form of life cannot be determined independently of the concrete situation. Expressed in terms of Toulmin's scheme of argumentation, appropriateness argumentation refers only to the relation between C-D-W; reasons which affect the backing (B) of the validity of W do not play a part at this level. For this reason, the criterion of coherence can be employed meaningfully only at the first level. Whereas validity depends on the fact that the norm can be universalized in view of the evidence (B) put forward for its general observance, appropriateness is guided by whether the norm, in all its semantic variants and in relation to all the other applicable norms, is applicable to a situation described completely. The criterion of coherence only makes sense in appropriateness argumentation; in justification discourses, it cannot be used as an argument. For this reason, it is superfluous to formulate norms in the following way: if q, then it is prescribed to do p, unless there is an exception.

Rather, the consideration of exceptions is taken care of by appropriateness argumentation itself—in such a way that the requirement of considering all the other situation features forces the proponent to justify why these features, and not others, are relevant.

Thus, the criterion of coherence introduced here differs from theories of ethical life, in which validity is always combined with appropriateness, as well as from moral theories of coherence in the narrow sense, which determine not only the application of a norm, but also the justification of its validity according to its position in the balance with other norms.[99]

Finally, however, the question of how we should construe a coherent relation within a set of applicable norms still remains to be answered. Here it is scarcely possible to specify the criterion of appropriateness in an exclusively formal way. The only goal which can be specified consists in measuring compatibility in terms of what norm can best be justified in relation to all the other norms applicable in a situation.

Because this justification refers only to the decision on the selection of a norm, not to the universal reciprocity of a norm, it has a meaning independent of validity. In order to construct such a justification, we require an implicit theory which establishes an internal context of justification for the otherwise disordered valid norms of a form of life. In view of the unforeseeable constellations of features, we are faced with this constructive task over and over again in each situation. Coherence, which we have to construct, does not express a given system of transitive relations; rather, it must be established for each particular case. This does not rule out the fact that there are "paradigms" which determine what features are normatively relevant in a situation. Practical reason places the elements of these paradigms under the requirement of completeness, on the one hand, and that of validity, on the other. They can thus be changed by criticizing the validity of each individual norm, as well as by successively extending the description of the situation. In this sense, one could designate them as "schemes" in which empirical assumptions, ideas of the good life, valid norms, and more or less standardized situation descriptions are coherently connected with one another. Constituting a part of such a system of transitive relations, which can be changed by justification and application discourses at any time, are a specific schematization of possible application situations, structured situation descriptions, and combinations of situation features—all of which come with the set of valid norms given in each situation.

Part Four:

Appropriateness Argumentation in Law

In his study on the concept of *raison d'état*, Herfried Münkler presents, without further comment, a terse definition by Christoph Besold from 1614: *"Ratio politica quam nunc vocant de Statu (olim aequitas et epieikeia) transgreditur legibus, scripto vel voce promulgatae; literam, sed non sensum et finem."*[1] How is it that *raison d'état* and equity can be synonymous in the understanding of contemporaries? It can be assumed from the quotation that the possibility of suspending conventionally given laws in the name of equity was viewed as a common feature. Equity would then have been one of the precursory concepts that prepared the way for the main principle of the *raison d'état*, the *"princeps legibus solutus."* If the *raison d'état* slips into the function of equity, the goals are of course changed. What matters now is not to realize, corresponding to the nature of the thing, natural law against the general law, which is inadequate in the particular case, but to make law as a whole serve the purposes of the state. Equating equity and the *raison d'état* thus stands at the beginning of the positing of law—and positing means that law can be changed at will. In addition, taking recourse to "equity" provides the decisive reason for this: Because equity is closer to the "the things," or, as Aristotle calls it, to the "fullness of life," than the general law, the state can break the law, if the situation requires it. Carl Schmitt and Ernst Forsthoff are also in this tradition, according to which the law remains limited to semantic generality, and the exceptional case, which cannot be decided by simple subsumption, is the responsibility of the state: "For true statehood is above the competition between societal interests. It is neutral toward these interests and, in this neutrality, together with the freedom this creates to decide truly substantive matters, it has its specific authority and dignity."[2]

Following the stage model proposed by Kohlberg, the interpretation of the development of concepts of justice demonstrated that a conventional idea of equality and equity reaches its limits in the

247

"social system's morality," which is anchored in the context of a community. Postconventional Stages 5 and 6 break the rigid rule-exception scheme tied to given norms. Stage 6 can be reconstructed in such a way that equality and equity become indistinguishable at this stage because now every difference in a situation can become the starting point for constructing an appropriate and universally justifiable norm. If Besold's definition of the *raison d'état* may be considered more or less representative of current understanding,[3] then the obvious supposition is that the postconventional transformation of equity was not the only way to cope with the problems it stands for, namely, those of a case-specific normative regulation appropriate to the matter. This is supported by the emergence of political theories of prudence as a sign of the incipient emancipation of politics from a concept of justice fused with theology and morality.[4] *Phronesis,* which—still in its particular form as a judge's *phronesis* serving equity—was taken by Gadamer as evidence for his thesis of the exemplary significance of legal hermeneutics, becomes pure cleverness, *"deinotes,"* from the Aristotelian viewpoint.[5] This is wisdom without an ethical habitus. For this reason, Kant separates it strictly from the categorical imperative of morality. Prudence becomes means-ends rationality. What is important now is to grasp those features of the situation which are relevant to the successful attainment of any end whatever—primarily that of the self-preservation of the state and of one's own body; and this, as precisely as possible, and above all fast. For the situations are changing faster and, with increasing knowledge, appear more complex than Aristotle still believed when he assigned *phronesis* the task of mediating between the contingent and the end of the good life. On this presupposition, it is obvious that the decision on situation features relevant to success is left not to an application discourse, but to "experts" who are competent in dealing with the "thing"—for example, leaving it to a governmental agency. If we can never consider all the features of a situation and are always confronted with a scarcity of time, then there is a need for certain specialized institutions which can take over the old task of equity. Because validity and appropriateness are no longer interwoven with one another in a societal context but separate in the dimensions of justification and application, every difference in a situation can become relevant. That is why specific structures of relevance have to crystallize, ones which make it possible to cope quickly and appropriately with certain recurring constellations of features, without having to first relate all the normatively relevant viewpoints to one another in time-consuming procedures. These structures of relevance are the political system, positive law, and the economy.

Up to this point, it has not been necessary to distinguish between legal and moral norms because our aim consisted in constructing a theory of the impartial application of valid norms in general. Insofar as, in law, it is also a matter of applying legitimately created norms, this application falls under the requirement of impartiality too. Before going into appropriateness argumentation in law, I shall thus sketch briefly the reasons which follow from discourse ethics for the distinction between law and morality.[6]

law as reduction of cognitive overload (efficiency gains) stores of previous trade-offs

eg. when nonobservance
results in illegitimacy
(rather than rights)

1

Discourse Ethics' Reasons for
the Distinction Between Law and Morality

With the principle (U), the validity of norms is tied to the condition that the consequences and side effects arising for the interests of each individual as a result of a general observance of these norms under unchanging circumstances can be collectively accepted by all those affected. This moral principle can be applied only as a rule of argumentation in discourses in which the generalizability of interests is expressed in the acceptability of the reasons put forward by participants having equal rights. But the acceptability of good reasons does not imply a motive for actually observing the norm justified in that sense. Reasons which are rationally plausible do, by virtue of their claim to be binding, possess a direct relevance to the de facto orientation of action, but they cannot produce a corresponding action orientation on their own power. Whoever orients himself differently in action simply does not have good reasons.

If, according to the thesis discussed here, application discourses constitute a part of practical reason, then the problem of motivation exists in the same way for the realization of appropriate singular normative propositions as it does for the observance of valid norms. In justification and application discourses, we can only discover what we ought to do here and now. They do not however guarantee that what ought to be done will actually become what we wish to do in this situation.

Cognitivist ethics would not need to concern itself with the problem of motivation any further if, in the case of a nonobservance of valid and appropriate norms, a violation of the principle of universal reciprocity did not in turn occur. The criterion of validity which is established with the moral principle (U) expressly links the validity of a norm to the presupposition of its general observance. The acceptability of reasons advanced by the participants in discourse thus rests on the condition subsequent that the norm is actually observed by everyone. If ego brings about the occurrence of this resolutive condition in that he exempts himself from the duty to actually observe the norm, he destroys the reciprocity of validity. The condition on which alter, for his part, agreed to the duty to actually observe the norm is thus annulled.

But because good reasons alone cannot prevent the occurrence of the condition subsequent, it can be reasonably expected of alter to fulfill the duty to actually observe the norm if he can stabilize the expectation that ego can be motivated, not only by rational insight, but also by empirical influence, to fulfill the condition of reciprocity. That is to say, it can be reasonably expected of alter to observe a valid and appropriate norm only on the condition that he may, if necessary, constrain ego to observe the norm by employing means for empirically effectuating a decision. The only point of this "right" consists in making the de facto validity of the principle of reciprocity possible. It is only on these strict presuppositions that the Kantian equation of law and mutual constraint is justified.[7] Law constitutes a relation between virtual participants in discourse who may reasonably expect of one another that valid norms be actually observed. They thereby mutually recognize one another as "legal persons."

With the moral justification of a right to implement valid norms by employing means for empirically effectuating a decision, there is of course still no guarantee of general, de facto observance. It is not self-evident that these means serve the implementation of valid norms. Every individual's right to expect the general observance of norms cannot be protected against abuse, which in turn violates the principle of reciprocity, as long as the presuppositions for exercising this right are not impartially laid down. According to Locke, the moral reason for the justification of a civil constitution lies not so much in the danger of civil war as in the latter's underlying violation of the principle of reciprocity if everyone were a "judge for himself."[8] Thus, possessing the means for empirically effectuating a decision may not be exposed to the same motivational weaknesses, for the sake of whose compensation law is morally justified. However, to avert this danger we have in turn only law available. It must therefore lay down the preconditions of its own exercise in procedures which guarantee impartial decisions and, at the same time, are empirically effective, that is, institutionalized in a society. In this way, the de facto validity of the principle of reciprocity is effectuated by procedures in which positive legal norms are laid down as being generally valid, and these legal norms are impartially applied in "judgments founded on the present circumstances of the fact"[9] and implemented only on the basis of this decision process.

The fact that legal norms are justified and applied according to this scenario in institutionalized discourses does not change anything in respect of their claim to validity and situational appropriateness. This claim is restricted only insofar as the discourses must satisfy two conditions. On the one hand, there is a need for instruments of power, which are themselves organized in procedures, in order to neutralize disequilibriums of power. On the other hand, the means for empirically effectuating a decision can be implemented only if a clear and distinct decision has been made about the conditions of implementation. General and singular legal norms must therefore follow from discourses which can be terminated by decision. Unlike practical discourses, they are thus conducted under conditions of limited time and incomplete knowledge.

The legitimacy of the results of such restricted discourses depends on the extent to which argumentation that can give effect to reasons is possible and admissible in these discourses. In accordance with the distinction between justification and application proposed here, it must be possible for these reasons to bear a relation to the consideration of all the interests, in the case of argumentation on the validity of a norm; and to the consideration of all the features of a situation, in the case of argumentation on the appropriateness of a norm. The way in which the employment of these different types of reasons is optimally institutionalized is a question of historical experience. In debate with Alexy's distinction between rules and principles, it was already pointed out that, in easy-to-grasp cases, the legislator can also decide on the situational appropriateness of a norm. But even on the presupposition of a positive law which can be changed at will, it must be required of legal argumentation that the normative statement pronounced as a judgment be "rationally justified within the framework of the prevailing legal order."[10] As the reflections on a logic of appropriateness argumentation have shown, what is important in the case of indeterminate norms and conflicts of norms is an impartial consideration of all the features of the situation.

In what follows I shall first examine those positions which, due to the lack of empirical effectiveness of good reasons and due to the need to decide action conflicts under conditions of limited time and incomplete knowledge, have drawn the conclusion that law is to be regarded from the outset according to its function of stabilizing generalized expectations. From this viewpoint, appropriateness argumentation only has the value of contributing rhetorical means to the implementation of decisions. But, precisely in the case of indeterminate norms and conflicts on norms, it will be seen that impartial appropriateness argumentation is unavoidable. Following this I shall consider some proposals to reconstruct this kind of argumentation within legal theory. In conclusion I shall discuss Dworkin's theory of "integrity" as an example of a theory of coherence for the justification and application of law.

2

Systems Theory's Concept of Law

2.1 Double Contingency

We are now confronted with the problem which we persistently excluded in the preceding sections. So far I have simply assumed that it is possible to consider all the relevant features in every situation in order to form an appropriate norm hypothesis. The requirement of such a possibility followed from the interpretation of the moral principle (U) in its strong version, as well as from the developmental logic of moral consciousness, according to which validity and appropriateness must be separated from one another at the postconventional level. These determinations were reconstructed from an internal perspective. On this presupposition it was possible, with Durkheim, to speak in terms of a "free application" of highly abstract and indeterminate norms to an immeasurable number of different individual cases. Of course, Durkheim also adopted the other, external perspective, which allowed him to perceive those social phenomena which in turn compensate for the deficiencies of a lack of firmness and determinacy which necessarily follow from the internal development; these social phenomena are the professional groups into which a society organized according to the division of labor is functionally differentiated and which furnish the individual with fixed role ascriptions.

From the observer's perspective, a situation whose features are no longer determinable by a given, valid structure of relevance appears completely indeterminate. Because we would have to have infinite time and knowledge at our disposal in order to consider complex, continuously changing situations with all their relevant features, the exceptional situation, which has become the rule, appears as a risk. Prudence resorts to calculating the probable. With its help, stable patterns of behavior and expectation can be constructed, which are, at the same time, very much capable of change in order to exploit the varying latitude created by contingency.

Here, a different theoretical trajectory begins, one which is interested not in the evolution of the conditions of validity and appropriateness, but in the production and reproduction of specialized, noninterchangeable action systems under conditions of high complexity and accelerated change.

Since Hobbes, it has been possible to describe the inevitable indeterminacy of situations according to the aspects of existential uncertainty or double contingency in the relations between alter and ego. What is at the center of interest is no longer the problem of *reaching understanding* by mutual perspective-taking, as is the case with Mead, but the successful calculation of the probable behavior of others. For the purposes of determining these aspects more closely, I shall refer back to the model of the development of different types of application in association with the stages of moral consciousness, which we presented in the second part of this study.[11]

Three levels could be distinguished in rough outline. The first one is characterized by a weak generalization of context-dependent expectations that are first formed in the medium of a situation-determined perspective-taking. A common ground emerges in virtue of a situational process of bilateral perspective-taking here and now, or is generalized in systems of roles which need to be activated for the particular situation. At this level, validity and appropriateness are either still completely identical or linked to a concrete context of reciprocity. At the second level, the neutral third position of the generalized other can already be recognized, the position from which concrete interaction can be viewed and by which mutual perspective-taking can orient itself. Systems of temporally, substantively, and socially generalized norms do exist at this level, but their validity remains intertwined with a group or community-specific context which guarantees them their appropriateness within the horizons of a clear set of situations. Justification and application can now be separated institutionally—e.g., in legislation and adjudication—but this can succeed only because (and as long as) the institution deciding the question of validity simultaneously judges in advance the appropriateness of a norm in a clear context of possible constellations of situations. At the third level, the perspective change is universal-reciprocal. The validity of norms is detached from given contexts, with the result that it can no longer concurrently guarantee appropriateness in situations. This must now be independently established in accordance with the idea of impartial application, which requires that all the features of a situation be considered.

This model operates with an implicit premise which we now wish to question. We have assumed that, through the medium of reaching understanding in language, all perspectives can be coordinated with one another in such a way that the interests of all those affected and all the features of a situation can be thematized. Because a grammatically differentiated language with common meanings always generates illocutionary bonds as well, ones which can be thematized in terms of a specific validity claim in cases of conflict, the coordination of actions by norms can in turn be made—through the medium of practical discourse—the subject matter of reaching understanding in language under ideal conditions. The idea of impartiality, functioning here as a rule of argumentation, also includes a principle of the appropriate application of valid norms in consideration of all the relevant contexts.

From the viewpoint of a situation description under the circumstances of double contingency, the interactive generation, justification, and appropriate application of common norms which can coordinate action appear not as a problem of reaching understanding, but as one of stability. Because alter's and ego's perspectives cannot be made fully transparent on the presupposition of rapid changes and incomplete knowledge, coordinating actions in situations is concerned less with a discursively thematizable, common knowledge of identical meanings than with the external conditions of the initiation, continuation, and termination of communication.

Action situations can be stylized in such a way that the possibility of interaction between alter and ego appears as an extremely improbable event. To increase its probability, complex preconditions must be fulfilled, ones which can no longer be calculated with the help of de-moralized theories of prudence. They elude intentional steering as such. If there is no common ground at all between ego and alter, ego adapts his behavior to the fact that alter's behavior is not foreseeable, and vice versa. Then it is highly improbable that an action will occur at all because each one is waiting for orientating indicators which the respective other could give for his own action in order to limit the range of unforeseeable behavioral events. A common ground which makes communication based on mutual expectations possible can only be established behind the backs of those involved, as it were. The moment ego not only has to calculate the contingencies of his nonsocial environment, but also recognizes that his action depends on the contingencies of an alter who in turn is adapting to ego's behavioral contingencies, the situation can no longer be controlled by intentional actions. This uncertainty in prognosticating behavior disturbs the complementarity of expectations—as Parsons called it. Ego cannot orient his actions to alter's expectations, nor vice versa,[12] as long as both are oriented, in a way neither can comprehend, to arbitrarily chosen ends. This becomes possible only if the expectations are generalized and thereby rendered independent of a contingent, indeterminate situation. Whether expectations are fulfilled or disappointed can then be measured according to a generalized criterion which ego and alter share. "There is a *double contingency* inherent in interaction. On the one hand, ego's gratifications are contingent on his selection among available alternatives. But in turn, alter's reaction will be contingent on ego's selection and will result from a complementary selection on alter's part. Because of this double contingency, communication, which is the precondition of cultural patterns, could not exist without both generalization from the particularity of the specific situations (which are never identical for ego and alter) and *stability* of meaning which can only be assured by 'conventions' observed by both parties."[13] For Parsons, the doubly contingent situation brings forth commonly shared cultural patterns. Luhmann detached the concept of double contingency from this reference to the emergence of normative orientations and radicalized it to a factor in the formation of social systems in general.[14] The situation becomes the "crystallization core for an emerging system-environment relation."[15] The instability produced by double contingency becomes the ferment for a particular kind of system formation: systems which reproduce themselves by exclusively referring to themselves in every operation, and thereby become autonomous vis-à-vis their environment. It is thus this situation itself which gives rise to emerging structures from which communication can take its orientation (in a nonintentional way). In what follows, this process is to be traced for the social system of law.

The structures developing from the problematic situation of double contingency must be able to make not only complementary expectations possible, but also the expectation of expectations. If ego limits his expectations only to a certain conformable or deviant behavior on alter's part, the horizon of expectations remains concretist. Rather, ego's expectation must consider alter's own selection of behavioral possibilities, that is, must refer to alter's own expectations.[16] For Luhmann, the function of normativity and law lies in integrating and securing this reflexive expectancy structure. The need for this function increases in proportion to the increasing complexity of situations. The more behavioral possibilities there are in a situation, the greater is the danger of errors and disappointments. Laying down rules makes it possible to orient expectations according to a generalized medium instead of the other's as yet undetermined possibilities in every situation.

If laying down systems of rules or structures is the decisive step which makes stable expectancy formations possible, then of course a problem arises for Luhmann that is related to the problem of the appropriateness of valid norms. It arises, however, not as a result of a differentiation of justification and application at a postconventional level of morality, but from the attempt to derive certainty in expectation from the function of norms. Precisely because situations are experienced as complex and contingent, it must be possible to change rules and adapt them to changing situations. The changeability of rules must be compatible with their established validity.[17]

Luhmann solves this problem on three levels: structurally, by distinguishing between two societal mechanisms for coping with disappointments in expectations—science and law; within law, by combining cognitive and normative expectancy orientations; and by analyzing limited possibilities for learning within normative orientations.

This solution aims at a concept of positive law in which cognitive openness must be combined with normative closure in such a way that legal norms are changeable, that is, adaptable, and, at the same time, can be maintained in the particular case, that is, can guarantee certainty in expectation.

Structures inevitably produce disappointments because they are founded on selections (i.e., selections from the selections from one's own experiences and actions). They reduce the indeterminate number of possibilities in a situation,[18] are thus however exposed to the risk of being surprised, that is, disappointed, in a serious way by what has not been considered. Since disappointments are unavoidable on this presupposition, mechanisms must be created to make it possible to cope with them. Luhmann envisions two mechanisms: the structure can be changed or it can be maintained. In the first case, we cope with disappointments cognitively by changing our knowledge, in view of unexpected events, about what may be selected as being regularly expectable. For this purpose, we "learn" and introduce a new code which operates with the distinction "true/untrue." In the other case, we cope with disappointments normatively by demonstrating, in view of unexpected events, that we nevertheless maintain our expectations and that one should continue to be oriented by this expectation and not by changes in expectation which could be triggered by the unexpected. We do not "learn." On this rests the "security and social integration of expectation,"[19] which we link to a code that operates with the distinction "lawful/ unlawful." In this way, highly artificial structures can be protected against the threat from contingency and complexity and, at the same time, changed. Normative and cognitive attitudes can be combined, but not interchanged.

It is possible to link these two attitudes to any expectation whatsoever. In this respect, all *"counterfactually stabilised behavioural expectations"* are norms.[20] Law emerges only from the fact that certain expectations are selected and placed under the protection of the normative handling of disappointments. It is only if a certain number of expectations are temporally, socially, and substantively generalized to a body of norms that one may speak of a structure which can be designated as law. Luhmann develops the selective character of law as a structure of social systems in the three dimensions constitutive of systems of meaning: temporal, social, and substantive. In the temporal dimension, it is a matter of the variability of the selective structure of law in relation to other normative expectations. In this respect, a presupposition for the emergence of law is that certain expectations are equipped with a prescriptive quality, that is, fixated on the attitude of not learning, and that mechanisms for handling disappointments, such as ascriptions of guilt and sanctions, are made available. It is only then that expectations can be permanently secured through temporally different cases of disappointment. In the social dimension, it is a question of selecting those expectations which are condensed into the selective structure of law. Not every privately held expectation, or one commonly shared by chance in a small group, is suitable for this, but only those which can be supported by the position of a neutral third party, in the sense of the generalized other. It must be possible to assume that the *"presupposed expectations of expectation on the part of a third party"*[21] form a general consensus and are therefore dependent on procedures of institutionalization. In law, the institutionalizing function itself can be reflexively institutionalized, namely, first in the function of the judge, later by differentiating between legislation and adjudication. In the substantive dimension, it is a matter of materially condensing the selected expectations into an identifiable system of meaning. It is only in this way that behavioral expectations can also be stabilized. The levels of meaning at which individual concrete expectations are synthesized can attain different degrees of abstraction. Luhmann distinguishes between persons, roles, programs, and values. What is important here too is to locate the golden mean between situationally flexible changeability and certainty in expectation. For the function of identification, this problem presents itself as the relation between the concreteness and abstraction of syntheses of meaning. Luhmann opts for roles and programs as suitable levels because persons are too concrete and values too indeterminate and abstract.[22]

Each of these dimensions of experiencing meaning generalizes expectations according to a particular aspect: temporally, by abstracting from individual cases of possible disappointment; socially, by abstracting from the agreement of different individuals; and substantively, by abstracting from the material differences in expectations. Those expectations which can be simultaneously generalized in all three dimensions are selected as law. Law is a mechanism of selection that meaningfully synthesizes those expectations to a structure which, first, can be equipped with prescriptive quality and connected with sanctions for handling disappointments; secondly, can be selected by institutionalized procedures as a generally assumed consensus; and finally, as programs of decision, can be cast in a recognizable form. Because all three dimensions of generalization can vary in relation to one another, we can distinguish as law only those expectations which have been selected on account of compatible mechanisms of generalization. "We will classify the thus *congruently generalised normative behavioural expectations* as the *law* of a social system. Law attains selective congruence and therefore forms a structure of social systems" (italics in the original).[23]

For Luhmann, positivized law is that form of law which can congruently generalize behavioral expectations in a complex society differentiated into specialized subsystems. It satisfies this requirement by means of its autonomy vis-à-vis all the other societal systems. Complexity and contingency can be managed by arbitrary decisions on the part of the political legislator, whereas adjudication has to tend to the handling of disappointment in application situations. In this manner, the changeability and stabilization of behavioral expectations can be combined in such a way that a flexible adaptation to changing situational circumstances becomes possible without falling back into the state of nature constituted by double contingency. The tasks of changing and stabilizing the structure are distributed across various situations and institutionalized in various procedures: "The function of a structure does not presume absolute constancy, but requires merely that the structure in the situations which it structures is not problematised. Thus it is absolutely consistent for it to be made the subject of decision in *other* situations (at other points of time, for other roles or persons), i.e. that it is variable. The only thing that is thus required is that a clearly recognisable, firmly institutionalised boundary separates these situations."[24]

The internal differentiation into a legislation which deals with social problems cognitively and an adjudication which secures structures normatively leads to law itself being differentiated as a system. Its decisions do indeed remain tied to the legislator's political programs, but, as decisions in law, are independent of politics, natural law, and morality. The typical program structure is therefore the conditional program that links the decision in law to an if-then relation between the facts circumscribed by a legal norm and the legal consequence. Conditional programs can refer to limited and detailed sections of a situation, that is, can cope with contingent circumstances faster and more appropriately. Decisions in law are just subject to the principle of deciding like cases alike,[25] which is guaranteed by a consistent dogmatic catalogue of decisions. On considering new developments in general systems theory, Luhmann further radicalized this distinction between the cognitive and normative aspects of the legal system. Law appears as a normatively closed and cognitively open system.[26] It is closed in its function of deciding what is lawful and what unlawful, a function which cannot be substituted, controlled, or steered by any other system. It can characterize whatever it wishes with this decision, as long as it adheres to its own presuppositions in doing so. Only then does it reproduce itself from event to event as an autonomous system. Reducing the normative function of law to the allocation of the predicates lawful and unlawful permits a greater openness to arbitrary events in the environment. What matters is not the quality of these events themselves, but simply whether they affect the conditions internal to the system for triggering the allocation of the positive or negative value. The legal system can thus learn within the limits of its normative closure. "It can transfer normative validity from element to element only by its own action; but it is precisely this autopoietic closedness that makes high demands on a cognitive disposition in relation to the environment. The system secures its closedness by the fact that it maintains self-reference in all its operations and makes them dependent upon whether the moment-to-moment produced elements can or cannot adopt a normative quality. It secures its openness by the fact that it adapts the semantics of this reproduction to environmental conditions."[27] The combination of conditional programming and binary coding in lawful/unlawful thus proves to be the pivotal point for the reproduction of the legal system.

2.2 Law as an Autopoietic System: Differentiation into Code and Programming

Following Luhmann's conception of an autonomous legal system could be a way of solving the problem of stabilizing behavioral expectations under conditions of high complexity and contingency. However, from the viewpoint of cognitivist ethics, a high price would have to be paid for this: because their prescriptive quality only signals a refusal to learn, (legal) norms can be neither universally justified nor appropriately applied. The autonomy of the legal system consists precisely in having been emancipated from natural law's requirements for justification. The validity of the code "lawful/unlawful" is also independent of a positivist basic norm (Kelsen) or of a rule of recognition (H. L. A. Hart).[28] Similarly, the application of individual norms is simply a decision regulated according to internal criteria, one which, viewed externally, consists in attributing the positive or negative value of the code to a behavioral expectation. The internal foundations for creating a norm to decide the individual case are merely a matter for legal rhetoric.[29] The fact that there are nevertheless demands for justifying validity, for legitimate procedures, and for the necessity of distinguishing between correct and incorrect application only serves the purpose of concealing internally the externally observable, absolute contingency of the legal system. Because there is no legal right for the introduction of the distinction between lawful and unlawful, the paradox present here has to be concealed with the help of systematic self-deception. Since the establishment of the Areopagus in ancient Athens, such attempts, like all justifications, have had only a placebo function.

This diagnosis would indeed be correct if law could actually be described in Luhmann's intended sense as a societal subsystem that has been completely differentiated functionally from all other subsystems. It is only then that it would seem as if we had to furnish law with the idea of impartial justification and application from without. This assumption appears problematic for two reasons. In the first place, the paradox identified by Luhmann himself points to the fact that justifications in law cannot be rejected *a limine*. They appear as futile efforts to resolve the paradox only because Luhmann has to exclude the internal perspective on these attempts at de-paradoxicalization. It may well be the case that the sociological observer perceives moral justifications of the validity of legal norms only as strategies to avoid contingency. However, the observer would have to change his perspective in order to explain why those involved connect—for the most part—their willingness to follow legal norms with the expectation of contingent force *and* with the recognition of the legitimacy of the legal foundation for exercising this force.

For our purposes, however, another problem is more important. By differentiating the legal code into a binary schematism exclusively administered by the legal system, a problem arises—again from the viewpoint of moral cognitivism—namely, that of the appropriateness of the code in relation to other societal subsystems and their specific codes. On the presuppositions of functional differentiation, the legal system can neither adopt nor intervene in other codes. The consequence of this would be dedifferentiation.

For this reason, Luhmann permits only two possibilities as to how the legal system can adapt itself to changes in its environment in such a way that it changes itself in the process. In the dimension of the code, this is achieved by introducing a third value which enlarges the original binary schematism and functions as a so-called "rejection value." In this way, the codes of different subsystems can refer to one another without having to adopt the other's coding; this is repulsed by the "rejection value" in each case. In this manner, the code represented by the third value can be considered, and not considered, concurrently; it is both a *tertium non datur* and a *tertium datur:* "What is rejected . . . is the *standard-setting character* [*Maßgeblichkeit*] of other systems' *codes* (their actual code function) for one's own system, *not the relevance of their valuations.*"[30] In this manner, the perspective of other codes can be reflected in the system without following the other code itself. The "polycontextuality of society" can thus be represented in the subsystem.[31] The disadvantage of the trivalency consists however in the fact that the decision between the values lawful/unlawful is, for its part, again up for decision, relative to the third value in each case. Thus, the very paradox which is to be avoided reappears in order to reject the question concerning the legal right for introducing the distinction between lawful and unlawful.

Thus, the only alternative which remains is the possibility of tackling the problem of de-paradoxicalization itself and of solving it by a further internal differentiation, now that the external differentiations (natural law) have been used up and the system is in danger of dedifferentiating. Luhmann assigns this task to programs, which decide the correct use of the code. The structural differentiation between legislation and adjudication, still favored in *A Sociological Theory of Law,* proves to be overstrained in view of the polycontextuality of society. Luhmann now appears to locate the differentiation into code and program at right angles to the distinction between legislation and adjudication. He begins with the following observation: "An alternative seems to be developing directly from the practice of law [in society], and, in an unreflected manner as it were, under the sheer pressure of problems—an alternative that could be characterized as a softening of legal doctrine, as a change over to indeterminate legal concepts or prescriptions on weighing, and as a switching of decision-making processes from structural directives to concrete deliberations on consequences."[32] This is how the problem of appropriateness is characterized. Luhmann assigns its resolution to programs, which have to become more indeterminate in order to be open to situational differences which are relevant from the perspective of "values" and make it necessary to go beyond the rule character of formal programs. The code is restricted to its mere deciding function independent of the situation, whereas programs are subject to the situational pressure to adapt.

> "With the unavoidable exaggerations of a very abstract presentation, one can say: the binary code remains intact. A decision still has to be made between lawful and unlawful. *Tertium non datur.* But the programs that guide these decisions and limit the conditions of their correctness (and thereby make them expectable and decidable) are subject to changes—be it in the direction of indeterminacy, or be it in the direction of a rapid and frequent change of their determinations—and this, as if what mattered was giving greater control of current decision making to the changing situations themselves (at a time when it is in any case not possible to look with certainty to the future)."[33]

Switching the perspective to the situational change of programs has revealing consequences. The code now only takes care of the unequivocal decision in favor of one of the two values; it is otherwise normatively inactive. It renders itself completely independent in its deciding function, and it now bears the names "lawful/ unlawful" really only by chance. Instead, programs decide the " 'correct' ascription of the circumstances of the case to the values of the code,"[34] but they provide only "viewpoints on what is correct."[35]

Under these conditions, the allocation of the values "lawful/un-lawful" can no longer be unequivocally conditioned because viewpoints on what is correct can be changed at any time as a result of the impressions generated by situations. It is an open question whether viewpoints can then still fulfill their original function of "giving aid in matters of decision or expectation" by determining in advance "a verbally fixed rule of decision, the application of which is guaranteed by institutionalisation."[36] The code seems to adopt this function, whereas programs, independently of this, are confined to the permanent cognitive changes which stable expectations can no longer connect up with. "Then it is understandable that a legal system that finds itself prevented from adapting to the polycontextuality of modern society at the level of coding is compelled to transfer adaptation to the programming of the system. If sufficient logical and structural complexity of coding cannot be attained, then inexactness, situation dependency, and fluctuations have to be the response in the programs."[37] The code necessitating unequivocal decisions is subsumed under a program which is itself constantly changing and highly equivocal because it has to consider the differences in complex situations. The relationship between code and programming becomes a precarious balancing act; and producing a unity in the legal system between determinacy and indeterminacy becomes a permanent problem. On the one hand, the deciding capacity must be maintained in order not to jeopardize the societal function of stabilizing behavioral expectations. On the other hand, however, the same recipients of unequivocal decisions demand situationally flexible programs which consider their specifically different requirements (appropriately).

With this argumentation, Luhmann seems to maneuver himself into a precarious situation. If everything depends on programs being sufficiently sensitive to changes, justifications and appropriateness argumentation can no longer be dismissed as merely system-internal legal rhetoric.[38] What is it supposed to mean that programs decide the "correct" classification of the circumstances of the case and the code value, if this decision can no longer be programmed or controlled unequivocally? Luhmann has to implicitly ascribe great importance to appropriateness argumentation, which decides *in casu* about the consideration of all the relevant features of a situation, but he cannot permit himself to appreciate this in its argumentative significance. An argumentative zone is pushed in between code and program, one which cannot be completely reconstructed using the means of sociological observation. To make allowance for this, Luhmann seems to assimilate programs to values, which do not lay down in advance what is to be done in a situation. *A Sociological Theory of Law* still distinguishes programs by the fact that they integrate behavioral expectations at a medium level of abstraction, in contrast to values, on the one hand, and roles and persons, on the other. Situational concreteness is ruled out as a dysfunctional alternative: "persons who integrate their expectations too concretely, and nevertheless set norms, will be living with many disappointments and will have difficulties in learning."[39] To become situationally flexible, programs now seem to switch to the level of abstraction of values. Because they now only provide "viewpoints on what is correct," they become as indeterminate as values, which are simply "points of view on the preferability of actions."[40] However, in considering material contexts of value, which break through the conditional rule character of programs, we find ourselves being again referred back to the problem of coherent situation interpretations, which can only be reconstructed from an internal perspective—which is why they do not interest Luhmann any further: "the ensuing mixed relations between values are treated as a problem of interpretation."[41]

What leads to the same dilemma is the attempt to construe the legal system reflexively from the outset and thereby raise the sensitivity and appropriateness of law in relation to other subsystems to the *explanandum* of systems theory. This relation then appears as a "regulatory trilemma" (Teubner) in which the problem of how normative steering and cognitive evolution in law can be made compatible under conditions of high complexity and contingency is radicalized: "External influence on areas of social life is possible but— and this is crucial—only within the paths and limits of the respective self-reproduction. These are described by the *regulatory trilemma: Every regulatory intervention which goes beyond these limits is either irrelevant or produces disintegrating effects on the social area of life or else disintegrating effects on regulatory law itself* (. . .)" (italics in the original).[42]

To avoid this trilemma, law has to cut back significantly on its steering interventions and limit itself to laying down the conditions which make it possible for individual subsystems to steer themselves in a manner compatible with every subsystem. Here too, the deciding function, centered on the code, forms the core of the functional differentiation of the legal system, a function which is however subject to a programming decision that must be situationally flexible. The precarious task of the legal system consists in reflexively tying its steering interventions back to the conditions of possibility of a nonconflicting self-steering of subsystems. In this way, the legal system accomplishes the paradoxical assignment of providing for the maintenance of the steering capacity of subsystems on the strength of its own reflexively controlled self-steering. This necessitates not that the aspects of a situation be considered according to the relevance criteria of principles which need to be weighed and justified, but that the subsystems' self-descriptions themselves be adopted and the *functional* imperatives embodying these be brought into a relation with one another in such a way that they do not run counter to the conditions of reproduction of the system affected. Appropriateness argumentation then consists in developing a reflexive doctrine that maintains the compatibility of different and changing self-descriptions of other systems and lays down the conditions on which these descriptions may be connected to the legal code. For Teubner too, the task of looking after the legal system's adequate capacity to respond [*Resonanzfähigkeit*] to the demands of the environment falls to programming. Like Luhmann, Teubner diagnoses the increasing indeterminacy of programs as a consequence of reflexivity and as a precondition for a law that can learn:

> "The system has one possibility to avoid a catastrophe in its capacity to respond [*Resonanzkatastrophe*]: to integrate the self-descriptions of the other system into its own description of it. But this leads in principle to a new problem. Integrating an external code into a system's own operations means disintegration of this system; it means the end of its own operations, which are tied to the specific code. Therefore, as a compromise, there is only one, unsatisfactory way out: to leave the system's own code untouched and just adapt its program structures to other systems' self-descriptions; that is, adapt them while maintaining compatibility with its own code. This presupposes a clear separation between the system's code and its program. But at a price: high indeterminacy of the system's own program."[43]

3

The Indeterminacy of Legal Rules

We can now describe the problem more precisely. With the help of the model of double contingency and the theories based on it, it was to be shown how certainty in expectation can become possible under conditions of limited time and incomplete knowledge. We thus confronted those very conditions which were previously excluded when we endeavored to reconstruct concurrently appropriate and valid norms. Systems theory in sociology characterizes positive law as a social system which makes certainty in expectation, and thus communication, possible in situations of double contingency. Law appears as a structure of the societal system that emerges from selecting congruently generalized behavioral expectations. These selected expectations are protected against possible disappointments by being ascribed a prescriptive quality. From the moment the process of generalization and abstraction (which, for Parsons, is decisive for the possibility of certainty in expectation) is carried out according to its own criteria, independently of politics and morality, it leads to the development of positive law as an emerging, autonomous system. By means of binary coding, this system is normatively closed toward its environment and, through conditional programming, it is open to the reception of changes in the environment.

In order to find out how appropriateness argumentation is possible under conditions of double contingency, we can refer back to the proposal we made in our discussion of Alexy, namely, to relate the distinction between rules and principles not to the structure of norms, as with Alexy, but to the presuppositions of action on which norms are applied. As definitive rules, conditional programs require an unequivocal application which is tied to the presence of the "if-component" in a concrete situation.[44] The selective character of a norm is expressed in this conditional connecting of presupposition and consequence: only the features laid down in the presupposition count. Not all the features of a situation are relevant, only those that belong to the semantic extension of the "if-component," which triggers a specific legal consequence and thus a decision on the allocation of the values "lawful/unlawful." This description is true for our proposal to understand "rules" as a specific *procedure of application;* and it is essential for this procedure that a situation's "irrelevant" features, those not belonging to the semantic extension of the legal norms, are screened out. This form of an application procedure can now be explained as a consequence of double contingency. It is institutionalized in specific procedures for applying norms, such as programmed decisions with rule character, professionalized role systems, and sanctions based on the state's monopoly of force.

How does this form of application now relate to the one Alexy characterized as "principles"? I modified Alexy's definition to the degree necessary and proposed that we then speak of applying a norm as a principle when we enter an argumentative procedure which obligates us to consider all the features of a situation and to weigh the relevant normative viewpoints. When applying norms as rules, that is precisely not the case. Luhmann's description of the legal system as the combination of conditional programming and binary coding is tailored to the application of norms as rules with definitive character.

It has however become apparent that suspending appropriateness argumentation when applying norms is justified only to the extent that we are dealing with unequivocal decisions under conditions of limited time and incomplete knowledge, because otherwise a symmetrical observance of justified norms in every situation, at all times, and by every person cannot be guaranteed. This qualification rests however on a special premise: that the appropriateness of the norm be decided elsewhere. After the dissolution of the conventional fusion of validity and appropriateness, screening out appropriateness argumentation can now only be justified by handing this argumentation over to the legislator. Against the background of a postconventional level of justifying and applying norms, the artificial conventionalization of legal norms as positivized "rules" requires an additional justification. It is only on this premise that one can justify, from an *internal* perspective, why situational contexts may be left unconsidered when applying norms as rules. If a particular institution, such as the legislature, has decided the appropriateness of the norm in advance, it can be applied like a rule. In this way, positive law corresponds to the postconventional level of justifying and applying norms. The positing of legal norms must be institutionalized in procedures which correspond to the rules of practical discourse, so that the interests of each individual can receive their due regard. The application of norms must be institutionalized in procedures which make it possible to consider all the particular features of a situation. It is only in this manner that the apparent paradox of positive law can be dissolved, the arbitrary changeability of positive law made compatible with the requirement of universally recognizing its validity, and the selectivity of norms (as rules) combined with the idea of impartial application.

Luhmann screens out this background completely; and it is only against this background that the artificial conventionalization of norms as rules is possible and justified. His thesis about the autonomy of the legal system negates this background in both dimensions. In the dimension of justification, law is valid independent of the fact that the procedures of its production can be justified morally. In its code function, it is autonomous, and in its programming, it is dependent on the political legislator who, for his part, subsumes his measures under the code function of law. The application of norms is limited to cognitively checking whether the internally given presuppositions are present. Appropriateness argumentation is not permissible because it would rupture the scheme of conditional programming.

Luhmann can generate the illusion of the legal system's autonomy by rejecting, in the dimension of coding, the justifiability of the distinction between lawful/unlawful (but permitting it as an expectation, so that paradoxes arise which have to be covered up internally), and by ruling out, in the dimension of programming, the appropriate application of conditional rules. Conditionality and binary schematization only achieve the "simultaneous processing of normative and cognitive aspects of meaning . . . as a system."[45] However, both he himself and Teubner have observed that this description of the legal system is unable to grasp the problems of law's coping with accelerated structural change which is becoming increasingly situation-dependent, that is, is no longer generalizable in advance. The polycontextuality of society presses for appropriate consideration by law, and indeed *in casu*.

Consequently, both authors register an increasing *indeterminacy* of law. This is not surprising on the premise of a concept of law as a corpus of conditional rules. However, what appears, from an *external* perspective, as an increasing indeterminacy of law proves to be, from an *internal* perspective, an increasing indispensability of appropriateness argumentation when applying legal norms as rules. Durkheim already described the indeterminacy of norms as a consequence of the greater division of labor in society and therefore considered only a "free application" by autonomous individuals possible; but of course, in a complementary step, he regarded professional groups with conventional articles of association as organizational principles of society. We have, in the meantime, reconstructed the reference to "free application" as the idea of the impartial application of universally justified norms. If our hypothesis is correct that the idea of an impartial application which considers all the features of a situation is constitutive of the postconventional level of moral norms, then the increase in appropriateness argumentation is as such not at all surprising. What changes, however, is the institutional assignment of this type of argumentation to a legislator who decides appropriateness in advance, so that adjudication remains confined to an application of norms as rules. Because the number and types of conflict situations are no longer easy to grasp, the task of applying norms appropriately is increasingly assigned to adjudication.

Nevertheless, it is still an open question whether, with these changes, it is a matter of an increase in appropriateness argumentations. The same result could also be inferred from Teubner's description: Law has to perceive its function (anchored in the code) of providing for clear and distinct decisions in such a way that—at the level of programs and in every situation—it simultaneously reflects on the consequences and side effects of a decision for the subsystem affected—a decision, that is, which attributes the values "lawful" or "unlawful" to a particular behavioral expectation. The functionally adequate perception of its code function under conditions of high complexity and contingency thus compels law to be *open* to appropriateness argumentation, which Luhmann can only describe at the level of values. To the extent that law permits appropriateness argumentation when applying its programs, it is socially functional in the employment of its code, that is, it can do justice to the "polycontextuality" of the system of society.

Although both reconstructions, one conducted from an internal and the other from an external perspective, lead to the same outcome, they are not interchangeable. Two aspects have to be considered. (a) The loss of determinacy entails an impairment of that function of law for the sake of whose fulfillment (according to our description of situations of double contingency) law has developed, namely, to provide for certainty in expectation under conditions of limited time and incomplete knowledge. Teubner avoids this problem by tying the reflexivity of law to the integration of other systems' self-descriptions and by recognizing law as autonomous only in its code function. Thus, a further problem of a conflict of norms arises for impartial appropriateness argumentation. Certainty in law must be weighed against other principles *in casu*. (b) Not all the arguments which appear in appropriateness argumentation are compatible with the idea of impartial application. From the problem of the legal system's impending incapacity to respond [*Resonanzunfähigkeit*], Teubner concluded that other systems' self-descriptions have to be considered in the dimension of the program. In this way, the application of law is tied to functional imperatives. Constituting a part of the idea of impartial application, however, is the consideration of all the normatively relevant situation features. For this reason, it is tied to the weighing of principles and to procedures which make a complete and appropriate consideration possible. The application of law must be able to create a free space where—*in casu*—appropriateness argumentation, which can be based on a multitude of relevant principles, is possible. In order to bring as many factual and normative aspects of a situation as possible into relation with one another, there has to be latitude within the application of law itself, so that effect can also be given to the political and moral principles which embody the postconventional level of moral reasoning. In this way, the application of norms itself is again "proceduralized" and thereby linked back to impartial appropriateness argumentation.[46]

In conclusion, I would like to discuss the following possibilities as two proposals for describing appropriateness argumentation in law: hermeneutical models, which differentiate Engisch's metaphor of "casting one's glance back and forth," and Dworkin's concept of "integrity."

3.1 Hermeneutical Models

H. L. A. Hart traces the unavoidable indeterminacy of legal rules back to two "handicaps." The first one consists in "our relative ignorance of fact," so that we cannot foresee all the possible feature combinations of individual application situations when laying down a rule.[47] Connected to our inability to anticipate future experiences is the second handicap: "our relative indeterminacy of aim," that is, the aim we follow with a legal rule; it can also change in view of an unforeseen constellation of features.[48] That is why legal rules have an "open texture," from which a "paradigm" for clear cases may be drawn, whereas what matters in difficult cases is the discretion of the judge.

Hart assesses the consequences of this structural indeterminacy of legal rules to be so serious that they necessarily lead to rule-skeptical conclusions. His argument is an empirical one: Because in most cases we succeed in applying rules to our conduct according to their necessary and ordinarily sufficient conditions of application, the few cases where the conditions of application are unclear need not bother us.[49]

In contrast to that, the hermeneutical insight that we cannot understand a text independently of the situation of its interpretation has radicalized the thesis of structural indeterminacy to the claim that every norm becomes a determinate one only in the act of interpretation itself. If future experiences cannot be anticipated, then a norm acquires its obligating validity only in the particular interpretative situation itself. This is implied in Engisch's famous image of "casting one's glance back and forth between the major premise and the circumstances of life."[50] This metaphor has led to regarding the relation between norm and circumstances of the case as a circle because the indeterminate norm can only be determined by the circumstances of the case, and the indeterminate circumstances of the case only by the norm in its relevant features.

The reflections so far have, however, demonstrated that indeterminacy is not a problem of norm structure; it is simply a circumscription of the procedure of impartial application. If a norm can be applied impartially only on considering all the situation features, then the property of indeterminacy applies to every norm. Thus, with every norm we have an obligation to enter an appropriateness argumentation, and indeed independently of how "determinate" those unchanging circumstances are under which the norm was recognized as valid.

Our reflections on the logic of appropriateness argumentation led us to the point that only a coherent exhaustion of all the norms and their semantic variants which are applicable to a complete situation description fulfills the principle of impartial application. An analogous conception can be found in those hermeneutical theories of application in law which locate the situation-specific context of consideration between the normative viewpoints relevant within a situation in—admittedly—the "preunderstanding" of the person applying the norm.

Against this thesis of hermeneutics, the objection has been raised that an indeterminacy of the norm arises only in cases of ambiguous, vague, porous, or value-deficient concepts, as well as in the use of concepts of disposition.[51] Thus, a meaning would have to be determined, and then justified with the help of canons of interpretation, precedents, and principles of legal doctrine. As the above reflections on the logic of appropriateness argumentation have demonstrated, word usage rules are necessary to guarantee the internal justification of a legal decision. Its external justification cannot, however, ground the selection of relevant situation features taken from a complete situation description—a selection tied to the determination of a meaning. With external arguments, such as the historical will of the legislator, only a rule already containing the selected situation feature and screening out all other aspects is justified. Establishing such a relation with, for example, the ends of the historical legislator is necessary if it is a matter of the validity of the corresponding rule within the framework of the accepted legal order. But hermeneutics' thesis of the unavoidable circle is aimed at the situation dependency of discovering a determination of meaning.[52] Between the situation-independent justification of a rule and its situation-dependent discovery, however, there is still the separate step of justifying its situational appropriateness, as I attempted to show. It is only by reflecting on this process that one can avoid a danger which became clear in debate with Gadamer, namely, that of also adopting hermeneutics' implicit Aristotelian ethics and thus assimilating the norm to the "demands of the situation."

Martin Kriele differentiated Engisch's "glance metaphor" into two levels for discovering law [Rechtsgewinnung]. At the first level, it is a matter of discovering norm hypotheses in relation to the circumstances of the case to be decided. To clarify the structure of this process, Kriele begins with a "hypothetically conceived situation free of all given legal norms."[53] A norm hypothetically considered in this situation differs from every other norm in that (a) it "declares more or different facts of the circumstances of life" to be relevant, (b) it refers to "the same facts in the facts circumscribed by the legal norm [Tatbestand] with concepts varying in degree of abstraction," and (c) "different legal consequences are ascribed to the same facts circumscribed by the legal norm."[54] Kriele immediately confounds this level of situation description with evaluative and normative lines of argumentation. The norms hypothetically considered in the thought experiment, that is, considered not against a positive law background, are to be weighed in terms of "rational law" [*vernunft-rechtlich*]. The person applying the law has "to check the individual variants of his norm hypotheses according to where the one or the other leads, in order then to select the most reasonable one, that is, the one which serves the general interest or the relatively most fundamental interest in the case of group interests."[55] It is not until the ensuing second level that it is to be considered whether the norm hypotheses, "which issue from deliberations based on rational law, are included in positive law or not."[56] Here, rational-law viewpoints continue to play the leading part.

In this proposal to construct levels for discovering law, the selection of situation features is directly connected to the consideration of interests and the consideration of the consequences for rational law. However, the generalization of the interests supporting a norm hypothesis avails itself of a type of reasons different from the examination of the situational appropriateness of various applicable norm hypotheses. At this level, the situation description itself would first have to be related to all the applicable norm hypotheses, including their applicable semantic variants. The applicable, and possibly conflicting, norm hypotheses then require a coherent justification and weighing from the viewpoint of their greatest possible compatibility.

According to Josef Esser, the act of applying a law is embedded in a valuating preunderstanding that integrates every norm into an open teleological system guided by principles. Like Kriele, Esser is guided here by the model of case law thinking, which views every new situation in the light of the *ratio decidendi* of cases already decided and of their interrelationship as established by principles. The principle "governs the interpretation of norm and rule, namely, the direction taken by the preselection and recognition of the legally relevant facts in the circumstances of the case and of the legally relevant comments in precedent."[57] If, for Kriele, it is the rational-law deliberations which determine the selection of the relevant features of the circumstances of the case as well as the manner of interrelating possibly applicable normative viewpoints, then, for Esser, it is "the wisdom preceding the truth of the *lex*"[58] that achieves this. Here it is a matter not just of legal principles already established, but of extralegal valuations which come from the ethical context of the legal system. For this, there are transformational rules, or "transforming topoi,"[59] available, the most prominent of which is the argument from the nature of the thing.[60] This argument serves to transform functional determinations which are particular to certain spheres into law (the best known example being the role of "prevailing practice" [*Verkehrssitte*] in civil law): "It remains a secret how 'positive' legal principles can be integrated from 'prepositive' ones, if one does not comprehend the process of interpretation itself as an act of integration, i.e., here, of positivizing— that is to say, an act of integrating the substantive and linguistic logics of the codified system, as well as the whole legal order, including the standards of customs or habits that have not been condensed to norms."[61]

Esser thus presupposes an organically thinking jurist, that is, one thinking functionally in reference to the entire corpus of law, who can reproduce every change and fit it into the system of legal principles. This *corpus juris* of all "civilized" societies—a corpus which is organized and integrated by principles, casuistically anchored, and flexible in the particular case—acquires an objective value of its own, has, as an "institution," its own "tradition," and competes, on the basis of a normative claim sui generis, with the "extremely busy political legislator."[62] Thus, ultimately, "finding issue-conditioned postulates of justice with the help of the Ariadne thread provided by concepts"[63] is dependent on the historical level which the culture of law has reached in civilization. True, principles are thereby assigned the argumentative function of transforming hitherto unconsidered situation features into law. But their status is tied to the existing form of law and life; they determine the pre-understanding of the person who applies the law—a preunderstanding bound to effective history.[64] If, however, one understands principles in the manner proposed here, namely, as the expression of an argumentative procedure which makes an impartial consideration of all situation features possible, then their meaning changes. They serve the coherent justification of those norms, and their semantic variants, which can bear a relation to a complete description of the situation.

This claim presupposes the ideal of a judge who, in every individual case, considers all the applicable norms and semantic variants in a coherent context of justification in order to comply with the requirement of a complete description of the situation. This context of justification would not be closed in on itself; rather, it would press forward to those moral principles that legitimate the legal order and the political community in toto—and it would have to be changed in every individual case in which the constellation of situation features changes. Dworkin has characterized a similar procedure as that of formulating a coherent political theory.

3.2 *"Integrity": In Search of the Best Justification (Dworkin)*

Dworkin argues that the indeterminacy of legal rules necessitates going back to rights or arguments of principle, which are located outside of the positive legal order and cannot therefore be identified with the help of a rule of recognition. These rights, the most fundamental one being each person's right to equal concern and respect in all political decisions, can be relevant in hard cases. They have to be discovered with the help of a "sense of appropriateness" and asserted.[65] Arguments of principle differ from rules in that they can be weighed against one another only in the dimension of importance and without losing their validity, whereas rules are only applicable in an all-or-nothing manner. Dworkin describes in detail how arguments of principle can become effective in hard cases. They have their function in justifying legal decisions which grant or deny legal rights. Since it is never the case that one principle alone is relevant, what matters is the compatibility of principles and policies. It must be possible to combine them into a general and appropriate political theory in which every element can be justified. Here, the will of the legislator and the principles of common law function as a bridge between general theory and concrete legal rights. Through the justification of the legislator's will and the principles that, in view of a particular case, can be drawn from common law, the judge has to establish a coherent connection between his decision and the general political theory. The decisions must "be brought within some comprehensive theory of general principles and policies that is consistent with other decisions also thought right."[66] Thus, those precedents to which principles can be linked also form a part of this context of "articulate consistency."[67]

The advantage of Dworkin's theory is that it explicates the idea of an impartial consideration of all the relevant situation features. It is not limited to the interpretation of laws. When the judge "interprets statutes he fixes to some statutory language . . . arguments of principle or policy that provide the best justification of that language in the light of the legislature's responsibilities."[68] In this way, the norm itself is again moved into a context of justification which can be linked to various other (virtually all) principles and policies. Included here are, on the side of the legislator, the constitution and statutes, and on the side of common law, precedent, the "seamless web"[69] (other precedents and statutes), as well as mistakes.[70] The theory thus envisioned describes, in the ideal case, a set of principles "that reconciles all standing statutes and precedents."[71] The justification "must be plausible and not sham. If the justification he constructs makes distinctions that are arbitrary and deploys principles that are unappealing, then it cannot count as a justification at all."[72] And that means that one can demolish it by pointing out aspects left unconsidered.

With this requirement of fitting arguments of principle into a coherent interpretation, the weighing procedures which go beyond a concrete rule find their "institutional support."[73] In handling precedents, this takes effect in the necessity of considering the "gravitational force" they generate in the context of comparable cases.[74] A judge who ignored this would apply the political decision which was the precedent in an unlike, and therefore unfair manner.

By employing the concept of "integrity," Dworkin has enlarged and specified the ideal of making decisions about legal norms in accordance with a completely coherent political theory.[75] Though it first appears as an independent principle, this ideal acquires its importance only in association with other fundamental principles, such as fairness, justice, and procedural due process; its importance, that is, as a virtue of the coherent handling of these principles—as this is expressed in the maxim of treating like cases alike.[76]

However, Dworkin uses this ideal of integrity not as a semantic rule for consistently applying an individual norm in like cases, but in the sense of a relational concept that prescribes the compatibility of a decision with virtually all principles. The political community should act with integrity, just as we expect a concrete other to act toward us, even if we do not agree with his particular views on the content of justice or fairness. We thus expect treatment in compliance with a "single, coherent set of principles"[77] according to which the other leads his life, and rule out capricious or whimsical decisions from one case to the next. Just as the individual strives for a coherent manner of living, the political community is subject to the requirement of being able to justify coherently every single one of its decisions in the light of the principles it accepts, and may not act according to different principles in like cases.[78] Thus, this ideal of integrity refers not to individual rights and the arguments of principle they embody, but to the way in which a political community treats them in legislation and adjudication. Because rights cannot be applied in an isolated manner, nor limited to a privileged group of people, it is necessary that they be coherently considered in every decision about legal norms. The internal force developed by the principle of coherence takes effect in the requirement that all the persons in a political community be treated as subjects with equal rights, that is, with equal concern and respect, and consequently that no right be denied its place in the context of consideration.

Dworkin distinguishes between a principle of integrity in legislation and one in adjudication. In the two spheres, the prescription of nonarbitrary treatment asserts itself in a specific way. In legislation it functions as a principle "which asks those who create the law by legislation to keep that law coherent in principle."[79] It is only at first glance that this strikes one as being trivial. The coherence requirement includes all the arguments of principles from which a political community draws its legitimation. Legitimacy itself is at stake with every arbitrary treatment which violates one of the principles that have been availed of for legitimating reasons. A legislation which creates a new law without considering its coherence with other laws, or which pursues certain political goals in such a manner that it makes arbitrary compromises which lead to the preferential treatment of a given legal position—such a legislation does not treat everyone with equal concern and equal respect. In a thought experiment of sorts, Dworkin thus relates the principle of integrity to a "principled community" whose members behave with equal respect to one another. A community structured by concrete relations of recognition does not permit any other decisions about what should be regarded as fair and just than those which can be justified by universally accepted principles. It is thereby distinguished from other models of community whose establishment can be traced back to either purposive-rational considerations or submission to an abstract system of rules.[80] "Its rationale tends to equality . . . : its command of integrity assumes that each person is as worthy as any other, that each must be treated with equal concern according to some coherent conception of what that means."[81]

Just as in legislation a principle or a political end may not be implemented if this means relinquishing other rights, the "principle of integrity in adjudication" requires that like cases be treated alike not in respect of an individual norm or a certain precedent, but in respect of a coherent set of principles which, in the final analysis, has to be brought into agreement with the political morality of the community. Here too, it functions actually as a relational principle which, going beyond the application of a single specific rule, points to a coherent context of consideration of virtually all the relevant rights and principles. A political community treats its members underhandedly if, though applying given rules and principles consistently, it does so arbitrarily. The requirement of equal treatment applies to *all* rights and principles whose borders are open to the fundamental political and moral principles of a community. This implies that, when applying laws, precedents, and doctrinal arguments, we operate on the presupposition that each individual one can be justified within a comprehensive context. The principle of integrity in adjudication "requires our judges, so far as this is possible, to treat our present system of public standards as expressing and respecting a coherent set of principles, and, to that end, to interpret these standards to find implicit standards between and beneath the explicit ones."[82] Discovering or finding implicit norms does not happen arbitrarily or with a presumptuous legislative intention. Dworkin insists that judges do not invent new rights, but discover existing rights, and this they do continually, though possibly often in an implicit manner.[83] Dworkin's argumentation here is consistent because rights are essentially of a moral nature, that is, not open to positivizing change. They are derived not from a legislative or judicial act, but from the "right to equal concern and respect," which is anchored in the fundamental legitimating principles of a community. The competence to enact norms, and the adjudicative authority to decide, must themselves be able to be justified in the light of this principle, just as the laws and precedents to be considered when deciding an individual case have to be.

This complex network of principles that are to be interpreted in terms of their coherent interconnection can be traced out to its smallest branches. Dworkin employs the fictional figure of a superhuman judge, Hercules, who in every individual case can unfold an interpretative chain of laws, precedents, and doctrinal principles, and construe them in their comprehensive context of justification, which includes all the rights relevant in the political community. In this manner, he implements the principle of integrity all the way down to the particular case. Every right which is discovered in an individual case and has become a precedent is relevant in every other similar case. The requirement of coherence applies not only to the "grand rights," which more or less abstractly serve only rhetorical purposes,[84] but also to the complex network of "concrete" rights, which are tied to specific cases, but take effect in certain branches of legal doctrine. They have to be taken into consideration in the same way in every new case that is similar. "Law as integrity asks judges to assume, so far as this is possible, that the law is structured by a coherent set of principles about justice and fairness and procedural due process, and it asks them to enforce these in the fresh cases that come before them, so that each person's situation is fair and just according to the same standards."[85] Since conflicts of rights and principles are unavoidable and, indeed, systematically produced by this method, only the better interpretation can be decisive in each case, that is, the interpretation that is able to construct the most comprehensive, coherent context of justification by, for example, integrating a large number of precedents, or some very important ones, which could not be considered by a competing interpretation. Ultimately, the best interpretation can only be conducted "from the standpoint of political morality."[86] For the application of law, the principle of integrity thus requires that all members of the political community be treated with equal respect; and it does this by subjecting every decision to the demand that it be compatible with the best interpretation.

The requirement that legislative and adjudicative decisions be justified according to a coherent, general political theory establishes a bridge between moral arguments of principle and decisions about legal norms. The disadvantage of this proposal is that the principles to be considered are limited to the context of a political community by Dworkin. In this way, de facto morality becomes the integrating point of reference.[87] However, the principle of integrity does not necessarily have to reach its limits within the given context of a political morality. For the right to equal concern and respect, the embodiment of which is "integrity" for Dworkin, displays a universalist content which first allows this right to become operative in the way Dworkin claims. If one reconstructs this content, three different meanings of this principle can be distinguished.

(a) By "equal concern and respect," one could mean the idea of impartiality, just like the one we explicated above, following Habermas's suggestion, as a rule of argumentation in practical discourses. For this rule operationalizes only the universal-reciprocal sense of the idea of impartiality, namely, that of equally considering the interests of each individual when justifying a norm. In this way, the legitimating principles of a political community become, for their part, the topic of a proceduralized justification argumentation. Thus, insofar as the ideal of integrity aims at treating each individual as a subject with equal rights, it can be better explicated in a procedural theory. One would then capture more precisely the meaning that Dworkin associates with the right to be treated as an equal: "This is the right, not to an equal distribution of some good or opportunity, but the right to equal concern and respect in the political decision about how these goods and opportunities are to be distributed."[88]

(b) By connecting the principle of integrity to the ideal of a political community in this thought experiment, Dworkin makes it clear that this principle is dependent on relations of solidarity in a form of life. Legislation has to bring to expression the fact that all the members of the community respect one another as equals. Here too, it can be shown that reciprocal relations of recognition are not excluded by a universalist concept of justice, but presupposed by it.[89] Habermas traced the complementarity of justice and solidarity back to the fragility of human beings who can become individuals only through socialization.[90] Guided by a similar insight, Dworkin construes his model of the principled community: "It insists that people are members of a genuine political community only when they accept that their fates are linked in the following strong way: they accept that they are governed by common principles, not just by rules hammered out in political compromise."[91] If however, as Mead attempted to show, the individual's becoming a self cannot be conceived of without taking the perspective of a generalized other, the thesis of rights can only be understood intersubjectively, and not individualistically. The principle of coherence, to which legislation is also subject, implicitly manifests this interconnection between societal solidarity and an intersubjectivist concept of law. Because every new right is valid always only in the context of consideration of other rights, they are embedded in relations of mutual recognition from the very beginning. This is how Dworkin also introduces the fundamental principle of equal concern and respect, on the basis of which all other rights have to be able to be justified: "Government must treat those whom it governs with concern, that is, as human beings who are capable of suffering and frustration, and with respect, that is, as human beings who are capable of forming and acting on intelligent conceptions of how their lives should be lived."[92] An intersubjectivist concept of law thus also prompts the discovery of more rights.[93] This results in the fact that conflicting rights can now only be balanced by preserving coherence, that is, by weighing the principles they embody.

(c) For this reason, the principle of integrity can be understood as a principle for appropriateness argumentation. In this form of argumentation, societal relations of recognition are given effect in such a way that the network of concrete rights is applied equally in each particular case. Dworkin's characterization of principles as "considerations beyond the rules themselves"[94] places the application of laws, precedents, and legal doctrine under the requirement of exhausting all those aspects of a case which can be interpreted in the light of principles. The right to be treated as an equal with concern and respect appears here as the right to equal treatment—that is to say, treating like cases alike not with reference to an individual norm, but with reference to a coherent set of principles as rights. This kind of equal treatment systematically creates differences and conflicts. But the very structure of such conflicts—a structure leading to the consideration of differences—is the structure of appropriateness argumentation, as we attempted to describe it above.

Notes

Translator's Introduction

1. The distinction between normative ethics and metaethics need not concern us here.

2. On the "revival" of applied ethics, see Peter Singer, "Introduction," in *Applied Ethics,* ed. Peter Singer (Oxford: Oxford University Press, 1986), pp. 1–7; Jonsen and Toulmin read this revival as a "revival of casuistry," see A. R. Jonsen and S. Toulmin, *The Abuse of Casuistry. A History of Moral Reasoning* (Berkeley: University of California Press, 1988), chap. 16.

3. See, for example, the division in the reader edited by Peter Singer, *A Companion to Ethics* (Oxford: Blackwell, 1991).

4. Fox and DeMarco, for instance, recognize the need to mediate between the two aspects but, like many other critics of formalism, tend to solve the problem by proposing a *substantive* ethics; see "The Challenge of Applied Ethics," in *New Directions in Ethics. The Challenge of Applied Ethics,* ed. R. M. Fox and J. P. DeMarco (New York: Routledge & Kegan Paul, 1986), pp. 1–18.

5. See *Part One,* 6 below; for a defense of deontological moral philosophy, see J. Habermas, "Erläuterungen zur Diskursethik," in *Erläuterungen zur Diskursethik* (Frankfurt am Main: Suhrkamp, 1991), pp. 166–76.

6. On this reading of contextualist critiques, see *Part Two,* 4 below.

7. See K. Günther, "Ein normativer Begriff der Kohärenz für eine Theorie der juristischen Argumentation," *Rechtstheorie* 20 (1989): 163–90; abridged English translation: "A Normative Conception of Coherence for a Discursive Theory of Legal Justification," *Ratio Juris* 2 (1989): 155–66; "The Pragmatic and Functional Indeterminacy of Law," in *Critical Legal Thought: An American-German Debate,* ed. C. Joerges and D. M. Trubek (Baden-Baden: Nomos, 1989), pp. 435–60; "Universalistische Normbegründung und Normanwendung in Recht und Moral," in *Generalisierung und Individualisierung im Rechtsdenken,* ed. M. Herberger, U. Neumann and H. Rüßmann (Stuttgart: Franz Steiner, 1992), pp. 36–76.

285

8. See *Part One,* 3 and *Part Three,* 1 below.

9. See Günther's critique of *phronesis* in the second excursus below.

10. See *Part One,* 4 below.

11. See *Part Two,* 6 below. Further, empirical research on application consciousness remains a desideratum.

12. See *Part Three* below.

13. See "A Normative Conception of Coherence."

14. See *Part Four,* 2 below, and Günther, "The Idea of Impartiality and the Functional Determinacy of the Law," *Northwestern University Law Review* 83 (1989): 151–83.

15. Günther's analysis has sparked a major debate on the status of legal discourse, see Ingrid Dwars, "Application Discourse and the Special-Case Thesis. On a Discussion between Robert Alexy and Klaus Günther," *Ratio Juris* forthcoming; Robert Alexy "Justification and Application of Norms," *Ratio Juris* forth coming; K. Günther, "Some Critical Remarks on Robert Alexy's 'Special-Case Thesis'," *Ratio Juris* forthcoming; J. Habermas, *Faktizität und Geltung. (Frankfurt am Main: Suhrkamp, 1992), pp. 282–86; Günther, "Universalistische Normbegründung," see part VI (pp. 68–76) for the distinction between moral and legal application discourses.*

16. "Erläuterungen zur Diskursethik," p. 164; on Habermas's reception of Günther's model for moral theory, see also pp. 137–142; "Vom pragmatischen, ethischen und moralischen Gebrauch der praktischen Vernuft," in *Erläuterungen zur Diskursethik,* pp. 113f; for legal theory, see *Faktizität und Geltung,* esp. pp. 265–72, 316–8.

17. See Günther, "Universalistische Normbegründung," pp. 63–8; "Ein normativer Begriff der Kohärenz," pp. 181–3.

18. Jonsen and Toulmin, op. cit. See Günther's critique, "Universalistische Normbegründung," pp. 67f.

19. Jonsen and Toulmin, op. cit., p. 318. But see their interesting analysis of the part historically played by "circumstances" in casuistry, pp. 131–6, 253f.

20. Günther, "Universalistische Normbegründung," p. 68.

21. Michael Walzer, *Spheres of Justice* (reprint, Oxford: Blackwell, 1985).

22. "Jürgen Habermas: Morality, Society and Ethics. An Interview with Torben Hviid Nielsen," *Acta Sociologica* 33 (1990): 96f.

23. Jon Elster, *Local Justice. How Institutions Allocate Scarce Goods and Necessary Burdens* (Cambridge: Cambridge University Press, 1992), pp. 11–14.

24. On this problem in the welfare state paradigm of law, see Habermas, *Faktizität und Geltung,* pp. 504–6.

25. Elster, op. cit., pp. 236–45.

26. Ibid., pp. 5f, 139–43, 180–3.

Author's Preface

1. Ronald Dworkin, *Taking Rights Seriously* (1977; New impression with a reply to critics; London: Duckworth, 1978), p. 40.

Author's Introduction

1. For the sake of simplicity, I regard the intention to lie as one of the objective facts in this example and do not take into consideration the ascription of subjective attitudes to the concept of the subjective world.

2. Jürgen Habermas, *The Theory of Communicative Action,* vol. 1, trans. Thomas McCarthy (Boston: Beacon, 1984), p. 85.

3. On this, see the comprehensive model by Ursula Wolf, *Das Problem des moralischen Sollens* (Berlin/New York: Walter de Gruyter, 1984).

4. Hans-Georg Gadamer, *Truth and Method* (London: Sheed & Ward, 1975), p. 279.

5. See, for example, Philippa Foot, "Moral Beliefs," in *Virtues and Vices and Other Essays in Moral Philosophy* (Oxford: Basil Blackwell, 1978), p. 121.

6. True to his approach, this step is demanded by Wellmer. See Albrecht Wellmer, "Ethics and Dialogue: Elements of Moral Judgement in Kant and Discourse Ethics," in *The Persistence of Modernity. Essays on Aesthetics, Ethics, and Postmodernism,* trans. David Midgley (Cambridge, Mass.: MIT Press, 1991), pp. 204ff. I shall return to this below (*Part One,* 5).

7. On this, see Herfried Münkler, "Staatsraison und politische Klugheitslehre," in *Pipers Handbuch der politischen Ideen.* Band 3. *Neuzeit: Von den Konfessionskriegen bis zur Aufklärung,* ed. I. Fetscher and H. Münkler (Munich/Zürich: Piper, 1985), pp. 23–72. This process is lamented by Aristotelian positions in political theory as a loss of political judgment and *topos.* For a typical example, see Wilhelm Hennis, *Politik und praktische Philosophie* (Neuwied/Berlin: Luchterhand, 1963).

8. Immanuel Kant, *Critique of Practical Reason,* trans. Lewis White Beck (1956; Indianapolis: Bobbs-Merrill, 1980), (A 122) p. 72.

9. In his neo-Aristotelian transformation of Kant, Wellmer attempts to defuse the problem by interpreting the categorical imperative as a negatory moral principle that only has the purpose of prohibiting nonuniversalizable maxims of action. Since this critique of Kant follows the objective of demonstrating that the need for a consensual justification principle is superfluous and thereby the objective of revoking the distinction between justification and application, I shall return to this again below (*Part One*, 5). Wellmer, op. cit., pp. 127ff.

10. See the energetic presentation of this aspect in Rüdiger Bubner, *Geschichtsprozesse und Handlungsnormen* (Frankfurt am Main: Suhrkamp, 1984), pp. 35ff.

11. One could compare this with Gadamer's "standpoint of finiteness" (op. cit., p. 89) which is indeed only chosen in order to regain the certainty of effective-historical consciousness.

12. As a characteristic example, see Niklas Luhmann, *Soziale System-Grundriß einer allgemeinen Theorie* (Frankfurt am Main: Suhrkamp, 1984), p. 599, and *Ökologische Kommunikation* (Opladen: Westdeutscher Verlag, 1986), pp. 259ff.

13. See, for example, Luhmann, *A Sociological Theory of Law*, trans. Elizabeth King and Martin Albrow (London: Routledge & Kegan Paul, 1985), p. 31.

14. Luhmann, *Soziale Systeme*, pp. 77, 389.

15. Ibid., p. 70.

16. Ibid., p. 76.

Part One:
The Problem of Application in Discourse Ethics

1. Jürgen Habermas, "Discourse Ethics: Notes on a Program of Philosophical Justification," in *Moral Consciousness and Communicative Action*, trans. C. Lenhardt and S. Weber Nicholsen (Cambridge, Mass.: MIT Press, 1990), p. 65.

2. Supra, pp. 6f.

3. R. M. Hare, *Freedom and Reason* (Oxford: Oxford University Press, (1963), *The Language of Morals* (Oxford: University Press, 1978), and *Moral Thinking* (Oxford: Clarendon Press, 1981).

4. Wellmer, op. cit., pp. 130, 204.

5. Gadamer, op. cit., pp. 278ff; Winfried Hassemer, "Juristische Herme-neutik," *Archiv für Rechts- und Sozialphilosophie* 72 (1986): 195–212.

6. Jean-Paul Sartre, *Existentialism and Humanism*, trans. Philip Mairet (London: Methuen, 1973), pp. 35f.

7. Hare, *Moral Thinking*, p. 41; "Universalisability," *Proceedings of the Aristotelian Society* LV (1954/55): 301, 305ff, 311f.

8. Hare, *Freedom and Reason*, pp. 89f.

9. Ibid., pp. 21f, 30.

10. Ibid., pp. 89f, p. 199.

11. Ibid., p. 23.

12. Ibid., p. 30; see p. 37 for a similar comment—hence the title "uni-versal presecriptivism," p. 16.

13. Hare, *Moral Thinking*, pp. 90ff.

14. George Herbert Mead, *Mind, Self, and Society* (Chicago: University of Chicago Press, 1962), pp. 379ff.

15. This does not rule out the possibility that I extend my perspective to include not only the concrete other, but also many or all others (Hare, *Freedom and Reason*, p. 116).

16. Ibid., p. 98.

17. Ibid., p. 32.

18. Ibid., pp. 44, 48, 94, 126.

19. Ibid., p. 88, p. 193. In *Moral Thinking*, Hare developed this thought into a model with two levels; I shall return to this below, in the context of the description of application argumentation.

20. See, for instance, Hare, *Freedom and Reason*, p. 92. Only the fol-lowing decision may not be hypothetical: whether we can will a norm hy-pothesis under changed conditions without self-contradiction; it may not be hypothetical because otherwise we could maneuver ourselves out of the pre-scriptivity of the "ought" (see ibid., p. 108).

21. See, above all, Hare, *Moral Thinking*, pp. 90ff.

22. On this, see Habermas, "Discourse Ethics," p. 64.

23. See the formulation of the moral principle (U) above, pp. 11f.

24. On the role of the principle of semantic universalizability in prac-tical justifications, see Robert Alexy, *A Theory of Legal Argumentation*,

trans. Ruth Adler and Neil MacCormick (Oxford: Oxford University Press, 1989), pp. 188, 190, and Habermas, "Discourse Ethics," pp. 86f.

25. Habermas, ibid., p. 66.

26. Habermas, *The Theory of Communicative Action,* vol. 1, pp. 98ff.

27. Thomas McCarthy, *The Critical Theory of Jürgen Habermas* (Cambridge, Mass,: MIT Press, 1978), pp. 312f.

28. Ibid., p. 313.

29. Stephen Toulmin, *The Uses of Argument* (Cambridge: Cambridge University Press, 1964), p. 99.

30. Ibid., p. 98.

31. Ibid., pp. 97f.

32. Ibid., p. 100, as well as S. Toulmin, Richard Rieke, and Allan Janik, *An Introduction into Reasoning* (London: Macmillan, 1979), p. 324. See also Kurt Baier, *The Moral Point of View* (Ithaca, N.Y.: Cornell University Press, 1958), p. 94, and Marcus George Singer, *Generalization in Ethics,* 2d ed. (New York: Atheneum, 1971), pp. 41f.

33. Alexy, *A Theory of Legal Argumentation,* p. 86.

34. For an exact logical reconstruction, one would, of course, have to add that Fx is then both a sufficient and a necessary condition for the acceptable prescriptiveness of Gx.

35. Toulmin, *The Uses of Argument,* p. 98.

36. Nevertheless, Toulmin sees—in connection with "set[ting] out a piece of applied mathematics"—that, when using a system of mathematical relations (in the sense of a warrant), a distinction must be observed: " . . . the correctness of the calculations will be one thing, their appropriateness to the problem in hand may be quite another" (ibid., pp. 102, 225ff, 209f).

37. Habermas, "Discourse Ethics," pp. 63, 66, as well as "Wahrheitstheorien," in *Vorstudien und Ergänzungen zur Theorie des kommunikativen Handelns* (Frankfurt am Main: Suhrkamp, 1984), pp. 166f, 172f.

38. On this, see Toulmin, *The Uses of Argument,* pp. 103ff.

39. Habermas, "Discourse Ethics," p. 65.

40. Ibid.

41. Ibid., p. 67.

42. Ibid., "Wahrheitstheorien," pp. 165ff.

43. *Idem.,* "Discourse Ethics," p. 65; "Wahrheitstheorien," p. 173.

44. Ludwig Wittgenstein, *Philosophical Investigations,* trans. G. E. M. Anscombe (Oxford: Basil Blackwell, 1978), §225 (p. 86).

45. John Rawls, *A Theory of Justice* (Oxford: Oxford University Press, 1973), pp. 126ff, 136ff.

46. At this point, if not earlier, Kant's example of lying becomes problematic—a norm justification and application in the sense of discourse ethics would presuppose the possibility of allowing the potential executioners to participate in a practical discourse.

47. Habermas, "Discourse Ethics," p. 67f; "Wahrheitstheorien," p. 173.

48. And everyone must have the authorization to judge for himself whether his interests could possibly be affected.

49. On this, see the impressive description of the structure of situations by Sartre, *Being and Nothingness,* trans. Hazel E. Barnes (London: Methuen, 1969), pp. 481ff.

50. This argument is also used by Ernst Tugendhat, "Kann man aus der Erfahrung moralisch lernen?" in *Probleme der Ethik* (Stuttgart: Reclam, 1984), pp. 102ff.

51. Ibid., pp. 87ff.

52. On what follows, see Habermas, "Discourse Ethics," passim.

53. On what follows, see ibid., pp. 87ff; *The Theory of Communicative Action,* vol. 1, pp. 24ff.

54. Habermas, "Discourse Ethics," p. 93.

55. John L. Austin, *How To Do Things with Words,* 2d ed. (Oxford: Oxford University Press, 1980).

56. Habermas, "Discourse Ethics," p. 87.

57. Ibid., p. 66.

58. Habermas, *The Philosophical Discourse of Modernity,* trans. Frederick G. Lawrence (Cambridge, Mass.: MIT Press, 1988), p. 323.

59. Wellmer, op. cit., pp. 203ff.

60. Ibid., pp. 209f.

61. Ibid., p. 210.

62. Ibid., p. 153 and passim. [Translator's note: an alternative translation of this expression could be "action mode in situations of one type."] On this manner of expression, see Wittgenstein, *Philosophical Investigations,* §206 (p. 82).

...ellmer, op. cit., p. 143. [Translator's note: translation altered

4. Ibid., pp. 154f.

65. Ibid., pp. 195ff.

66. Ibid., pp. 160ff.

67. Ibid., p. 167.

68. This is how I understand Wellmer's critique of equating "consensus rationality" with "truth"—see ibid., pp. 160ff. (This follows, in some points, Rolf Zimmermann, *Utopie–Rationalität–Politik* [Freiburg/Munich: Alber, 1985], pp. 314f.)

69. "Habermas suppresses the problem of *situation-related* truth in favor of that of *situation-independent* truth" (Zimmermann, op. cit., p. 314). Here, the analogy to Wellmer's option for a "situationist" ethics is especially clear. However, the consequence is that truth, in accordance with the presuppositions of verificationist semantics (on this: Zimmermann, op. cit., p. 325), is indeed semantically definable (and purely so) by referring to statements of perception, but, for actions and their justification, there only remains the relativism of appropriate situation interpretations. On the consequences of this one-sided privileging of propositional utterances over other utterances of reason, see Habermas, "A Reply," in *Communicative Action. Essays on Jürgen Habermas's "The Theory of Communicative Action,"* eds. A. Honneth and H. Joas and trans. Jeremy Gains and Doris L. Jones (Cambridge, Mass.: MIT Press, 1991), pp. 233ff.

70. To my mind, it can be asked at this point whether, with reference to truth, we have at our disposal any perspective other than the "internal" one—that is, after the Enlightenment. If it is not the painting in Sais [translator's note: this is a reference to Friedrich Schiller's poem *Das verschleierte Bild zu Sais*], Wellmer would have to indicate how we can experience truth from a standpoint of pure observation. In my opinion, the consensus theory of truth has the advantage of not needing anything more than the internal perspective in order to explicate pragmatically the meaning of truth. This does not rule out the possibility of our being able to distinguish, within consensus theory, between "truth" and "hold to be true," which is subsequently observable (on this objection, see Wellmer, op. cit., pp. 161f). The difference consists in the fact that, in the "internal perspective," recognizing a validity claim is required of us as participants in a theoretical discourse, whereas we do not find ourselves at all in this role in the case of merely "hold to be true."

71. Zimmermann, op. cit., p. 326.

72. Ibid., pp. 182ff.

73. Wellmer, op. cit., p. 197. [Translator's note: translation altered slightly.]

74. Ibid., pp. 201f.

75. Ibid., pp. 202f. [Translator's note: translation altered slightly.]

76. Explicitly, ibid., pp. 204–7.

77. Ibid., p. 206.

78. Otherwise disparate methodologies in jurisprudence should agree on this point, for instance, the hermeneutical orientation of Josef Esser, *Vorverständnis und Methodenwahl in der Rechtsfindung* (Kronberg im Taunus: Scriptor, 1972), and the formal semantic orientation of Hans-Joachim Koch and Helmut Rüßmann, *Juristische Begründungslehre* (Munich: C. H. Beck, 1982).

79. Wellmer, op. cit., pp. 120, 193f.

80. Zimmermann traces this compulsion to universalize back to the *"factum"* 1789 and ascribes to parliaments a pioneering function for politically establishing societal communication processes, which would have to be extended to the relations of production too. Because Zimmermann adopts Carl Schmitt's explication of the basic principles of parliamentary democracy (Zimmermann, op. cit., p. 200), his proposal is however open to criticism. Zimmermann would have to show, in opposition to Carl Schmitt, that the principles of parliamentary democracy can cope with those "[g]reat political and economic decisions" which, according to Schmitt, are too much for them (Carl Schmitt, *The Crisis of Parliamentary Democracy*, trans. Ellen Kennedy [Cambridge, Mass.: MIT Press, 1985], p. 49). Zimmermann's proposal to transform *ratio* into *voluntas* is then unavoidably exposed to Schmitt's simplifying question concerning the *quis iudicabit* [who will decide].

81. Wellmer, op. cit., pp. 188ff.

82. Wittgenstein, op. cit., §199 (p. 81).

83. Gadamer, *Truth and Method,* p. 279. [Translator's note: "concrete" does not appear in the English edition.]

84. Thus, for Wellmer, questions of politics, jurisprudence, economics, technology, aesthetics, and morality all belong in practical discourse (see, op. cit., pp. 228f).

85. Ibid., pp. 154f.

86. Ibid., pp. 156f.

87. Ibid., p. 150; Habermas, "Discourse Ethics," p. 53.

88. Habermas, "Discourse Ethics," p. 53. [Translator's note: translation altered slightly.]

89. Wellmer, op. cit., p. 157.

90. On this, see Zimmermann, op. cit., p. 325, with reference to Dummet and Tugendhat. For a critique, see Habermas, "A Reply," pp. 233ff.

91. This does not exclude the fact that the structure of forms of life must "facilitate" a universalist morality. Habermas, "Über Moralität und Sittlichkeit—Was macht eine Lebensform 'rational'?" in *Rationalität*, ed. H. Schnädelbach (Frankfurt am Main: Suhrkamp, 1984), p. 228.

92. Wellmer, op. cit., pp. 197ff.

93. Seel characterizes the process of "experiencing" [*eine Erfahrung zu machen*] quite in Wellmer's sense as follows: " . . . that is the case when the possibility of an appropriate and reliably pertinent appraisal only exists in the course of changing an existing *attitude*. In contrast to a concept of experience tailored to directly ascertaining the facts, I consider (. . .) a conception productive that comprehends experiencing as a singular process of changing orientations in given areas of action" (Martin Seel, *Die Kunst der Entzweiung* [Frankfurt am Main: Suhrkamp, 1986], pp. 77f). This combines with a skepticism about the "cheap temptation to play off the pragmatic-performative and the cognitive-propositional aspects of having experiences [*Haben von Erfahrungen*] and experiencing [*Machen von Erfahrungen*] against each other" (ibid., p. 76). Zimmermann (op. cit., p. 303) also advocates a rehabilitation of a concept of experience which has its origin in simple statements of perception. One is tempted to designate this in the same way as Wellmer characterizes his ethics, viz., as a "semantic situationism" which has emerged in the wake of Tugendhat's analysis of assertoric sentences. On tracing back situation-independent experiences/truths/moral attitudes to situation-dependent ones, see the almost identical statements by Seel, op. cit., p. 75; Zimmermann, op. cit., p. 314; and Wellmer, op. cit., pp. 133f, passim.

94. When Wellmer states "that positive norms command us to act in a particular way" (op. cit., p. 131), then this not only applies to positive duties, but to universally valid principles as such—they can conflict with other principles in application situations without becoming invalid as a result. On the corresponding distinction between principles and rules, see Dworkin, op. cit., pp. 28ff; Robert Alexy, *Theorie der Grundrechte* (Baden-Baden: Nomos, 1985), pp. 71ff; and infra, *Part Three* and *Part Four*.

95. Tugendhat, "Kann man aus der Erfahrung moralisch lernen?"; Günter Frankenberg and Ulrich Rödel, *Von der Volkssouveränität zum Minderheitenschutz* (Frankfurt am Main: Europäische Verlagsanstalt, 1981), pp. 20ff; Klaus Eder, *Geschichte als Lernprozeß?* (Frankfurt am Main: Suhrkamp, 1985).

96. On what follows, see Habermas, "Discourse Ethics," passim, as well as "Moral Consciousness and Communicative Action," in *Moral Consciousness and Communicative Action,* pp. 119ff.

97. Habermas, "Discourse Ethics," p. 66.

98. In this way—but on completely different foundations—Ernst Vollrath interprets political practice as the problem of "founding and preserving the association of a group of human beings." Accordingly, it is primarily a matter of perpetuating this association by political action under the guidance of judgment [*Urteilskraft*]. Ernst Vollrath, *Die Rekonstruktion der politischen Urteilskraft* (Stuttgart: Klett-Cotta, 1977), p. 74, passim.

99. Immanuel Kant, "Concerning the Common Saying: That May Be True in Theory But Does Not Apply to Practice," in *The Philosophy of Kant. Immanuel Kant's Moral and Political Writings,* ed. Carl J. Friedrich (New York: Random, 1949), p. 414.

100. Immanuel Kant, *Critique of Practical Reason,* trans. Lewis White Beck (1956; Indianapolis: Bobbs-Merrill, 1980), p. 34.

101. Habermas, "Metaphysik nach Kant," in *Theorie der Subjektivität,* ed. Konrad Cramer et al. (Frankfurt am Main: Suhrkamp, 1987), p. 429.

102. This deduction forms the argumentative core of the transcendental-pragmatic and universal-pragmatic justification of ethics by Apel and Habermas. Since it is not the topic of this study, it can only be presented in a roughly abridged form here.

103. Of course, the ambivalence in the presentation of these three dimensions of the problem of the relation between form of life and universalist moral principle should not be overlooked. The presentation is inspired by the threatening and, for the most part, already transpired destruction of traditional forms of life by the rationalist culture of modernity and by the tendency to overtax concrete interpersonal relations of solidarity by means of abstract principles of justice. However, it should not be forgotten that repression, suffering, and injustice were often enough coupled with traditional forms of life and small group solidarity (and this, viewed not only from the perspective of the observer!).

104. Apel, "Kann der postkantische Standpunkt der Moralität noch einmal in substantielle Sittlichkeit 'aufgehoben' werden?" in *Moralität und Sittlichkeit. Das Problem Hegels und die Diskursethik,* ed. W. Kuhlmann (Frankfurt am Main: Suhrkamp, 1986), pp. 231f.

105. Apel, "Kant, Hegel und das aktuelle Problem der normativen Grundlagen von Moral und Recht," in *Kant oder Hegel? (Stuttgarter Hegel-Kongreß 1981),* ed. Dieter Henrich (Stuttgart: Klett-Cotta, 1981), p. 623.

106. Apel, "Kann der postkantische Standpunkt der Moralität noch einmal in substantielle Sittlichkeit 'aufgehoben' werden?" pp. 223ff.

107. Ibid., p. 236.

108. Ibid., p. 248.

109. In law, "reasonable expectation" is a standard category for solving problems of a conflict of obligations. For the area of criminal law, see the representative study by Peter Frellesen, *Die Zumutbarkeit der Hilfeleistung* (Frankfurt am Main: Metzner, 1980).

110. Apel, "Kann der postkantische Standpunkt der Moralität noch einmal in substantielle Sittlichkeit 'aufgehoben' werden?" p. 240.

111. Habermas, "Über Moralität und Sittlichkeit," p. 228.

112. On the relation between purposive rationality and reaching understanding, see Habermas "A Reply," pp. 239ff.

Part Two:
The Problem of the Application of Norms in the Development of Moral Consciousness

1. Emile Durkheim, *The Division of Labor in Society,* trans. W. D. Halls (New York: Free Press, 1984), pp. 226ff.; French edition: *De la division du travail,* 8th ed. (Paris: Presses Universitaires de France, 1967).

2. Ibid., p. 201 and p. 203.

3. Ibid., p. 122; René König, "Emile Durkheim," in *Klassiker des soziologischen Denkens,* vol. 1, ed. D. Käsler (Munich: C. H. Beck, 1976), p. 323.

4. König, op. cit., p. 325; Hans-Peter Müller, "Gesellschaft, Moral und Individualismus. Emile Durkheims Moraltheorie," in *Gesellschaftlicher Zwang und moralische Autonomie,* ed. H. Bertram (Frankfurt am Main: Suhrkamp, 1986), pp. 71–105.

5. Durkheim, op. cit., pp. 226f.

6. Ibid., pp. 71, 83f.

7. Ibid., pp. 60, 35, 36.

8. Ibid., pp. 39ff, p. 60. On law in general as a "visible symbol" (p. 24) for the type of solidarity: "In fact, social life, wherever it becomes lasting, inevitably tends to assume a definite form and become organised. Law is nothing more than this very organisation in its most stable and precise form" (p. 25). Law is characterized by Durkheim through its "determinacy," independently of its separation into criminal law—repressive sanctions, and civil law—restitutive sanctions.

9. Ibid., p. 39.

10. Ibid., pp. 43, 94, 131.

11. Ibid., p. 172.

12. Ibid., p. 242.

13. Ibid., p. 231.

14. Ibid., pp. 206, 208.

15. Ibid., pp. 83, 219f.

16. Ibid., p. 85.

17. Ibid., pp. 172f.

18. Ibid., p. 106.

19. Ibid., pp. 119ff.

20. Durkheim gathers together all the anathemas of postmodern thought when he characterizes this universality as follows: "That alone is rational that is universal. What defies the understanding is the particular and the concrete. We can only ponder effectively upon the general. Consequently, the closer the common consciousness is to particular things, the more exactly it bears their imprint, and thus the more unintelligible it is." Ibid., p. 232.

21. Ibid., p. 232 (italics added).

22. Ibid., p. 233: "Because the collective consciousness becomes more rational, it therefore becomes less categorical and, for this reason again, is less irksome to the free development of individual variations."

23. Ibid., pp. 236f.

24. *Equip yourself to fulfil usefully a specific function*" (italics in the original). Ibid., p. 4.

25. Ibid., p. 243, and the *Preface to the Second Edition,* pp. xxxi–lix.

26. König, op. cit., p. 325.

27. Durkheim, op. cit., p. 243.

28. Ibid., p. 338. Durkheim summarizes the rules which remain abstract in the collective consciousness as follows: "It [morality] requires us only to be charitable and just towards our fellow-men, to fulfil our task well, to work towards a state where everyone is called to fulfil the function he performs best and will receive a just reward for his efforts. The rules constituting this morality have no constraining power preventing their

being fully examined. Because they are better made for us and, in a certain sense, by us, we are free in relation to them." Ibid., pp. 338f.

29. Mead, op. cit. On the history of the development of Mead's work, see Hans Joas, *G. H. Mead. A Contemporary Re-Examination of His Thought*, trans. Raymond Meyer (Cambridge, Mass.: MIT Press, 1985).

30. On the characterization of the "moral situation," see Joas, op. cit., pp. 133f; on the connection between the model of role-taking and universalist ethics: ibid., p. 135.

31. On this, see Joas, op. cit., pp. 90ff.

32. Mead, op. cit., p. 47.

33. Habermas, *The Theory of Communicative Action*, vol. 2, trans. Thomas McCarthy (Boston: Beacon, 1987), p. 15.

34. Mead, op. cit., p. 54.

35. Ibid., p. 120; see also p. 123.

36. Ibid., p. 78; see also pp. 79f.

37. Joas, op. cit., p. 104.

38. Mead, op. cit., p. 85; see also p. 125.

39. Ibid., p. 88.

40. Ibid., p. 89.

41. Ibid., p. 149.

42. Wittgenstein, op. cit., §146 (p. 58).

43. On this, see Habermas, *The Theory of Communicative Action*, vol. 2, p. 22.

44. Wittgenstein, op. cit., §§225 (p. 86) and 136 (pp. 52f).

45. On this, see Wolfgang Stegmüller, *Main Currents in Contemporary German, British and American Philosophy*, trans. Albert E. Blumberg (Dordrecht: Reidel, 1969), pp. 452ff. More specifically on the "accompaniments" of rule-following, see Wittgenstein, op. cit., §§152–79 (pp. 60ff).

46. Habermas, *The Theory of Communicative Action*, vol. 2, p. 18.

47. Peter Winch, *The Idea of a Social Science and its Relation to Philosophy* (London: Routledge & Kegan Paul, 1958), p. 30.

48. Habermas, *The Theory of Communicative Action*, vol. 2, p. 18.

49. On this and what follows, see Andreas Kemmerling, "Regel und Geltung im Lichte der Analyse Wittgensteins," *Rechtstheorie* 6 (1975): 104–31.

50. Wittgenstein, op. cit., §§232ff (pp. 87ff).

51. Ibid., §219 (p. 85).

52. Kemmerling, op. cit., p. 106.

53. Wittgenstein, op. cit., §§104 (p. 55) and 222 (p. 86).

54. Ibid., §84 (p. 39); see also Kant, who justifies the necessity of judgment with this argument: *Critique of Pure Reason,* trans. Norman Kemp Smith (1933; London: Macmillan, 1973), A 133 (p. 177).

55. Kemmerling, op. cit., p. 105; H. L. A. Hart has shown that the skeptic is actually a disappointed Platonist: "he has found that rules are not all they would be in a formalist's heaven, or in a world where men were like gods and could anticipate all possible combinations of fact, so that open-texture was not a necessary feature of rules. The sceptic's conception of what it is for a rule to exist may thus be an unattainable ideal, and when he discovers that it is not attained by what are called rules, he expresses his disappointment by the denial that there are, or can be, any rules" (*The Concept of Law* [Oxford: Clarendon Press, 1961], p. 135). On this, see also Wittgenstein, op. cit., §100 (p. 45).

56. Wittgenstein, op. cit., §107 (p. 46).

57. I shall not go into the extensive discussion of Wittgenstein's "behaviorism." On this, see Stegmüller, op. cit., pp. 482ff.

58. See the following paragraph (§199) in Wittgenstein, op. cit., pp. 80f.

59. Ibid., §§202 (p. 81), 206 (p. 82).

60. Ibid., §219 (p. 85); Robert J. Fogelin, *Wittgenstein* (London: Routledge & Kegan Paul, 1976), p. 141.

61. Wittgenstein, op. cit., §25 (p. 12)

62. Kemmerling, op. cit., p. 115 (fn 15), pp. 124f; Fogelin, op. cit., pp. 144f.

63. Kemmerling, op. cit., p. 114.

64. For this reason, Habermas rejects Wittgenstein's "positivism of language games." See Habermas, *The Philosophical Discourse of Modernity,* p. 199. See also "Vorlesungen zur sprachtheoretischen Grundlegung der Soziologie," in *Vorstudien und Ergänzungen zur Theorie des kommunikativen Handelns,* pp. 65ff.

65. On this thematization of rule-following at the level of a "transcendental language game," see Apel, "Sprechakttheorie und transzendentale Sprachpragmatik zur Frage ethischer Normen," in *Sprachpragmatik und Philosophie,* ed. Karl-Otto Apel (Frankfurt am Main: Suhrkamp, 1976), pp. 123f, and "The A Priori of the Communication Community and the Foundations of Ethics," in *Towards a Transformation of Philosophy,* trans. Glyn Adey and David Frisby (London: Routledge & Kegan Paul, 1980), p. 269.

66. Habermas, *The Theory of Communicative Action,* vol. 2, p. 19.

67. To my mind, this is clearly the case above all in *The Theory of Communicative Action,* vol. 2, pp. 18f, and in "Vorlesungen zur sprachtheoretischen Grundlegung der Soziologie," p. 66; Habermas begins with the problem of reaching understanding about the incorrect application of rules, then however only speaks about the identity of rules or reaching understanding about rules.

68. Wittgenstein, op. cit., §241 (p. 88). See also the quotation from Wittgenstein's *Remarks on the Foundations of Mathematics* (ed. G. H. von Wright, R. Rhees and G. E. M. Anscombe and trans. G. E. M. Anscombe [Oxford: Blackwell, 1956], p. 184ᵉ) in Kemmerling, op. cit., p. 155: "And does this mean e.g. that the definition of 'same' would be this: same is what all or most human beings with one voice take for the same?—Of course not./For of course I don't make use of the agreement of human beings to affirm identity. What criterion do you use, then? None at all."

69. See the explicit reference to this aphorism (§241) from Wittgenstein in "Vorlesungen zur sprachtheoretischen Grundlegung der Soziologie," p. 72.

70. Wittgenstein, op. cit., §217 (p. 85).

71. Habermas, *The Theory of Communicative Action,* vol. 2, p. 23.

72. Ibid., pp. 28ff, 31ff, 40ff.

73. Mead, op. cit., p. 138. Since I shall not pursue the genesis of self-consciousness any further, I shall not consider the current controversy about whether Mead's interpretation of self-consciousness as the outcome of a social process does not perhaps presuppose a primordial, nonsocial self-understanding.

74. Ibid., pp. 150f; Habermas, *The Theory of Communicative Action,* vol. 2, pp. 33ff; Joas, op. cit., pp. 119f.

75. Mead, op. cit., p. 151; see pp. 151ff.

76. Ibid., pp. 154ff.

77. Habermas, *The Theory of Communicative Action,* vol. 2, pp. 33ff; as well as Piaget, who refers to Durkheim, and not Mead: *The Moral Judgment of the Child,* trans. Marjorie Gabain (New York: Free Press, 1965).

78. On the social-psychological aspect of this, see Wolfgang Edelstein and Monika Keller, "Perspektivität und Interpretation. Zur Entwicklung des sozialen Verstehens," in *Perspektivität und Interpretation,* ed. W. Edelstein and M. Keller (Frankfurt am Main: Suhrkamp, 1982), p. 27; as well as Dieter Geulen, "Soziales Handeln und Perspektivenübernahme," in *Perspektivenübernahme und soziales Handeln. Texte zur sozial-kognitiven Entwicklung,* ed. D. Geulen (Frankfurt am Main: Suhrkamp, 1982), p. 53.

79. Habermas, *The Theory of Communicative Action,* vol. 2, pp. 35f; Edelstein and Keller, op. cit., p. 26.

80. Mead, op. cit., pp. 157f. On Mead's thesis of the continuity between the child's self-consciousness and abstract thought processes, see Joas, op. cit., pp. 110f; on the transition from the concept of generalized other to universalist ethics, see ibid., pp. 119f.

81. Mead, op. cit., p. 162.

82. Ibid., p. 175.

83. Ibid., p. 277.

84. Ibid., pp. 227f, 280.

85. Ibid., pp. 280f.

86. Ibid., p. 270.

87. Ibid., p. 199, 201; Joas, op. cit., p. 118.

88. Mead, op. cit., p. 209.

89. Ibid., p. 198.

90. Ibid., p. 261.

91. Ibid., p. 262.

92. Ibid., p. 387.

93. On Mead's concept of value and its origins in pragmatism, see Joas, op. cit., pp. 130f.

94. "In order truly to resolve a problem-situation, the individual must examine the values, expectations, and impulses he has brought to the situation, and should he become convinced of the necessity for changing them, he must then re-structure them. Only through the elaboration of a practicable moral strategy which is suited to a given situation is a resolution of a conflict of values and a re-integration of the self possible" (Joas, op. cit., p. 134).

95. Mead, op. cit., p. 388.

96. On the parallels in Mead's work between experimental method in the empirical sciences and in ethics, see Joas, op. cit., pp. 128f.

97. On this, see Habermas, *The Theory of Communicative Action,* vol. 2, p. 95.

98. Mead, op. cit., p. 381. For more on Mead's critique of Kant with reference to situation relatedness, see Joas, op. cit., pp. 123f.

99. Mead, op. cit., p. 388.

100. On this, see the critique of Habermas in the light of Mead's proposal in Joas, op. cit., p. 130: " . . . Mead links here the sphere of moral reflection or moral discourse to the specific problem encountered in action which gave rise to the reflection or discourse. In Mead's view, there is not a yawning chasm between discourse and action—as is the case in Habermas's theory. The discourse remains functionally related to the action-situation; in the discourse only those validity-claims can be considered as problematical which are in fact called into question by the conflict of values." [Translator's note: The reference to Habermas is omitted in the published translation.] Joas, who, admittedly, restricts his critique to the early writings on discourse theory, does not quite grasp the problem with this; controversial action norms are "fed into" practical discourse from the outside (Habermas, "Discourse Ethics," p. 103). What remains questionable, however, is how this is congruent with Habermas's thesis (which follows Mead) that constructive hypothesis formation and practical (justification) discourse are not to be separated (Habermas, *The Theory of Communicative Action,* vol. 2, p. 95). If processes of discovery and application are reversible, they do not belong at all in justification discourses, but in application discourses. For a summary of the constructive method of Mead's universalist ethics, see Joas, op. cit., p. 137.

101. Piaget, op. cit.

102. Lawrence Kohlberg, "Stage and Sequence: The Cognitive-Developmental Approach to Socialization," and "Moral Stages and Moralization: The Cognitive-Developmental Approach," in *Essays on Moral Development,* vol. 2 (San Francisco: Harper & Row, 1984), pp. 7–169 and 170–205.

103. Piaget, op. cit., pp. 14f, 29ff.

104. Ibid., pp. 37, 40f.

105. Ibid., p. 46.

106. Ibid., pp. 49f.

107. Ibid., p. 47.

108. Ibid., p. 64.

109. Ibid., pp. 111, 186f, 188, and passim.

110. Ibid., pp. 94ff, 197ff.

111. See the numerous references to Durkheim and discussions of his position in Piaget, op. cit., as well as the collection of papers edited by Hans Bertram, *Gesellschaftlicher Zwang und moralische Autonomie* (Frankfurt am Main: Suhrkamp, 1986), especially the introduction by the editor, p. 23.

112. Ibid., p. 267. [Translator's note: Translation altered slightly.]

113. Ibid., pp. 282f. [Translator's note: The English translation reads "mere quality" instead of "pure equality," which is obviously an oversight; see the French edition *Le jugement moral chez l'enfant* (Paris: Librairie Félix Alcan, 1932), p. 324 (*"l'égalité pure"*).]

114. Ibid., p. 317.

115. Ibid., p. 97. Correspondingly, the distinction between "constitutive rules" and "constituted rules" is essential for the third stage (see op. cit., p. 98).

116. Ibid., p. 83; Carol Gilligan, *In a Different Voice. Psychological Theory and Women's Development* (Cambridge, Mass.: Harvard University Press, 1982), pp. 9f.

117. Kohlberg, "Moral Stages and Moralization," p. 177; "Stage and Sequence," p. 44. On his critique of Piaget, see ibid., p. 43.

118. Kohlberg, "Stage and Sequence," p. 44.

119. Kohlberg, "Moral Stages and Moralization," p. 173.

120. Ibid., p. 177; on this, see Robert L. Selman, *The Growth of Interpersonal Understanding. Developmental and Clinical Analyses* (New York: Academic Press, 1980).

121. Kohlberg, "Moral Stages and Moralization," pp. 177ff.

122. See table 2.1 in Kohlberg, ibid., pp. 174ff.

123. Kohlberg, "The Six Stages of Justice Judgment," in *Essays on Moral Development*, vol., 2, pp. 621–39.

124. See ibid., pp. 624ff, and the table of six stages reproduced here (p. 130) from Kohlberg, "Moral Stages and Moralization," pp. 174ff.

125. I attempted to reconstruct the development of the concept of equality in this sense in "Verrechtlichung durch Gleichbehandlung?" in *Thema: Ungleichheit, Gesellschafts- und Sozialpolitische Texte Band 4*, ed. Evelyn Gröbl (Linz: Forschungsinstitut für Sozialplanung, Johannes Kepler University, 1986), pp. 51–64.

126. Dworkin, *Taking Rights Seriously,* p. xi.

127. In German criminal law, these circumstances, insofar as they do not belong to the constituent facts of being guilty, are considered separately when punishment is conferred; see §46 Criminal Code. Here too, person-related features play a considerable role.

128. Kohlberg, "The Six Stages of Justice Judgment," pp. 626f.

129. Aristotle, *Nicomachean Ethics,* trans. W. D. Ross, in *The Complete Works of Aristotle,* vol. 2, ed. Jonathan Barnes (Princeton: Princeton University Press, 1984), Book 5 1137b12f and 1137b19ff (pp. 1795 and 1796).

130. Ibid., 1137b19 (pp. 1795f).

131. Kohlberg, "The Six Stages of Justice Judgment," p. 632.

132. See for the German discussion, especially for the 1920s, Gerhard Leibholz, *Die Gleichheit vor dem Gesetz,* 2d ed. (Munich/Berlin: Beck, 1959), p. 76. This change is clearly expressed in the fact that the rule of equality *before* the law is interpreted in the temporal sense. See ibid., p. 35.

133. Kohlberg, "Moral Stages and Moralization," p. 178.

134. Kohlberg, "The Six Stages of Justice Judgment," p. 638.

135. Ibid., pp. 637f.

136. From a different perspective, namely, in terms of the aspect of the functional differentiation of societal subsystems, Luhmann comes to the same conclusion:

"If one forgoes presupposing in nature or in a system of values fixed viewpoints which normatively dictate what is to be treated as equal and what as unequal, it must be possible to find the meaning of this scheme in the comparative orientation itself. And it reveals itself in the fact that *the equal/unequal scheme serves as a specifically constituted scheme of the question concerning a sufficient reason.* It is the very emptiness of the principle of equality—viz., it contains *absolutely no* indication as to what is to be treated equally and what unequally—that gives it its special function: the sufficient justification of *every* unequal treatment" (italics in the original). (Luhmann, *Grundrechte als Institution* [Berlin: Duncker & Humblot, 1986], p. 169).

Leibholz also interprets the principle of equality in the sense of a "prohibition of arbitrariness" which is to be used negatively: "The concept of arbitrariness itself *cannot be unequivocally determined in material terms* and cannot be formally demarcated by a criterion. 'Arbitrary law' is simultaneously 'incorrect law' and differs from the latter only in a purely quantitative manner: in the sense that absolutely no reason at all, or perhaps at the most an essentially irrational reason, can be advanced for action on the part of the state (passing a law, making a judgment, issuing an administrative directive); besides, 'rational' cannot be defined in a once-and-for-all manner, just as little as the public interest or public welfare can" (italics in the original) Leibholz, op. cit., p. 87. This determination of the principle of equality has entered the rulings of the German Federal Constitutional Court as the "prohibition of arbitrariness." See the proof provided by Manfred Gubelt, marg. 11 and 18 on Article 3, in *Grundgesetz-Kommentar,* ed. von Münch (Munich: Beck, 1981).

137. Kohlberg, "The Six Stages of Justice Judgment," p. 638. On the difference principle, see Rawls, op. cit., pp. 75, 83.

138. See the description of the social perspective of Stage 5 in Kohlberg's table of moral stages: "Moral Stages and Moralization," p. 175.

139. Kohlberg, "The Six Stages of Justice Judgment," pp. 621f.

140. Ibid., p. 637.

141. Ibid.

142. Ibid., p. 638.

143. Gilligan, op. cit.

144. John Michael Murphy and Carol Gilligan, "Moral Development in Late Adolescense and Adulthood: a Critique and Reconstruction of Kohlberg's Theory," *Human Development* 23 (1980): 83.

145. Ibid., p. 99.

146. Ibid., p. 97.

147. Norma Haan "Two Moralities in Action Contexts: Relationships to Thought, Ego Regulation, and Development," *Journal of Personality and Social Psychology* 36.3 (1978): 287.

148. Ibid., p. 290.

149. Ibid., p. 303.

150. Gilligan, op. cit., p. 19. A neo-Aristotelian interpretation of Gilligan's critique of Kohlberg can be found in Owen Flanagan, Jr. and Jonathan E. Adler, "Impartiality and Particularity," *Social Research* 50 (1983): 576–96, especially p. 586. See also Owen Flanagan, Jr., "Virtue, Sex, and Gender: Some Philosophical Reflections on the Moral Psychology Debate," *Ethics* 92 (1982): 499–512, and Kohlberg's response: "A Reply to Owen Flanagan and Some Comments on the Puka-Goodpaster Exchange," *Ethics* 92 (1982): 513–28.

151. Gilligan, op. cit., p. 30.

152. Carol Gilligan and Mary Field Belenky, "A Naturalistic Study of Abortion Decisions," in *Clinical-Developmental Psychology,* no. 7, ed. R. Selman and R. Yando (San Francisco: Jossey-Bass, 1980), pp. 69–88; Gilligan, op. cit., pp. 64ff.

153. Gilligan, op. cit., p. 74.

154. Ibid., p. 31. This determination of the subject matter of morality corresponds to Aristotelian ethics: see Flanagan and Alder, "Impartiality and Particularity," op. cit., and in this study, pp. 171ff, infra.

155. Lawrence Kohlberg, Charles Levine, and Alexandra Hewer, "The Current Formulation of the Theory," in Kohlberg, *Essays on Moral Development,* vol. 2, op. cit., pp. 227ff.

156. Ibid., p. 229.

157. Ibid., p. 232.

158. Lawrence Kohlberg, Charles Levine, and Alexandra Hewer, "Synopses and detailed Replies to Critics," in Kohlberg, "Essays on Moral Development, vol. 2, op. cit., p. 356.

159. Habermas, "Justice and Solidarity: On the Discussion Concerning Stage 6," in *The Moral Domain. Essays in the Ongoing Discussion between Philosophy and the Social Sciences,* ed. Thomas E. Wren (Cambridge, Mass.: MIT Press, 1990), pp. 224–51.

160. Habermas, "Morality and Ethical Life: Does Hegel's Critique of Kant Apply to Discourse Ethics?" in *Moral Consciousness and Communicative Action,* p. 200.

161. Habermas, "Justice and Solidarity," p. 247.

162. Ibid., pp. 43f, 50; "Morality and Ethical Life," pp. 205ff; "Discourse Ethics," pp. 104f; for the direct discussion of Gilligan, Haan, and Murphy, see "Moral Consciousness and Communicative Action," pp. 175ff.

163. Habermas, "Discourse Ethics"; "Moral Consciousness and Communicative Action." For a critique of the moral-theoretic implications of this, see my paper "Vorläufige Überlegungen zu einer Theorie der prozeduralen Applikation," in *Workshop zu Konzepten des postinterventionistischen Rechts,* ed. G. Brüggemeier and C. Joerges (Bremen: Zentrum für europäische Rechtspolitik—Materialen 4, 1984), pp. 74–90.

164. Kohlberg, Levine, and Hewer, "Synopses and Detailed Replies to Critics," p. 367.

165. Ibid., pp. 366, 368.

166. Lawrence Kohlberg, D. R. Boyd, and C. Levine, "The Return of Stage 6: Its Principle and Moral Point of View," in *The Moral Domain*, p. 179.

167. Kohlberg, Levine, and Hewer, "Synopses and Detailed Replies to Critics," p. 368. On Rawls' constructivism, see Rawls, "Kantian Constructivism in Moral Theory," *The Journal of Philosophy* 77 (1980): 515–72.

168. Kohlberg, Levine, and Hewer, "Synopses and Detailed Replies to Critics," p. 365, 301.

169. Gilligan and Murphy, op. cit., p. 83.

170. Haan, op. cit., p. 303.

171. Gilligan and Murphy, op. cit., pp. 98, 99.

172. Ibid., p. 83.

173. On this, see Gertrud Nunner-Winkler, "Moral Relativism and Strict Universalism," in *The Moral Domain*, pp. 109–26.

174. Haan, op. cit.

175. Hannah Arendt, "Thinking and Moral Considerations: A Lecture," *Social Research* 38 (1971): 435f.

176. Hegel, "Der Geist des Christentums und sein Schicksal," in *Werke*, vol. 1 (Frankfurt am Main: Suhrkamp, 1971), p. 323.

177. On this, see my paper "Dialektik der Aufklärung in der Idee der Freiheit. Zur Kritik des Freiheitsbegriffs bei Adorno," *Zeitschrift für philosophische Forschung* 39 (1985): 229–60.

178. On this, see Axel Honneth, *The Critique of Power. Reflective Stages in a Critical Social Theory*, trans. Kenneth Baynes (Cambridge, Mass.: MIT Press, 1991).

179. Wolf, op. cit., pp. 47ff.

180. Ibid., pp. 3f.

181. Ibid., pp. 52, 56.

182. Ibid., p. 166.

183. Ibid., pp. 167, 170f.

184. G. E. M. Anscombe, "Modern Moral Philosophy," *Philosophy* 33 (1958): 18.

185. Ibid., pp. 14f.

186. Foot, op. cit., pp. 121ff.

187. Hart, op. cit., pp. 19ff.

188. Habermas, "Morality and Ethical Life," p. 200.

189. Habermas, *The Philosophical Discourse of Modernity,* p. 322.

190. Habermas, "Moral Consciousness and Communicative Action," pp. 182ff.

191. Kant, *Critique of Practical Reason,* A 122ff (pp. 71ff), A 74ff (pp. 45ff).

192. Singer, op. cit., p. 226.

193. Hegel, *Hegel's Philosophy of Right,* trans. T. M. Knox (Oxford: Oxford University Press, 1967), Addition to §135 (p. 254).

194. Mead, op. cit., p. 381. On this, see supra, pp. 109f.

195. Hegel, *Natural Law,* trans. T. M. Knox (Philadelphia: University of Pennsylvania Press, 1975), pp. 78f.

196. Singer, op. cit., p. 238.

197. On this, see my paper "Verrechtlichung durch Gleichbehandlung?" p. 58; Habermas, "Justice and Solidarity," pp. 248f.

198. On this, see Dieter Simon, "Historische Beiträge zur Rechtsprechungslehre," in *Rechtsprechungslehre,* ed. N. Achterberg (Cologne/Berlin: Heymann, 1986), p. 231, where he summarizes the discussion: "Separating conflict resolution from the general locus of power, assigning it to the judiciary, and cementing this process in decades of discourses—still continuing—on the question concerning the essence of the judiciary and the administrative authorities—all this stood under the then plausible premise that the number of conflicts would remain visible at a glance."

Excursus:
"Phronesis" *as an Example of Context-bound Application*

1. Höffe, "Kants kategorischer Imperativ als Kriterium des Sittlichen," in *Ethik und Politik. Grundmodelle und -probleme der praktischen Philosophie* (Frankfurt am Main: Suhrkamp, 1979), pp. 84–119. See also Bubner, op. cit., pp. 245f.

2. See, for example, Kant, *Groundwork of the Metaphysic of Morals,* 3rd ed., trans. H. J. Paton (New York: Harper & Row, 1956), p. 69, first footnote.

3. Höffe, op. cit., p. 90.

4. Ibid., p. 97. Bubner characterizes maxims as a "modern variant of classical *phronesis*" (op. cit., p. 234). There are however indications that Kant saw this problem. Höffe himself refers to the "casuistic questions" Kant discussed in connection with each particular virtue in the doctrine of virtues (Höffe, ibid.). In the introduction to the doctrine of virtues, Kant himself distinguishes between "narrow" and "wide" duties. The former belong in the doctrine of Right and must be precisely determined, with the consequence that the doctrine of Right "has no more need of general directions (method) as to how to proceed in judging than does pure mathematics; instead, it certifies its method by what it does." In contrast to that, ethics, "because of the latitude it allows in its imperfect duties, inevitably leads to questions that call upon judgment to decide how a maxim is to be applied in particular cases, and indeed in such a way that judgment provides another (subordinate) maxim (and one can always ask for yet another principle for applying this maxim to cases that may arise). So ethics falls into a casuistry, which has no place in the doctrine of Right" (Kant, *The Metaphysics of Morals*, trans. Mary Gregor [Cambridge: Cambridge University Press, 1991], p. 211).

5. Höffe, op. cit., p. 95.

6. Bubner, op. cit., p. 238.

7. Herbert Schnädelbach, "What is Neo-Aristotelianism?" *Praxis International* 7 (Winter 1987/8): 228f.

8. Aristotle, *Nicomachean Ethics,* Book 1, 1094al (p. 1729).

9. Ibid., 1098a3 (p. 1735). Greek edition: *Aristotelis Ethica Nicomachea, recognovit I. Bywater,* Oxonii: Scriptorum classicorum bibliotheca oxoniensis (Oxford: Oxford University Press, 1984).

10. Ibid., 1098b1ff; 1099alff (pp. 1736f).

11. Ibid., 1102a26ff (p. 1741).

12. Ibid., Book 2 1103a14 (p. 1741).

13. Ibid.

14. Günther Bien, "Aristotelische Ethik und Kantische Moraltheorie," *Freiburger Universitätsblätter* 73 (1981): 67. [Translator's note: "circumstantial" is a translation of *peristatisch,* and *Peristasen* will be translated as "circumstances." On the original Greek term, *peristasis,* see the section on "Circumstances" in A. R. Jonsen and S. Toulmin, *The Abuse of Casuistry. A History of Moral Reasoning* (Berkeley: University of California Press, 1988), pp. 131–36. I thank Federico Hermanin De Reichenfeld for drawing my attention to this.]

15. Aristotle, *Nicomachean Ethics,* Book 2, 1106b20 (p. 1747).

16. See also ibid., 1109b28 (p. 1752); Book 3, 1111a3 (p. 1754); Book 4, 1120a25 (p. 1768); Book 4 1126a9 (p. 1777). On the significance of circumstances [*Peristasen*] in Greek thinking, see Erich Auerbach, *Mimesis. The Representation of Reality in Western Literature*, trans. W. R. Trask (1953; reprint, Princeton: Princeton University Press, 1974), p. 6. On their function in the speech scheme of classical rhetoric, especially for a speech in court (as part of the *narratio*, prior to the actual presentation of evidence, the *prothesis*), see Manfred Fuhrmann, *Die antike Rhetorik* (Munich/Zürich: Artemis, 1984), p. 87. There are seven circumstances in the theory of status: "persons, actions, time, place, motive, manner, and means—*quis, quid, ubi, quibus auxiliis, cur, quomodo, quando*" ibid., p. 99. There has been an interesting reception of the theory of circumstances in ethnomethodology, see H. Garfinkel and H. Sacks, "On Formal Structures of Practical Actions," in *Theoretical Sociology: Perspectives and Development*, ed. J. C. McKinney and E. A. Tiryakian (New York: Appelton-Century-Crofts, 1970), pp. 355f.

17. Aristotle, *Nicomachean Ethics*, Book 3, 1111a18 (p. 1754).

18. See Schnädelbach, "What is Neo-Aristotelianism?" p. 230.

19. Aristotle, *Nicomachaen Ethics*, Book 6, 1140a25 (p. 1800).

20. Ibid., 1140b20 (p. 1801).

21. Ibid., 114b14f (p. 1802).

22. Ibid., 1142a30 (p. 1803).

23. Ibid., 1142b15 (p. 1804).

24. Ibid., 1142a32 (p. 1803).

25. Ibid., 1142b22 (p. 1804).

26. Ibid., 1143a9 (p. 1805).

27. Ibid., Book 6, Chap. 13 (1143b18ff).

28. Ibid., 1144a7 (p. 1807).

29. Ibid., 1144b31 (p. 1808).

30. Ibid., 1144b27 (p. 1808).

31. Schnädelbach, "What is Neo-Aristotelianism?" p. 233. [Translator's note: translation altered slightly.]

32. Ernst Tugendhat, *Selbstbewußtsein und Selbstbestimmung* (Frankfurt am Main: Suhrkamp, 1979), p. 178; Hans-Georg Gadamer, "Heideggers Rückgang auf die Griechen," in *Theorie der Subjektivität*, ed. Konrad Cramer et al. (Frankfurt am Main: Suhrkamp, 1987), p. 408.

33. Aristotle, *Politics,* trans. B. Jowett, in *The Complete Works of Aristotle,* vol., 2, 1253a3 (p. 1987); Greek edition: *Aristotelis Politica, post Fr. Susemihilium recognovit O. Immisch* (Lipsiae: In Aedibus B. G Teubner, 1909).

34. Ibid., 1253a14 (p. 1988).

35. *Nicomachean Ethics,* Book 1, 1097b9 (p. 1734), 1094a26 (p. 1729).

36. Ibid., 1094b7 (p. 1730).

37. Gadamer, "A Letter by Professor Hans-Georg Gadamer," in Richard J. Bernsetin, *Beyond Objectivism and Relativism: Science, Hermeneutics, and Praxis* (Oxford: Basil Blackwell, 1982), p. 263.

38. Aristotle, *Nicomachean Ethics,* Book 10, 1179b31 (p. 1864).

39. Ritter, " 'Politik' und 'Ethik' in der praktischen Philosophie des Aristoteles," in *Metaphysik und Politik* (Frankfurt am Main: Suhrkamp, 1979), p. 110.

40. Ibid.

41. Ibid., p. 118.

42. Ibid., p. 120.

43. Ibid., p. 125.

44. Ritter, "Das bürgerliche Leben. Zur aristotelischen Theorie des Glücks," in *Metaphysik und Politik,* pp. 64, 75.

45. Gadamer, "Hermeneutics as Practical Philosophy," in *Reason in the Age of Science,* trans. Frederick G. Lawrence (Cambridge, Mass.: MIT Press, 1982), pp. 88–112.

46. Gadamer, "Über die Möglichkeit einer philosophischen Ethik," in *Kleine philosophische Schriften I* (Tübingen: J. C. B. Mohr, 1976), pp. 184, 181.

47. Ibid., see also the almost identical statement in *Truth and Method,* p. 279.

48. "Über die Möglichkeit einer philosophischen Ethik," p. 186.

49. Ibid., p. 87. Gadamer's reception of Hegel's critique of Kant is especially clear here.

50. Ibid.

51. Tugendhat, "Antike und moderne Ethik," in *Probleme der Ethik* (Stuttgart: Reclam, 1984), p. 43.

52. Ibid., pp. 39f. In the second of three lectures on problems of ethics, "Kann man aus der Erfahrung moralisch lernen?," Tugendhat put this argument more precisely. I shall return to this in *Part Three* of this study.

53. Ibid., pp. 40f.

54. Ibid., p. 41.

55. Ibid., p. 52.

56. Höffe, "Ethik als praktische Philosophie—Die Begründung durch Aristoteles," in *Ethik und Politik,* p. 44.

57. Ibid., p. 45.

58. Ibid., p. 52.

59. Ibid., p. 55.

60. Ibid., p. 57.

61. Ibid., p. 61. Günther Bien aims not at a synthesis of, but at a complementary relation between, Kant and Aristotle, see "Aristotelische Ethik und Kantische Moraltheorie," p. 73. This leads to the peculiar consequence that Kant's ethics is reserved for exceptional situations (ibid.). Gadamer comes to the same result, see "Über die Möglichkeit einer philosophischen Ethik," p. 184.

62. Höffe, "Ethik als praktische Philosophie," pp. 66ff.

63. Ibid., p. 68.

64. Eric Voegelin does not have any difficulties with this because of his onto-theological presuppositions, see *Anamnesis. Zur Theorie der Geschichte und Politik* (Munich: Piper, 1966), pp. 130ff.

65. Tugendhat introduces this idea via the truth validity of empirical propositions; see "Antike und moderne Ethik," pp. 36f, 43. However, precisely when it is a question of impartiality, the psychologistic manner of speaking about a "faculty" would have to be replaced by a rationally reconstructable procedure. On this, see infra, *Part Three.*

66. David Wiggins, "Deliberation and Practical Reason," in *Essays on Aristotle's Ethics,* ed. Amélie O. Rorty (Berkeley: University of California Press, 1980), p. 232.

67. Ibid., p. 236.

68. Ibid., p. 232.

69. Wiggins translates *aisthesis* with "situational appreciation" (ibid., p. 233); see supra, pp. 176f.

70. Ibid., p. 233.

71. Ibid., p. 234.

72. Ibid.

73. See supra, pp. 139, 150f.

74. Gadamer, *Truth and Method,* pp. 277f. [Translator's note: translation altered slightly.]

75. Ibid., p. 279.

76. Ibid., p. 234.

77. Ibid., p. xiii.

78. See above all ibid., p. 261: "The anticipation of meaning that governs our understanding of a text is not an act of subjectivity, but proceeds from the communality that binds us to the tradition. But this is contained in our relation to tradition, in the constant process of education. Tradition is not simply a precondition into which we come, but we produce it ourselves, inasmuch as we understand, participate in the evolution of tradition and hence further determine it ourselves. Thus the circle of understanding is not a 'methodological' circle, but describes an ontological structural element in understanding."

79. Ibid., p. 16. It is only in passing that the conspicuous proximity to a theory of social systems is to be noted again. See, for instance, the conclusion Luhmann draws from the existence of functional differentiation in complex societies: "In strategies of individual self-presentation, in the tactfully revealing, dispassionate courtesies of the expectant civilization, in the trust in the fictitious satisfaction value of money, in the unperturbed indifference in the face of the profusion of the state's decisions about problems, and in the sensitiveness of all these attitudes to critical disturbances that question the systems' capacity to function—in all these phenomena, a new kind of behavior of man toward the world is becoming apparent, and the interpretation of this behavior sets philosophy a new task" (*Grundrechte als Institution,* p. 216).

80. Gadamer, *Truth and Method,* pp. 17f.

81. Ibid., pp. 30f. [Translator's note: translation altered slightly.]

82. Ibid.; see also ibid., p. 36, following Gracian. The relation to Aristotle's *Politics,* 1253a3 is obvious.

83. Ibid., pp. 31f, 34ff, 39ff.

84. Ibid., pp. 76, 81ff.

85. Ibid., p. 104. [Translator's note: translation altered slightly.]

86. Ibid., p. 118.

87. Ibid., pp. 204, 199f.

88. Ibid., p. 227.

89. Ibid., p. 232. [Translator's note: translation altered slightly.]

90. Ibid., p. 245.

91. Ibid., p. 238. [Translator's note: translation altered slightly.] On this critique, see also Dietrich Böhler, "Philosophische Hermeneutik und hermeneutische Methode," in *Text und Applikation (Poetik und Hermeneutik IX)*, ed. M. Fuhrmann et al. (Munich: Fink, 1981), pp. 483–511.

92. Gadamer, *Truth and Method,* pp. 272, 323.

93. Ibid., p. 261.

94. Ibid., p. 273.

95. Ibid., pp. 274ff.

96. Ibid., pp. 17f.

97. Ibid., p. 324. [Translator's note: translation altered slightly.]

98. Ibid., pp. 348, 400f. [Translator's note: translation altered slightly.]

99. Ibid., p. 399: "Linguistic form and content that has been handed down cannot be separated in the hermeneutical experience." On the critique of the assimilation of "truth" and "thing," see also Bernstein, op. cit., p. 154.

100. Gadamer, *Truth and Method,* p. 345. [Translator's note: translation altered slightly.]

101. On the critique of this exemplary function, see Ulfried Neumann, "Neuere Schriften zur Rechtsphilosophie und Rechtstheorie," *Philosophische Rundschau* 28 (1981): 197ff. See the detailed presentation of the controversy about this function in Monika Frommel, *Die Rezeption der Hermeneutik bei Karl Larenz und Josef Esser* (Ebelsbach: R. Gremer, 1981), pp. 97ff. Frommel comes to the conclusion that application in law acquires a "model function" if one limits it to the problem of the application of the text of statutes (ibid., p. 105).

102. Bernstein, op. cit., p. 157. On this, see also Gadamer's letter to Bernstein, ibid., pp. 261–65.

103. Gadamer, *Truth and Method,* p. 279. [Translator's note: in the second quotation, "concrete" does not appear in the English edition.]

104. Ibid., p. 240. [Translator's note: translation altered slightly.]

105. Böhler, op. cit., pp. 504f.

106. Ibid., p. 505.

107. Thomas S. Kuhn, "Objectivity, Value Judgment, and Theory Choice," in *The Essential Tension. Selected Studies in Scientific Tradition and Change* (Chicago: University of Chicago Press, 1977), p. 330. Bernstein links his thesis of the internal connection between the postempiricist philosophy of science and hermeneutics with this characterization of the theory-choice situation in empirical research. See Bernstein. op. cit., pp. 52ff.

108. Bernstein, op. cit., p. 158.

Part Three:
Appropriateness Argumentation in Morality

1. In case this point of contact appears arbitrarily chosen, Mead's draft of a universalist ethics should be recalled. The problem of a conflict of norms is the reason for him to overcome Kant's ethics. "Mead stresses very strongly that the self-examination called for by the categorical imperative reaches its limit when it is not a matter of determining just what one's duty is, but of resolving a conflict of duties, or, better, of establishing a constructive way of fulfilling one's duty" (Joas, op. cit., p. 124).

2. Alexy, *Theorie der Grundrechte*, p. 77.

3. Baier, *The Moral Point of View*, pp. 92ff.

4. Ibid., pp. 99ff.

5. Ibid., p. 106.

6. Ibid., p. 101.

7. Ibid., pp. 102, 103.

8. Ibid., p. 103.

9. Ibid.

10. John Searle, *"Prima Facie* Obligations," in *Practical Reasoning,* ed. J. Raz (Oxford: Oxford University Press, 1978), pp. 81–90.

11. Ibid., p. 82.

12. Ibid., p. 86. The question whether it follows from the fact of promising that X has an obligation to keep his promise is also relevant to Searle in connection with his attempt to criticize the is-ought dichotomy. The problem can however be discussed independently of this. One could say that the *(prima facie)* promise had no obligatory character from the beginning.

13. Ibid.

14. Ibid., pp. 88f.

15. Ibid., p. 88.

16. On this, see Singer, *Generalization in Ethics,* p. 238.

17. We thereby adopt the insight, formulated by Kohlberg for Stage 6, that what requires justification now is not equality, but the unequal treatment which accompanies each case of equal treatment. See supra, pp. 125ff.

18. Modifying a term borrowed by Hintikka from modal logic, one could refer the justification of the validity of a norm under unchanging circumstances to a "deontically perfect world" where it is possible to fulfill the obligation requiring justification along with all the other obligations belonging to the ideal deontic world concerned. In the real world, by contrast, conflicts are possible. See Jaakko Hintikka, "Some Main Problems of Deontic Logic," in *Deontic Logic: Introductory and Systematic Readings,* ed. R. Hilpinen (Dordrecht: D. Reidel, 1971), pp. 70ff, 87ff. The difference consists in the fact that, in the deontically perfect world, the relation of obligation between p and q is a matter of a material implication: $p -> Oq$ (ibid., p. 78), whereas in the real world there is only a deontic relation between p and q: $O(p -> q)$.

19. Alexy, *Theorie der Grundrechte,* pp. 71ff. The distinction originates from Dworkin, *Taking Rights Seriously,* pp. 22ff. On the critique of Dworkin, see Alexy, "Zum Begriff des Rechtsprinzips," *Rechtstheorie* Beiheft 1 (1979): 59–87.

20. Alexy, *Theorie der Grundrechte,* p. 88.

21. Ibid., p. 75.

22. Ibid., p. 76.

23. Alexy, "Zum Begriff des Rechtsprinzips," p. 82, fn 96, with a reference to Luhmann's concept of conditional program.

24. *Theorie der Grundrechte,* pp. 77ff.

25. Ibid., p. 79.

26. This does not preclude the fact that rules, in connection with principles, can also have a *prima facie* character, which does however differ from the *prima facie* character of principles. Ibid., p. 89.

27. This would correspond to Dworkin's point that rules only have a "functional" weight in regulating social behavior, see *Taking Rights Seriously,* p. 27. I shall return to this in *Part Four.*

28. *Theorie der Grundrechte,* p. 81.

29. Ibid., pp. 84, 87.

30. Paralleling normative and evaluative judgments (ibid., p. 133) is not without its problems. However, we cannot go into this any further here.

31. Ibid., p. 146.

32. Ibid., pp. 149f, 152.

33. Ibid., p. 80. It is thus a matter of conflicts *per accidens*, and not *per se*.

34. That is why this objection affects Alexy's proposal only in part. He refers to the norms of fundamental rights and simple legal rules. Nonetheless, the moral-theoretic objection advanced here has consequences for jurisprudence because it entails tying the distinction between principles and rules to procedural presuppositions. For more details on this, see infra, *Part Four*.

35. Ibid., p. 89.

36. On this see Alexy, *A Theory of Legal Argumentation*, pp. 240ff; Koch and Rüßmann, *Juristische Begründungslehre*, pp. 222ff (from a critical viewpoint); Karl Larenz, *Methodenlehre der Rechtswissenschaft*, 5th ed. (Berlin/New York: Springer, 1983), pp. 319f. On the development and (political) significance of teleological arguments in the application of law, see Görg Haverkate, *Gewißheitsverluste im juristischen Denken* (Berlin: Duncker & Humblot, 1977), pp. 115ff.

37. *Theorie der Grundrechte.*

38. This is the structure of the principle of proportionality [*Verhältnismäßigkeit*], see ibid., p. 100.

39. Ibid., p. 149.

40. Ibid., pp. 128, 132. See also Esser, *Vorverständnis und Methodenwahl in der Rechtsfindung*, p. 59: "The norm as a paradigm of regulation, whose grounds are a value judgment or a combination of value judgments."

41. This critique of values would have to be possible at least at the highest level of the four-stage model proposed by Alexy, the level of universal practical discourse. He does not however maintain that there is such a possibility there. See *Theorie der Grundrechte*, pp. 498ff.

42. Ibid., pp. 98f; "Zum Begriff des Rechtsprinzips," p. 61, fn 19. On the confounding of constitutional values and functional imperatives, see Erhard Denninger, "Verfassungsrechtliche Schlüsselbegriffe," in *Festschrift für R. Wassermann*, ed. Christian Broda et al. (Neuwied/Darmstadt: Luchterhand, 1985), p. 295. On the critique of modes of weighing in the form of concepts of value, see also Frankenberg and Rödel, *Von der Volkssouveränität zum Minderheitenschutz*, p. 230: "Moreover, those who support

the weighing of goods have yet to provide a conclusive justification for how private and public interests, how individual rights, political liberty, and the functional efficiency of state authority can be made commensurable and be 'weighed' against one another, without the priority of one or another of the legal goods already being covertly assumed."

43. In this sense, Günther Patzig proposed distinguishing a first level for the weighing of interests in a situation from a second level for universalist justification, "Der kategorische Imperativ in der Ethik-Diskussion der Gegenwart," in *Tatsachen, Normen, Sätze* (Stuttgart: Reclam, 1980), p. 170. I shall return to the appropriateness of need interpretations and the problems of a utilitarian interpretation later in this part of the study.

44. Hare, *Freedom and Reason,* p. 88.

45. *Moral Thinking,* p. 26.

46. Ibid.

47. Ibid., p. 39.

48. Ibid., p. 40.

49. Ibid., pp. 41f.

50. Ibid., p. 43.

51. Ibid., p. 44.

52. Ibid., p. 47.

53. Ibid., pp. 89f.

54. Ibid., p. 90; see also ibid., pp. 63, 216f, 217f.

55. Tugendhat, "Kann man aus der Erfahrung moralisch lernen?" p. 91.

56. Ibid., p. 97. This would result in the rigoristic consequences objected to by Kant's critics. On the problems of a direct participation of individual norms in the deontological meaning of the categorical imperative, see Singer, op. cit., pp. 225f; Patzig, op. cit., p. 166.

57. Ibid., p. 98.

58. It is still contentious whether simple "application" does not perhaps change the norm. Semantic theories limit themselves to justifying rules of word usage. Hermeneutical theories claim differently that it is only with and through situational interpretation that a norm realizes itself as a deciding norm. It goes without saying that changing norms within, or by means of, the deductive scheme is impossible.

59. Tugendhat, "Kann man aus der Erfahrung moralisch lernen?" p. 100.

60. Ibid.

61. Ibid., p. 101.

62. Ibid., p. 102.

63. See also ibid., p. 103: "The moral principle that makes such a learning process possible cannot be an arbitrary one because only a normative utterance that claims adequacy and, if possible, impartiality can be invalidated by aspects that were overlooked."

64. See supra, pp. 25f, as well as Toulmin et al., *An Introduction into Reasoning*, pp. 85f, 323f; see also Singer, op. cit., pp. 41f.

65. Alexy, *A Theory of Legal Argumentation*, p. 188.

66. Ibid., pp. 195f; Singer, op. cit., pp. 19f, 31, 42.

67. Alexy, *A Theory of Legal Argumentation*, pp. 197ff.

68. Toulmin et al., op. cit., pp. 323ff.

69. *A Theory of Legal Argumentation*, p. 226. See also H. L. A. Hart, op. cit., p. 123. Toulmin seems to proceed from the same assumption, Toulmin et al., op. cit., pp. 323, 325.

70. Alexy, *A Theory of Legal Argumentation*, p. 226.

71. Ibid., p. 226. See also Koch and Rüßmann, *Juristische Begründungslehre*, p. 113.

72. Alexy, *A Theory of Legal Argumentation*, pp. 227f.

73. Horst Zimmermann, "Rechtsanwendung als Rechtsfortbildung," in *Juristische Methodenlehre und analytische Philosophie*, ed. H.-J. Koch (Kronberg im Taunus: Athenäum, 1976), p. 76; Alexy, *A Theory of Legal Argumentation*, p. 235; Koch and Rüßmann, op. cit., p. 15.

74. Alexy, *A Theory of Legal Argumentation*, p. 230.

75. Ibid., pp. 231ff.

76. Koch and Rüßmann, op. cit., pp. 126ff. On the expediency of this distinction for the application of law, see ibid., p. 145.

77. This definition is from Maximilian Herberger and Dieter Simon, *Wissenschaftstheorie für Juristen* (Frankfurt am Main: Metzner, 1980), p. 209; Koch and Rüßmann, op. cit., p. 130.

78. Koch and Rüßmann, op. cit., p. 131.

79. Ibid., pp. 24, 126.

80. Karl Engisch, *Logische Studien zur Gesetzesanwendung,* 3d ed. (Heidelberg: Winter, 1963), p. 15. Engisch distinguishes between "subordinating" features to a concept and "subsuming" the circumstances of a case under the interpreted features. The concept designates cases and case groups, so that in "application" it is a matter of "identifying the cases and case groups at which the law is aimed and which are to be subordinated to this law on the strength of interpretation; and the concrete case to be decided has to be equated subsumptively to these cases and case groups" (ibid., p. 29). See also Engisch, *Die Idee der Konkretisierung in Recht und Rechtswissenschaft unserer Zeit,* 2d ed. (Heidelberg: Winter, 1968), p. 155.

81. On this, see Joachim Hruschka, *Die Konstitution des Rechtsfalles* (Berlin: Duncker & Humblot, 1965), pp. 41f; Winfried Hassemer, *Tatbestand und Typus* (Cologne/Berlin: Heymanns, 1968), p. 55; Klaus Lüderssen, *Erfahrung als Rechtsquelle* (Frankfurt am Main: Suhrkamp, 1972), p. 97.

82. Alexy, *A Theory of Legal Argumentation,* pp. 228f; Koch and Rüßmann, op. cit., p. 118.

83. Koch and Rüßmann, op. cit., p. 145.

84. Justifying this doubt would presuppose a comprehensive debate with the semantic theory of meaning, which cannot be conducted here. On this, see Habermas's remark "that the understanding of linguistic expressions already calls for an orientation toward validity claims," "A Reply," p. 327 and *The Theory of Communicative Action,* vol. 1, p. 297.

85. On this, see Toulmin et al., op. cit., pp. 323ff; Martin Kriele, *Theorie der Rechtsgewinnung,* 2d ed. (Berlin: Duncker & Humblot, 1976), pp. 163, 198.

86. Toulmin et al., op. cit., p. 315.

87. Wolfgang Wieland, "Praxis und Urteilskraft," *Zeitschrift für philosophische Forschung* 28 (1974): 32f. See also Charles Larmore, "Moral Judgment," *Review of Metaphysics* 35 (1981): 287. In this connection, see again the arguments presented by contextual relativism, supra, pp. 137ff.

88. Larmore, op. cit., p. 280. However, as a condition for appropriate choice, Larmore introduces character features, in Aristotle's sense, see ibid., p. 287.

89. Toulmin et al., op. cit., p. 75.

90. Ibid., p. 329.

91. Ibid., p. 161.

92. Reiner Wimmer, *Universalisierung in der Ethik* (Frankfurt am Main: Suhrkamp, 1980), p. 232.

93. See also Bernard Gert, "Moral Theory and Applied Ethics," *The Monist* 67 (1984): 536f.

94. Baier, op. cit., p. 106.

95. Alexy, *Theorie der Grundrechte,* p. 152.

96. "Concerning the Common Saying," p. 414.

97. *Critique of Pure Reason,* p. 177. It is on this circumstance that Schnädelbach bases his critique of the transcendental-pragmatic reconstruction of the unity of reason. "How can one represent rationality in a priori rules, if indeed it is apparent that, for the application of rules which belong to rationality, no a priori rules can exist?" ("Remarks about Rationality and Language," in *The Communicative Ethics Controversy,* ed. S. Benhabib and F. Dallmayr [Cambridge, Mass.: MIT Press, 1990], p. 278). Because language is subject to a process of historical change, rationality cannot be completely represented in rules (ibid., pp. 279f). In relation to a moral principle which is reconstructed in formal-pragmatic terms and functions as a rule of argumentation in practical discourses, the problem sketched by Schnädelbach arises, in my opinion, in two respects: when applying the moral principle in a historically contingent form of life, and, indirectly, when applying universalistically justified norms. At least with regard to the latter, reason can be taken a little further, as we are attempting to show here.

98. Kant, *Critique of Pure Reason,* p. 177; "Concerning the Common Saying," p. 412.

99. Theories of coherence of this kind are advanced by John Rawls, "Outline of a Decision Procedure for Ethics," *The Philosophical Review* 60 (1951): 177–90; Joel Feinberg, "Justice, Fairness and Rationality," *The Yale Law Journal* 81 (1972): 1019ff; Norman Daniels, "Wide Reflective Equilibrium and Theory Acceptance in Ethics," *The Journal of Philosophy* 76 (1979): 256–82; Neil MacCormick, "Coherence in Legal Justification," in *Theorie der Normen. Festgabe für O. Weinberger,* ed. W. Krawietz et al. (Berlin: Duncker & Humblot, 1984), pp. 37–53. What these theories of coherence have in common is that the criterion of coherence serves the justification of validity. I shall deal with Dworkin's theory of coherence below.

Part Four:
Appropriateness Argumentation in Law

1. Herfried Münkler, *Im Namen des Staates. Die Begründung der Staatsraison in der frühen Neuzeit* (Frankfurt am Main: Fischer, 1987), p. 169. [Translator's note: What follows is the English version of Münkler's

German translation: "Political rationality, which is now called *raison d'état* (once it was called equity), transgresses the laws, those promulgated both in writing and orally, but only the letter, not the end and meaning of the laws."]

2. Ernst Forsthoff, "Verfassungsprobleme des Sozialstaats," in *Rechtsstaatlichkeit und Sozialstaatlichkeit,* ed. E. Forsthoff (Darmstadt: Wissenschaftliche Buchgesellschaft, 1968), p. 159; Carl Schmitt, *Political Theology,* trans. G. Schwab (Cambridge, Mass.: MIT Press, 1985), pp. 5f, 12f. See also the determination of he who issues an emergency decree as *"ratione temporis ac situationis"*: "Forcing its way through all the normativist fictions and obscurations, a simple jurisprudential truth comes to light in him, namely, that norms apply only to normal situations, and that the presupposed normality of the situation is a legal component of their 'validity'." Schmitt, "Legalität und Legitimität," in *Verfassungsrechtliche Aufsätze,* 2d ed. (Berlin: Duncker & Humblot, 1973), p. 321.

3. On the dissolution of equity in the *raison d'état* as the attempt "to leave the problem of the logical incompleteness of the legal order buried here," see Luhmann, "Die Theorie der Ordnung und die natürlichen Rechte," *Rechtshistorisches Journal* 3 (1984): 142f.

4. For a detailed presentation of this, see Münkler, "Staatsraison und politische Klugheitslehre."

5. Aristotle, *Nicomachean Ethics,* Book 6, 1144a27.

6. On what follows, see Habermas, "Law and Morality," trans. Kenneth Baynes, in *The Tanner Lectures on Human Values,* vol. 8, ed. S. McMurrin (Cambridge, Mass.: Harvard University Press, 1988), pp. 217–79. A demarcation similar to the one proposed here has been made by Klaus Lüderssen, "Recht, Strafrecht und Sozialmoral," in *Kriminalpolitik auf verschlungenen Wegen* (Frankfurt am Main: Suhrkamp, 1981), pp. 39–79. According to this, the essential difference between law and morality consists in the fact that "there are not the same possibilities for a consensus on the rules involved, and that a more or less strong congruence between consensus and validity is assumed. With increasing congruence, there is a greater probability that it is (also) a matter of morality, with decreasing congruence, that it is (only) a matter of law, whereby . . . at some point (depending on historical consciousness), the degree of consensus is so minimal that the demarcation to power has been reached" (pp. 63ff). Instead of an empirical justification according to the degree of consensus, we propose a moral justification here. See also the comprehensive orientation provided by Heinrich Geddert, *Recht und Moral—Zum Sinn eines alter Problems* (Berlin: Duncker & Humblot, 1984).

7. On this, see Wolfgang Kersting, *Wohlgeordnete Freiheit* (Berlin/New York: Walter de Gruyter, 1984), pp. 26ff. There is an analogous argument in

Martin Kriele, *Recht und praktische Vernunft* (Göttingen: Vandenhoeck & Ruprecht, 1979), p. 48.

8. John Locke, *Two Treatises of Government* (1924; London: Dent-Everyman's Library, 1990), pp. 159 and 180.

9. Ibid., p. 160.

10. Alexy, *A Theory of Legal Argumentation*, p. 214. On the argument of the need for decision making, see ibid., p. 287, as well as Kriele, *Recht und praktische Vernunft*, pp. 40ff.

11. See supra, pp. 167ff.

12. Talcott Parsons, Edward A. Shils, et al., *Toward a General Theory of Action* (Cambridge, Mass.: Harvard University Press, 1954), p. 15.

13. Ibid., p. 16.

14. Luhmann, *Soziale Systeme*, pp. 148.ff.

15. Ibid., p. 167.

16. Luhmann, *A Sociological Theory of Law*, pp. 26f.

17. Ibid., pp. 30f.

18. Ibid., p. 32.

19. Ibid., p. 34.

20. Ibid., p. 33 (italics in the original).

21. Ibid., p. 49 (italics in the original).

22. Ibid., p. 72.

23. Ibid., p. 77. Luhmann still uses this characterization as a determination of the function of the legal system. See "The Unity of the Legal System," in *Autopoietic Law. A New Approach to Law and Society*, ed. G. Teubner (Berlin/New York: Walter de Gruyter, 1988), pp. 27f.

24. Luhmann, *A Sociological Theory of Law*, pp. 161f, 182.

25. Ibid., pp. 176, 178, 180.

26. Ibid., pp. 281ff.

27. Ibid., p. 283. See also "The Unity of the Legal System," p. 20.

28. Luhmann, "The Unity of the Legal System," p. 22.

29. Luhmann, *Die soziologische Beobachtung des Rechts* (Frankfurt am Main: Metzner, 1986), pp. 31ff. The function of arguments is to reduce the surprise effect which could be generated by newly emerging viewpoints. They thereby contribute to the absorption of uncertainty and thus belong to

the series of attempts to solve the problem of double contingency. However, this "redundant" function can only be observed; it is not accessible to the participant in argumentation because only reasons are essential for him: "Redundancy itself is a contextual fact, that is, a feature of the system, whereas argumentation must trust the intrinsic properties of arguments, their inherent ability to justify positions convincingly. Redundancy itself cannot be counted as an argument, whereas it is precisely this that is claimed for an attempted justification" (ibid., p. 37).

30. Luhmann, "Die Codierung des Rechtssystems," *Rechtstheorie* 17 (1986): 182.

31. Ibid., p. 183.

32. Ibid., p. 193. On the consideration of consequences, see Gertrude Lübbe-Wolff, *Rechtsfolgen und Realfolgen* (Freiburg/Munich: Alber, 1981). Here, concept formation in law is itself determined as the appropriate connecting of consequences and presuppositions (see pp. 66ff).

33. "Die Codierung des Rechtssystems," p. 194.

34. Ibid.

35. Ibid., p. 195.

36. *A Sociological Theory of Law,* p. 68. [Translator's note: Translation altered slightly.]

37. "Die Codierung des Rechtssystems," pp. 197f.

38. *Die soziologische Beobachtung des Rechts.*

39. *A Sociological Theory of Law,* pp. 65f.

40. "Die Codierung des Rechtssystems," p. 195, for programs; *A Sociological Theory of Law,* p. 69, for values.

41. "Die Codierung des Rechtssystems," p. 198. The dissolution of the structuring function, still ascribed by Luhmann to law in *A Sociological Theory of Law,* was already announced in *Soziale Systeme.* The concept of structure conflicts with the idea of autopoiesis. Luhmann notes that the concept of structure "is losing its central position" for a theory of self-referential systems (*Soziale Systeme,* p. 382). The alternative of explaining the behavior of a system in terms of its own structural features or by features of the situation is changed: "There might then be highly individuated constrictions which make it easier to find connecting modes of behavior quickly; however, ones which must at the same time remain sufficiently sensitive toward situation-specific requirements, and which can thus expand or contract the cognitive domain of the choice of behavior, if the established ways do not lead to the goal convincingly enough" (ibid., pp. 381 f). Specially for the legal system, see also:

"This [i.e., conditionality], however, is only half of the truth and only one way to relate normative and cognitive components of the legal system. Conditionality is the general and indispensable device, but there are also more subtle, subcutaneous ways to infuse cognitive controls into normative structures. Judges are supposed to have particular skills and contextual sensitivities in handling cases. They apply norms according to circumstances, and if necessary generate exceptions to confirm the rule. They try to do justice—and postpone the perishing of the world from case to case." (Luhmann, "The Self-Reproduction of Law and Its Limits," in *Essays on Self-Reference* [New York: Columbia University Press, 1990], p. 234)

42. Gunther Teubner, "Juridification—Concepts, Aspects, Limits, Solutions," in *Juridification of Social Spheres,* ed. G. Teubner (Berlin/New York: Walter de Gruyter, 1987), p. 21.

43. Teubner, " 'And God laughed . . . ': Indeterminacy, Self-Reference and Paradox in Law," in *Critical Legal Thought: An American-German Debate,* ed. Christian Joerges and David M. Trubek (Baden-Baden: Nomos, 1989), pp. 412f. [Translator's note: The passage quoted by K. Günther is taken from a manuscript, and this is not identical with the above-cited published version of the paper.]

44. See again the equating of rules and conditional programs in Alexy, "Zum Begriff des Rechtsprinzips," p. 82, fn 96.

45. Luhmann, "The Unity of the Legal System," p. 23. He is more precise in "Die Codierung des Rechtssystems," p. 198: Argumentation in law is dispensable "because the complementarity of coding and programming produces an autopoietic, self-substitutive order."

46. On the category of the "proceduralization of law," see Rudolf Wiethölter, who, with this notion, also aims at a reconstruction of law as the embodiment of societal appropriateness: "The proceduralization of law aims at the reconstitutionalization of 'liberty,' that is, at a new acquisition of criteria, forums, and procedures for 'doing justice' [*Recht-Fertigungen*] (justification is not affirmation, but a category for the unity of 'critique and construction'!)" (Wiethölter, "Sanierungskonkurs der Juristenausbildung?" *Kritische Vierteljahresschrift für Gesetzgebung und Rechtswissenschaft* 1 (1986): 32); "Materialization and Proceduralization in Modern Law," in *Dilemmas of Law in the Welfare State,* ed. G. Teubner (Berlin/New York: Walter de Gruyter, 1986), pp. 221–49.

47. Hart, *The Concept of Law,* p. 125.

48. Ibid.

49. Ibid., pp. 123, 128ff. On this, see G. P. Baker, "Defeasibility and Meaning," in *Law, Morality and Society. Essays in Honour of H. L. A. Hart,* ed. P. M. S. Hacker and J. Raz (Oxford: Clarendon, 1979), p. 32.

50. Engisch, *Logische Studien zur Gestzesanwendung,* p. 15. On the mutual determinacy of norm and circumstances of the case, see above all Arthur Kaufmann, *Analogie und 'Natur der Sache'. Zugleich ein Beitrag zur Lehre vom Typus,* 2d ed. (Heidelberg: C. F. Müller, 1982), p. 42:

> "But why does the 'meaning of the law' change when its wording stays the same? That is solely the case because this 'meaning of the law' is not only in the law, but equally in the concrete circumstances of life, for which the law is determined. In truth, the 'objective interpretation' of the law is thus not just interpretation of the law; rather, it is that complex, 'deductive-inductive' analogical process, that casting of one's glance back and forth between the law and the circumstances of life . . . It is only because of this analogousness, this 'polarity' between the circumstances of life and the circumstances of the norm, that law lives and grows, that it has the ontological structure of historicality."

Hassemer enlarged this image to that of a "spiral-like" progress by alternating between induction and deduction. With this, the *process* of exhausting a norm in different situations comes into view: "Both factors in the interpretative process, the facts circumscribed by the legal norm [*Tatbestand*] and the circumstances of the case [*Sachverhalt*], determine each other not just once or at the same hermeneutical level, but many times and at different, 'higher' hermeneutical levels in each case" (Hassemer, *Tatbestand und Typus,* p. 108).

51. Zimmermann, "Rechtsanwendung als Rechtsfortbildung"; Hans-Joachim Koch, "Einleitung," in *Seminar: Die juristiche Methode im Staatsrecht,* ed. H.-J. Koch (Frankfurt am Main: Suhrkamp, 1977), pp. 41ff.

52. Hassemer, *Tatbestand und Typus,* pp. 35f, 102ff.

53. Kriele, *Theorie der Rechtsgewinnung,* pp. 198, 326ff.

54. Ibid., pp. 163, 198, 200.

55. Ibid., p. 200; see also Esser, *Vorverständnis und Methodenwahl in der Rechtsfindung,* pp. 75f.

56. Kriele, *Theorie der Rechtsgewinnung,* p. 202.

57. Esser, *Grundsatz und Norm in der richterlichen Fortbildung des Privatrechts,* 2d ed. (Tübingen: Mohr, 1964), pp. 192f; *Vorverständnis und Methodenwahl in der Rechsfindung,* pp. 47f.

58. *Grundsatz und Norm in der richterlichen Fortbildung des Privatrechts*, p. 182.

59. Ibid., p. 61.

60. Ibid., p. 182. Despite all attempts at reconstruction, Engisch's skeptical question (raised in connection with his own earlier efforts) still applies to the topos of the "nature of the thing": "what does 'nature' mean in this expression, and what are all the things intended by 'thing' here?" (Engisch, *Einführung in das juristische Denken*, 7th ed. [Stuttgart/Berlin: Kohlhammer, 1977], p. 196). The origins in Aristotelian and Thomist ontology cannot be easily left behind (on this, see the pertinent remarks in Lübbe-Wolff, *Rechtsfolgen und Realfolgen*, p. 88, fn 139). Lüderssen attempts to reconstruct rationally what is meant by this topos, but limits himself to the empirical side of the legal value judgment (Lüderssen, *Erfahrung als Rechtsquelle*, pp. 90ff). What is concealed behind the ideology-laden manner of speaking about the "thing" would thereby seem to be unmasked to a considerable extent. The question is, however, whether one needs an empirical criterion of validity for this. If only a "recognition of topoi that can be empirically tested" is permissible (Lüderssen, "Dialektik, Topik und 'konkretes Ordnungsdenken' in der Jurisprudenz," in *Kriminalpolitik auf verschlungenen Wegen*, p. 127), then the other half, the *normative* content of that "topos," is left unexplicated.

61. Esser, *Grundsatz und Norm in der richterlichen Fortbildung des Privatrechts*, pp. 182, 81.

62. Ibid., p. 287. The similarity to Gadamer's concept of "effective-historical consciousness" is clear, despite the fact that the first edition of Esser's book appeared in 1956. Later he adopted explicitly hermeneutical motifs: *Vorverständnis und Methodenwahl in der Rechtsfindung*, passim.

> "It is exactly at that point where the law does not consider certain interests, or does so inappropriately, that the object of knowledge is that *horizon of expectation* which can be designated 'legitimate' in the prepositive sense by comparing it with other recognized expectations, be it in a larger context of law or in terms of the present societal consciousness of law. The work of the jurist, characterized by [legal] methodology as finding justice, begins with the search for analogies or cogent doctrinal references into which the legal proposition in question can be constructively embedded or argumentatively fitted; but this work already presupposes the basis provided by the prepositive judgment of the problem and the appreciation of interests, both of which take a certain direction" p. 150.

On the historical emergence of "organic thinking" in legal doctrine and the subsequent decline of empirical, inductively generalizing methods, see

Maximilian Herberger, *Dogmatik. Zur Geschichte von Begriff und Methode in Medizin und Jurisprudenz* (Frankfurt am Main: Klostermann, 1981), pp. 389ff.

63. On Esser's reception of hermeneutics, see Monika Frommel, *Die Rezeption der Hermeneutik bei Karl Larenz und Josef Esser* (Ebelsbach: R. Gremer, 1981).

64. Esser, *Grundsatz und Norm in der richterlichen Fortbildung des Privatrechts*, p. 304.

65. Dworkin, *Taking Rights Seriously*, p. 40.

66. Ibid., p. 87.

67. Ibid., p. 89.

68. Ibid., p. 111, fn 1.

69. Ibid., p. 115.

70. Ibid., p. 118.

71. Ibid., p. 119. Dworkin thereby links up with arguments from legal realism, which has processed experiences similar to those processed by the *Freirecht* school and the jurisprudence of interests in Germany. The application situation in law presents itself from the outset because various indeterminate viewpoints must be related to one another in a particular case. "In any single case, then, there were multiple potential points of indeterminacy due to vagueness, not a single point as Hart's account sometimes seems to suggest" (Andrew Altman, "Legal Realism, Critical Legal Studies, and Dworkin," *Philosophy and Public Affairs* 15 [1986]: 208). The arguments of legal realism have been radicalized, especially by Critical Legal Studies, so much so that they are now in the vicinity of a rule-skeptical position, so that bringing contradictory principles into a (weighing) relation with one another in a particular case (e.g., freedom of contract versus consumer protection) appears hopeless (on this, see Altman, ibid., pp. 222ff). If one accepts the distinction between justification and application, it can be objected that contradictions between principles arise in a particular case only if one applies them "like rules," that is, without considering all the features of the situation.

72. Ibid., p. 119.

73. Ibid., pp. 40, 64ff.

74. Ibid., pp. 112ff, 118. Alexy raises doubts about this kind of "legal holism" ("Zum Begriff des Rechtsprinzips," p. 86), which calls to mind the talk about the unity of the legal and constitutional orders as the interpretative principle for basic rights. But Dworkin is concerned not only with the coherence of an objectively given order, but with the equal consideration of

all subjects having rights. It is only from this requirement that the pre-scription of coherence follows, and not from the institutional stabilization needs of an independent order of values. Dworkin's statements about this point are not, however, very clear. They have to be made more precise by again relating the justification and application of rights to discourses. On this, see the suggestions at the end of this section.

75. *Law's Empire* (London: Fontana Press, 1986).

76. Ibid., pp. 165f.

77. Ibid., p. 166.

78. The political community is thus to be conceived of as a "community personified," and we may expect it to possess integrity in character, ibid., pp. 167ff.

79. Ibid., p. 167.

80. Ibid., pp. 209ff.

81. Ibid., p. 213.

82. Ibid., p. 217.

83. *Taking Rights Seriously,* p. 44; *Law's Empire,* p. 244.

84. *Taking Rights Seriously,* pp. 89, 93.

85. *Law's Empire,* pp. 243, 255.

86. Ibid., p. 256. This is also the point at which a discourse-theoretic transformation would have to begin.

87. On this critique, see Alexy, "Zum Begriff des Rechtsprinzips," pp. 86f.

88. *Taking Rights Seriously,* p. 273.

89. See supra, pp. 143ff.

90. Habermas, "Morality and Ethical Life," p. 200.

91. *Law's Empire,* p. 211.

92. *Taking Rights Seriously,* p. 272.

93. And thereby becomes subject to the critique that it arbitrarily mul-tiplies claims. See Arnold Gehlen, *Moral und Hypermoral* (Wiesbaden: Aula, 1981), pp. 64f, as well as Luhmann, *A Sociological Theory of Law,* p. 188, and "Subjektive Rechte. Zum Umbau des Rechtsbewußtseins für die moderne Gesellschaft," in *Gesellschaftsstruktur und Semantik,* Band 2 (Frankfurt am Main: Suhrkamp, 1981), p. 97: "limitless need and greed," which are satisfied by the allocation of more and more rights to the subject.

The concept of "subject" functions here as a "formula of inclusion par excellence" (see "Wie ist soziale Ordnung möglich?" in *Gesellschaftsstruktur und Semantik*, Band 2, p. 239).

94. *Taking Rights Seriously*, p. 27.

Bibliography

Alexy, Robert. "Zum Begriff des Rechtsprinzips." *Rechtstheorie* Beiheft 1 (1979): 59–87.

———. *Theorie der Grundrechte*. Baden-Baden: Nomos, 1985.

———. *A Theory of Legal Argumentation*. Trans. Ruth Adler and Neil Mac-Cormick. Oxford: Oxford University Press, 1989.

Altman, Andrew. "Legal Realism, Critical Legal Studies, and Dworkin." *Philosophy and Public Affairs* 15 (1986): 205–35.

Anscombe, G. E. M. "Modern Moral Philosophy." *Philosophy* 33 (1958): 1–19.

Apel, Karl-Otto. "Sprechakttheorie und transzendentale Sprachpragmatik zur Frage ethischer Normen." In *Sprachpragmatik und Philosophie*. Ed. Karl-Otto Apel. Frankfurt am Main: Suhrkamp, 1976, pp. 10–173.

———. "The A Priori of the Communication Community and the Foundations of Ethics." In *Towards a Transformation of Philosophy*. Trans. Glyn Adey and David Frisby. London: Routledge & Kegan Paul, 1980, pp. 225–300.

———. "Kant, Hegel und das aktuelle Problem der normativen Grundlagen von Moral und Recht." In *Kant oder Hegel? (Stuttgarter Hegel-Kongreß 1981)*. Ed. Dieter Henrich. Stuttgart: Klett-Cotta, 1981, pp. 597–624.

———. "Kann der postkantische Standpunkt der Moralität noch einmal in substantielle Sittlichkeit 'aufgehoben' werden?" In *Moralität und Sittlichkeit. Das Problem Hegels und die Diskursethik*. Ed. W. Kuhlmann. Frankfurt am Main: Suhrkamp, 1986, pp. 217–64.

Arendt, Hannah. "Thinking and Moral Considerations: A Lecture." *Social Research* 38 (1971): 417–446.

Aristotle. *Aristotelis Politica, post Fr. Susemihilium recognovit O. Immisch*. Lipsiae: In Aedibus B. G. Teubner, 1909.

——. *Nicomachean Ethics*. Trans. W. D. Ross. In *The Complete Works of Aristotle*. Vol. 2. Ed. Jonathan Barnes. Princeton: Princeton University Press, 1984, pp. 1729–1867.

——. *Politics*. Trans. B. Jowett. In *The Complete Works of Aristotle*. Vol. 2. Ed. Jonathan Barnes. Princeton: Princeton University Press, 1984, pp. 1986–2129.

——. *Ethica Nicomachea, recognovit I. Bywater*. Oxonii: Scriptorum classicorum bibliotheca oxoniensis, Oxford: Oxford University Press, 1984.

Auerbach, Erich. *Mimesis. The Representation of Reality in Western Literature*. 1953. Trans. W. R. Trask. Reprint. Princeton: Princeton University Press, 1974.

Austin, John L. *How To Do Things with Words*. 2d ed. Oxford: Oxford University Press, 1980.

Baier, Kurt. *The Moral Point of View*. Ithaca, N. Y.: Cornell University Press, 1958.

Baker, G. P. "Defeasibility and Meaning." In *Law, Morality and Society. Essays in Honour of H. L. A. Hart*. Ed. P. M. S. Hacker and J. Raz. Oxford: Clarendon, 1979, pp. 26–57.

Bernstein, Richard J. *Beyond Objectivity and Relativism: Science, Hermeneutics, and Praxis*. Oxford: Basil Blackwell, 1983.

Bertram, Hans. *Gesellschaftlicher Zwang und moralische Autonomie*. Frankfurt am Main: Suhrkamp, 1986.

Bien, Günther. "Aristotelische Ethik und Kantische Moraltheorie." *Freiburger Universitätsblätter* 73 (1981): 57–74.

Böhler, Dietrich. "Philosophische Hermeneutik und hermeneutische Methode." In *Text und Applikation (Poetik und Hermeneutik IX)*. Ed. M. Fuhrmann et al. Munich: Fink, 1981, pp. 483–511.

Bubner, Rüdiger. *Geschichtsprozesse und Handlungsnormen*. Frankfurt am Main: Suhrkamp, 1984.

Daniels, Norman. "Wide Reflective Equilibrium and Theory Acceptance in Ethics." *The Journal of Philosophy* 76 (1979): 256–82.

Denninger, Erhard. "Verfassungsrechtliche Schlüsselbegriffe." In *Festschrift für R. Wassermann*. Ed. Christian Broda et al. Neuwied/Darmstadt: Luchterhand, 1985, pp. 279–98.

Durkheim, Emile. *The Division of Labor in Society*. Trans. W. D. Halls. New York: Free Press, 1984.

———. *De la division du travail*. 8th ed. Paris: Presses Universitaires de France, 1967.

Dworkin, Ronald. *Taking Rights Seriously*. 1977. New Impression with a Reply to Critics. London: Duckworth, 1978.

———. *Law's Empire*. London: Fontana Press, 1986.

Edelstein, Wolfgang, and Monika Keller. "Perspektivität und Interpretation. Zur Entwicklung des sozialen Verstehens." In *Perspektivität und Interpretation*. Ed. W. Edelstein and M. Keller. Frankfurt am Main: Suhrkamp, 1982, pp. 9–43.

Eder, Klaus. *Geschichte als Lernprozeß?* Frankfurt am Main: Suhrkamp, 1985.

Engisch, Karl. *Logische Studien zur Gesetzesanwendung. Sitzungsberichte der Heidelberger Akademie der Wissenschaften (Phil.-hist.)*. 3d ed. Heidelberg: Winter, 1963.

———. *Die Idee der Konkretisierung in Recht und Rechtswissenschaft unserer Zeit. Abhandlungen der Heidelberger Akademie der Wissenschaften (Phil.-hist.)*. 2d ed. Heidelberg: Winter, 1968.

———. *Einführung in das juristische Denken*. 7th ed. Stuttgart/Berlin: Kohlhammer, 1977.

Esser, Josef. *Grundsatz und Norm in der richterlichen Fortbildung des Privatrechts*. 2d. ed. Tübingen: Mohr, 1964.

———. *Vorverständnis und Methodenwahl in der Rechtsfindung*. Kronberg im Taunus: Scriptor, 1972.

Feinberg, Joel. "Justice, Fairness and Rationality." *The Yale Law Journal* 81 (1972): 1004–31.

Flanagan, Jr., Owen. "Virtue, Sex, and Gender: Some Philosophical Reflections on the Moral Psychology Debate." *Ethics* 92 (1982): 499–512.

Flanagan, Jr., Owen, and Jonathan E. Adler. "Impartiality and Particularity." *Social Research* 50 (1983): 576–96.

Fogelin, Robert. *Wittgenstein*. London: Routledge & Kegan Paul, 1976.

Foot, Philippa. "Moral Beliefs." In *Virtues and Vices and Other Essays in Moral Philosophy*. Oxford: Basil Blackwell, 1978, pp. 110–31.

Forsthoff, Ernst. "Verfassungsprobleme des Sozialstaats." In *Rechtsstaatlichkeit und Sozialstaatlichkeit*. Ed. E. Forsthoff. Darmstadt: Wissenschaftliche Buchgesellschaft, 1968, pp. 145–64.

Frankenberg, Günter, and Ulrich Rödel. *Von der Volkssouveränität zum Minderheitenschutz.* Frankfurt am Main: Europäische Verlagsanstalt, 1981.

Frellesen, Peter. *Die Zumutbarkeit der Hilfeleistung.* Frankfurt am Main: Metzner, 1980.

Frommel, Monika. *Die Rezeption der Hermeneutik bei Karl Larenz und Josef Esser.* Ebelsbach: R. Gremer, 1981.

Fuhrmann, Manfred. *Die antike Rhetorik.* Munich/Zürich: Artemis, 1984.

Gadamer, Hans-Georg. *Truth and Method.* London: Sheed & Ward, 1975.

――――. "Über die Möglichkeit einer philosophischen Ethik." In *Kleine philosophische Schriften I.* Tübingen: J. C. B. Mohr, 1976, pp. 179–91.

――――. "Hermeneutics as Practical Philosophy." In *Reason in the Age of Science.* Trans. Frederick G. Lawrence. Cambridge, Mass.: MIT Press, 1982, pp. 88–112.

――――. "A Letter by Professor Hans-Georg Gadamer." In Richard J. Bernstein. *Beyond Objectivism and Relativism: Science, Hermeneutics, and Praxis.* Oxford: Basil Blackwell, 1982, pp. 261–65.

――――. "Heideggers Rückgang auf die Griechen." In *Theorie der Subjektivität.* Ed. Konrad Cramer et al. Frankfurt am Main: Suhrkamp, 1987, pp. 397–424.

Garfinkel, H., and H. Sacks. "On Formal Structures of Practical Actions." In *Theoretical Sociology: Perspectives and Development.* Ed. J. C. McKinney and E. A. Tiryakian. New York: Appelton-Century-Crofts, 1970, pp. 337–66.

Geddert, Heinrich. *Recht und Moral—Zum Sinn eines alten Problems.* Berlin: Duncker & Humblot, 1984.

Gehlen, Arnold. *Moral und Hypermoral.* Wiesbaden: Aula, 1981.

Gert, Bernard. "Moral Theory and Applied Ethics." *The Monist* 67 (1984): 532–48.

Geulen, Dieter. "Soziales Handeln und Perspektivenübernahme." In *Perspektivenübernahme und soziales Handeln. Texte zur sozialkognitiven Entwicklung.* Ed. D. Geulen. Frankfurt am Main: Suhrkamp, 1982, pp. 24–72.

Gilligan, Carol. *In a Different Voice. Psychological Theory and Women's Development.* Cambridge, Mass.: Harvard University Press, 1982.

Gilligan, Carol, and Mary Field Belenky. "A Naturalistic Study of Abortion Decisions." In *Clinical-Development Psychology.* No. 7. Ed. R. Selman and R. Yando. San Francisco: Jossey-Bass, 1980, pp. 69–88.

Gubelt, Manfred. "Kommentierung zu Artikel 3 des Grundgesetzes." In *Grundgesetz-Kommentar.* Ed. Ingo von Münch. Munich: Beck, 1981.

Günther, Klaus. "Vorläufige Überlegungen zu einer Theorie der prozeduralen Applikation." In *Workshop zu Konzepten des postinterventionistischen Rechts.* Ed. G. Brüggemeier and C. Joerges. Bremen: Zentrum für europäische Rechtspolitik—Materialien 4, 1984, pp. 74–90.

———. "Dialektik der Aufklärung in der Idee der Freiheit. Zur Kritik des Freiheitsbegriffs bei Adorno." *Zeitschrift für philosophische Forschung* 39 (1985): 229–60.

———. "Verrechtlichung durch Gleichbehandlung?" In *Thema: Ungleichheit, Gesellschafts- und sozialpolitische Texte Band 4.* Ed. Evelyn Gröbl. Linz: Forschungsinstitut für Sozialplanung, Johannes Kepler University, 1986, pp. 51–64.

Haan, Norma. "Two Moralities in Action Contexts: Relationships to Thought, Ego Regulation, and Development." *Journal of Personality and Social Psychology* 36.3 (1978): 286–305.

Habermas, Jürgen. "Wahrheitstheorien." In *Vorstudien und Ergänzungen zur Theorie des kommunikativen Handelns.* Frankfurt am Main: Suhrkamp, 1984, pp. 127–83.

———. "Über Moralität und Sittlichkeit—Was macht eine Lebensform 'rational'?" In *Rationalität.* Ed. H. Schnädelbach. Frankfurt am Main: Suhrkamp, 1984, pp. 218–35.

———. "Vorlesungen zur sprachtheoretischen Grundlegung der Soziologie." In *Vorstudien und Ergänzungen zur Theorie des kommunikativen Handelns.* Frankfurt am Main: Suhrkamp, 1984, pp. 11–126.

———. *The Theory of Communicative Action.* Vol. 1: *Reason and the Rationalization of Society;* Vol. 2: *The Critique of Functionalist Reason.* Trans. Thomas McCarthy. Boston: Beacon, 1984, 1987.

———. "Metaphysik nach Kant." In *Theorie der Subjektivität.* Ed. Konrad Cramer et al. Frankfurt am Main: Suhrkamp, 1987, pp. 425–43.

———. *The Philosophical Discourse of Modernity.* Trans. Frederick G. Lawrence. Cambridge, Mass.: MIT Press, 1988.

———. "Law and Morality." Trans. Kenneth Baynes. In *The Tanner Lectures on Human Values.* Vol. 8. Ed. S. McMurrin. Cambridge, Mass.: Harvard University Press, 1988, pp. 217–79.

———. *Moral Consciousness and Communicative Action.* Trans. C. Lenhardt and S. Weber Nicholsen. Cambridge, Mass.: MIT Press, 1990.

————. "Discourse Ethics: Notes on a Program of Philosophical Justification." In *Moral Consciousness and Communicative Action,* pp. 43–115.

————. "Moral Consciousness and Communicative Action." In *Moral Consciousness and Communicative Action,* pp. 116–94.

————. "Morality and Ethical Life: Does Hegel's Critique of Kant Apply to Discourse Ethics?" In *Moral Consciousness and Communicative Action,* pp. 195–215.

————. "Justice and Solidarity: On the Discussion Concerning Stage 6." In *The Moral Domain. Essays in the Ongoing Discussion between Philosophy and the Social Sciences.* Ed. Thomas E. Wren. Cambridge, Mass.: MIT Press, 1990, pp. 224–51.

————. "A Reply." In *Communicative Action. Essays on Jürgen Habermas's "The Theory of Communicative Action."* Ed. A. Honneth and H. Joas. Trans. Jeremy Gaines and Doris L. Jones. Cambridge, Mass.: MIT Press, 1991, pp. 214–64.

Hare, R. M. "Universalisability." *Proceedings of the Aristotelian Society* LV (1954/55): 295–312.

————. *Freedom and Reason.* Oxford: Oxford University Press, 1963.

————. *The Language of Morals.* Oxford: Oxford University Press, 1978.

————. *Moral Thinking.* Oxford: Clarendon Press, 1981.

Hart, H. L. A.. *The Concept of Law.* Oxford: Clarendon Press, 1961.

Hassemer, Winfried. *Tatbestand und Typus.* Cologne/Berlin: Heymanns, 1968.

————. "Juristische Hermeneutik." *Archiv für Rechts- und Sozialphilosophie* 72 (1986): 195–212.

Haverkate, Görg. *Gewißheitsverluste im juristischen Denken.* Berlin: Duncker & Humblot, 1977.

Hegel, Georg Wilhelm Friedrich. *Hegel's Philosophy of Right.* Trans. T. M. Knox. Oxford: University Press, 1967.

————. "Der Geist des Christentums und sein Schicksal." In *Werke.* Vol. 1. Frankfurt am Main: Suhrkamp, 1971, pp. 274–418.

————. *Natural Law.* Trans. T. M. Knox. Philadelphia: University of Pennsylvania Press, 1975.

Hennis, Wilhelm. *Politik und praktische Philosophie.* Neuwied/Berlin: Luchterhand, 1963.

Herberger, Maximilian. *Dogmatik. Zur Geschichte von Begriff und Methode in Medizin und Jurisprudenz.* Frankfurt am Main: Klostermann, 1981.

Herberger, Maximilian, and Dieter Simon. *Wissenschaftstheorie für Juristen.* Frankfurt am Main: Metzner, 1980.

Hintikka, Jaakko. "Some Main Problems of Deontic Logic." In *Deontic Logic: Introductory and Systematic Readings.* Ed. R. Hilpinen. Dordrecht: D. Reidel, 1971, pp. 59–104.

Höffe, Otfried. "Ethik als praktische Philosophie—Die Begründung durch Aristoteles." In *Ethik und Politik. Grundmodelle und -probleme der praktischen Philosophie.* Frankfurt am Main: Suhrkamp, 1979, pp. 38–83.

———. "Kants kategorischer Imperativ als Kriterium des Sittlichen." In *Ethik und Politik. Grundmodelle und -probleme der praktischen Philosophie.* Frankfurt am Main: Suhrkamp, 1979, pp. 84–119.

Honneth, Axel. *The Critique of Power. Reflective Stages in a Critical Social Theory.* Trans. Kenneth Baynes. Cambridge, Mass.: MIT Press, 1991.

Hruschka, Joachim. *Die Konstitution des Rechtsfalles.* Berlin: Duncker & Humblot, 1965.

Joas, Hans. *G. H. Mead. A Contemporary Re-Examination of His Thought.* Trans. Raymond Meyer. Cambridge, Mass.: MIT Press, 1985.

Kant, Immanuel. *Critique of Pure Reason.* 1933. Trans. Norman Kemp Smith. London: Macmillan, 1973.

———. "Concerning the Common Saying: That May Be True in Theory But Does Not Apply to Practice." In *The Philosophy of Kant. Immanuel Kant's Moral and Political Writings.* Ed. Carl J. Friedrich. New York: Random, 1949, pp. 412–29.

———. *The Critique of Judgment.* Trans. J. C. Meredith. Oxford: Clarendon Press, 1952.

———. *Groundwork of the Metaphysic of Morals.* 3d ed. Trans. H. J. Paton. New York: Harper & Row, 1956.

———. *Critique of Practical Reason.* 1956. Trans. Lewis White Beck. Indianapolis: Bobbs-Merrill, 1980.

———. *The Metaphysics of Morals.* Trans. Mary Gregor. Cambridge: Cambridge University Press, 1991.

Kaufmann, Arthur. *Analogie und 'Natur der Sache'. Zugleich ein Beitrag zur Lehre vom Typus.* 2d ed. Heidelberg: C. F. Müller, 1982.

Kemmerling, Andreas. "Regel und Geltung im Lichte der Analyse Wittgensteins." *Rechtstheorie* 6 (1975): 104–31.

Kersting, Wolfgang. *Wohlgeordnete Freiheit*. Berlin/New York: Walter de Gruyter, 1984.

Koch, Hans-Joachim. "Einleitung." In *Seminar: Die juristische Methode im Staatsrecht*. Ed. Hans-Joachim Koch. Frankfurt am Main: Suhrkamp, 1977, pp. 13–157.

Koch, Hans-Joachim, and Helmut Rüßmann. *Juristische Begründungslehre*. Munich: C. H. Beck, 1982.

König, René. "Emile Durkheim." In *Klassiker des soziologischen Denkens*. Vol. 1. Ed. D. Käsler. Munich: C. H. Beck, 1976, pp. 312–64.

Kohlberg, Lawrence. "A Reply to Owen Flanagan and Some Comments on the Puka—Goodpaster Exchange." *Ethics* 92 (1982): 513–28.

———. *Essays on Moral Development*. Vol. 2: *The Psychology of Moral Development*. San Francisco: Harper & Row, 1984.

———. "Stage and Sequence: The Cognitive-Developmental Approach to Socialization." In *Essays on Moral Development*. Vol. 2, pp. 7–169.

———. "The Six Stages of Justice Judgment." In *Essays on Moral Development*. Vol. 2, pp. 621–39.

———. "Moral Stages and Moralization: The Cognitive-Developmental Approach." In *Essays on Moral Development*. Vol. 2, pp. 170–205.

Kohlberg, Lawrence, D. R. Boyd, and C. Levine. "The Return of Stage 6: Its Principle and Moral Point of View." In *The Moral Domain. Essays in the Ongoing Discussion between Philosophy and the Social Sciences*. Ed. Thomas E. Wren. Cambridge, Mass.: MIT Press, 1990, pp. 151–81.

Kohlberg, Lawrence, Charles Levine, and Alexandra Hewer. "The Current Formulation of the Theory." In Lawrence Kohlberg. *Essays on Moral Development*. Vol. 2, pp. 212–319.

———. "Synopses and Detailed Replies to Critics." In Lawrence Kohlberg. *Essays on Moral Development*. Vol. 2, pp. 320–86.

Kriele, Martin. *Theorie der Rechtsgewinnung*. 2d ed. Berlin: Duncker & Humblot, 1976.

———. *Recht und praktische Vernunft*. Göttingen: Vandenhoeck & Ruprecht, 1979.

Kuhn, Thomas S. "Objectivity, Value Judgment, and Theory Choice." In *The Essential Tension. Selected Studies in Scientific Tradition and Change*. Chicago: University of Chicago Press, 1977, pp. 321–39.

Larenz, Karl. *Methodenlehre der Rechtswissenschaft.* 5th ed. Berlin/New York: Springer, 1983.

Larmore, Charles. "Moral Judgment." *Review of Metaphysics* 35 (1981): 275–96.

Leibholz, Gerhard. *Die Gleichheit vor dem Gesetz.* 2d ed. Munich/Berlin: Beck, 1959.

Locke, John. *Two Treatises of Government.* 1924. London: Dent-Everyman's Library, 1990.

Lübbe-Wolff, Gertrude. *Rechtsfolgen und Realfolgen. Welche Rolle können Folgenerwägungen in der juristischen Regel- und Begriffsbildung spielen?* Freiburg/Munich: Alber, 1981.

Lüderssen, Klaus. *Erfahrung als Rechtsquelle.* Frankfurt am Main: Suhrkamp, 1972.

———. "Dialektik, Topik und 'konkretes Ordnungsdenken' in der Jurisprudenz." In *Kriminalpolitik auf verschlungenen Wegen.* Frankfurt am Main: Suhrkamp, 1981, pp. 115–42.

———. "Recht, Strafrecht und Sozialmoral." In *Kriminalpolitik auf verschlungenen Wegen.* Frankfurt am Main: Suhrkamp, 1981, pp. 39–79.

Luhmann, Niklas. "Subjektive Rechte. Zum Umbau des Rechtsbewußtseins für die moderne Gesellschaft." In *Gesellschaftsstruktur und Semantik.* Band 2. Frankfurt am Main: Suhrkamp, 1981, pp. 45–104.

———. "Wie ist soziale Ordnung möglich?" In *Gesellschaftsstruktur und Semantik.* Band 2. Frankfurt am Main: Suhrkamp, 1981, pp. 195–285.

———. *Soziale Systeme—Grundriß einer allgemeinen Theorie.* Frankfurt am Main: Suhrkamp, 1984.

———. "Die Theorie der Ordnung und die natürlichen Rechte." *Rechtshistorisches Journal* 3 (1984): 133–49.

———. *A Sociological Theory of Law.* Trans. Elizabeth King and Martin Albrow. London: Routledge & Kegan Paul, 1985.

———. *Ökologische Kommunikation.* Opladen: Westdeutscher Verlag, 1986.

———. *Grundrechte als Institution.* Berlin: Duncker & Humblot, 1986.

———. *Die soziologische Beobachtung des Rechts.* Frankfurt am Main: Metzner, 1986.

————. "Die Codierung des Rechtssystems." *Rechtstheorie* 17 (1986): 171–203.

————. "The Unity of the Legal System." In *Autopoietic Law. A New Approach to Law and Society.* Ed. G. Teubner, Berlin/New York: Walter de Gruyter, 1988, pp. 12–35.

————. "The Self-Reproduction of Law and Its Limits." In *Essays on Self-Reference.* New York: Columbia University Press, 1990, pp. 227–45.

MacCormick, Neil. "Coherence in Legal Justification." In *Theorie der Normen. Festgabe für O. Weinberger.* Ed. W. Krawietz et al. Berlin: Duncker & Humblot, 1984, pp. 37–53.

McCarthy, Thomas. *The Critical Theory of Jürgen Habermas.* Cambridge, Mass.: MIT Press, 1978.

Mead, George Herbert. *Mind, Self, and Society.* Chicago: University of Chicago Press, 1962.

Müller, Hans-Peter. "Gesellschaft, Moral und Individualismus. Émile Durkheims Moraltheorie." In *Gesellschaftlicher Zwang und moralische Autonomie.* Ed. H. Bertram. Frankfurt am Main: Suhrkamp, 1986, pp. 71–105.

Münkler, Herfried. "Staatsraison und politische Klugheitslehre." In *Pipers Handbuch der politischen Ideen.* Band 3. *Neuzeit: Von den Konfessionskriegen bis zur Aufklärung.* Ed. I. Fetscher and H. Münkler. Munich/Zürich: Piper, 1985, pp. 23–72.

————. *Im Namen des Staates. Die Begründung der Staatsraison in der frühen Neuzeit.* Frankfurt am Main: Fischer, 1987.

Murphy, John Michael, and Carol Gilligan. "Moral Development in Late Adolescence and Adulthood: a Critique and Reconstruction of Kohlberg's Theory." *Human Development* 23 (1980): 77–104.

Neumann, Ulfried. "Neuere Schriften zur Rechtsphilosophie und Rechtstheorie." *Philosophische Rundschau* 28 (1981): 189–216.

Nunner-Winkler, Gertrud. "Moral Relativism and Strict Universalism." In *The Moral Domain. Essays in the Ongoing Discussion between Philosophy and the Social Sciences.* Ed. Thomas E. Wren. Cambridge, Mass.: MIT Press, 1990, pp. 109–26.

Parsons, Talcott, Edward A. Shils, et al. *Toward a General Theory of Action.* Cambridge, Mass.: Harvard University Press, 1954.

Patzig, Günther. "Der kategorische Imperativ in der Ethik-Diskussion der Gegenwart." In *Tatsachen, Normen, Sätze.* Stuttgart: Reclam, 1980, pp. 154–77.

Piaget, Jean. *Le jugement moral chez l'enfant*. Paris: Librairie Félix Alcan, 1932.

———. *The Moral Judgment of the Child*. Trans. Marjorie Gabain. New York: Free Press, 1965.

Rawls, John. "Outline of a Decision Procedure for Ethics." *The Philosophical Review* 60 (1951): 177–90.

———. *A Theory of Justice*. Oxford: Oxford University Press, 1973.

———. "Kantian Constructivism in Moral Theory." *The Journal of Philosophy* 77 (1980): 515–72.

Ritter, Joachim. "Das bürgerliche Leben. Zur aristotelischen Theorie des Glücks." In *Metaphysik und Politik*. Frankfurt am Main: Suhrkamp, 1979, pp. 57–105.

———. " 'Politik' und 'Ethik' in der praktischen Philosophie des Aristoteles." In *Metaphysik und Politik*. Frankfurt am Main: Suhrkamp, 1979, pp. 106–32.

Sartre, Jean-Paul. *Being and Nothingness*. Trans. Hazel E. Barnes. London: Methuen, 1969.

———. *Existentialism and Humanism*. Trans. Philip Mairet. London: Methuen, 1973.

Schmitt, Carl. "Legalität und Legitimität." In *Verfassungsrechtliche Aufsätze*. 2d ed. Berlin: Duncker & Humblot, 1973, pp. 263–350.

———. *Political Theology*. Trans. George Schwab. Cambridge, Mass.: MIT Press, 1985.

———. *The Crisis of Parliamentary Democracy*. Trans. Ellen Kennedy. Cambridge, Mass.: MIT Press, 1985.

Schnädelbach, Herbert. "What is Neo-Aristotelianism?" *Praxis International* 7 (Winter 1987/8): 225–37.

———. "Remarks about Rationality and Language." In *The Communicative Ethics Controversy*. Ed. S. Benhabib and F. Dallmayr. Cambridge, Mass.: MIT Press, 1990, pp. 270–92.

Searle, John. "*Prima Facie* Obligations." In *Practical Reasoning*. Ed. J. Raz. Oxford: Oxford University Press, 1978, pp. 81–90.

Seel, Martin. *Die Kunst der Entzweiung*. Frankfurt am Main: Suhrkamp, 1986.

Selman, Robert L. *The Growth of Interpersonal Understanding. Developmental and Clinical Analyses*. New York: Academic Press, 1980.

Simon, Dieter. "Historische Beiträge zur Rechtsprechungslehre." In *Rechtsprechungslehre*. Ed. N. Achterberg. Cologne/Berlin: Heymann, 1986, pp. 229–36.

Singer, Marcus George. *Generalization in Ethics*. 2d ed. New York: Atheneum, 1971.

Stegmüller, Wolfgang. *Main Currents in Contemporary German, British and American Philosophy*. Trans. Albert E. Blumberg. Dordrecht: Reidel, 1969.

Teubner, Gunther. "Juridification—Concepts, Aspects, Limits, Solutions." In *Juridification of Social Spheres*. Ed. G. Teubner. Berlin/New York: Walter de Gruyter, 1987, pp. 3–48.

————. " 'And God laughed . . . ': Indeterminacy, Self-Reference and Paradox in Law." In *Critical Legal Thought: An American-German Debate*. Eds. Christian Joerges and David M. Trubek. Baden-Baden: Nomos, 1989, pp. 399–434.

Toulmin, Stephen. *The Uses of Argument*. Cambridge: Cambridge University Press, 1958.

Toulmin, Stephen, Richard Rieke, and Allan Janik. *An Introduction into Reasoning*. London: Macmillan, 1979.

Tugendhat, Ernst. *Selbstbewußtsein und Selbstbestimmung*. Frankfurt am Main: Suhrkamp, 1979.

————. "Antike und moderne Ethik." In *Probleme der Ethik*. Stuttgart: Reclam, 1984, pp. 33–56.

————. "Kann man aus der Erfahrung moralisch lernen?" In *Probleme der Ethik*. Stuttgart: Reclam, 1984, pp. 87–108.

Voegelin, Eric. *Anamnesis. Zur Theorie der Geschichte und Politik*. Munich: Piper, 1966.

Vollrath, Ernst. *Die Rekonstruktion der politischen Urteilskraft*. Stuttgart: Klett-Cotta, 1977.

Wellmer, Albrecht. "Ethics and Dialogue: Elements of Moral Judgement in Kant and Discourse Ethics." In *The Persistence of Modernity. Essays on Aesthetics, Ethics, and Postmodernism*. Trans. David Midgley. Cambridge, Mass.: MIT Press, 1991, pp. 113–231.

Wieland, Wolfgang. "Praxis und Urteilskraft." *Zeitschrift für philosophische Forschung* 28 (1974): 17–42.

Wiethölter, Rudolf. "Sanierungskonkurs der Juristenausbildung?" *Kritische Vierteljahresschrift für Gesetzgebung und Rechtswissenschaft* 1.1–2 (1986): 21–36.

———— . "Materialization and Proceduralization in Modern Law." In *Dilemmas of Law in the Welfare State*. Ed. G. Teubner. Berlin/New York: Walter de Gruyter, 1986, pp. 221–49.

Wiggins, David. "Deliberation and Practical Reason." In *Essays on Aristotle's Ethics*. Ed. Amélie O. Rorty. Berkeley: University of California Press, 1980, pp. 221–40.

Wimmer, Reiner. *Universalisierung in der Ethik*. Frankfurt am Main: Suhrkamp, 1980.

Winch, Peter. *The Idea of a Social Science and its Relation to Philosophy*. London: Routledge & Kegan Paul, 1958.

Wittgenstein, Ludwig. *Philosophical Investigations*. Trans. G. E. M. Anscombe. Oxford: Basil Blackwell, 1978.

Wolf, Ursula. *Das Problem des moralischen Sollens*. Berlin/New York: Walter de Gruyter, 1984.

Zimmermann, Horst. "Rechtsanwendung als Rechtsfortbildung." In *Juristische Methodenlehre und analytische Philosophie*. Ed. H.-J. Koch. Kronberg im Taunus: Athenäum, 1976, pp. 70–95.

Zimmermann, Rolf. *Utopie–Rationalität–Politik*. Freiburg/Munich: Alber, 1985.

Index

Action: communicative, 24–26; coordination of, 1–2, 257; vs. discourse, 24–25, 67; and judgment, 160; presuppositions of, 210, 217, 269. *See also* Maxim; Mode of action; *Phronesis*
Act utilitarianism, 21
Adequacy, 139, 149, 189; principle of, 222, 228, 239. *See also* "Fit"
Adjudication, 256, 260, 261–62, 272, 279. *See also* Legislation
Adorno, Theodor W., 158
Aisthesis, 176, 189
Alexy, Robert, 26, 204, 205, 212–19, 227, 230, 232, 235, 240–41, 269–70
Altman, Andrew, 328n.71
Anscombe, Elizabeth, 158–59
Anthropology, 188
Apel, Karl-Otto, 13, 66–68, 71–72
Application, 1–2, 31, 38, 53, 68, 70–71, 91–93, 95–97, 164, 200, 216, 218, 270–71; as belonging to practical reason, 40; and character features, 241; as a cognitive process, 2; coherent, 70–72; context-bound, 162, 170, 172; context-bound vs. impartial, 75, 82, 84, 170; context-sensitive, 40, 118, 147, 148, 170; conventional concept of, 161–62; discourse, 13, 28, 39, 41–45, 52, 54–57, 69, 70, 124–25, 150, 152, 161, 191, 197, 203, 204, 211–12, 221, 229, 245, 251; free, 80–83, 113, 116, 152, 169–70, 201, 203, 255, 272; impartial, 13, 57, 68, 69–70, 72, 147–48, 150–51, 156, 160–61, 165, 201, 204, 214, 216, 234–35, 272, 273; indeterminacy of, 7; and judgment, 41; and loss of certainty in norms, 201; of norms a response of self to social

situation, 108; partial, 236; and *phronesis,* 184, 197; problem of, 7–9, 21, 27, 32–33, 66, 75, 82, 98, 111, 112, 184, 201; problems in law, 51; procedural, 241; prudent, 67–69, 147; rationality of, 229, 243–44; rational reconstruction of, 9; and reason, 44; rigoristic, 161; situation-appropriate, 68, 98–99, 118; situation-related, 40; situation-specific, 56; of texts and application of norms, 191; types of, 119–25, 137, 151, 156, 167–70, 256; of (U), 24, 29–30, 32, 36, 40, 47, 54; and understanding, 191, 196, 198; and universalist morality, 82; *See also* Appropriateness; Appropriateness and validity; Justification; Justification and application; Moral principle, application of
Application rules, paradox of, 93, 241–42
Application situations, 11–12, 15, 16, 18, 20, 21, 26, 28, 34–35, 54, 69, 115, 161, 261; anticipate various possible, 37; cannot anticipate all, 36, 43, 239; complexity of, 169; diversity of, 31; indeterminacy of, 10; new experiences in, 40; required consideration of, 24; rule fetishism in, 117
Appropriateness, 67, 162–63, 193, 203, 214, 216, 242, 256; and coherence, 70, 242, 244–45; and completeness of situation descriptions, 53–54, 225; and consideration of situation features, 43–44, 52, 164, 241, 253; and impartiality, 37, 111; and practical reason, 224; as predicate of norm not situation description, 52; procedural

345

33

0171
278 2477